Monera
Protista
Fungi
Plantae
Animalia

INVESTIGATING
AQUATIC
ECOSYSTEMS

CONTOURS: STUDIES OF THE ENVIRONMENT
Second Edition

EDITOR AND PRINCIPAL AUTHOR
William A. Andrews
Professor and Chairman of Science Education
Faculty of Education, University of Toronto

Investigating Terrestrial Ecosystems
Investigating Aquatic Ecosystems
Investigating Natural Resources
Investigating Environmental Issues

THE MEANING OF THE CONTOURS SYMBOL

The symbol for *Contours* embodies two basic elements: the Greek letter theta and receding and rising contours. The letter theta is the first letter of the Greek word *thanatos*, meaning death, which has come to symbolize the urgency with which we must examine our "use" of our home, Earth. The receding and rising contours within the letter theta represent the conflicting sides in every issue and the need for careful study and analysis of those issues.

William A. Andrews

EDITOR AND PRINCIPAL AUTHOR
Faculty of Education, University of Toronto

Sandra J. McEwan

Anderson Collegiate and Vocational Institute

INVESTIGATING AQUATIC ECOSYSTEMS

Prentice-Hall Canada Inc., Scarborough, Ontario

Canadian Cataloguing in Publication Data

Andrews, William A., date
  Investigating aquatic ecosystems

(Contours, studies of the environment)
Includes index.
ISBN 0-13-503129-X

1. Aquatic ecology   2. Aquatic biology.   I. McEwan,
Sandra J.   II. Title.   III. Series.

QH541.5.W3A53 1987   574.5'263   C86-093831-X

©1987 by Prentice-Hall Canada Inc., Scarborough,
Ontario.

Prentice-Hall Inc., Englewood Cliffs, *New Jersey*
Prentice-Hall International, Inc., *London*
Prentice-Hall of Australia, Pty., *Sydney*
Prentice-Hall of India Pvt., Ltd., *New Delhi*
Prentice-Hall of Japan, Inc., *Tokyo*
Prentice-Hall of Southeast Asia (Pte.) Ltd., *Singapore*
Editora Prentice-Hall do Brasil Ltda., *Rio de Janeiro*
Prentice-Hall Hispanoamericana, S.A., *Mexico*
Whitehall Books Limited, *Wellington, New Zealand*

ISBN 0-13-503129-X

Communications Branch, Consumer and Corporate Affairs Canada,
has granted use of the National Symbol for Metric Conversion.

Project Editor: Lesley Wood
Production Editor: Mary Beth Leatherdale
Design: Joe Chin
Production: Irene Maunder
Illustrator: James Loates
Composition: CompuScreen Typesetting Ltd.
Cover Illustration: Julian Mulock

Printed and bound in Canada by Bryant Press

3   4   5   BP   91   90

Policy Statement

Prentice-Hall Canada Inc., Educational Book Division, and the authors of *Investigating Aquatic Ecosystems* are committed to the publication of instructional materials that are as bias-free as possible. The student text was evaluated for bias prior to publication.

The authors and publishers also recognize the importance of appropriate reading levels and have therefore made every effort to ensure the highest degree of readability in the student text. The content has been selected, organized, and written at a level suitable to the intended audience. Standard readability tests have been applied at several stages in the text's preparation to ensure an appropriate reading level.

Research indicates, however, that readability is affected by much more than word or sentence length; factors such as presentation, format and design, none of which are considered in the usual readability tests, also greatly influence the ease with which students read a book. These and many additional features have been carefully prepared to ensure maximum student comprehension.

Contents

UNIT FIVE: THE ECOLOGY OF MARINE ECOSYSTEMS

Acknowledgments

The authors wish to acknowledge the competent professional help received from the staff of Prentice-Hall Canada Inc. in the production of this text. In particular, we extend our thanks to Lesley Wood and Mary Beth Leatherdale for their editorial work and to Irene Maunder for her coordination of the production aspect of this book. We also thank Steve Lane for his assistance in the planning and development of this text. This book owes its final shape and form largely to the efforts of Joe Chin.

We wish, further, to thank the many teachers who consulted with us in the developmental phase of this text. Our thanks also go to the students who volunteered to serve as models in the photographs. In particular, we wish to acknowledge the assistance of Sandra McEwan and her Science Club at Anderson Collegiate and Vocational Institute, and students from the classes of Donna Moore at David and Mary Thomson Collegiate Institute. We are grateful for the photographs that these people and those mentioned in the photo credits below provided in order to make our book more appealing and useful.

We would be remiss if we did not express our appreciation of the imaginative, attractive, and accurate artwork of James Loates and the cover illustration drawn by Julian Mulock. Finally, we extend a special word of appreciation to Lois Andrews for her skillful and dedicated preparation of the final manuscript and index.

W.A. Andrews
Editor and Principal Author

Credits

Every reasonable effort has been made to find copyright holders of the following material. The publishers would be pleased to have any errors or omissions brought to their attention. For permission to use the following material in this textbook, we thank:
Figs. 1-0; 2-3,A; 2-3,B: Ontario Ministry of Natural Resources. Fig. 1-8: This map is based on information taken from 31E/1 ©1975 Her Majesty the Queen in Right of Canada with permission of Energy Mines and Resources Canada. Fig. 2-2: J. Coleman Fletcher/Miller Services. Fig. 2-3,E: NASA. Fig. 2-12: H. Armstrong Roberts/Miller Services. Fig. 3-8: U.S.D.A. Fig. 18-10: Sandra McEwan. All other photos by W.A. Andrews.

To the Student

This book is one of four in a series which deals with the ecology of the world in which you live. Ecology is the study of the relationships between living things and their environments. Such relationships occur everywhere on earth. They occur in freshwater ecosystems such as ponds, lakes, and streams. They occur in terrestrial (land) ecosystems such as forests, grasslands, and deserts. They occur in marine (saltwater) ecosystems such as oceans and tidal marshes. They occur in the soil under terrestrial, freshwater, and marine ecosystems. They even occur in towns and cities. *Investigating Terrestrial Ecosystems* deals with the basic principles of ecology in considerable detail. It then uses those principles to explore terrestrial ecosystems. This book briefly reviews those principles. Then it uses them to explore both freshwater and marine ecosystems.

Why study freshwater and marine ecology? There are two good reasons. First, it's fun; you will enjoy doing the activities in this book and figuring out how everything is related. But there is a more important reason. Almost everyone knows that relationships exist between all things on earth. As well, most people know that the well-being of humans depends upon the well-being of all other parts of the natural world. In other words, most people know how important ecology is. However, most people do not know enough about ecology to help look after this earth and the life on it. As a result, environmental problems are quite common. Noise, water, and air pollution plague cities. Agricultural land is being lost through soil erosion and urbanization. Also, natural resources such as forests and wildlife are being exploited.

The purpose of this book is to help you learn the ecology of freshwater and marine ecosystems. Then you should be ready to help solve and prevent environmental problems in those ecosystems. Two other books in this series will give you further ideas on how to do this: *Investigating Environmental Issues* and *Investigating Natural Resources*.

UNIT ONE

Introduction to Freshwater Ecosystems

Oceans . . . lakes . . . ponds . . . bogs . . . marshes . . . rivers . . . estuaries. . . . Aquatic ecosystems seem to be everywhere! And there are so many kinds of them! But this is not surprising. Over 70% of the earth's surface is covered by water. Most of this, of course, is made up of the oceans. In fact, 97% of the earth's water is salt water. Only 3% is fresh water. Of that 3%, about 98% is frozen in the icecaps of Antarctica and Greenland. But the 2% that is not frozen makes a wide variety of freshwater ecosystems. This unit surveys the ecology of those freshwater ecosystems.

This lake is a freshwater ecosystem. The word "ecosystem" means that the living (biotic) and nonliving (abiotic) things in this lake are interdependent.

1 Types of Freshwater Ecosystems

The first three units of this book explore the ecology of freshwater ecosystems. This chapter introduces that topic by looking at the types and importance of freshwater ecosystems.

1.1 Why Study Freshwater Ecosystems?

Water, water everywhere,
Nor any drop to drink.
S.T. Coleridge

Freshwater Resources

The above quote comes from Coleridge's poem, *The Rime of the Ancient Mariner*. In this poem the storyteller was adrift at sea. Though he was surrounded by water, he could not drink it because the water was too salty. Had he been adrift on a lake, he could have drunk the water—at least in 1798, when the poem was written. Today many lakes are so polluted that it is dangerous to drink the water unless it is treated.

Only 3% of the water on earth is fresh water (water without salt). All but 2% of that is frozen in icecaps. Much of the earth's unfrozen fresh water is in big lakes like the Great Lakes. But a surprisingly large amount is in rivers. The Amazon River of South America, with about 1100 tributaries and a length of over 6000 km, contains at least 65% of the world's river water.

From its mouth each day comes 20% of all the river water that enters the oceans. Fresh water is also found in countless small lakes, ponds, rivers, streams, and wetlands that dot the earth.

Importance

Freshwater ecosystems, large and small, are vital to all of us. They provide us with drinking water and water for irrigating food crops. They provide habitats for fish we can eat. They provide places of recreation. They also help return water to the atmosphere to keep the water cycle going.

Without water, life on earth would cease to exist. Your body is almost 80% water. Lettuce, cabbage, and tomatoes are over 90% water. Eggs and lean beef are about 75% water. In fact, all plants and animals contain large amounts of water in their tissues. Unless they live in the oceans, they must get this water from freshwater sources.

Of vital concern to humans today is the need for water to produce food. Growing just 1 kg of wheat requires 600 L of water; 1 kg of rice 2000 L; 1 kg of meat 25 000 to 60 000 L; 1L of milk 9000 L. A single corn plant absorbs over 200 L of water from the soil in one growing season.

Industry also uses large amounts of water. At least 500 000 L of water are needed to make one car!

Each of us uses directly or indirectly about 9000 L of water a day. This includes water for drinking and bathing as well as a share of the water used by agriculture and industry. In 1900 each person in North America used only 2400 L. Industrialization and irrigation of farmland have caused the increase.

Since the earth has so little fresh water, care must be taken not to use large amounts needlessly. Global studies show that humans are now removing fresh water from the land faster than the water cycle can replace it. In North America we use about twice as much water as the water cycle returns. Every time we want more water, we pump it from a lake or river or we drill a new well. Sooner or later a limit will be reached. Some scientists say that, within a few years, we will no longer be able to find all the fresh water we need. Perhaps it would be more accurate to say the fresh water we *want*.

This situation is causing some concern in North America. In a country such as India that is short of food, has a large population, and a low average rainfall, the situation is desperate. In an attempt to find more water to grow more food, India drilled about 80 000 wells in just one year. In the same year it installed about 250 000 pumps to bring water from lakes and rivers. How long can this continue?

Freshwater ecosystems are used as dumps for domestic sewage and industrial wastes (Fig. 1-1). They are being polluted by agricultural runoff. As well, they are being depleted by overuse. But this situation need not continue. There are solutions. The first step in finding these solutions is to understand the ecology of freshwater ecosystems. This book should help you do that.

Fig. 1-1 This river flows through a city. It is so polluted that you should not even wade in it. Yet it flows into a lake from which the city gets its drinking water. What should we do about this problem?

Section Review

1. **a)** What percent of the earth's water is fresh water?
   b) What percent of fresh water is liquid water?
2. State five uses of freshwater ecosystems.
3. Why does life on earth depend on water?
4. By how much has the daily water use by an individual in North America increased from 1900 to today?
5. Why should we be concerned about pumping more and more water from the ground for irrigation purposes?

1.2   Types of Standing Waters

Freshwater ecosystems can be grouped into two categories, standing waters and flowing waters. A pond is an example of standing water. A river is an example of flowing water. In some cases it is difficult to classify a body of water as standing or flowing. For example, some rivers flow very slowly near their mouths. Thus, they appear to be standing waters. Most ponds have inlets and outlets and as a result they have a slow flow of water through them.

A

B

Fig. 1-2 The two main types of standing waters are a pond (A) and a lake (B). How are they alike? How do they differ?

There are just two main types of standing waters that are wholly aquatic. These are ponds and lakes (Fig. 1-2). The rest—marshes, carrs, swamps, fens, and bogs—are partly terrestrial. In fact, they are often called wetlands. You can read about all of these in Chapter 3.

There is not a sharp distinction between ponds and lakes. However, most limnologists (those who study standing waters) define a pond as a body of water in which light can reach the bottom at all places. In contrast, light cannot reach the bottom in the deeper regions of lakes. In general, then, ponds are smaller and more shallow than lakes.

All types of standing waters, including wetlands, occur right across the United States and Canada. Even the prairies, often thought of as dry, are dotted with numerous ponds and small lakes. These have very high concentrations of nutrients. They are often called sloughs [sloos] or potholes. Table 1-1 describes the main types of standing waters, including wetlands.

Table 1-1 Types of Standing Waters

Name	Description
Pond	• shallow • light can reach bottom in most places • considerable vegetation, mostly submerged
Lake	• deeper than a pond • light cannot reach bottom in many places • no vegetation in deeper areas
Marsh	• very shallow • no open expanses of water • contains "islands" of soggy land • dominated by cattails, bulrushes, reeds, and grasses
Carr	• very shallow • drier "islands" of land • dominated by shrubs
Swamp	• like a carr, except "islands" of land have trees on them
Bog	• waterlogged spongy area (peat) • contains acidic water • dominated by sphagnum moss
Fen	• waterlogged spongy area (peat) • contains neutral or basic water • dominated by sedges, grasses and mosses
Slough or pothole	• small lake or pond • nutrient-rich • in low areas of prairies

1. Why is it difficult to classify a freshwater ecosystem as either standing or flowing?
2. Name five kinds of wetlands.
3. **a)** How does a pond differ from a lake?
   b) What is a slough or pothole?
4. **a)** How does a marsh differ from a pond or lake?
   b) How does a carr differ from a marsh?
   c) How does a swamp differ from a carr?
5. **a)** How are a bog and a fen alike?
   b) How do they differ?

1.3 Types of Flowing Waters

You likely call flowing waters by names such as brook, creek, stream, and river. In general, brooks and creeks are the smallest, streams larger, and rivers the largest. Creeks and brooks are often fed by springs. They may also drain ponds, lakes, and wetlands. However, sooner or later, they join together to form streams. Streams, in turn, join together to form rivers. The rivers carry the water to a lake or, in some cases, to the sea.

Stream Orders

Clearly, the use of the terms creek, brook, stream, and river can cause confusion. How big, for example, must a creek be before we start calling it a stream? And at what size does a stream become a river? To avoid such confusion, many stream ecologists do not use these terms. Instead, they classify flowing waters by a system called stream orders.

According to the stream order system, streams with no tributaries are called **first order** streams. When two first order streams join, they form a **second order** stream. When two second order streams join, they form a **third order** stream. Figure 1-3 shows a river system with five such orders. Note that tributaries of lower order than that of the receiving stream do not change its order.

Low order streams are often much cooler than higher order streams on the same river system. There are three reasons for this. First, low order streams often originate in hilly country. Therefore the slope is high and, as a result, the stream speed is high. The resulting turbulence causes evaporation of water. This, in turn, cools the stream. Second, these low order streams are small. As a result, they are often shielded from the heat of the sun by overhanging vegetation. Finally, many low order streams get much of their water from springs, sub-surface runoff, and the water table (Fig. 1-4). Such sources usually contain cool water.

Fig. 1-3 A typical river system has many stream orders. What orders are a, b, c, and d?

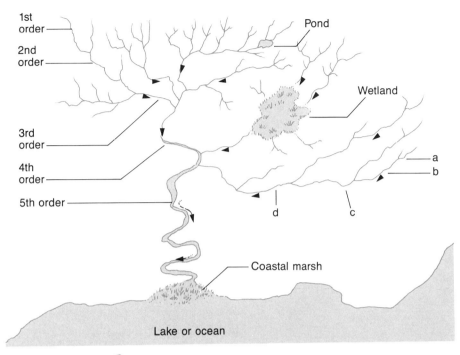

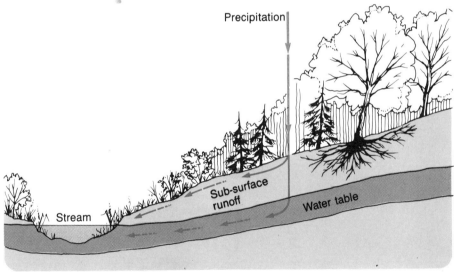

Fig. 1-4 Cool water often enters streams from such sources as sub-surface runoff and the water table.

Stream Orders and Ecology

Two main things usually happen as the stream order increases.
- The water becomes warmer.
- The stream speed decreases.

These two changes cause a gradual change in the ecology of the stream. Table 1-2 shows how striking the change can be between a first and fifth order stream. The fast water in the first order stream washes away small particles

Table 1-2 Stream Orders and Ecology

Stream order	Stream speed (m/s)	Stream temperature (°C)	Stream bottom	Oxygen concentration (μg/g)	Fish
first	2.2	12	cobble	11	trout
fifth	0.6	27	sand	5	carp

on the bottom. Only cobble (particles between 64 mm and 256 mm in diameter) remains. In contrast, the slower water of the fifth order stream allows sand to accumulate on the bottom. The cool fast water in the first order stream holds a high concentration of oxygen. This, in turn, allows trout to live in the water. However, the fifth order stream is slow and warm. It cannot dissolve enough oxygen to support trout, but other fish like carp can live there.

You can expect, then, to find a gradual change in the ecology of a stream as you move from the headwaters (source) to the mouth. All ecological factors—geophysical, chemical, and biological—gradually change along the stream. Such a gradual change is called an environmental gradient.

Section Review

1. Why are the terms brook, creek, stream, and river not used by ecologists to indicate sizes of flowing waters?
2. Describe the stream order system for classifying flowing waters.
3. Give three reasons why low order streams are often cooler than higher order streams.
4. Give a description of the environmental gradient that exists along most streams.

1.4 How Standing and Flowing Waters Differ

Since standing waters don't move and flowing waters do, three other important differences occur between these types of water.

Source of Oxygen

In standing waters, photosynthesis by producers (plants and algae) is the main source of oxygen. However, it is not the main source in most flowing waters. In fact, most plants and algae are swept away by the current. Fast water gets most of its oxygen by aeration. The water of low order streams, in

Fig. 1-5 Fast water becomes aerated by the turbulence created as the water rushes over rocks.

Fig. 1-6 A stonefly nymph. Note how it is adapted to fast water.

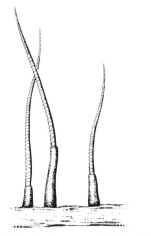

Fig. 1-7 The sludgeworm, *Tubifex*. Note how it is adapted to a muddy bottom habitat.

particular, usually rushes over rocks (Fig. 1-5). Therefore air circulates through the water (aeration).

A few producers do live in flowing waters. Clinging to the rocks are blue-green algae, green algae, diatoms, and mosses. These organisms photosynthesize. As a result, they add oxygen to the water. The amount of oxygen added is usually small compared to that which enters by aeration.

Source of Food

The producers of ponds and lakes support most of the food chains. Such food chains are called autotrophic food chains (self-feeding food chains). Producers may also support some food chains in streams. For example, herbivores such as snails may graze on algae and mosses on the rocks. The snails, in turn, may be eaten by carnivores such as fish. However, only a small part of the total food supply of a fast stream comes from the producers. Most of it enters the water from the surrounding land. This can happen in two ways. First, leaves, twigs, grass, and other organic matter fall into the water or are washed in by rain. Scavengers feed on this organic matter. They, in turn, are eaten by carnivores. Food chains which begin with non-living organic matter such as this are called detritus food chains. Second, insects and other small terrestrial animals also often fall into the water. These are eaten by fish and other predators. Such food chains, like detritus food chains, have their first steps outside the stream. As a result, they are called heterotrophic food chains (other-feeding food chains).

High order streams are generally wider, slower, warmer, and more nutrient-rich than low order streams. Therefore plants and algae are often more abundant in them. Also, decaying organic matter builds up on the bottom of slower streams. In fact, a wide slow stream has many of the properties of a pond or small lake.

Adaptations of Organisms

The organisms of both standing and flowing waters have special adaptations which suit them to their habitats. For example, stonefly nymphs that live under the rocks in fast streams are streamlined in shape. They have muscular legs and hooks on their feet (Fig. 1-6). In contrast, sludgeworms are adapted to the bottom ooze of ponds, lakes, and slow streams. They have no adaptations for holding on in fast water. Instead, they are adapted to the muddy bottom. They build a tube in the muddy bottom material and feed head-down in this tube. To capture oxygen in this low-oxygen environment, they rotate their "tails" through the water (Fig. 1-7).

Section Review

1. a) What is the main source of oxygen in standing waters?
   b) What is the main source of oxygen in most flowing waters?

2. **a)** With what do most food chains in ponds and lakes begin?
   b) Give an example of an autotrophic food chain in a stream.
   c) What is a detritus food chain?
   d) Why do most streams have detritus food chains?
3. **a)** How are stoneflies adapted to fast water?
   b) How are sludgeworms adapted to muddy bottom habitats?

1.5   ACTIVITY   Freshwater Ecosystems in Your Area

Water is often called our most precious natural resource. We use it for agricultural irrigation, transportation, recreation, and industry. We also use it for a wide variety of purposes in our homes. Most important, without water, life on earth would cease to exist.

Even though water is so important to us we often treat our rivers and lakes carelessly. We dump sewage and industrial wastes into them, often into the same bodies of water from which we get our drinking water. We drain some rivers and lakes almost dry to irrigate crops, lawns, and golf courses. We dam rivers and divert them to suit our needs and wants. Some of the things we do to our freshwater ecosystems are necessary; others are not. What is the situation like where you live?

In this activity you will investigate the locations, nature, and uses of the main freshwater ecosystems in your area. You will do this investigation using topographical maps (Fig. 1-8). You may also wish to examine aerial photographs and, if possible, visit some of the ecosystems.

Problem

What freshwater ecosystems occur in your area? What are they like and what are they used for?

Materials

topographical map(s)   camera (optional)
aerial photographs (optional)   binoculars (optional)

Procedure

a. Form a group with four or five other students.
b. Get the topographical map(s) from your teacher. The map(s) shows the area where you live and some of the area around it. For example, if you live in a town the map(s) shows the town and some of the surrounding countryside. Therefore, you should be able to see where a river begins and where it ends.

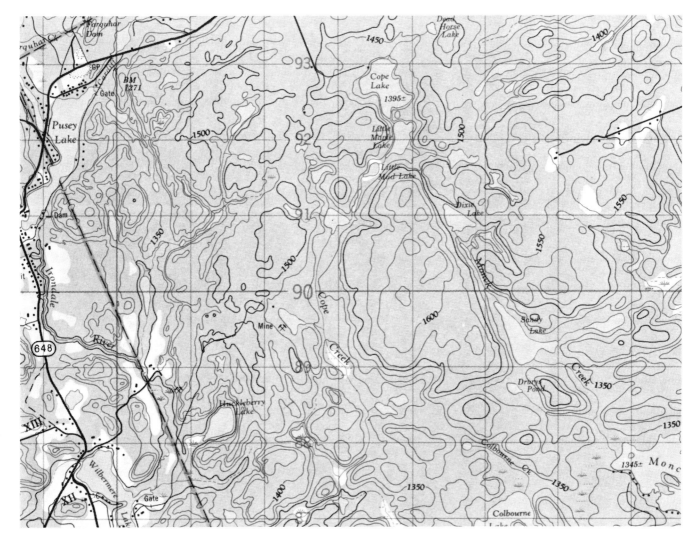

Fig. 1-8 Part of a topographical map. How many types of freshwater ecosystems can you see? Always check the date of a topographical map. Changes may have occurred since the map was made.

c. Make a full-page copy of Table 1-3. The examples are included to give you an idea of how much you should write in each column. Do not copy them.

d. Complete your table for all freshwater ecosystems within a given radius from your school. Your teacher will give you this radius. Include lakes, ponds, all orders of streams, and wetlands.

e. Answer the discussion questions for each ecosystem. If there are too many ecosystems, your teacher will tell you which ones to investigate.

f. You may find aerial photographs helpful for steps (d) and (e). Your teacher will have these if they are available.

g. If conditions permit, visit two or three of the main ecosystems. Take photographs which you can use in class to illustrate answers to the discussion questions.

Table 1-3   Freshwater Ecosystems

Name	Type of ecosystem	Size	Location	Surroundings
Crystal Lake	lake	about 1.5 km long and 0.5 km wide at the widest place	north end of town near the highway and south of a new subdivision	homes at north end; two factories at south end; large wooded park on the east; public dock and homes on the west
Belgrave Creek	fourth order stream	about 6 km long	joins the Maitland River (which flows into Crystal Lake) about 2 km north of the lake	grassy meadow for about 2 km then a subdivision (relatively new)
Huron Wildlife Refuge	marsh	about 20 ha in area	about 35 km northwest of town	surrounded by agricultural land; drains into a first order stream which is part of the Maitland River system

Discussion

1. *If the ecosystem is a stream, answer these questions:*
    a) What stream order is the stream?
    b) What is the origin of the stream?
    c) Where does it end?
    d) What factors along its path may affect the water quality of the stream? In what ways?

e) Does the future look good or bad for the stream? Explain your answer.

f) What is the stream used for? Which uses may change in the future?

g) Who has jurisdiction over the stream? Is it in private property or is it in property administered by some level of government?

2. *If the ecosystem is a lake, pond, or wetland, answer these questions:*

a) From where does this ecosystem get its water?

b) Where does the water go when it leaves this ecosystem?

c) What is the lake or pond used for? Which uses may change in the future?

d) How good is the water quality of the ecosystem? (You may wish to discuss this matter with local people.)

e) What factors affect the water quality of the ecosystem?

f) Does the future look good or bad for the ecosystem? Explain your answer.

g) What species of wildlife use the ecosystem? (A visit to the ecosystem with binoculars will help you answer this question. Also, you could contact your local nature club.)

3. Find out where your drinking water comes from. Then explain how the freshwater ecosystems in your area affect the quantity and quality of that drinking water.

Main Ideas

1. Only 3% of the water on earth is fresh water.
2. Freshwater ecosystems are used for drinking water, irrigation, recreation, transportation, fish production, industrial processes, and waste disposal.
3. Freshwater ecosystems can be classified as either standing or flowing.
4. Ponds and lakes are the only wholly aquatic standing ecosystems.
5. The five types of wetlands are marshes, carrs, swamps, fens, and bogs.
6. All flowing waters can be classified by a system of stream orders.
7. Standing and flowing waters differ in their sources of oxygen and food, and in the adaptations of their organisms.

Key Terms

aeration	environmental gradient	pothole
autotrophic food chain	fen	slough
bog	heterotrophic food chain	stream order
carr	lake	swamp
detritus food chain	pond	wetland

Chapter Review

A. True or False

Decide whether each of the following statements is true or false. If the sentence is false, rewrite it to make it true. (Do not write in this book.)
1. Lettuce is mainly water.
2. Streams get most of their oxygen by photosynthesis of plants and algae.
3. Pond life is supported mainly by autotrophic food chains.
4. Stream organisms have adaptations that make it possible for them to live in streams.

B. Completion

Complete each of the following sentences with a word or phrase that will make the sentence correct. (Do not write in this book.)
1. All plants and animals contain large amounts of ▨▨▨▨ in their tissues.
2. All freshwater ecosystems can be grouped into two categories, and ▨▨▨▨ .
3. A gradual change in ecological factors over a distance is called an ▨▨▨▨ .
4. Food chains supported by non-living organic matter are called ▨▨▨▨ food chains.

C. Multiple Choice

Each of the following statements or questions is followed by four responses. Choose the correct response in each case. (Do not write in this book.)
1. Which one of the following wetlands contains trees?
   a) swamp   **b)** carr   **c)** marsh   **d)** slough
2. A wetland is dominated by sphagnum moss growing on acidic water. This wetland is a
   a) marsh   **b)** carr   **c)** bog   **d)** fen
3. Two streams without tributaries combine to form a larger stream. The larger stream is a
   a) first order stream   **c)** third order stream
   b) second order stream   **d)** fourth order stream
4. As the stream order increases, the water usually becomes
   a) faster and cooler   **c)** faster and warmer
   b) slower and cooler   **d)** slower and warmer

Using Your Knowledge

1. Compare the methods by which a pond and a first order stream get most of their food supply.
2. A first order stream is usually quite narrow. As a result, grasses, shrubs, and other vegetation growing along the banks often hang over and shade much of the stream.
   a) In what ways will this vegetation affect the ecology of the stream?
   b) The landowners cleared away this overhanging vegetation in order to "beautify the stream". Then they discovered that the stream no longer contained trout. Why?
3. The owner of a small lake added an algicide (algae-killer) to the lake to "kill the unsightly algae". What other effects could the algicide have?
4. Why do lakes have no vegetation growing on the bottom in deeper areas?
5. Look back to Figure 1-3. What orders are the streams designated by a, b, c, and d?

Investigations

1. How much water do you use in a day? Keep track of the amount of water you use in a week. Then divide the amount by seven to get your daily use. Include individual activities such as baths, toilet flushing, drinks, and teeth brushing. Include your share of family activities such as cooking, watering lawns, washing clothes, and washing cars.
2. Select a freshwater ecosystem in your area. Research its history. How has it changed over the years? How have its uses changed?
3. Interview five people about the water quality of a local freshwater ecosystem. Summarize your findings. What did you learn from these interviews?

2 The Ecology of Freshwater Ecosystems

In Units 2 and 3 of this book, you will do a detailed study of the ecology of freshwater ecosystems. However, before you can do that you need to understand some basic ecological terms. This chapter will help you gain that understanding.

2.1 Basic Ecological Terms

This section is simply a list of basic ecological terms you should understand before you proceed with your study of freshwater ecology. The list is provided so you can, at a glance, get an idea of the terms you should know.

If you have studied ecology before, you may know many of these terms. You will likely discover that, if you read Sections 2.2 to 2.5, you will understand all of them. (Sections 2.2 to 2.5 explain the terms using freshwater examples.)

If you have not studied ecology before, you may need additional help with the terms. They are explained briefly in Sections 2.2 to 2.5. These explanations may not be, in some cases, detailed enough for you. If necessary, you can find more detailed explanations in most introductory biology books and in this book's companion, *Investigating Terrestrial Ecosystems*.

Note: These terms are listed in the order in which they appear in the remaining sections of this chapter.

General Terms

ecology	biome	biotic
photosynthesis	biosphere	abiotic
population	ecosystem	respiration
community		

Structure of an Ecosystem

habitat	second-order consumer	pyramid of numbers
niche	first-order carnivore	pyramid of biomass
competition	top carnivore	pyramid of energy
trophic level	omnivore	symbiosis
producer	predator	parasitism
autotroph	prey	parasite
consumer	scavenger	host
heterotroph	saprophyte	mutualism
first-order consumer	decomposer	commensalism
herbivore	food chain	range of tolerance
carnivore	food web	optimum condition

Flow of Matter and Energy

energy flow	macronutrient	precipitation
nutrient	micronutrient	percolation
mineral nutrient	nutrient cycle	capillarity
non-mineral nutrient	transpiration	

Section Review

Make sure you understand the terms before you proceed with your study of freshwater ecology. Your teacher will tell you the kind of record you should make in your notebook.

2.2   The Ecosystem Concept

The scene in Figure 2-1 was photographed in the mountains of western North America. This area may look quite unlike the area where you live. However, to people who live there, your area may look unusual. Yet, whether you live in the northern tundra, a forested area, a grassland, a desert, or a city, you and your environment are governed by the same set of ecological principles. Likewise, those same ecological principles apply to all aquatic ecosystems. This chapter summarizes those principles and shows you how they apply to freshwater ecosystems.

Fig. 2-1 All parts of the earth, like the area shown here, are governed by the same set of ecological principles.

Fig. 2-2 Numerous relationships exist between this fish and its environment.

What Is Ecology?

No organism lives completely on its own. It depends on other organisms and they depend on it. An organism also depends on the non-living environment in which it lives, and it affects that environment. Ecology is the study of the relationships between organisms and their environments. That is, ecology describes and explains how organisms interact with other organisms and with their non-living environments.

An Example   The fish in Figure 2-2 lives in a small lake. The fish depends on plants for most of the oxygen it needs for respiration. During respiration the fish produces carbon dioxide that plants need for photosynthesis. The fish feeds on small plants and animals. Waste products from the fish provide nutrients that plants and animals need. The plants provide hiding places for the fish. The bottom of the lake provides a place for the fish to lay its eggs. The fish and some of its offspring may be eaten by birds, turtles, mammals, or larger fish. These are just a few of the many relationships between the fish and its living and non-living environment.

Levels of Biological Organization

No individual organism lives completely on its own. It may live with other individuals of the same species to form a population. Several populations may live together in a community. Several communities may make up a biome. And several biomes occur in the biosphere (Fig. 2-3). These five terms —individual, population, community, biome, and biosphere—are called levels of biological organization. Ecology deals largely with the latter four levels. Definitions and descriptions of these four levels follow.

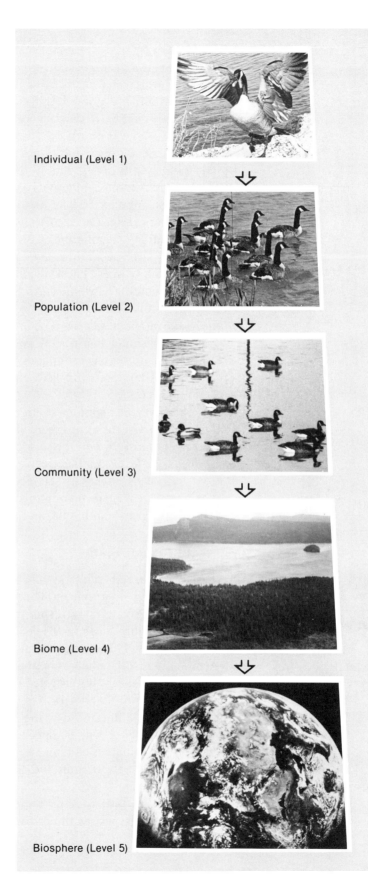

Individual (Level 1)

Population (Level 2)

Community (Level 3)

Biome (Level 4)

Biosphere (Level 5)

Fig. 2-3   Individuals of the same species make up a population; populations make up a community; communities make up a biome; biomes make up the biosphere.

- A population is a group of individuals of the same species, living together in the same area. The Canada geese in level 2 of Figure 2-3 are an example of a population. The pond with the geese in it may also have a bullfrog population. It might also have a perch population and a water lily population.
- A community is *all* the living things in an area. A community consists of several populations. The pond community in level 3 of Figure 2-3 is an example. Look closely and you will see a Canada goose population and a mallard duck population. The pond community also has many populations that you cannot see in this photograph—a water lily population, a perch population, a snail population and others.
- A biome is a large geographic area with a characteristic climate. Canada has seven main biomes. The United States has the same seven plus three additional biomes. The whole earth has only thirteen main biomes.

  The coniferous forest that stretches across Canada and into Alaska is a biome. Like all biomes, it has a characteristic set of plants and animals. A biome like this one consists of several communities. The plants and animals occur in these communities. Among the communities that make up the coniferous forest are lake communities, pond communities, and bog communities.
- The biosphere is the region on earth in which all life exists. Organisms live in the lower part of the atmosphere. They live in almost all bodies of water on earth. They also live on the surface and in the first metre or two of the soil. This thin layer on the earth, from the lower atmosphere to the bottoms of oceans, makes up the biosphere.

  The biosphere is made up of biomes. Among them are the desert biome, tundra biome, grassland biome, and coniferous forest biome.

What Is an Ecosystem?

An ecosystem is an interacting system that consists of groups of organisms and their non-living environment. Thus an ecosystem has two main parts, a biotic (living) part and an abiotic (non-living) part (Fig. 2-4). The biotic part includes all the living things in the ecosystem—animals, plants, fungi, protists, and monerans. The abiotic part includes all the non-living factors in the ecosystem—water, soil, temperature, light, wind, and others.

The ecosystem concept is illustrated in Figure 2-5. As you can see, climate is the overriding factor that determines the general nature of an ecosystem. If the climate is always hot and dry, the soil will likely be sandy. The plants, animals, and other life will be special organisms that can live in desert conditions. If the climate is cool and wet, the area will likely have many cold streams and lakes. These streams and lakes will probably contain cold-water fish such as trout.

Remember, *all* parts of an ecosystem are interrelated. Each part is affected by *all* the other parts, just as the arrows in Figure 2-5 suggest. Thus, if the

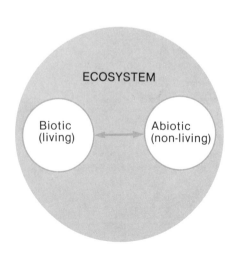

Fig. 2-4   An ecosystem has two interacting parts, biotic and abiotic.

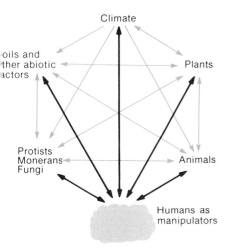

Fig. 2-5 The main parts of most ecosystems. Each part, biotic or abiotic, is affected by the other parts. Can you name some other abiotic factors which could be placed in this diagram?

Fig. 2-6 What are some of the ecological consequences of building a weir in a river?

plants in a lake change, the animals, the soil in the bottom, the amount of oxygen in the water, and all other factors will be affected. The chain of events that occurs when one factor in an ecosystem is changed is long and complex. These events are certain to take place.

An ecosystem can be any size. Any community of living things interacting with its environment is an ecosystem. Terrestrial ecosystems range in size from a handful of soil to a woodlot, a city park, and even the entire Arctic tundra. Freshwater ecosystems range in size from a balanced aquarium to ponds and lakes.

Humans and Ecosystems

Humans are animals. Therefore, like other animals, we are part of the interactions shown by the blue arrows in Figure 2-5. However, unlike other animals, we change ecosystems in dramatic ways. As shown by the black arrows in Figure 2-5, we manipulate ecosystems. For example, we kill fish we don't want in lakes and replace them with desirable sport species such as trout. We change the structure of streams to produce trout habitat. Yet such changes may make life impossible for other species. We add nutrients to streams and lakes through farm runoff and sewage. We change the course of streams, and build marinas and cottages around lakes. We use the water from streams and lakes as a coolant for electrical generating plants.

All these things are not necessarily "bad". Humans do have to eat and have a place to live. We need electricity and farms. Sometimes, though, the *way* we do these things is "bad". We often do not consider the ecological consequences of our actions. For example, the weir (small dam) shown in Figure 2-6 was built to produce trout habitat so humans could fish for trout. It worked, but only downstream from the weir. The water gained oxygen as it rushed over the weir. The water also became cooler due to increased evaporation. As well, the turbulent water scoured the bottom, washing away fine sediments and leaving cobble and gravel. All these conditions are desirable for trout. But upstream from the weir, the water was trapped as in a lake or pond. It became slow-moving and warmer. Fine sediments built up on the bottom. These conditions are not good for trout. What, then, was accomplished by building the weir? Would a succession of several weirs do the job? Was building the weir the wrong thing to do?

We should always remember that we are part of the earth ecosystem. Therefore, our survival as a species depends on *all* the other parts of the ecosystem. We must develop an ecological awareness of our actions. Then we must act in accord with the ecosystem concept.

Section Review

1. **a)** What is ecology?
   b) Describe how a fish interacts with its environment in a lake.

2. **a)** Name, in order from smallest to largest, the four levels of biological organization that ecology deals with.
   b) Define each of those four levels.
3. **a)** What is an ecosystem?
   b) What are the two main parts of an ecosystem?
4. **a)** Explain the relationships represented by the blue arrows in Figure 2-5.
   b) What is meant by "Humans as manipulators" in Figure 2-5?
5. What sizes can freshwater ecosystems be?
6. The building of a weir may seem like a good way to create trout habitat. However, if this is done without ecological thinking, the project could "backfire". Describe how this could occur.
7. Give a good reason why we should remember that we are part of the earth ecosystem.

2.3   *ACTIVITY* **Making a Model Ecosystem**

If you studied the first unit of *Investigating Terrestrial Ecosystems* you may have done this activity. If you did, review your results. If you did not, you should now do this activity.

In this activity you will build a model ecosystem. Then you will study how it works. The basic principles you learn here also apply to natural ecosystems such as lakes and forests. How many of these principles can you discover?

Problem

What are the basic parts of an ecosystem? How does an ecosystem work?

Materials

large bottle or jar with top (at least 3-4 L)	khuli loach or another plant-eating fish
table lamp with 60 W bulb	pond snails (8-10)
strands of an aquatic plant (3 or 4)	clean gravel and/or sand

Procedure

a. Place sand or gravel to a depth of 2-3 cm in the jar.
b. Fill the jar with water. If you use tap water, let the jar stand with the top removed for 48 h. This lets the chlorine leave the water.
c. Add a few strands of an aquatic plant. Any submerged aquatic plant will do. *Cabomba* (fanwort) and *Ceratophyllum* (hortwort or coontail) do particularly well in closed ecosystems.
d. Add 8-10 pond snails to the water.

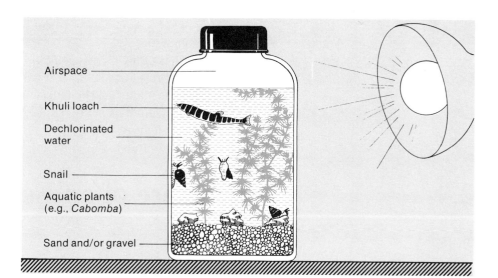

Fig. 2-7 A model ecosystem. Where do the plants, fish and snails get their nutrients? Why is light needed? Why don't the organisms die with the top on?

Labels in figure:
Airspace
Khuli loach
Dechlorinated water
Snail
Aquatic plants (e.g., *Cabomba*)
Sand and/or gravel

e. Place a khuli loach in the water. You may use one or two small guppies instead of the khuli loach, or you may use both types of fish.

f. Put the top on the jar and seal it tightly.

g. Place a table lamp with a 60 W bulb in it close to the jar as shown in Figure 2-7.

h. Place the setup in a location away from windows and other places where light and temperature conditions change greatly during the day.

i. Leave the lamp on 24 h per day. Or, place it on a timer that provides at least 16 h of light per day. Do not depend on your memory to turn the light off and on!

j. A healthy ecosystem of this kind will have a pale green colour in the water. This colour is caused by algae. They develop from spores present on the plants and animals. Algae are important in the ecosystem. They provide both food and oxygen for the animals. As the days pass, move the light closer if the water does not develop a green colour. Move it further away if the green becomes intense.

k. Observe your ecosystem closely, from time to time, for several months. Make careful notes of any changes that occur.

Discussion

Many days may pass before you can answer all these questions. You must read Sections 2.4 and 2.5 to get the information you need to answer some of these questions. Further, you should have a clear idea of what photosynthesis and respiration are. You can read about these in any introductory biology text or in Section 1.5 of *Investigating Terrestrial Ecosystems.*

1. Your ecosystem is called a *closed* ecosystem. How does this differ from natural ecosystems?

2. Why do you think we used a closed ecosystem for this activity?

3. From what source do the plants and algae get carbon dioxide for photosynthesis?
4. From what source do the organisms (plants, animals, and algae) get oxygen for respiration?
5. How do the plants get the nutrients they need?
6. How do the animals get the nutrients they need?
7. Why is the light required?
8. What do you think will happen if a fish or snail dies?

2.4   Structure of an Ecosystem

An ecosystem has two main parts, a biotic (living) part and an abiotic (non-living) part. The lake in Figure 2-8 is an ecosystem. Its biotic part includes all the living things in the lake—plants, animals, fungi, protists, and monerans. It also includes animals such as mammals and birds that visit the lake on occasion to feed. Its abiotic part includes all the non-living factors in the lake —temperature, depth profile, nature of the bottom, oxygen concentration, and others. This section gives an overview of both the biotic and abiotic factors. It also shows you how they interact to give an ecosystem its structure. You will do a detailed study of abiotic factors in Unit 2 and biotic factors in Unit 3.

Habitat and Niche

Habitat   The habitat of an organism is the place in which it lives. An ecosystem such as a lake has many habitats. For example, the habitat of a trout is the deep cool water. The habitat of a sunfish is the warm weedy shallows at the edge of the lake. The habitat of a turtle is also the edge of the lake. The habitat of a sludgeworm is the bottom ooze of the lake (see Figure 1-7, page 9).

Habitats may overlap. For example, a trout may on occasion visit warm water to feed on small fish. As well, a turtle may swim into deep water to escape a predator.

Niche   The niche of an organism is its total role in the community. For example, the niche of the frogs in a pond is to feed on insects and to become food for snakes and other animals. The niche of beavers in a small stream is to feed on plants, to dam the stream, and to become food for wolves and other predators.

Comparing Habitat and Niche   Many people confuse habitat and niche. This may help you remember the difference. Think of the habitat as the "address" of the organism and the niche as the organism's "occupation" or "job" (Fig. 2-9).

Fig. 2-8   A lake ecosystem. What factors make up its biotic and abiotic parts?

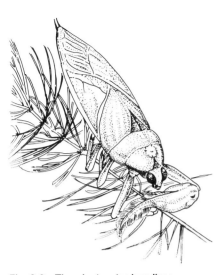

Fig. 2-9 The giant water bug lives among plants in lakes and ponds. It feeds on other animals, including tadpoles, crayfish, and fish. It, in turn, is fed upon by fish and mammals. Can you describe its habitat and niche?

The niche of an organism decides its main habitat. For example, the niche of a sludgeworm is, in part, to feed on decaying organic matter. Such matter is common on the bottoms of most lakes, ponds, and slow streams. But it is uncommon on the bottoms of fast streams. Therefore the habitat of sludgeworms is the bottoms of lakes, ponds, and slow streams.

Competition   If two species have the same habitat and similar niches, they will compete with one another. For example, both red-winged blackbirds and yellow-headed blackbirds live in the marshes of western North America. Both species have similar niches. For example, they have similar diets and both prefer to search for food on tall aquatic plants. Clearly, then, they will compete if they both try to use the same part of a marsh as a habitat. Often competition causes one species to leave the habitat. In this case, however, both species can remain in the same marsh. The yellow-headed blackbirds occupy the deeper areas, while the red-winged blackbirds occupy the shallow areas near the shore.

The red-winged blackbirds arrive first in the spring. They set up territories that cover much of the marsh. Then the yellow-headed blackbirds arrive and begin to set up territories in the deeper areas. The red-winged blackbirds now contract their territories to the shallow areas of the marsh. If a marsh has no red-winged blackbirds in it, the yellow-headed blackbirds expand their territories into the shallow areas. By splitting up a marsh in this way, the birds avoid competing in the same habitat.

Trophic (Feeding) Levels

All organisms in an ecosystem depend on one another in many ways. One way is for food. Every organism belongs to at least one of three main feeding levels—producers, consumers, and decomposers. Ecologists call feeding levels trophic levels. Let's look more closely at these levels.

Producers   All living things need energy to support life processes. Plants, many protists, and many monerans contain chlorophyll. Therefore they can carry out photosynthesis. That is, they store some of the sun's energy in sugar, starch, and other molecules. They make, or produce, their own food. Therefore they are called producers.

Organisms that produce their own food are also called autotrophs (self-feeders). They are said to occupy the trophic level of producer. The diatoms of a lake, the cattails of a marsh, the water lilies of a pond, and the algae on a rock in a river are all producers.

Consumers   Some organisms cannot make their own food. They must feed on, or consume, other organisms. Therefore they are called consumers. Most consumers are animals that feed on plants or other animals. Consumers are also called heterotrophs (other feeders).

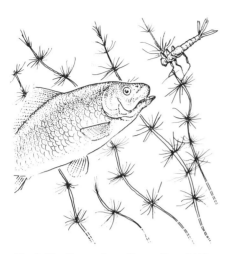

Fig. 2-10 Carp eat small aquatic animals like insect larvas. They also eat plant fragments and algae. What kind of consumer are they: herbivore, carnivore, or omnivore?

Fig. 2-11 A predator-prey relationship exists between bald eagles and fish. Which one is the predator? Which one is the prey?

Animals that feed directly on producers are called **first-order consumers** or **herbivores** (plant-eaters). Beavers feed on aquatic plants and tree bark. Therefore they are **herbivores**. Animals that eat other animals are called **carnivores** (flesh-eaters). Trout, mink, and otters are carnivores.

Those carnivores that feed on herbivores are called **first-order carnivores**. (They can also be called **second-order consumers**. Why is this so?) Most snails are herbivores. Therefore a racoon is a first-order carnivore when it eats snails.

Those carnivores that feed on first-order carnivores are called second-order carnivores (and also third-order consumers). If a trout eats small fish that ate herbivorous insects, the trout is a second-order carnivore. You are a **third-order carnivore** if you eat the trout just referred to. However, you would be a second-order carnivore if you ate trout that feed mainly on fish and insects which are herbivores.

Some ecosystems have five or more orders of carnivores. These are all trophic levels within the main trophic level of consumer. All ecosystems have top carnivores. What do you think that means?

Some animals are both herbivores and carnivores (Fig. 2-10). For example, carp feed on insect larvas, small crustaceans, small snails, and worms. But they also eat algae and pieces of plants. Animals which are both herbivores and carnivores are called **omnivores** ("all-feeders"). Are you a herbivore, carnivore, or omnivore?

Carnivores that feed on live animals are called **predators**. The animals that are eaten are called **prey**. The bald eagle in Figure 2-11 is, at times, a predator, while the fish and other animals that it eats are the prey. Another bird of prey, the osprey, lives entirely on fish. It captures these by spectacular dives from the air. The osprey hovers over the water until it spots a fish. Then it hits the water with a powerful splash. Often it disappears underwater for a few moments. Then, if it has caught a fish, the osprey flies away, carrying the fish in both sets of claws. It holds the fish parallel with the bird's body and head first. Why does the osprey carry the fish in this position?

The bald eagle also eats mainly fish. Sometimes it makes its own kill, and sometimes it robs an osprey of its kill. Most often it eats fish that are already dead. For example, eagles that live along the sea-coast eat dead fish cast up on the beach by the waves (Figure 2-12). Animals like the bald eagle that feed on dead organisms are called **scavengers**. Like the eagle, an animal may be a predator one day and a scavenger the next. The dead organisms need not be animals for the consumer to be called a scavenger. Snails and crayfish in ponds eat both dead plants and animals. Even when they eat only dead plants, they are called scavengers.

Have you ever seen a dead fish lying in shallow water and covered with a fuzzy grey growth? This growth is a fungus. It is feeding on the fish. Though you cannot see them, bacteria will also be feeding on that fish. Fungi and bacteria that feed on dead organisms (both plant and animal) are called **saprophytes**.

Fig. 2-12 The bald eagle is usually a scavenger.

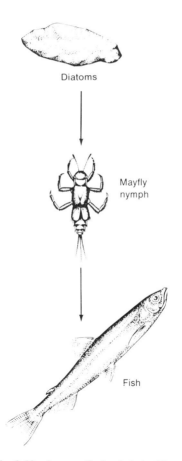

Fig. 2-13 An aquatic food chain. The diatoms, a form of algae, are producers. In this case they are growing on rocks in a stream. They are eaten by mayflies which, in turn, are eaten by fish.

Decomposers All ecosystems have a feeding level made up of decomposers. These organisms are mainly bacteria and fungi such as yeasts and moulds. They break down (decompose) and feed on non-living organic matter such as dead plants, dead animals, and animal wastes. When could decomposers also be called saprophytes?

All organisms eventually die. As well, all animals produce wastes. If decomposers were not present, aquatic ecosystems would soon clog up with wastes and dead organisms. But decomposers perform an even more important function. As they break down or feed upon the organic matter, they return valuable nutrients to the water. These nutrients can now be used again to help producers grow.

Food Chains and Food Webs

Food Chains You may have gathered as you read about trophic levels that organisms may be linked together in feeding relationships. These feeding relationships are called food chains. Many food chains follow the pattern shown in Figure 2-13. That is, they begin with producers that are eaten by herbivores that, in turn, are eaten by carnivores. However, some food chains begin with dead plants or animals. An example is a crayfish feeding on a dead fish in a lake. In a sense, even this food chain began with a producer. The fish, when it was alive, was in a food chain that began with a producer. The fish may have eaten smaller animals that, in turn, had eaten algae or plants.

Though many food chains have just the three steps shown in Figure 2-13 (producer, herbivore, carnivore), others can be quite long. That's because they have several "orders" of carnivores. In other words, they have more predator-prey relationships. Figure 2-14 shows a food chain with three orders of carnivores. Even a long food chain like this usually has the three main trophic levels—producer, consumer, and decomposer. The decomposers feed at all levels along the food chain. The consumer level, in this case, has four sub-levels—herbivore, first-order carnivore, second-order carnivore, and top carnivore. Thus it is proper to say that the mayflies occupy the trophic level of herbivore and the dace the level of second-order carnivore.

Fig. 2-14 This food chain has the three main trophic levels—producer, consumer, and decomposer. (Decomposers are "busy" at all steps in this food chain when organisms die.) The consumer level is divided into four sub-levels. At a different time or place, some of these organisms may feed at different trophic levels. For example, the trout may eat mayflies. Then what would it be?

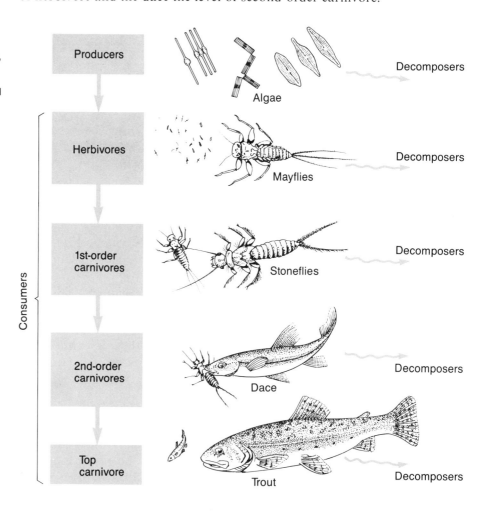

Food Webs Most organisms are in more than one food chain. A certain species of plant could be eaten by several species of animal. Also, a certain species of animal could eat more than one type of food. For example, one species of mayfly could be part of the following food chains:

Algae ⟶ Mayflies ⟶ Fish
Algae ⟶ Microscopic animals ⟶ Mayflies ⟶ Fish
Plants ⟶ Microscopic animals ⟶ Mayflies ⟶ Fish
Algae ⟶ Mayflies ⟶ Stoneflies ⟶ Small fish ⟶ Larger fish

Since organisms are often in more than one food chain, the food chains in an ecosystem are connected. The connected food chains are called a food web. Figure 2-15 shows a simple aquatic food web. Follow the arrows in this food web to find out what eats what.

Fig. 2-15 An aquatic (freshwater) food web.

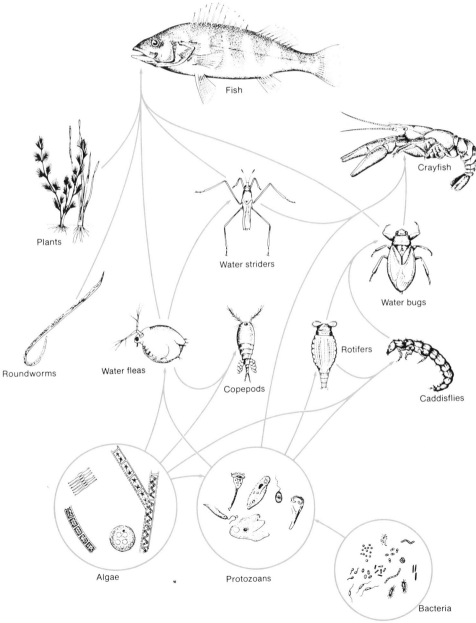

Fish

Crayfish

Plants

Water striders

Water bugs

Roundworms

Water fleas

Copepods

Rotifers

Caddisflies

Algae

Protozoans

Bacteria

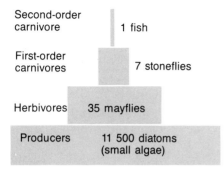

Fig. 2-16 A pyramid of numbers for a stream.

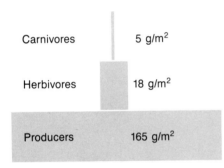

Fig. 2-17 A pyramid of biomass for a lake.

Ecological Pyramids

Pyramid of Numbers   As you may have guessed, food chains usually proceed from very small organisms to larger and larger ones. Therefore the number of organisms at each trophic level tends to decrease as you move along the food chain. In other words, many small producers feed fewer larger herbivores that, in turn, feed still fewer and larger carnivores. Such relationships are often represented by a pyramid of numbers (Fig. 2-16).

Not all pyramids of numbers have such a regular shape. In fact, some aren't pyramids at all! Think about the hundreds of mould organisms that feed on a dead fish. What will this "pyramid" of numbers look like?

Although the pyramid of numbers is simple, it is not used much by ecologists. That is because it treats all organisms only in terms of numbers. It ignores differences in size. Yet to a hungry fish, size is important. One stonefly with a mass of 1.2 g makes a better meal than one mayfly with a mass of 0.4 g.

Pyramid of Biomass   To avoid the fault in the pyramid of numbers, ecologists often use a pyramid of biomass. Each trophic level in this pyramid shows the biomass (total mass of the organisms) at that level. Figure 2-17 is a pyramid of biomass for a small lake. Studies showed that for every square metre of surface area, this lake has 165 g of producers, 18 g of herbivores, and 5 g of carnivores.

It makes much more sense to talk about *masses* of organisms at each trophic level than about *numbers* of organisms. After all, the important thing for a trout is the total mass not the number of stoneflies it eats. (In like manner, you probably don't care *how many* potatoes you eat for dinner. Rather, you care about the *total amount*, or mass, of potato. One big potato may feed you better than three small ones.)

There is just one small problem with pyramids of biomass. They imply that equal masses of all organisms have equal energy contents. This is not so. Different types of tissues have different energy contents. The most noticeable difference occurs between plant and animal tissue. An organism can usually obtain about 20% more energy by eating 1 g of animal than by eating 1 g of plant.

Pyramid of Energy   The most useful pyramid then is one which shows energy instead of masses or numbers. All animals need energy to live. Some eat plants to get this energy. Other animals eat animals to get their energy. The more easily animals can get the energy they need, the better. Therefore the efficiency with which energy is passed along the food chain is more important than either the numbers of organisms or their biomasses. Ecologists today direct most of their attention toward pyramids of energy (see Fig. 2-23). You will learn more about these in Section 2.4.

Special Feeding Relationships

Many unusual relationships exist between organisms. One of these is called symbiosis. This word means "living together". Symbiosis is a close association between two organisms of different species in which at least one of the two benefits. There are three kinds of symbiosis:

- parasitism
- mutualism
- commensalism

In each of these relationships, organisms provide food and/or other benefits for different organisms without being killed and eaten themselves.

Parasitism Parasitism is a symbiotic relationship between two organisms in which one organism benefits and the other suffers harm. Frogs and turtles often have leeches ("bloodsuckers") attached to them. The leeches are feeding on blood from the other animals. Clearly the leeches benefit from this relationship. The other animals are harmed, though seldom killed. The organism that benefits is called the parasite. The organism that is harmed is called the host.

Mutualism Mutualism is a symbiotic relationship between two organisms in which both organisms benefit. One species of hydra, *Chlorohydra viridissima*, is green. That is because it contains green algae in its interior (Fig. 2-18). This tiny animal is only about 1 cm long. The green algae live in the cells that surround the hydra's body cavity. These algae make food by photosynthesis. They donate about 10% of the food they make to the hydra. In return, the hydra provides the algae with water and a secure place to live.

Commensalism Commensalism is a symbiotic relationship in which one organism benefits and the other organism neither benefits or suffers harm. Freshwater turtles may often be seen with green "hair" on their backs. This "hair" is the green alga *Basicladia*. It grows only on the backs of freshwater turtles. It needs keratin, a substance present in the shells of turtles. It gets the keratin from the shells in such low quantities that the turtles are not harmed. Since the turtles do not need or benefit from the alga the relationship is called commensalism. On rare occasions, the alga grows thick enough to camouflage the turtle, thereby protecting it from its enemies. What is the relationship now called?

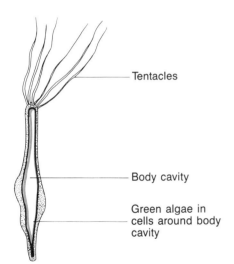

Tentacles

Body cavity

Green algae in cells around body cavity

Fig. 2-18 The hydra, *Chlorohydra viridissima*, showing green algae in its interior (in blue).

Abiotic Factors in Freshwater Ecosystems

An ecosystem has two main parts, a biotic part and an abiotic part. So far in this section we have directed our attention to the biotic part. Let us now take a brief look at the abiotic part. You will study this part, in detail, in Unit 2.

Fig. 2-19 A fast stream (A) and a slow stream (B) were compared on a warm summer day. The fast stream was cooler and had a higher oxygen concentration. Also, the bottom of the fast stream had larger particles.

A   B

Life in a stream is affected by many abiotic factors. Among these are the temperature, the speed of the water, the nature of the bottom, the oxygen concentration, and the acidity. For example, a fast stream like the one in Figure 2-19(A) will likely be cool, have a cobble bottom, and have abundant oxygen. In contrast, a slow stream like the one in Figure 2-19(B) will likely be warmer, have a sandy or muddy bottom, and have less oxygen. The cobble bottom, cool water, and abundant oxygen of a fast stream make an ideal habitat for stoneflies and mayflies. These, in turn, are food for trout which also prefer cool highly oxygenated water. In contrast, the slow stream supports none of these organisms.

Life in a pond or lake is also affected by many abiotic factors. Among these are temperature, light, depth, nature of the bottom, oxygen concentration, and acidity.

Each organism has a range of tolerance for each abiotic factor. This range depends on the factor and on the organism. When the range is exceeded, in either direction, the organism suffers. Within each range of tolerance there is a point at which the organism lives best. This is called the optimum condition. However, conditions are seldom optimum. Therefore organisms with the broadest range of tolerance generally survive best. Figure 2-20 illustrates range of tolerance and optimum condition as they apply to the environmental temperature of lake trout.

Section Review

1. a) What is the difference between habitat and niche?
   b) What happens if two species with similar niches move into the same habitat?

Fig. 2-20 Range of tolerance to temperature of lake trout.

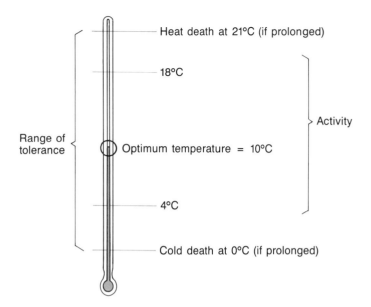

Heat death at 21°C (if prolonged)

18°C

Range of tolerance

Optimum temperature = 10°C

Activity

4°C

Cold death at 0°C (if prolonged)

2. **a)** Describe the habitat of the fish in the model ecosystem you set up in Section 2.3.
   b) Describe the niche of the fish in the model ecosystem.
3. **a)** Name the three main trophic levels.
   b) What are producers?
   c) Why are producers called autotrophs?
   d) Name four aquatic producers?
4. **a)** What are consumers?
   b) What is the difference between a first-order and a second-order consumer?
   c) What is a top carnivore?
   d) How do herbivores, carnivores, and omnivores differ?
5. **a)** What is the difference between predator and prey?
   b) What is a scavenger?
   c) What is a saprophyte?
   d) What are decomposers?
   e) Give two reasons why decomposers are important in ecosystems.
6. **a)** What is a food chain?
   b) What is the general pattern for food chains that begin with producers?
   c) What is a food web?
7. **a)** List four food chains that are in the food web in Figure 2-15. Indicate the niche of each organism in each food chain.
   b) List three food chains in your model ecosystem.
8. Describe each of the following: pyramid of numbers, pyramid of biomass, pyramid of energy.

9. **a)** Define symbiosis.
   b) Define each of the following terms and give an example to illustrate your definition: parasitism, mutualism, commensalism.
10. **a)** Name five abiotic factors that affect life in a stream.
    b) Name five abiotic factors that affect life in a lake.
    c) What is meant by these terms: range of tolerance, optimum condition?

2.5 Flow of Matter and Energy in Ecosystems

All living things need matter and energy. The matter is needed to make new cells and to repair worn-out parts. The energy is needed to "power" life processes such as movement and growth.

How does energy get into an ecosystem? And how does it reach every organism in the ecosystem? How does matter get into an ecosystem? And how does each organism in the ecosystem get the matter it needs? This section explains how matter and energy move into and through ecosystems.

Energy Flow in Ecosystems

Perhaps you have spent a few quiet moments by the edge of a lake (Fig. 2-21). If you have, you probably noticed the constant activity of the organisms around you. Fish cause ripples in the water as they break the surface to capture food. Birds fly back and forth over the water and land. Insects crawl, hop, and fly just about everywhere. The air is filled with the sounds of animals you cannot see.

Fig. 2-21 All living things need energy. How do fish, birds, mammals, insects, and trees get their energy?

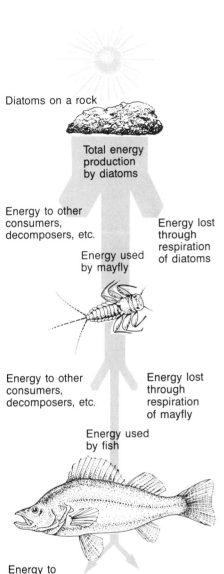

Diatoms on a rock

Total energy production by diatoms

Energy to other consumers, decomposers, etc.

Energy lost through respiration of diatoms

Energy used by mayfly

Energy to other consumers, decomposers, etc.

Energy lost through respiration of mayfly

Energy used by fish

Energy to other consumers, decomposers, etc.

Energy lost through respiration of fish

Fig. 2-22 Energy flow along a food chain.

Activity is the essence of life. In order to have activity, energy is needed. Where do organisms get the energy they need? What happens to energy in ecosystems like the lake?

Energy from the Sun to Carnivores   All the energy used by living things comes, in the first place, from the sun. Producers store some of the sun's energy in the foods they make by photosynthesis. They use some of this food for their own life processes. The rest is stored. Herbivores get their energy by eating producers, while carnivores get their energy by eating herbivores or other carnivores. In this way the sun's energy is passed along food chains to carnivores.

Energy Flow is One-Way   The passing of energy along a food chain is not very efficient. A great deal of energy is lost at each trophic level. As an example, consider the following food chain. (It is illustrated in Figure 2-13, page 27.)

$$\text{Diatoms} \longrightarrow \text{Mayflies} \longrightarrow \text{Fish}$$

Follow Figure 2-22 as you read on. The diatoms, through photosynthesis, store some of the sun's energy in foods. Much of this energy is lost as heat through respiration by the diatoms. However, when the mayflies eat the diatoms, the mayflies get some of the stored energy.

Like the diatoms, the mayflies lose much of the energy they took in through life activities such as respiration. When the fish eats the mayflies, the fish gets some of the energy stored in the mayflies. It does not get all this energy, however. For instance, parts of the exoskeletons of the mayflies cannot be digested by the fish.

The fish also loses much of its acquired energy through life activities such as respiration. Parasites and decomposers also use some of the fish's energy. In the end, little energy remains to be passed onto higher trophic levels.

As Figure 2-22 shows, energy is gradually lost along a food chain. Much of this energy leaves the food chain as heat. It cannot be recaptured by any organisms in the food chain. It is lost forever to that ecosystem. Thus energy flow is one-way along a food chain. For an ecosystem to keep operating, energy must always enter it from the sun

Pyramid of Energy   In Section 2.4 you saw that there are three kinds of ecological pyramids: pyramids of numbers, biomass, and energy. The most important of these is the pyramid of energy. How well an ecosystem functions depends on how well each trophic level captures energy and passes it on to the next level. This is much more important than the numbers of organisms or their sizes (biomasses).

Since energy is lost along a food chain, all pyramids of energy look like the one in Figure 2-23. They taper off to almost nothing. Each level in this pyramid represents the total energy flow at that level. This includes the

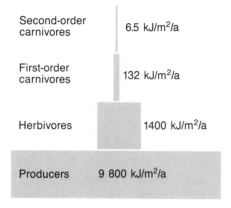

Second-order carnivores   6.5 kJ/m²/a

First-order carnivores   132 kJ/m²/a

Herbivores   1400 kJ/m²/a

Producers   9 800 kJ/m²/a

Fig. 2-23 A pyramid of energy for a lake. Each numeral represents the total energy flow at that level in kilojoules per square metre of surface per year.

energy tied up in the formation of new cells and the energy given off by respiration.

Flow of Matter in Ecosystems

Nutrients: The Elements of Life   An ecosystem needs more than energy in order to function. It also needs matter. The matter is used by organisms in the ecosystem for life processes such as growth. Most ecosystems need over 20 elements. Among these are nitrogen and oxygen. Just the plants in most ecosystems need 16 elements. Because these elements are so important to living things, they are called nutrients.

Figure 2-24 shows a classification system for the 16 elements which most plants need. As you can see, three elements are classified as non-mineral nutrients and the others as mineral nutrients. Mineral nutrients are those which originally entered the ecosystem from bedrock. The non-mineral nutrients entered the ecosystem in the form of water and carbon dioxide.

The three non-mineral nutrients (carbon, hydrogen, and oxygen) are often called the building blocks of life. Every organism, including you, is made almost entirely of them.

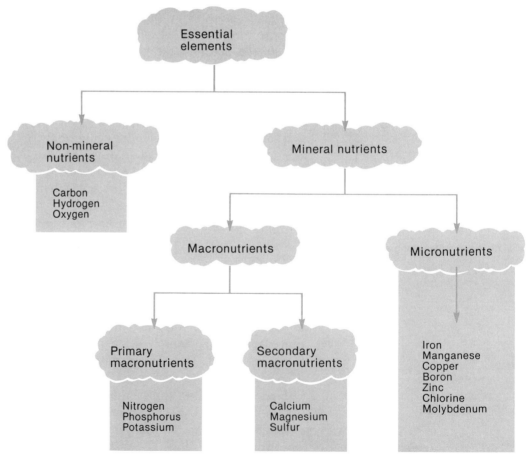

Fig. 2-24 Classification of plant nutrients.

The mineral nutrients are divided into macronutrients and micronutrients. (*Macro* means large and *micro* means small.) The macronutrients are required in greater amounts than the micronutrients. Of the macronutrients, the three primary macronutrients (nitrogen, phosphorus, and potassium) are required in the greatest amounts. In fact, commercial fertilizers usually contain these three nutrients. Magnesium, a secondary macronutrient, is one of the atoms in a chlorophyll molecule. Thus all plants and algae need this nutrient. Iron, a micronutrient, is needed to make hemoglobin molecules in red-blooded animals.

Most ecosystems need a few more nutrients than the 16 which plants require. For example, most of the animals in ecosystems need sodium and cobalt. As well, the plants which grow in salt marshes along the oceans generally need sodium.

Nutrient Cycles In the early part of this section you learned that energy is lost along a food chain. Little or no energy is left at the end of the food chain to be recycled to the producers. However, this is not the case for nutrients. Nutrients flowing through the food chain are returned to the producers. Producers get their nutrients from the soil, water, and air. Herbivores get these nutrients when they eat the producers. Carnivores also get the same nutrients when they eat the herbivores. Then decomposers break down animal wastes and dead organisms. This releases the nutrients back into the soil, water, and air so producers can use them again. In this way, nutrients are recycled through an ecosystem. The path each nutrient follows is called a nutrient cycle. Figure 2-25 compares energy flow and nutrient recycling in an ecosystem. Study this comparison closely. Then read on to find out how four basic nutrient cycles operate.

The Water Cycle

The hydrogen and oxygen atoms in water are nutrients that organisms need. Clearly there is no problem obtaining these nutrients in aquatic ecosystems. However, they are sometimes in short supply in terrestrial ecosystems. The overall cycling of water in nature involves both aquatic and terrestrial ecosystems and the air above them. Let's see how this occurs.

Water vapour enters the atmosphere through transpiration from vegetation. (Transpiration is the loss of water through pores in the leaves of plants.) It also enters the atmosphere by evaporation from bodies of water and the soil (Fig. 2-26). In the cool upper atmosphere this vapour condenses, forming clouds. In time, enough water collects in the clouds to cause precipitation. When this occurs, some of the water falling on the ground runs along the surface of the ground to a stream, pond, or other body of water. This water is called surface runoff. Some of the water also soaks into the ground by a process called percolation. Some water percolates down to the bedrock. Then it becomes ground water and gradually runs back to lakes and other bodies of water.

Fig. 2-25 Energy flow and nutrient cycles in an ecosystem. The blue arrows show the direction of energy flow. Note that energy is lost at each level (wavy lines). The black arrows show the path of nutrient flow. Note that nutrients complete the cycle. The broken blue arrow represents both energy and nutrient flow to decomposers as they break down dead producers.

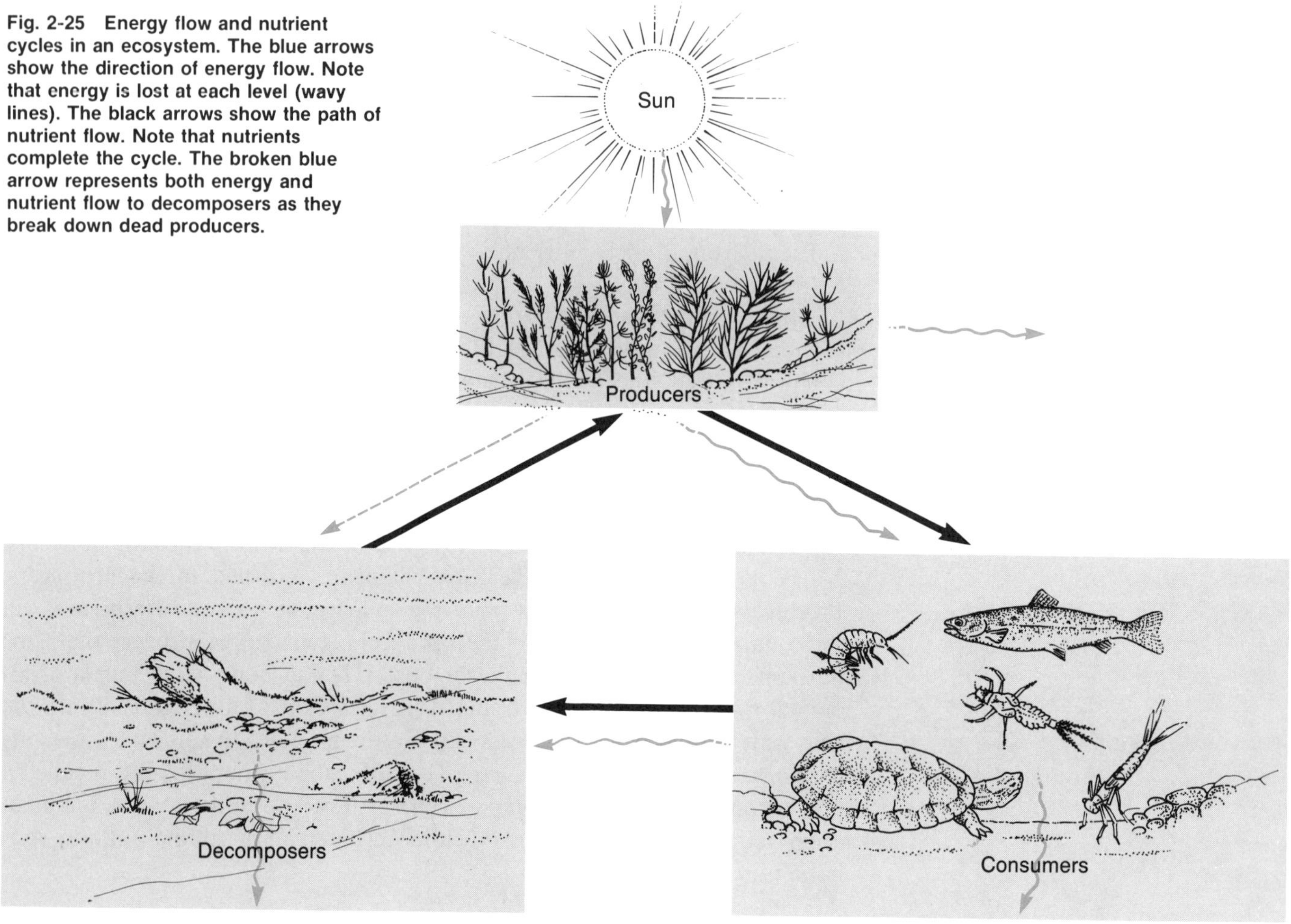

Sun

Producers

Decomposers

Consumers

Some of the water in the soil moves up to the roots of plants by capillarity. The roots absorb the water. This is how most plants get the hydrogen and oxygen they need. Animals can obtain water by eating plants or by eating other animals. Of course, they can also obtain water by drinking it directly from a body of water. When plants and animals die, they decompose. During this process, the water present in their tissues is released into the environment.

The Carbon Cycle

Carbon is another nutrient that all organisms need. In fact, it is the basic building block of all living things. Like water, carbon moves through an ecosystem in a cycle (Fig. 2-27). Here is how the cycle works.

Carbon is present in the atmosphere as carbon dioxide. Producers (plants and algae) use it to make food. Now the carbon is in the producers. Herbivores eat the plants, and carnivores eat the herbivores. Now the carbon is in

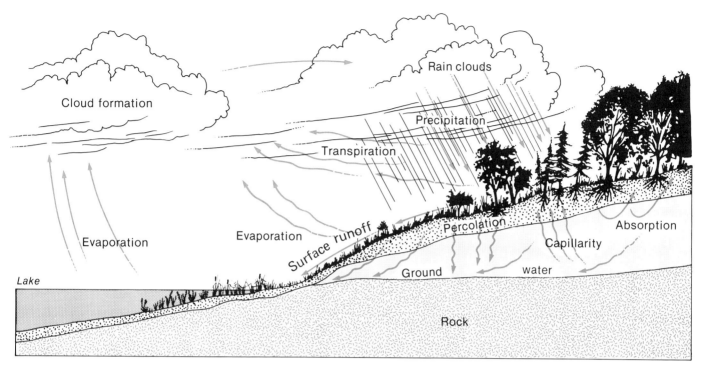

Fig. 2-26   The water cycle.

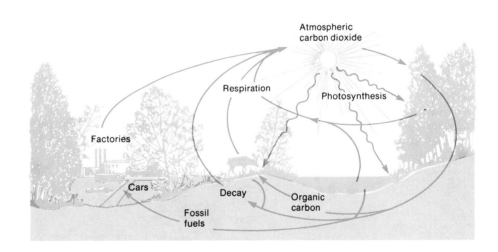

Fig. 2-27   The carbon cycle.

animals. Both plants and animals respire. Their respiration returns carbon dioxide to the atmosphere. Decomposers break down dead plants and animals as well as animal waste. This, too, returns carbon dioxide to the atmosphere.

Some organic matter does not decompose easily. Instead, it builds up in the earth's crust. Oil and coal were formed from the build-up of plant matter millions of years ago.

At one time, the carbon cycle was almost a perfect cycle. That is, carbon was returned to the atmosphere as quickly as it was removed. Lately, however, the increased burning of fossil fuels has added carbon to the atmosphere faster than producers can remove it.

The cycle just described occurs on, in, and above the land. A similar cycle also occurs in aquatic ecosystems such as lakes and oceans. In fact, water (mainly in the oceans) holds over 50 times as much carbon dioxide as the air.

The Nitrogen Cycle

Nitrogen is another important nutrient. All living things need nitrogen to make proteins. Let's see how this nutrient is recycled in ecosystems (Fig. 2-28).

Almost 78% of the atmosphere is nitrogen (N_2). However, neither plants nor animals can use this form of nitrogen directly. Usually, the nitrogen must be in the form of a nitrate (NO_3). Then plant roots can absorb it. Lightning forms some nitrate by causing oxygen and nitrogen in the atmosphere to join. *Rhizobium* bacteria can do the same thing. You may recall that these bacteria live on the roots of legumes. Many bacteria and blue-green algae also form nitrates. The changing of nitrogen to nitrates is called nitrogen fixation

Plants use the nitrates that they absorb to make plant proteins. Animals get the nitrogen that they need to make proteins by eating plants or other animals.

When plants and animals die, bacteria change their nitrogen content to ammonia (NH_3). The nitrogen in the urine and fecal matter of animals is also changed to ammonia by bacteria. The pungent odour of outhouses, chicken pens, hog yards, cat litter boxes, and wet baby diapers is ample evidence of this fact. (If you are not sure what ammonia smells like, smell some ammonium carbonate . . . *cautiously!*) Ammonia, in turn, is converted to nitrites and then to nitrates by bacteria. This completes the main part of the cycle. Bacteria convert some nitrites and nitrates to nitrogen (N_2) to complete the total cycle. The nitrogen cycle need not and often does not involve this last step.

Many plants are able to use some ammonia directly. Therefore all of it does not have to be converted to nitrate before plants absorb it.

The Phosphorus Cycle

Phosphorus is another nutrient which is important to all living things. Many important molecules within cells contain phosphorus atoms. For example, adenosine triphosphate (ATP) is a phosphorus-bearing compound found in every living cell. There it plays a key role in energy storage and supply.

Fig. 2-28 The nitrogen cycle.

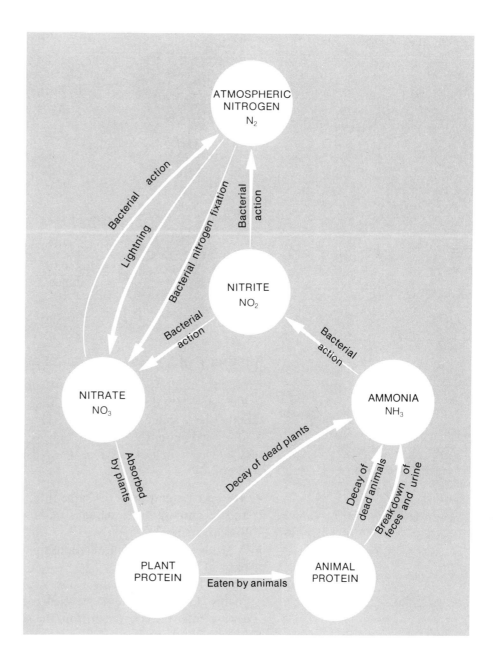

Phosphorus, like other nutrients, follows a cycle through the ecosystems. Let us begin in the upper left corner of Figure 2-29 and trace this cycle.

Phosphorus normally occurs in water and soil as inorganic compounds. Phosphates (PO_4) are a common form. These compounds are absorbed by plants and used to make organic compounds such as ATP. When animals eat plants, phosphorus is passed on to them. When dead plants, dead animals, and fecal matter decay, organic forms of phosphorus are released into the water or soil. Bacteria decompose these organic forms into inorganic forms. The cycle begins again.

Fig. 2-29 The phosphorus cycle.

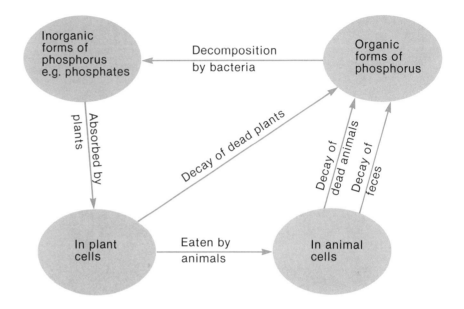

Summary of the Structure and Functioning of Ecosystems

An ocean, pond, forest, desert, park, alpine (mountain) meadow, and your model ecosystem don't look much alike. Yet they are all ecosystems. Therefore they have a common structure. They also function in the same basic way. You learned about the structure of ecosystems in Section 2.4 and about how they function in this section. Let's list those things ecosystems have in common.

- Most ecosystems have the same three biotic parts: producers, consumers, and decomposers. The actual species will, of course, differ from ecosystem to ecosystem.
- A highly interdependent relationship exists between the biotic and abiotic parts of an ecosystem.
- Energy flow in ecosystems is one-way. Energy is gradually lost along food chains. Little or none is recycled to producers. Therefore energy must always enter the ecosystem from the sun.
- Most ecosystems need the same 20 or so nutrients. These nutrients are recycled within each ecosystem.

Section Review

1. **a)** Describe the path of energy from the sun to carnivores.
   b) Describe how energy is lost along a food chain.
   c) What is meant by the phrase "energy flow is one-way in ecosystems"?
   d) Why is a pyramid of energy more useful to ecologists than a pyramid of numbers or biomass?

e) Account for the shape of a pyramid of energy.
   f) Describe the flow of energy through your model ecosystem.
2. **a)** Why are some elements called nutrients?
   b) What is the difference between mineral and non-mineral nutrients?
   c) Name the three primary macronutrients.
   d) Discuss one example which shows that micronutrients are important to ecosystems.
   e) What evidence do you have that nutrient cycles exist in your model ecosystem?
3. **a)** Why is the water cycle important?
   b) Make a point form summary of the water cycle.
4. **a)** Why is the carbon cycle important?
   b) Make a point form summary of the carbon cycle.
   c) Describe the carbon cycle as it might occur in a lake. Begin with carbon dioxide in the water.
5. **a)** Why is the nitrogen cycle important?
   b) Make a point form summary of the nitrogen cycle.
6. **a)** Why is the phosphorus cycle important?
   b) Make a point form summary of the phosphorus cycle.
7. Make a summary in your notebook of the four things most ecosystems have in common.

2.6   *ACTIVITY*   Upsetting the Nutrient Balance in an Ecosystem

If you didn't do this activity while studying *Investigating Terrestrial Ecosystems*, you should do it now.

Nutrients pass through cycles in ecosystems. They move from producers through consumers. Then they are returned to producers by decomposers. Also, the nutrients in dead producers are recycled to producers by decomposers. As a result, a balance usually exists in an ecosystem. That is, some of each nutrient is in the producers, some of it is in the consumers, and some of it is in the free state, ready to be absorbed by producers.

What do you suppose would happen to an ecosystem if we added extra nutrients in the free state? How might this affect the cycles; the producers; and the consumers?

In this activity you will make a simple aquatic ecosystem. Then you will add some lawn fertilizer to it. This fertilizer contains three main nutrients, nitrogen, phosphorus, and potassium.

Problem

How will lawn fertilizer affect the balance in an ecosystem?

Materials

wide-mouthed jars, with
   a capacity of at least 1 L (2)
pond water (2 L)
pond snails (6)

strands of *Cabomba, Elodea,* or other
   aquatic plant, each about 10-20 cm
   long (6)
fertilizer

Procedure

a. Fill both jars with pond water.
b. Add half the *Cabomba* to each jar.
c. Add 3 pond snails to each jar.
d. Label one jar "Control". Label the other jar "Experimental" (Fig. 2-30).
e. Add a *very small* pinch of lawn fertilizer to the experimental jar.
f. Place the jars, side by side, in a bright location.
g. Observe the jars each day for 2-3 weeks. Make notes on changes in the
    appearance of the *Cabomba* and the snails.

Fig. 2-30 How will fertilizer affect the experimental jar?

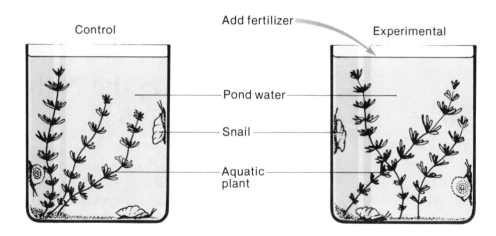

Discussion

1. What are the producers in your ecosystems?
2. What are the consumers in your ecosystems?
3. **a)** What important invisible organisms are in your ecosystems?
    b) What is their role?
4. What is the purpose of the control?
5. Why are the jars placed side by side?
6. **a)** Describe the changes the fertilizer caused in your ecosystem.
    b) Explain these changes.
7. Explain why sewage can cause plant and algal growth in lakes.

Main Ideas

1. Ecology is the study of the relationships between organisms and their environments.
2. Ecology deals with four levels of biological organization: population, community, biome, and biosphere.
3. An ecosystem is an interacting system that consists of groups of organisms and their non-living environment.
4. Organisms with similar niches will compete if they attempt to live in the same habitat.
5. Ecosystems have three main trophic levels: producers, consumers, and decomposers.
6. The main trophic level of consumer contains several trophic levels called orders.
7. Organisms in ecosystems are linked together in feeding relationships called food chains and food webs.
8. Feeding relationships can be illustrated with ecological pyramids.
9. Three types of symbiosis exist: parasitism, mutualism, and commensalism.
10. Organisms have a range of tolerance and an optimum condition for each abiotic factor.
11. Energy flow in ecosystems is one-way.
12. Nutrients in ecosystems are recycled.

Key Terms

The key terms for this chapter are listed in Section 2.1.

Chapter Review

A. True or False

Decide whether each of the following statements is true or false. If the sentence is false, rewrite it to make it true. (Do not write in this book.)

1. Ecology deals only with the relationships between organisms.
2. A biome contains several communities.
3. The biosphere is the region on earth in which life exists.
4. The niche of an organism is the place where it lives.
5. Omnivores eat both plants and animals.
6. A parasite usually kills its host.
7. Both organisms benefit in the symbiotic relationship called commensalism.
8. Energy flow in ecosystems is one-way.
9. Phosphorus can occur in water as a phosphate.

B. Completion

Complete each of the following statements with a word or phrase that will make the sentence correct. (Do not write in this book.)

1. The gravel, sand, water, air, and lamp make up the ▨▨▨▨▨▨ part of the model ecosystem.
2. A biome is a large area with a ▨▨▨▨▨▨ climate.
3. Animals that eat dead animals are called ▨▨▨▨▨▨ .
4. The food chains in an ecosystem are connected to form a ▨▨▨▨▨▨ .
5. Each trophic level in a pyramid of biomass shows the ▨▨▨▨▨▨ of the organisms at that level.
6. An organism thrives best at its ▨▨▨▨▨▨ temperature.
7. Nutrients needed in large amounts are called ▨▨▨▨▨▨ .

C. Multiple Choice

Each of the following statements or questions is followed by four responses. Choose the correct response in each case. (Do not write in this book.)

1. All the snapping turtles in a lake are best called a
   a) population   b) community   c) ecosystem   d) organism
2. A trout feeds on insects, worms, and small fish. It, in turn, is food for some mammals. Leeches and lampreys often feed on the trout. This description is best called the trout's
   a) habitat   b) niche   c) community   d) ecosystem
3. Young suckers (a fish) feed on tiny aquatic organisms. They also feed on decaying organic matter. These fish are best called
   a) predators   b) carnivores   c) scavengers   d) omnivores
4. Studies show that, for every square metre of surface area, a lake has 150 g of producers, 16 g of herbivores, and 4.5 g of carnivores. These data can be used to draw
   a) a pyramid of numbers   c) a pyramid of energy
   b) a pyramid of biomass   d) the main food chain
5. Consider this food chain:

   algae ⟶ mayflies ⟶ stoneflies ⟶ trout ⟶ humans

   The trout in this food chain are
   a) first-order carnivores   c) third-order carnivores
   b) second-order carnivores   d) top carnivores
6. Nitrogen, phosphorus, and potassium are best classified as
   a) primary macronutrients   c) micronutrients
   b) secondary macronutrients   d) non-mineral nutrients
7. The nutrient that is the basic building block of all living things is
   a) hydrogen   b) oxygen   c) carbon   d) nitrogen
8. The owners of a swimming pool returned from a holiday to find the water in the pool green. An extensive growth of algae had occurred. The owners added an algicide (algae killer) to the water but did not clean the

filter. In two days the green colour was gone. However, in three more days it came back. The algae returned mainly because

a) energy flow is one-way through the pool
b) nutrients were recycled in the pool
c) the carbon cycle is no longer perfect
d) nutrients entered the pool from the air

Using Your Knowledge

1. Copy Table 2-1 into your notebook. Then complete it for the following food chain:

    algae → mayflies → stoneflies → minnows → trout → human

Table 2-1 Trophic Levels

Organism	Trophic or sub-trophic level
algae	
mayflies	
stoneflies	
minnows	
trout	
human	

2. What would happen to a pond ecosystem if all the decomposers died? Why?
3. Make a list of the foods you ate recently that came from freshwater food chains. Draw the food chains. Include yourself in them.
4. Human sewage is often allowed to run, partially treated, into streams and lakes.
    a) Name the two macronutrients that would likely be present in the greatest quantities in this sewage.
    b) Explain why sewage contains these nutrients.
    c) Describe the effects that these nutrients could have on a lake.
5. If the filter is not working properly, an aquarium containing fish and snails often develops an extensive algal growth (a green colour). Why does this occur?
6. Many municipalities pollute nearby aquatic ecosystems by allowing poorly treated sewage to run into them. When challenged about this matter, municipal authorities often say that the municipality cannot afford to do much to stop the pollution. How do you feel about this answer? Write a paper of about 200 words outlining your position.

7. Vegetarians (people who eat only plants) often say that they use less of the world's energy per person than meat-eaters do. Do you agree? Explain your answer.

Investigations

1. Visit a nearby aquatic ecosystem. Make notes on the habitat and niche of at least five animals. Binoculars would be helpful. You may also wish to photograph the habitats.
2. Write a short paper (150 words) on a waterborne parasite that causes a human disease.
3. Find an example of mutualism that is not described in this text. Write a short report (100 words) on it.
4. Find an example of commensalism that is not described in this text. Write a short report (100 words) on it.
5. Consult an advanced ecology text to get data on the pyramid of biomass for a lake. Write a report on your findings, including the experimental method, the results, and the pyramid.
6. Repeat Activity 2.6, but this time add just one macronutrient (nitrogen, phosphorus, or potassium) instead of lawn fertilizer. Describe and explain your results. *Note*: Nitrogen may be added by using a nitrate salt like sodium nitrate. Phosphorus may be added by using a phosphate salt like sodium phosphate. Potassium may be added by using a potassium salt like potassium chloride.
7. Find out if your municipality allows sewage effluent to run into a river or lake. Has this affected water quality? Is the water quality getting better or worse? What are the municipality's plans for the future? If you feel that conditions warrant improvement, write a letter to the appropriate person(s) explaining your position.

3

Succession in Ponds, Lakes, and Wetlands

All ecosystems undergo a gradual change with time. A vacant lot, left untouched, gradually changes from bare soil to a cover of grasses and weeds. As time passes, taller weeds, then shrubs, and finally trees take over the area. In like manner, a pond or a lake undergoes gradual changes. A freshly dug pond has a bare bottom. But, as time passes, plants colonize the bottom. Like the vacant lot, the plant community gradually changes as the years pass.

Changes in the animal community and in the abiotic environment accompany the changes in the plant community. The process by which all this occurs is called ecological succession. Just what is ecological succession? Why does it occur?

3.1   Succession in Ponds and Lakes

You may find it helpful to do two things before you proceed with this chapter.

- Review the types of standing waters and their characteristics. (See Section 1.2, page 4.)
- Read about terrestrial succession. (See for example, Sections 4.1 to 4.4 of *Investigating Terrestrial Ecosystems* or a biology text which covers this topic.)

Succession is the gradual replacement of one community of living things by another. It occurs in all types of ecosystems. Let us see how it takes place in ponds and lakes. Suppose that you sat in a boat at the centre of a freshly-dug, deep pond. If you could stay there for hundreds of years, you would see the complete succession of the pond. The following is what would likely happen.

Plant Succession

Since the pond is quite deep, sufficient light cannot reach the bottom to promote plant growth. Thus the bottom consists of nothing but the parent earth material. This is the first stage in pond succession. It is called the pioneer stage, or bare-bottom stage.

As the years pass, runoff from the land and the decay of dead organisms add soil to the bottom of the pond. The pond gradually becomes more shallow. Eventually it is shallow enough that green plants can grow on the bottom. These submergent or underwater plants soon cover the bottom. Among these are *Chara* (stonewort), *Elodea* (Canada waterweed), *Cerato-phyllum* (coontail), and *Cabomba* (fanwort). This stage in succession is called the submergent vegetation stage.

Over the years, the decay of these plants adds further humus to the bottom of the pond. In time, the pond is shallow enough that *floating-leafed* plants such as the water lilies can grow. These plants, in turn, make the pond still more shallow. Now it can support the growth of emergent plants such as cattails, rushes, and sedges. Such plants are called emergent because part of them sticks out or emerges from the water. This stage in succession is called the emergent vegetation stage. The pond is now called a reedswamp.

The decay of emergent vegetation fills the pond still further. Now no large open expanse of water remains. The reedswamp has changed into a marsh. As the "islands" of land become drier, shrubs may begin to grow on them. The marsh has changed into a carr. As the land becomes still drier, trees may begin to grow. The carr has become a swamp.

Fig. 3-1 The first three stages in pond and lake succession.

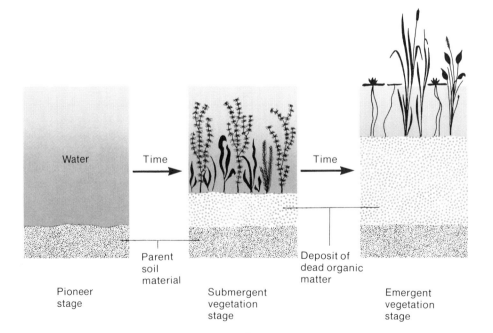

Water

Time

Time

Parent soil material

Deposit of dead organic matter

Pioneer stage

Submergent vegetation stage

Emergent vegetation stage

Given enough time, any pond or lake should fill in completely. However, the process of succession does not stop at this point. A whole series of terrestrial plant communities will continue the process. You can read about these in Chapter 4 of *Investigating Terrestrial Ecosystems*.

Figure 3-1 summarizes the process of pond succession from the pioneer stage to the emergent vegetation stage. These are the stages that you will likely study if your teacher takes you on a pond field trip. Fortunately, you will not have to wait in a boat for a few hundred years to see these stages. A pond is generally deepest near its centre. It gradually becomes more shallow towards the edge. Therefore, you can usually see the first three stages of succession if you look at the pond along a line that runs from the deepest spot to the edge (Fig. 3-2).

Fig. 3-2 Pond succession can be observed by looking at the vegetation along a line from the deepest spot to the edge.

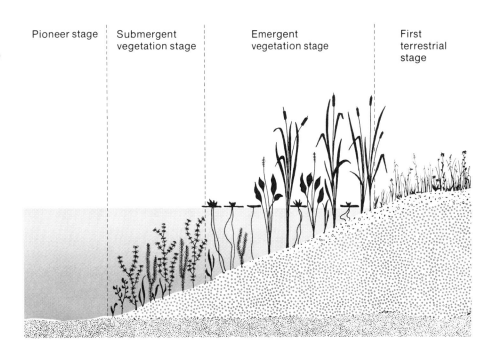

Pioneer stage | Submergent vegetation stage | Emergent vegetation stage | First terrestrial stage

Some Other Changes

The preceding discussion of pond succession dealt mainly with changes in plants. However, changes in other organisms accompany these changes in plants. Let us now look at these.

In the pioneer stage, most of the organisms are plankton. (The word "plankton" means small drifting organisms.) Most plankton are microscopic. A few are barely visible to the unaided eye. Some plankton are protists; others are animals. Some plankton are producers; others are consumers. The plankton that are producers are called phytoplankton (plant plankton). Most of these are algal protists such as diatoms and flagellates. Some are blue-green algae and green algae. The plankton that are consumers are called zooplankton (animal plankton). Some of these are protozoan protists. Many are animals such as rotifers and tiny crustaceans—cladocerans, copepods, and ostracods, to name a few. The zooplankton are mainly herbivores. They feed on the phytoplankton. Then they become food for carnivores such as aquatic insects and fish. The bottom of a pond contains large quantities of decaying organic matter. Decomposers such as bacteria, yeasts, and moulds break down this material. This returns nutrients to the water. These nutrients promote the growth of phytoplankton, thereby "feeding" the food chains of the pond.

The submergent vegetation stage of succession is dominated by plants that grow entirely under water. In like manner, the animals that live in this vegetation are adapted to life in a submerged stage. Most are gill-breathing insect larvas such as mayflies, damselflies, and dragonflies. In most ponds, the submerged vegetation is an important source of oxygen and food for the pond ecosystem.

The emergent vegetation stage is dominated by plants that grow partly in and partly out of the water. It is interesting to note that many of the animals that live in this vegetation are also adapted to a life that is partly aquatic and partly terrestrial. Amphibians such as frogs and toads are one example. Reptiles such as snakes and turtles are another.

Section Review

1. Copy Table 3-1 into your notebook. Then complete the column on the right.
2. Explain why ponds and lakes gradually change into marshes and even into carrs or swamps.
3. a) What are plankton?
   b) What is the difference between phytoplankton and zooplankton?

Table 3-1   Plant Succession in a Pond

Stage	Description
Pioneer	
Submergent	
Emergent (reedswamp)	
Marsh	
Carr	
Swamp	

3.2   *ACTIVITY*   **Succession in a Mini-Pond**

You can observe the early part of pond succession by setting up a "mini-pond" in a large jar. You must observe the jar from time to time for several weeks or, preferably, for several months. If there is not enough space in the classroom for the jars, your teacher may ask you to do this activity as a home project.

Problem

What is the nature of the early part of pond succession?

Materials

large jar (over 1 L)
pond water (1 L)
lamp (60 W)
hand lens
Pond Life (Golden Nature
   Guide Series) or other
   identification guides

microscope (optional)
microscope slide, flat (optional)
microscope slide, cavity (optional)
cover slip (optional)
dropper (optional)
1.5% methyl cellulose solution
   (optional)

Procedure

a. Put about 1 L of pond water in a large jar. The water should be collected in warm weather when the pond is active. Include 2 or 3 sprigs of submerged plant since these will carry eggs of a wide variety of animals.

b. Place a table lamp with a 60 W bulb in it over the jar as shown in Figure 3-3.

c. Place the setup in a location away from windows and direct heat. You must avoid locations where light and temperature conditions can change greatly during the day.

d. Leave the light on for at least 14 h each day. Top up the jar with dechlorinated tap water when necessary. (Water can be dechlorinated by letting it stand overnight preferably with aeration.)

e. Make a full-page copy of Table 3-2.

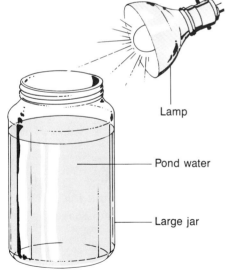

Lamp

Pond water

Large jar

Fig. 3-3   Succession in a mini-pond.

Table 3-2   Succession in a Mini-pond

Organism	Relative abundance	Date

f. After a day or two, do a biological inventory of the mini-pond. In other words, make a list of the types of organisms in the water. If you have access to a microscope, include protists (both algal and protozoan) and microscopic animals in your inventory. Your teacher will tell you how to use the microscope properly. Rank each organism as abundant (a), frequent (f), occasional (o), or rare (r). Put all this information in your table, along with the date.

g. Repeat the biological inventory in a week or so. Also, record any other changes which you observe.

h. Repeat the biological inventory every two weeks for as long as time permits. Continue to record other changes as well.

i. Return the organisms to a pond at the end of the study.

Discussion

Write a report on your findings. Include in your report a summary of your data and other observations. Then use that information to show that succession occurred in the mini-pond.

3.3   Succession from Lake to Peatland

In Section 3.1 you learned that lakes go through succession as follows:

Lake ⟶ Reedswamp ⟶ Marsh ⟶ Carr ⟶ Swamp Forest

This process occurs largely because of a gradual filling, from the bottom up, of the lake. There is, however, another route some lakes follow as they change from open water to forest. This route involves the formation of a peatland.

What Is a Peatland?

Peatlands occur in most parts of North America. They are best developed and most abundant, however, in the cool northern (boreal) forest. Regardless of where they are or what species grow in them, most peatlands have these characteristics in common.

• They contain an accumulation of partly decayed organic matter called peat.
• They have, at some stage, a floating mat of vegetation around the edge.
• They develop where drainage is poor.
• They develop a cushion-like mat of vegetation on top.
• They occur on flat or slightly undulating land.

There are two general types of peatlands—bogs and fens. Figure 3-4 shows each of these types. It also lists the main characteristics of each type.

Bog
- acidic water
- dominated by sphagnum moss, pitcher plants, sundews, and heaths
- nutrient poor
- little calcium
- little or no flow of water

Fen
- neutral or basic water
- dominated by sedges, grasses, and mosses other than sphagnum
- nutrient rich
- abundant calcium
- some flow of water

Fig. 3-4 The two main types of peatland.

Why Do Peatlands Form?

Formation of a peatland begins when drainage of a pond or lake becomes very slow. Sometimes this occurs because the outlet gets blocked by a beaver dam. Plant growth also helps to slow down drainage. In time, anaerobic (without oxygen) conditions are created. That is, the slow movement of water creates stagnant conditions, and the oxygen concentration goes down to almost zero. This causes the decay of dead plants to become slow and incomplete. As a result, partly decayed organic matter called **peat** forms. The peat releases **humic acids** into the water. They make the water brown.

If enough water flows through the peatland to bring in nutrients (including calcium), a **fen** forms (see Figure 3-4). If, however, this does not occur, the water turns acidic. Sphagnum moss begins to grow and a **bog** forms.

Succession in a Northern Bog

To see how succession occurs in peatlands, let us trace the process in North America's most common peatlands, the northern bogs. Follow Figure 3-5 as you read this description.

The process begins with open water (Step 1). As time passes, submerged plants appear (Step 2). These are followed by the first emergent plants, floating-leafed plants, such as the water lilies (Step 3). Then further emergent plants such as reeds, sedges, and cotton grass follow (Step 4).

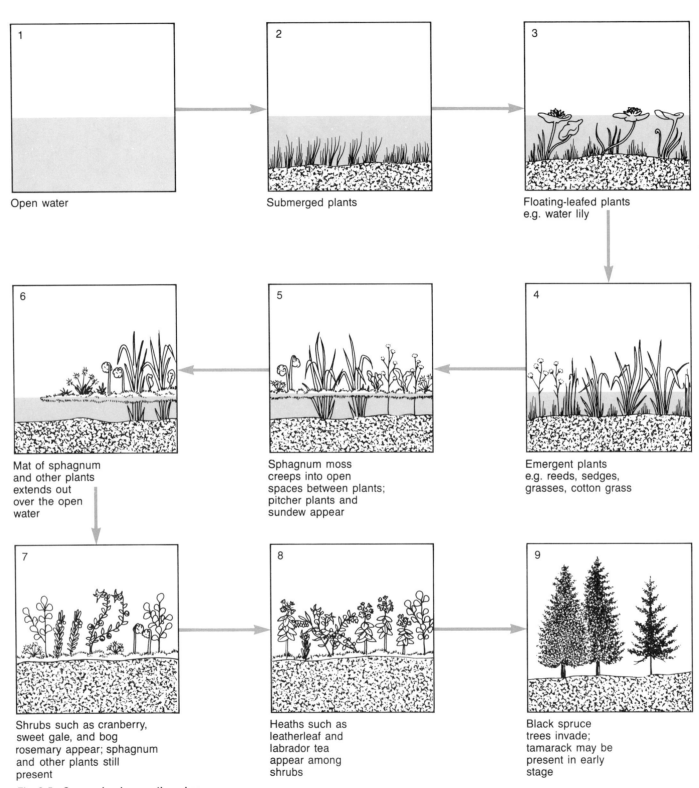

1 Open water

2 Submerged plants

3 Floating-leafed plants
e.g. water lily

4 Emergent plants
e.g. reeds, sedges,
grasses, cotton grass

5 Sphagnum moss
creeps into open
spaces between plants;
pitcher plants and
sundew appear

6 Mat of sphagnum
and other plants
extends out
over the open
water

7 Shrubs such as cranberry,
sweet gale, and bog
rosemary appear; sphagnum
and other plants still
present

8 Heaths such as
leatherleaf and
labrador tea
appear among
shrubs

9 Black spruce
trees invade;
tamarack may be
present in early
stage

Fig. 3-5 Succession in a northern bog.

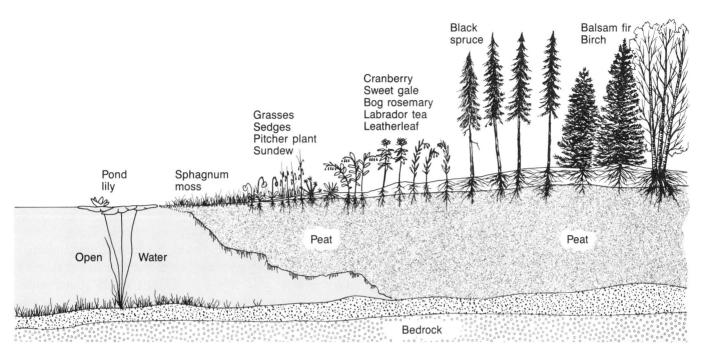

Fig. 3-6 Succession in a northern bog.

Fig. 3-7 Two carnivorous plants of northern bogs: sundew (A) and pitcher plant (B).

So far the succession has followed the pathway outlined in Section 3.1. Now, obstructed drainage causes the water to become acidic. Sphagnum moss appears and creeps into the open spaces between the plants (Step 5). Carnivorous plants—sundews and pitcher plants—also begin to appear.

As time passes, a mat of sphagnum and other plants extends over the open water (Step 6). This mat gets thicker and, as a result, drier. Shrubs such as cranberry, bog rosemary, and sweet gale now appear (Step 7). As well, heaths such as leatherleaf and labrador tea join the sphagnum and other plants under the shrubs (Step 8). Finally trees begin to appear. Black spruce trees soon dominate this stage (Step 9). In the early stages they may, however, be accompanied by tamarack. The sphagnum of the forest floor may be joined by partridge berry and bunchberry.

In some areas the succession climaxes at black spruce. In others it proceeds to a climax of black spruce, white cedar, and balsam fir. It may even proceed to a climax of balsam fir, red maple, and birch.

Hundreds of years are usually needed for this complete succession. But you can generally see most of the steps if you walk from the open water inland (Fig. 3-6).

Carnivorous Plants

Sphagnum moss is the dominant plant of a bog. However, the most interesting plants are the carnivorous (flesh-eating) plants. Two of these—pitcher plants and sundews—are found in northern bogs (Fig. 3-7). A third, the Venus' flytrap, occurs in bogs in the Carolinas (Fig. 3-8). It is often sold as a

Fig. 3-8 Venus' flytrap, a carnivorous plant in bogs in the Carolinas.

novelty house plant. All three have special ways for trapping insects and other small animals. They digest these organisms to obtain nitrogen. They need nitrogen to make proteins. Other plants get their nitrogen from the soil where it occurs as a nitrate. But bog soils contain little or no nitrate.

Succession: A Summary

As you have seen, succession is the gradual replacement of one community by another. Why does it occur?

Living things change their environment. In doing so, they make the environment less favourable for themselves. For example, a certain community of living things may become established in a lake because the acidity of the water is just right. But the life processes of the organisms can change the acidity. Now the lake is a less favourable environment for that community. But it may be more favourable for another community of living things. Therefore this second community gradually replaces the first one. Each stage in succession, then, brings about its own downfall.

Five things generally happen as succession proceeds.

- Species diversity (the number of species) increases.
- Population numbers (the number of individuals of each species) increase.
- The number of niches increases.
- The total biomass in the ecosystem increases.
- The amount of organic matter (living and non-living) increases.

All of these add to the complexity of the ecosystem. This complexity makes the ecosystem more stable. Many plant and animal species with numerous niches means more food chains and webs will be formed. Thus there is less chance of the entire community collapsing if one or two species disappear.

Section Review

1. List five characteristics which peatlands have in common.
2. What is peat?
3. Name the two main types of peatland.
4. What makes a bog form instead of a fen?
5. List five differences between fens and bogs.
6. Make a point form summary of the stages in the succession of a northern bog.
7. a) What are carnivorous plants?
   b) Name three common carnivorous plants.
   c) Why are animals like insects important in the diet of carnivorous plants?
8. a) Why does succession occur?
   b) What five things usually happen as succession proceeds?
   c) What do these five things do for the ecosystem?

3.4 *FIELD TRIP* **Investigating Pond Succession**

In this activity your class will investigate and compare the first three stages in pond succession: the pioneer stage, the submergent vegetation stage, and the emergent vegetation stage (Fig. 3-9). The emphasis will be upon the changes in biotic factors as succession proceeds.

You will be assigned to one of three groups by your teacher. Then your group will be asked to investigate one of the three stages. If time permits, your teacher will let your group study one or both of the other stages as well.

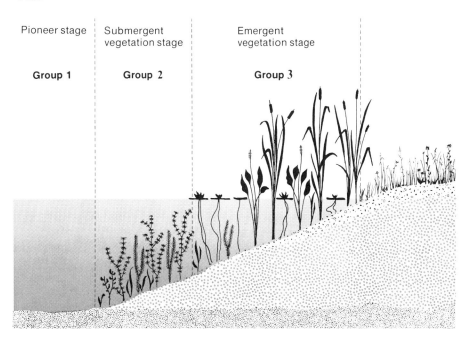

Pioneer stage | Submergent vegetation stage | Emergent vegetation stage

Group 1 | **Group 2** | **Group 3**

Fig. 3-9 Your class will investigate these three stages in pond succession.

Problem

How do the biotic factors change as pond succession proceeds from the pioneer stage to the emergent vegetation stage?

Materials (for the class)

In the field
plankton net (1)
plastic collecting jars (3)
dip nets (2)
white trays and sieves (8)
hand lens (6)
plastic buckets (2)
Pond Life (Golden Guide Series)
   or other identification guides (6)

In the classroom
microscopes (class set)
Pond Life or alternate (class set)
1.5% methyl cellulose solution (5)
droppers
cover slips
paper towels
lens paper
microscope slides

Procedure A   Group 1: Pioneer Stage

The task of this group is to collect plankton from the pioneer stage. The plankton will be taken back to the classroom for study.

a. Before you go on this field trip, read Chapter 7 to find out about plankton.

b. While hanging onto the tow rope, throw the plankton net as far out as you can into the pond (Fig. 3-10). Then tow the net toward the shore. Do not let the net go deep into the water. If you do, it will sample the submergent vegetation. Lift the net from the water just as soon as you can.

c. Make 4 or 5 drags as described in step (b).

d. Release the contents of the collecting tube into a plastic collecting jar.

e. Top up the jar with water. Do not cap the jar. *Note*: Do not overcrowd the jar or you will suffocate the organisms.

f. As soon as you return to the classroom, dump the contents of the jar into one of the white trays. Add dechlorinated tap water or pond water to a depth of 2 or 3 cm in the tray. The increased surface area that the tray provides will prevent the organisms from suffocating.

g. Make a full page copy of Table 3-3. Do not copy the example.

h. Study the plankton in the tray as described in Activity 7.4. Do not complete Table 7-2 in that activity. Instead, complete the first four columns of your table as you identify each organism.

i. Complete the *Niche* column of your table by looking up the information in Chapter 7.

j. Return all organisms to the tray after you have studied them. Your teacher will return them to a suitable habitat.

Fig. 3-10 Throw the net out to the pioneer stage. A plankton net, when pulled through the water, captures plankton.

Table 3-3 Planktonic Organisms

Organism	Phytoplankton (P) or zooplankton (Z)	Relative abundance (a,f,o,r)	Sketch	Niche
Daphnia	Z	f		filter feeder (algae, protozoans, bacteria, detritus); important trophic level in aquatic food chains; often most important herbivore in ponds and lakes

Procedure B Group 2: Submergent Stage

The task of this group is to collect organisms from the submergent vegetation stage. Invertebrates may be taken back to the classroom for study, although the study can be done at the pond if time permits. Vertebrates must be released immediately after examination.

a. Before you go on this field trip, read Chapters 8, 9, and 10 to find out about the organisms you may encounter.

b. Make a full page copy of Table 3-4. Do not copy the example.

Table 3-4 Animals in the Submergent Stage

Organism	Relative abundance (a,f,o,r)	Adaptations	Advantages to organism	Niche
Mayfly (vegetation dweller)	f	hook on each foot; gills on abdomen; gills and tail move strongly; brownish-green	can climb among plants; can remain submerged; strong swimmer; camouflaged	opportunistic feeder; mainly herbivore; key link in many food chains

Fig. 3-11 Short brisk strokes of a dip net will dislodge animals from the vegetation.

Fig. 3-12 In shallow water, a kitchen sieve works better than a dip net.

c. Sample the submergent stage for animals as follows. For deeper areas, move the dip net through the vegetation with short brisk strokes (Fig.3-11). Then dump the contents of the net into a white tray containing 2-3 cm of water. For shallow areas, use the sieve in place of the dip net (Fig. 3-12).

d. Sample the bottom ooze for organisms as follows. Scoop up some bottom ooze with the sieve. Swish it through the water to wash out as much of the "mud" as possible. Then dump the contents into a white tray containing 2-3 cm of water.

e. In the field or back in the classroom, study the invertebrates as described in Activity 8.5. Complete the first four columns of your table as you identify each organism. Your teacher may decide to leave the organisms in trays instead of putting them in an aquarium.

f. Complete the *Niche* column of your table by looking up the information in Chapters 8, 9, or 10.

g. Return all organisms to the tray or aquarium after you have studied them. Your teacher will return them to a suitable habitat.

Procedure C   Group 3: Emergent Stage

The task of this group is to collect organisms from the emergent vegetation stage. Invertebrates may be taken back to the classroom for study, although the study can be done at the pond if time permits. Vertebrates must be released immediately after examination.

The instructions for this procedure are the same as those for Procedure B. Keep the organisms in separate trays from those of Procedure B. Also put your data in separate tables.

Discussion

1. Make sure that you have completed the data tables for all three sites.
2. After the groups have shared information, write a paper of about 300 words which describes and explains the biotic changes that occur as succession progresses from the pioneer to the emergent stage.

Main Ideas

1. Succession is the gradual replacement of one community of living things by another.
2. Plant succession in a pond or lake often follows these stages: pioneer, submergent, emergent (reedswamp), marsh, carr, swamp.
3. An animal succession parallels a plant succession.
4. There are two types of peatlands, bogs and fens.
5. Sphagnum moss is the key plant in succession in a northern bog.
6. Carnivorous plants get needed nitrogen by digesting animals.
7. As succession proceeds, ecosystem stability usually increases.

Key Terms

bog	marsh	reedswamp
carnivorous plants	peat	submergent vegetation
carr	peatland	succession
emergent vegetation	phytoplankton	swamp
fen	pioneer stage	zooplankton
humic acids	plankton	

Chapter Review

A. True or False

Decide whether each of the following statements is true or false. If the sentence is false, rewrite it to make it true. (Do not write in this book.)
1. The pioneer stage of pond succession cannot change to the submergent vegetation stage until light can reach the bottom of the pond.
2. A swamp is a wetland with trees in it.
3. All plankton are microscopic animals.
4. Fens are a type of peatland.
5. A peatland becomes a fen if nutrients, including calcium, flow through it.
6. Carnivorous plants digest animals to obtain carbohydrates.

B. Completion

Complete each of the following sentences with a word or phrase that will make the sentence correct. (Do not write in this book.)
1. When a reedswamp eventually has no large open expanse of water, it has become a ▒▒▒▒▒ .
2. Amphibians such as frogs are most common in the ▒▒▒▒▒ stage of pond succession.
3. Partly decayed organic matter is called ▒▒▒▒▒ .
4. The key plant in bog formation is ▒▒▒▒▒ .
5. The most common tree in northern bogs is ▒▒▒▒▒ .

C. Multiple Choice

Each of the following statements or questions is followed by four responses. Choose the correct response in each case. (Do not write in this book.)
1. Suppose you are paddling a canoe through emergent plants in a lake. Then you come to an area where you keep bumping into "islands" of land with shrubs on them. You are probably in a
   a) reedswamp   **b)** marsh   **c)** carr   **d)** swamp
2. Which one of the following best describes the abiotic environment of a bog?
   a) acidic water, nutrient poor, little calcium, little flow of water
   b) acidic water, nutrient rich, abundant calcium, little flow of water
   c) neutral water, nutrient poor, little calcium, flow of water
   d) basic water, nutrient rich, abundant calcium, flow of water
3. A beaver dammed the drainage stream of a small northern lake. Water flow through the lake was reduced almost to zero and the water became anaerobic. Unless conditions changed, this lake will most likely become a
   a) marsh   **b)** bog   **c)** fen   **d)** swamp

Using Your Knowledge

1. The manager of a conservation area was observed removing the submergent vegetation from a small pond. When questioned about the reason for doing this he replied, ". . . to get rid of the unsightly weeds and make the pond healthier". What do you think of his answer? Defend your position.
2. Most of the animals of the pioneer stage of pond succession are zooplankton. Why?
3. Explain why some peatlands become bogs while others become fens.
4. Many small bogs near cities have been destroyed because people collect plants such as pitcher plants from them to plant in their gardens. But these plants soon die in gardens. Why is that so?
5. Well-preserved corpses of humans and other animals have been found deep in peatlands, some that are hundreds of years old. Why were they so well-preserved?
6. A pulp and paper company intends to harvest the black spruce in a peatland in northern Canada. At what time of year would you suggest they do this harvesting? Why?
7. Explain why ecosystems in advanced stages of succession are generally more stable than those in earlier stages.

Investigations

1. Put a large pan or bucket of tap water outside. Observe it carefully for several weeks. Describe any evidence of succession which you observed.
2. Write a paper of about 200 words on the uses of peat.
3. Select one of the following carnivorous plants and find out how it traps its prey: sundew, pitcher plant, Venus' flytrap.
4. Find out how to set up and maintain a bog terrarium. Set one up with a group of your classmates. Look after it for several months. Write a report on what you learned from this activity.
5. Research the importance of wetlands for one of the following:
   a) agriculture
   b) wildlife habitat
   c) recreation

UNIT TWO

Freshwater Ecosystems: Abiotic Factors

An ecosystem like this marsh has two main parts, a biotic (living) part and an abiotic (non-living) part. The abiotic part can, in turn, be divided into geophysical properties and chemical properties. This unit explores those properties.

Like all ecosystems, this marsh consists of a biotic part and an abiotic part which interact.

4 Geophysical Properties

Geophysical properties of freshwater ecosystems include such factors as temperature, colour, transparency, speed, depth, and the nature of the bottom. All these factors interact with one another. They also interact with chemical factors and with biological factors. For example, a slow stream tends to be warmer than a fast stream. The slow stream also has smaller particles on its bottom. Further, the slow stream usually has less oxygen in it (a chemical factor) than a fast stream does. As a result of all these factors, the slow stream usually has different organisms in it (a biological factor) than the fast stream does.

This chapter looks at the main geophysical properties that affect freshwater ecosystems. You will see in Chapters 5 and 6 how these geophysical properties interact with chemical factors. Finally, in Unit 3 you will learn how all these abiotic factors interact with biological or biotic factors.

4.1 Geophysical Properties of Standing Waters

Several geophysical properties affect the ecology of lakes and ponds. This section discusses five of them: temperature, nature of the bottom, colour, turbidity, and transparency.

Temperature

As you know, each species of organism has its own optimum or preferred temperature. For example, the optimum temperatures for three common species of fish are: 32°C for *Cyprinus carpio* (carp), 24°C for *Perca flavescens* (perch), and 15°C for *Salmo trutta* (trout). These and other aquatic organisms can stand some variation from the optimum temperature. However, if the temperature shifts too far from the optimum, the organism either dies or moves to a new location. With most species of fish, an increase of 5°C above the optimum can be quite harmful. This is particularly true if the increase is unexpected for that time of year. For example, if a stream has an average May temperature of 18°C and hot outflow from an industry raises the temperature to 25°C, a large number of fish will probably die. If, on the other hand, the temperature gradually rises to 25°C as a result of normal summer warming, a fish kill will probably not occur. The fish have time to migrate to cooler regions.

Why does an increase in temperature kill fish and other aquatic life? As the water temperature increases, the body temperature of any poikilothermic ("cold-blooded") animal in the water increases. This, in turn, results in an increase in the rate of metabolism in the animal. Of course, this increases the animal's need for oxygen. Yet, as the temperature of the water goes up, its ability to hold oxygen goes down. (See Section 5.1.) Eventually a temperature is reached at which the oxygen demand of the animal exceeds the available oxygen and the organism dies. This temperature is called the lethal temperature. It is unlikely that all members of a particular species will die at exactly the same temperature and time. Thus ecologists use what they call a tolerance limit median (TLm) when they are studying the effects of thermal pollution. They normally use either a 24 h TLm or a 12 h TLm. If a certain species of fish has a 24 h TLm of 30°C, then 50% of the fish die within a 24 h period if the water temperature is 30°C. What does a 12 h TLm of 35°C indicate?

High temperatures usually increase the toxic effects of chemical pollutants in water. For example, minnows placed in a 0.55 μg/g cyanide solution reacted to the cyanide in 72 min when the water temperature was 1.2°C; the reaction time decreased to 12 min when the temperature was raised to 20°C.

Nature of the Bottom

The bottom of a pond or lake normally consists of decaying plant and animal matter. This detritus is home to countless bacteria and fungi. They feed on the detritus. As they do so, they respire and use up oxygen. As a result, many other species cannot live near the bottom.

If light reaches the bottom, submerged plants may live there. They help provide oxygen. They also provide food and habitat for a wide variety of organisms.

Colour

The colour of water gives us an idea of the amount of suspended and dissolved matter in the water. If, for example, the water is green, we can assume that the water contains phytoplankton (algae). A light yellow or brown colour can be caused by a suspension of dead algae or by a suspension of clay, storm runoff may have carried into the water.

Fig. 4-1 A Secchi disc is used for finding the transparency of a body of water.

Turbidity

Water may be turbid or cloudy due to the presence of suspended solids. Some of these solids may be living organic matter such as phytoplankton and zooplankton. Also, they may be non-living organic matter such as small pieces of dead organisms and sewage. These solids may also be inorganic matter such as silt and clay.

Ecologists use an instrument called a turbidimeter to measure turbidity. Turbidity can also be measured roughly, using a Secchi disc (see *Transparency* below) or by finding the total suspended solids (T.S.S.) as described in Section 4.7.

Transparency

The transparency of water is a measure of how well light passes through the water. It is an indication of the amount of suspended solids in the water. Transparency is usually measured with a Secchi disc (Fig. 4-1). This metal disc is 20 cm in diameter. It is divided into four quarters, two of which are white and two black.

To obtain a Secchi disc reading, the disc is lowered into the water until it disappears. This depth is recorded. The disc is then lowered past this point and slowly raised until it can be seen again. This depth is recorded and averaged with the first reading. This entire procedure is repeated two more times. The final average of all three averages is the Secchi disc reading.

If the Secchi disc reading is low (for example 1 m), the water contains much suspended matter. If, however, it is high (for example 8 m), the water is quite clear and free of suspended solids. Lakes polluted with acid precipitation have high Secchi disc readings. That's because suspended matter such as phytoplankton and zooplankton have been killed and settled.

To get a reliable Secchi disc reading, ecologists take the reading as shown in Figure 4-2. The reading will, of course, depend on the location, time of day, and type of day (sunny or dull).

The Secchi disc reading corresponds roughly to what ecologists call the compensation depth. This is the depth at which oxygen production by phytoplankton in the upper water equals oxygen use by bottom organisms such as bacteria. (See also Section 4.5.)

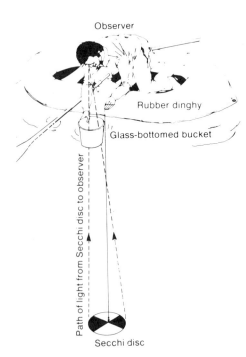

Observer

Rubber dinghy

Glass-bottomed bucket

Path of light from Secchi disc to observer

Secchi disc

Fig. 4-2 A Secchi disc reading is done on the shady side of the boat or through a glass-bottomed bucket to reduce error due to surface glare.

Section Review

1. Why might an increase in water temperature kill fish and other aquatic life?
2. **a)** What is meant by the "lethal temperature"?
   b) What does "TLm" mean?
3. Describe how the nature of the bottom affects life in a pond or lake.
4. What factors can give water a colour?

5. **a)** What causes turbidity?
   b) State three methods for measuring turbidity.
6. **a)** What is transparency?
   b) How is it measured?
   c) Why is water polluted with acid precipitation generally clear?
7. What is the compensation depth of a lake?

4.2 *ACTIVITY* The Abnormal Behaviour of Water

The survival of much of the life in ponds and lakes depends on the abnormal behaviour of water. "Abnormal" means strange or unusual. What is strange or unusual about the behaviour of water? Most liquids become more dense as they are cooled down. They become most dense at the freezing point. In other words, the solid state of most substances is more dense than the liquid state. Is this true for water? Or is water abnormal? How do you know? Try this experiment to test your ideas.

Problem

What is abnormal about the behaviour of water?

Materials

large beaker (1000 mL)	thermometer (-10°C to 110°C)
crushed ice	2-hole rubber stopper
salt	fine glass tubing
water	ruler
250 mL flask	ring stand
transparent tape	adjustable clamp

Procedure

a. Copy Table 4-1 into your notebook. Make it a full page long.
b. Set up the apparatus as shown in Figure 4-3. Your teacher will put the tubing and the thermometer into the stopper. Use transparent tape to attach the ruler to the tubing.
c. Every minute note and record the level of the water in the tube.
d. Stir the ice-salt-water mixture from time to time to make it as cold as possible.
e. Continue to take readings until the temperature of the water is 0°C.
f. Remove the flask from the mixture. Let it warm up. Note and record the level of the water in the tube every minute. Continue until the temperature of the water is back up near room temperature.

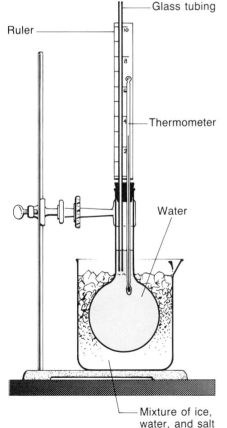

Fig. 4-3 **What will happen to the level of the water as the water cools?**

Table 4-1   Abnormal Behaviour of Water

Time (min)	Level of water (mm)
1	
2	
3	
4	
5	
•	
•	
•	

Discussion

1. Describe carefully what happens to the volume of water as the temperature drops to 0°C.
2. What happens to the density of water as the temperature drops to 0°C?
3. At what temperature does water have its smallest volume (and greatest density)?
4. Why does ice float on water?
5. What is abnormal about the behaviour of water?
6. Figure 4-4 shows a pond in mid-winter. Account for the various temperature readings.
7. If water did not have this abnormal behaviour, fish could not live in ponds and lakes in areas where freezing occurs. Why?

Fig. 4-4   The temperature profile of a pond in mid-winter.

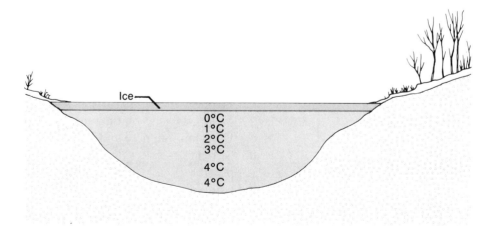

Layering and Overturn in Lakes

Light can reach the bottom at all places in a pond. As a result, submerged vegetation grows over the entire bottom of the pond. In contrast, light cannot reach the bottom at all places in a lake. As a result, submerged vegetation plays a lesser role in a lake ecosystem than in a pond ecosystem. In fact, phytoplankton form the base of most food chains in a lake. The phytoplankton live mainly in the upper few metres of a lake. They require light for photosynthesis. However, consumers are found at all depths in most lakes. Those that are herbivores dwell near the surface where they graze on phytoplankton. Those that are carnivores spend their time at various depths. Some live at a depth of several hundred metres in certain lakes. Of course, these consumers need oxygen. Most of the decomposers that live in the bottom ooze also need oxygen. Yet photosynthesis does not occur at such depths. How, then does oxygen get to the bottom of a deep lake? It does so by an interesting process called overturn. Let us see how it happens.

Spring Overturn

As the ice on a lake melts in the spring, the cold water that forms sinks to the bottom. (You learned in Section 4.2 that water is most dense at 4°C.) Therefore the lake gradually fills from the bottom with cold water. At some time in the spring, the lake is the same temperature throughout. As a result, it also has the same density throughout. Such water mixes easily when the spring winds blow over it (Fig. 4-5,A). This mixing of the water carries oxygen to the bottom. It also brings nutrients from the bottom to the top, where they support the growth of phytoplankton. This process is called spring overturn.

Summer Stagnation

As summer approaches, the sun warms the upper layer of water faster than the winds can mix it. By mid-summer, the lake usually has three layers in it (Fig. 4-5,B). The upper layer, or epilimnion, contains warmer water that circulates freely. The lower layer, or hypolimnion, contains colder water that does not circulate. In between is a layer of transition from warm to colder water. It is called the metalimnion, or thermocline. Usually the temperature drops about 1.0°C for every depth increase of 1.0 m. Because of density differences, the hypolimnion is cut off from circulation. It receives no further oxygen from the epilimnion. Limnologists say that the lake is now in summer stagnation. If the lake is eutrophic (nutrient-rich), much of the remaining oxygen is quickly used up. Then the hypolimnion becomes unsuitable for life that requires a large supply of oxygen.

Fall Overturn

As fall approaches, the epilimnion cools and gradually gets deeper. Finally the entire lake is a uniform temperature again. The fall winds are now able to cause another mixing of the water. This mixing is called the fall overturn (Fig. 4-5,C).

Fig. 4-5 Spring and fall overturn carry oxygen to the bottoms of many deep lakes.

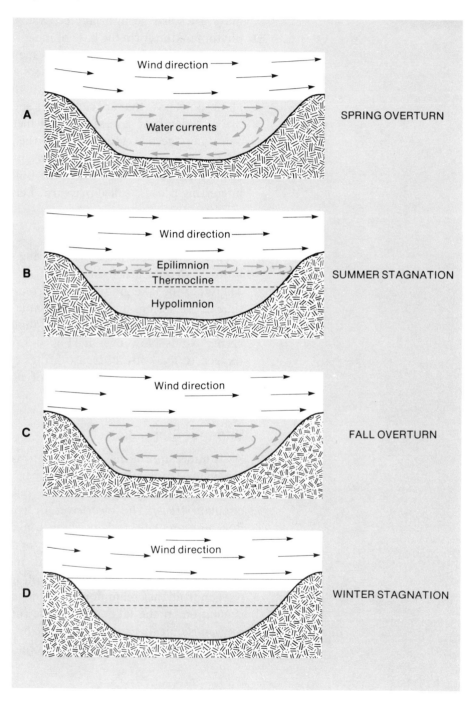

A   Wind direction   Water currents   SPRING OVERTURN

B   Wind direction   Epilimnion   Thermocline   Hypolimnion   SUMMER STAGNATION

C   Wind direction   FALL OVERTURN

D   Wind direction   WINTER STAGNATION

Winter Stagnation

With the coming of winter, the upper water cools still further. This cooling increases the density of the water. The resulting cool water sinks to the bottom. This process continues as long as the temperature of the water is above 4°C. Water with a temperature below 4°C is less dense. Therefore it stays on the top and eventually freezes (Fig. 4-5,D). Once again three layers form. The epilimnion is now ice and water near 0°C. The hypolimnion is water at or above 4°C. The thermocline is reversed. It goes from cold water at the top to warmer water below. Again, because of density differences, the hypolimnion is cut off from the epilimnion. No additional oxygen will reach the hypolimnion until the next spring overturn. The lake is said to be in winter stagnation.

Section Review

1. Why are phytoplankton most common near the top of a lake?
2. Explain why spring overturn occurs.
3. Give two reasons why overturn is important.
4. **a)** Draw a diagram of a lake in summer stagnation.
   b) Explain why the stagnation occurred.
   c) Why might the hypolimnion of an eutrophic lake be unsuitable for many forms of life?
5. Explain why fall overturn occurs.
6. Describe the structure of a lake during winter stagnation.

4.4   *ACTIVITY* Layering in a Model Lake

The purpose of this activity is to help you understand the explanation of layering in Section 4.3.

Problem

How does layering in a lake occur?

Materials

large glass container (2)   ring stand and clamp
coloured ice cubes   small fan
regular ice cubes   heat lamp
warm water   small beaker (250 mL)
food colouring (blue and red)   rubber tubing (optional)
thermometers (2)   marking pen

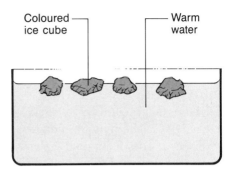

Coloured ice cube — Warm water

Fig. 4-6 What happens to the cold water which forms when the ice melts?

Procedure A What Happens When Ice Melts?

a. Fill one of the glass containers with warm water (about 25°C).

b. Carefully lower 3 or 4 coloured ice cubes onto the surface of the water. (Make the coloured ice cubes by putting food colouring in the water before you freeze it.)

c. Observe what happens as the ice cubes melt (Fig. 4-6).

Procedure B Layering

a. Half fill the other glass container with cold water (8°C or lower). (You can cool the water using the regular ice cubes.) Colour this water with blue food colouring.

b. Carefully add lukewarm water (about 22°C) to the surface of the cold water (Fig. 4-7). You can pour it on slowly using a small beaker or you can siphon it using the rubber tubing. In either case, be sure you do not disturb the bottom layer.

Fig. 4-7 A model of a lake during layering.

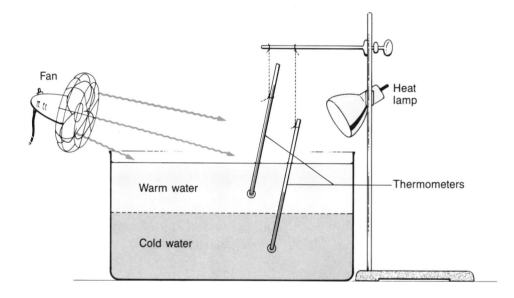

Fan

Heat lamp

Warm water

Cold water

Thermometers

c. Mark the position of the thermocline on the outside of the tank.

d. Warm the upper layer with a heat lamp placed 5-10 cm from the surface.

e. Blow air slowly over the surface of the water using a small fan.

f. Place a little red food colouring in the water.

g. Observe the temperatures and the position of the thermocline several times during this activity.

h. Continue the activity until overturn occurs.

1. a) What happens as the ice cubes melt?
    b) Why does this occur?
2. Why does this eventually lead to spring overturn in a lake?

Discussion B

1. Explain how this part of the activity illustrates summer stagnation in a lake.
2. What evidence did you see that wind can cause currents in the epilimnion of a lake but not in the hypolimnion?
3. a) What happened to the two temperatures and the position of the thermocline just before overturn occurred?
    b) Why did overturn occur?
    c) Is what happened here the same as spring overturn, fall overturn, or neither of these? How do you know?

4.5 Oxygen-Carbon Dioxide Balance in a Lake

Photosynthesis

Most of the oxygen in a lake comes from photosynthesis of producers (plants and algae). These organisms use up carbon dioxide and water during photosynthesis. They also produce oxygen and organic compounds such as glucose. Photosynthesis occurs only when light and chlorophyll are present. The oxygen which is produced dissolves in the water.

$$\text{Carbon dioxide} + \text{Water} + \text{Light Energy} \xrightarrow{\text{chlorophyll}} \text{Glucose} + \text{Oxygen}$$

PHOTOSYNTHESIS PRODUCES OXYGEN AND USES UP CARBON DIOXIDE.

Respiration

During respiration the producers and consumers (animals) use oxygen to "burn up" foods like glucose. Most decomposers (bacteria and fungi) do the same thing. Respiration gives the organisms the energy they need for life processes. Respiration produces two by-products, carbon dioxide and water.

$$\text{Glucose} + \text{Oxygen} \longrightarrow \text{Carbon dioxide} + \text{Water} + \text{Heat Energy}$$

RESPIRATION PRODUCES CARBON DIOXIDE AND USES UP OXYGEN.

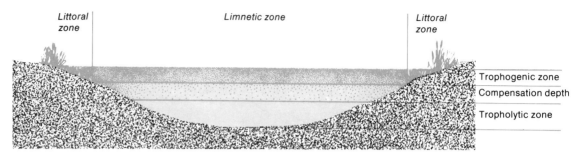

Fig. 4-8   The major zones of a lake.

The Balance Between Photosynthesis and Respiration

Organisms occur throughout a lake—from top to bottom. As a result, respiration takes place throughout the lake. Therefore oxygen is used up and carbon dioxide is produced at all depths. Often, though, respiration is greatest near the bottom. This is because dead organisms sink to the bottom where numerous decomposers feed on them. Thus the lower part of the hypolimnion often has high carbon dioxide and low oxygen values. This part of the lake is called the tropholytic zone (*Troph-* means feeding and -*lytic* means decomposition). The organisms in this zone feed by decomposing organic matter (Fig. 4-8).

If a lake is oligotrophic ("lacking food" or clean), the oxygen concentration decreases only slightly with depth. If, however, a lake is eutrophic ("adequate food" or nutrient-rich), the oxygen concentration decreases a great deal in the bottom of the hypolimnion, that is, in the tropholytic zone (Fig. 4-9).

In some lakes no oxygen occurs in the tropholytic zone. In such lakes the bacteria in the bottom ooze respire anaerobically (without oxygen). This forms methane and hydrogen sulfide ("rotten-egg") gases. Methane is the natural gas many people burn in their homes for cooking and heating. You can smell hydrogen sulfide if you push a stick into the black muck around a pond, lake, or marsh.

Although respiration occurs at all depths, photosynthesis does not. Photosynthesis requires light. Light can penetrate only so far into the water before it becomes too weak to cause much photosynthesis. Thus oxygen is not given off at all depths. Most of it is produced in an upper layer called the trophogenic zone. (*Troph-* means feeding and -*genic* means producing). The organisms in this zone produce food by photosynthesis.

Between the trophogenic zone (at the top) and the tropholytic zone (at the bottom) is a zone called the compensation depth. In this zone oxygen production and use are equal. Or, if you like, carbon dioxide production and usage are equal. The trophogenic zone produces more oxygen than it uses. In contrast, the tropholytic zone uses more oxygen than it produces. Therefore, between these zones there will be a zone where oxygen production and usage are equal. That is, oxygen production *compensates* for oxygen usage. Why are carbon dioxide production and usage also equal at the compensation depth?

Fig. 4-9   The oxygen-depth profiles for an oligotrophic and eutrophic lake.

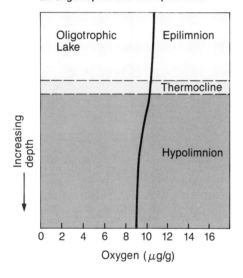

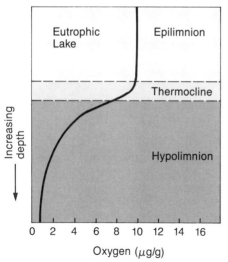

The trophogenic zone can be divided into two subzones. These are the littoral zone and the limnetic zone. The littoral zone (*littoral* means shore) is the region where light reaches the bottom. Thus submerged plants grow in this zone. Of course, it is normally around the edges of a lake. The limnetic zone (*limn-* means lake) is that part of the open water in which effective light penetration occurs. Phytoplankton are the main producers in this zone. In fact, they are the main producers of the lake. Note that the bottom of this zone meets the bottom of the littoral zone. Why is this so?

Section Review

1. Write a word equation for photosynthesis.
2. Write a word equation for respiration.
3. Describe the tropholytic zone.
4. Compare the oxygen-depth profiles of oligotrophic and eutrophic lakes.
5. What happens when the tropholytic zone runs out of oxygen?
6. Describe the trophogenic zone.
7. What does compensation depth mean?
8. Describe the two subzones of the trophogenic zone.

Geophysical Properties of Flowing Waters

4.6

The geophysical properties of standing waters were described in Section 4.1. What was said about four of those properties—temperature, colour, turbidity, and transparency—also applies here. Three other factors, however, apply especially to flowing waters—nature of the bottom, cross-section profile, and speed.

Nature of the Bottom

Table 4-2 Classification of Bottom Material

Name	Diameter (mm)
Boulder	over 256
Cobble	64-256
Pebble	2.0-64
Sand	0.063-2.0
Silt	0.004-0.063
Clay	less than 0.004

Table 4-2 gives a commonly used classification system for bottom material in flowing waters. Look at your ruler to get an idea of these sizes.

Usually fast water has larger material in the bottom than slow water does. Why is this so?

Cross-section Profile

Fast water often gouges out the centre of a stream. This gives the stream a triangular cross-section profile (Fig. 4-10,A). In contrast, slow water often has a rectangular cross-section profile (Fig. 4-10,B).

The cross-section profile of a stream can be mapped as follows. Suspend a string across the stream. Fasten both ends securely. Then, at suitable intervals

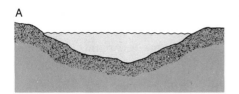

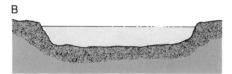

Fig. 4-10 Cross-section profiles of a fast stream (A) and a slow stream (B).

along the string, measure the depth of the water (Fig. 4-11). For a stream 10 m wide, a good interval is 1.0 m; for a stream 5 m wide, 0.5 m; for a stream 1 m wide, 5 cm. A typical set of data is shown in Table 4-3 and plotted in Figure 4-12.

Table 4-3   Cross-section Profile Data

Distance (m)	Depth (m)
0	0.00
1	0.15
2	0.27
3	0.55
4	0.72
5	0.71
6	0.62
7	0.42
8	0.31
9	0.14
10	0.00

Fig. 4-11 Finding the cross-section profile of a stream.

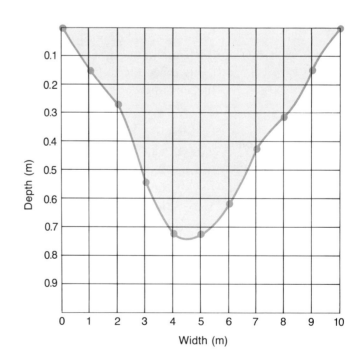

Fig. 4-12 Graph of the cross-section profile of a stream. The depth data are often plotted to a different scale than the width data to emphasize changes in depth.

Speed

The speed of the water is a very important geophysical property. As you have seen, the speed helps determine the cross-section profile and the nature of the bottom. It also influences the oxygen and carbon dioxide levels. Fast water tends to get oxygenated. It also loses excess carbon dioxide. Finally, speed also influences the water temperature. Fast water dashing over rocks evaporates. This evaporation causes the water to cool.

The speed of a stream can be determined as follows. Tie a string to an object that floats. (Don't use an object like a styrofoam ball that can be blown by the wind.) Tie the other end to one of your fingers. Stand near the centre of the stream. Hold a stopwatch in one hand and the object in the other. Place the object on the water and start the stop watch at the same time. As soon as the string becomes tight, stop the watch. Keep the hand to which the string is tied close to the water at all times (Fig. 4-13).

Fig. 4-13 Finding the speed of the water.

Sample Calculation
Suppose the string is 5 m long: Then d = 5 m
Suppose the elapsed time is 2.5 s: Then t = 2.5 s
Therefore the speed of water = $v = \dfrac{d}{t} = \dfrac{5m}{2.5s}$ = 2 m/s

Note: To get a more reliable value, repeat the experiment two or three times and average the results.

Section Review

1. Draw a piece of cobble, a pebble, and a grain of sand in your notebook. (Get the sizes from Table 4-2.)
2. **a)** Describe how to find the cross-section profile of a stream.
    b) Is the stream in Figure 4-12 a fast or slow one? How do you know?
3. Describe how to find the speed of a stream.
4. An object takes 4 s to travel 10 m. What is the speed of the water?

4.7 *ACTIVITY* Total Suspended Solids (T.S.S.)

Ponds and lakes usually contain suspended solids. These include tiny organisms, detritus, and inorganic matter such as clay. Rivers and streams also contain suspended solids. In fast water, little of this is organisms. In a city, part of the suspended solids could be sewage and street runoff. In the country (and also in the city) the suspended solids could contain clay and other soil particles which entered the water due to erosion. Perhaps you have seen brown water after a heavy rain. In this activity you will find the total suspended solids (T.S.S.) of a water sample. This is all the undissolved solids in the water.

Problem

What is the T.S.S. of a water sample?

Materials

fine filter paper	funnel
analytical balance ($\pm$0.1 mg)	beaker (L)
bottle (1 L)	

Procedure

a. Weigh the piece of filter paper to the nearest 0.1 mg.
b. Filter 1 L of the water to be tested through the filter paper.
c. Allow the filter paper to dry completely.
d. Weigh the filter paper again to the nearest 0.1 mg.
e. Calculate the mass of solid that collected on the filter paper.

Sample Calculation

Mass of filter paper + solid	= 0.5246 g
Mass of filter paper	= 0.3002 g
Mass of solid	= 0.2244 g

Thus 0.2244 g of solid were suspended in 1 L of water
or, 224.4 mg of solid were suspended in 1 L of water.
Therefore the T.S.S. = 224.4 mg/L = 224.4 μg/g.

Notes:

1. A balance which weighs to the nearest milligram (0.001 g) will work if the water contains a high T.S.S.
2. We can't tell you what constitutes an acceptable level for T.S.S. Therefore, to make this activity meaningful, you should have a definite purpose in mind before you start. For example, you may decide to find out how the T.S.S. changes due to a rainstorm. Or you may measure it in different seasons.
3. If you do not have an analytical balance, do the filtrations and lay the papers side by side. You will be able to see differences in T.S.S.

Main Ideas

1. Both standing and flowing waters have geophysical properties which help determine their ecology.
2. Water is most dense at 4°C.
3. Many lakes go through layering and overturn.
4. A lake can be divided into zones of high and low photosynthesis.

Key Terms

compensation depth
detritus
epilimnion
eutrophic
geophysical property
hypolimnion

lethal temperature
limnetic zone
littoral zone
oligotrophic
overturn
thermocline

tolerance limit median
transparency
trophogenic zone
tropholytic zone
turbidity

Chapter Review

A. True or False

Decide whether each of the following statements is true or false. If the sentence is false, rewrite it to make it true. (Do not write in this book.)

1. All abiotic factors can also be called geophysical factors.
2. Colour and turbidity are the same thing.
3. A certain species of fish has a 24 h TLm of 28°C. This means half of those fish will die within 24 h if the temperature is 28°C.
4. Turbidity can be caused by both living and non-living suspended matter.
5. During spring overturn, the epilimnion of a lake is cooler than the hypolimnion.

B. Completion

Complete each of the following sentences with a word or phrase that will make the sentence correct. (Do not write in this book.)

1. Warm water holds ▨▨▨▨ oxygen than cool water.
2. A Secchi disc is used to measure the ▨▨▨▨ of water.
3. Water is most dense at ▨▨▨▨ °C.

C. Multiple Choice

Each of the following sentences or questions is followed by four responses. Choose the correct response in each case. (Do not write in this book.)

1. High water temperatures can harm fish because
   a) oxygen demand goes up while oxygen availability goes down
   b) oxygen demand goes down while oxygen availability goes up
   c) both oxygen demand and availability go down
   d) both oxygen demand and availability go up

2. A Secchi disc reading of 3.0 m means that
   a) the tropholytic zone is 3.0 m deep
   b) the littoral zone is 3.0 m deeper than the limnetic zone
   c) the trophogenic zone is 3.0 m deep
   d) the compensation depth is about 3.0 m
3. The hypolimnion of an eutrophic (nutrient-rich) lake will likely be
   a) very warm   c) low in dissolved oxygen
   b) very deep   d) an ideal habitat for many species of fish
4. A floating object travels 15 m down a stream in 6 s. The speed of this stream is
   a) 2.5 m/s   b) 0.4 m/s   c) 4.0 m/s   d) 25 m/s

Using Your Knowledge

1. a) Why does an increase in temperature cause a fish to need more oxygen?
   b) Many electrical generating plants pollute lakes with hot water. When accused of such pollution, the manager of one plant replied that the pollution could not harm fish. It only raised the temperature of the lake near the plant by a few degrees. How would you respond to this person?
2. Which body of water will likely have the greater compensation depth, a lake polluted with acid precipitation or a lake that contains abundant suspended phytoplankton? Why?
3. Distinguish between the littoral zone and the limnetic zone of a lake.
4. a) Describe how the nature of the bottom in a stream changes with speed.
   b) Explain why this happens.
5. How might the weather affect T.S.S. values in a stream? Why?

Investigations

1. Plan and conduct a long-term study of the T.S.S. values in a local river or stream. Get approval of your plan from your teacher before you begin your study.
2. Find out all you can about the ecology of a local lake. Is it eutrophic? Does it stratify? Does it go through overturn? What fish species dominate the lake? What human uses are made of the lake? How do they affect the lake?

5

Chemical Properties: Five Key Factors

Several chemical factors affect life in freshwater ecosystems (Fig. 5-1). Some of these are natural. That is, these chemical factors are in the water regardless of human activity. Among these are oxygen and pH. Such factors may, however, be affected by human activity. Other chemical factors are not natural; they are the result of human activity. Among these are oil spills, pesticides, and other hazardous wastes.

This chapter and the next deal with the natural chemical factors. Another book in the series *Investigating Environmental Issues*, deals with the factors that are the result of human activity.

Fig. 5-1 Many chemical factors— oxygen, pH, and nitrogen, to name a few—help determine the species of organisms that live in this river.

5.1 Oxygen

Fig. 5-2 This river is being tested for its dissolved oxygen content.

Oxygen is a clear, colourless, odourless, tasteless gas. Air is about 21% oxygen by volume. Most living things need oxygen. Although oxygen doesn't dissolve very well in water, enough does dissolve to support a wide variety of living things.

How Much Oxygen Is Needed?

Most aquatic organisms depend on dissolved oxygen for survival. Also, most species have rather definite oxygen requirements. As a result, the test for oxygen is one of the most important tests to do when you are studying water quality (Fig. 5-2).

In general, water should contain at least 5 μg/g of oxygen (five micrograms of oxygen in one gram of water). Water with this concentration will support a fairly diverse community of organisms. Variations in oxygen requirements are wide, of course. The amount of oxygen required varies with the organism, its degree of activity, the water temperature, the pollutants present, and many other factors.

For example, under normal conditions the trout species, *Salmo trutta*, requires an oxygen concentration greater than 10 μg/g. The chub, *Leuciscus cephalus*, requires only 7 μg/g. The carp, *Cyprinus carpio*, can remain alive in water containing as little as 1-2 μg/g of oxygen.

Temperature, Metabolic Rate, and Oxygen

The amount of oxygen an animal needs depends on many factors. As mentioned earlier, one factor is activity. An animal normally needs more oxygen when it is active than when it is resting. That's because its metabolic rate goes up when it is active. (Metabolism is the sum of all the processes occurring in an organism. That includes respiration which, as you know, requires oxygen.)

The amount of oxygen a poikilothermic ("cold-blooded") animal needs also depends on the temperature. As the temperature of the water goes up, the metabolic rate goes up. Thus the need for oxygen increases. For example, one species of trout uses about 50 mg of oxygen per hour for each kilogram of body mass when it is resting at 5°C. But at 25°C, under similar conditions, it uses about 285 mg/h. In contrast, the values for one species of goldfish are 14 mg/h at 5°C and 140 mg/h at 25°C. Clearly the rate of oxygen use by fish depends on both temperature and species.

Solubility of Oxygen in Water

Fish such as trout, which need high-oxygen conditions, seek out cold water. In contrast, fish such as carp, which can tolerate low-oxygen conditions, seek

Table 5-1   Solubility of Oxygen in Water
(when air is the only source)

Temperature of water (°C)	Solubility (µg/g)
0	14.6
5	12.7
10	11.3
15	10.1
20	9.1
25	8.3
30	7.5

out warm water. This is because oxygen, like all gases, is more soluble in cold water. That is, cold water contains more oxygen than warm water.

Table 5-1 gives the solubility of oxygen gas in water when air (21% oxygen) is in contact with the water. That is, air is the only source of the oxygen. Note, as the temperature goes up, the amount of oxygen in the water goes down.

Sources of Oxygen

In fast streams and rivers, most of the oxygen comes from the air. As the water splashes over rocks, it picks up oxygen from the air. The data in Table 5-1 apply in such waters. For example, a fast stream at 15° C cannot have over 10.1 µg/g of oxygen in the water.

Lakes and ponds get some of their oxygen from the air. It enters the water by diffusion. But most of the oxygen comes from plants and algae. They make it by photosynthesis. On a sunny day, a pond or lake with abundant plants and algae may have oxygen values above those in Table 5-1.

Factors that Remove Oxygen

Thermal Pollution   Oxygen can be removed from water by thermal (heat) pollution. Power generating plants and some industries put warm water into lakes and rivers. As Table 5-1 shows, this will reduce the amount of oxygen in the water.

Even a little thermal pollution can be a very serious thing. The warm water *lowers* the amount of oxygen in the water. It also makes poikilothermic animals like fish need *more* oxygen. As a result, warm water kills some species of fish and other aquatic animals.

Respiration   Oxygen is also removed from water by the respiration of the organisms in the water. If the water has sewage in it, a great deal of oxygen will be used. Bacteria increase in great numbers as they feed on the sewage. Like other organisms these bacteria respire. Often they will reduce the oxygen level in the water to zero.

Fig. 5-3 This water has an algal bloom. When the algae die, their decay will use up oxygen in the lake. Then fish may die.

Oxygen and Algal Blooms

Sewage and farm runoff add nutrients to water. (Recall that nutrients are elements that living things need for growth. Examples are nitrogen and phosphorus.) Extra nutrients in a lake make algae grow very quickly. Thus large amounts of algae build up in the lake (Fig. 5-3). The water will likely turn green. This is called an algal bloom. When these algae are alive, they are good for the lake ecosystem. They produce oxygen by photosynthesis and are eaten by other organisms. Often, however, algae crowd themselves out of food and space and then die. Bacteria feed on the dead algae. This uses up oxygen that fish and other organisms need to survive.

Oxygen as a Limiting Factor

As you can see, oxygen can be a limiting factor in determining the species present in a body of water. This means if the oxygen level is too low, certain species will not be present.

Oxygen is generally not a limiting factor in fast clean rivers and streams. In such waters the oxygen level stays at the saturation point (see Table 5-1). In sluggish or polluted rivers, however, the oxygen level may be below saturation. Respiration by decomposers such as bacteria use oxygen faster than the air can replace it. Always take the temperature when you are doing an oxygen test on a stream or river. If the oxygen level is less than that indicated by Table 5-1, be suspicious of pollution with organic matter such as sewage.

Old and sewage-polluted lakes often have little oxygen near the bottom. It is used up by the many decomposers feeding on the sewage and dead algae on the bottom. At this time, the central basin of Lake Erie is below 10% saturation in its deeper regions. Lake Ontario is only 50-60% saturated in the deep water, and Lake Michigan is sometimes only 70-80% saturated in deep areas. In contrast, Lake Huron and Lake Superior are saturated at all depths.

In lakes like Lake Erie, oxygen is a limiting factor. The bottom of Lake Erie may have the right temperature and food supply for trout. Yet the low oxygen level prevents trout from living there as they did before we began to dump sewage in the lake.

Section Review

1. What is the minimum amount of oxygen needed in water to support a fairly diverse community?
2. **a)** How does activity affect oxygen demand?
   b) How does temperature affect oxygen demand in poikilotherms?
3. How does temperature affect the solubility of oxygen in water?
4. How do rivers and lakes differ in the way they get their oxygen?
5. Why can even a little thermal pollution be serious?
6. How does sewage affect oxygen levels? Why?

7. **a)** What is an algal bloom?
    b) Explain how algal blooms can both add oxygen to water and use it.
8. Explain why oxygen can be a limiting factor in polluted rivers and lakes.

Temperature, Metabolic Rate, and Oxygen

5.2 *ACTIVITY*

You learned in Section 5.1 that temperature plays an important role in determining the dissolved oxygen content of water. You also learned that temperature affects the metabolic rates of poikilotherms ("cold-blooded" organisms). In this activity you will study the solubility of oxygen in water. You will also study the effect of temperature on the metabolic rate of a goldfish.

Problem

How does temperature affect oxygen solubility and metabolic rate?

Materials

1 L beakers or other large containers (4)	ice cubes
	Hach oxygen test kit
aquarium aerators to service the 4 beakers	small goldfish of similar size (4)
	-10° C to 110° C thermometers (4)
aquarium heater (optional)	

Procedure A   Preparation for the Activity

Procedure A will be started by your teacher or by a small group of students at least 1 h before you begin this activity. These steps provide water, saturated with oxygen, at a range of temperatures from about 0° C to about 30° C.

a. Fill the 4 beakers with tap water. Begin aerating the water in all of them. Number the beakers from 1 to 4.
b. Maintain beaker 1 at about 0° C as follows. Add ice cubes to the water. Replace the ice as fast as it melts. Keep ice in the water at all times during the activity.
c. Maintain beaker 2 at about 10° C as follows. Add one ice cube to the water. Let it melt completely. Then add another. Continue this process throughout the activity.
d. Maintain beaker 3 at room temperature (about 20° C).
e. Maintain beaker 4 at about 30° C by using an aquarium heater or by adding warm water from time to time.
f. Place a small goldfish in each beaker.

Procedure B   The Activity

Perform Procedure B after the beakers have been allowed to stand (equilibrate) for at least 1 h.

a. Copy Table 5-2 in your notebook.

Table 5-2   Effect of Temperature on Oxygen and Metabolic Rate

Temperature (°C)	Oxygen Concentration (µg/g)	Movement of gill covers (number per minute)

b. Go to any one of the beakers. Record the temperature of the water. Find the oxygen concentration using the Hach kit. Find the breathing rate of the goldfish by counting the number of times the gill covers open and close in one minute. (This is a measure of the fish's metabolic rate.) Record all data in your table.

c. Now repeat step b) with each of the other 3 beakers.

Discussion

1. Use your data to plot a solubility curve for oxygen in water. Put the temperature on the horizontal axis and oxygen concentration on the vertical axis. On the same set of axes, plot the solubility data given in Section 5.1. Try to account for any differences between your data and the ideal data.
2. How does temperature affect the solubility of oxygen gas in water?
3. Describe the effect of temperature on the metabolic rate of goldfish, as measured by the rate of breathing.
4. Why can even a small temperature change have a great effect on poikilotherms?

5.3   Carbon Dioxide

Carbon dioxide is a clear, colourless, odourless, tasteless gas. It is the "fizz" in soda pop. Let us see how it gets into water and what it does to organisms.

Carbon Dioxide from the Air

Carbon dioxide, like oxygen, continually enters rivers and lakes from the air. However, air is only about 0.034% carbon dioxide by volume. Therefore, when air is the only source of carbon dioxide, very little carbon dioxide ends up in the water. For example, at $0°C$, the solubility of carbon dioxide in water is only 1 $\mu g/g$, when air is the only source. Thus a fast clean stream will not likely have over 1 $\mu g/g$ of carbon dioxide in it.

Carbon Dioxide from Respiration

In most natural bodies of water, the air is just a minor source of carbon dioxide. Respiration by living organisms is the major source. This is particularly true of lakes and slow or polluted rivers.

As a result of respiration, water near the surface of most bodies of water has up to 10 $\mu g/g$ of carbon dioxide in it. Water near the bottom ooze has even more. Decomposers feed on organic matter in the bottom ooze. As they respire, they add carbon dioxide to the water at the bottom.

Water that contains over 25 $\mu g/g$ of carbon dioxide is harmful to most gill-breathers. It interferes with breathing. Concentrations of 50-60 $\mu g/g$ will kill many species.

Carbon Dioxide in Rain and Groundwater

As raindrops fall, they dissolve carbon dioxide from the air. Usually the quantity dissolved does not exceed 0.6 $\mu g/g$. But if this rain falls on land and moves through soil, it picks up more carbon dioxide. The spaces between the soil particles have a fairly high level of carbon dioxide in them. This is due to respiration by the soil organisms, particularly the decomposers. If the groundwater runs to a lake, it will increase the carbon dioxide concentration of the lake.

Factors That Remove Carbon Dioxide

Atmospheric Exchange   Fast-moving rivers lose most of their carbon dioxide through atmospheric exchange. That is, they give up the carbon dioxide to the atmosphere. Suppose, for example, that a marsh drains into a river. The marsh water could have as much as 30 $\mu g/g$ of carbon dioxide in it at $20°C$. But a fast river which is not producing carbon dioxide can only hold about 0.5 $\mu g/g$ at $20°C$. Thus the excess carbon dioxide (29.5 $\mu g/g$) will get "knocked out" of the river in the turbulent regions.

Photosynthesis   Lakes and other standing waters lose most of their carbon dioxide through photosynthesis. Respiration will build up the carbon dioxide level at night, but photosynthesis will reduce it during the day.

1. What level of carbon dioxide can enter natural waters from the air?
2. What level of carbon dioxide would you expect to find in a fast clean stream? Why?
3. What is the main source of carbon dioxide in most natural bodies of water?
4. Why is there usually more carbon dioxide at the bottom of a lake than at the top?
5. State the levels of carbon dioxide that harm and kill most gill breathers.
6. Describe how rain and groundwater can add carbon dioxide to a lake.
7. a) How do fast waters lose most of their carbon dioxide?
   b) How do standing waters lose most of their carbon dioxide?

5.4 pH

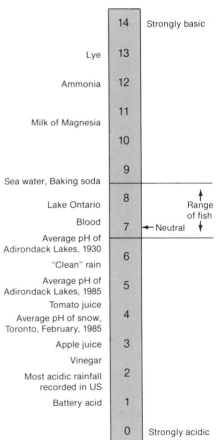

Fig. 5-4 The pH scale for acidity.

The pH Scale

The **pH** of water is a measure of its acidity. Values for pH run from 0 to 14 (Fig. 5-4). On this scale, a pH of 7 is neutral. A pH less than 7 is acidic and a pH greater than 7 is basic (alkaline). In other words, the lower the pH of water, the more acidic the water is. Water becomes less acidic and more basic as its pH increases.

The pH scale is logarithmic. This means that going from one number to the next is not a change of one, but a change of *ten*. For example, water with a pH of 6 is 10 times more acidic than water with a pH of 7. As well, water with a pH of 5 is 100 times more acidic than water with a pH of 7. Look at Figure 5-4. How much more acidic are the Adirondack Lakes than Lake Ontario?

pH and Life

A pH between 6.7 and 8.6 supports a well-balanced fish population. As long as the pH is within this range, it seems to have little effect on the life processes of most fish species. In fact, most species can tolerate, for a limited time, pH values beyond this range. Only a very few species, however, can tolerate pH values lower than 5.0 or greater than 9.0. Further, few gill breathers of any kind are found outside the range from 4.0 to 9.5. An improper pH interferes with gas exchange across the gill membranes. In other words, breathing becomes difficult.

Most plants and algae are also affected when the pH becomes very low or very high. An improper pH slows down nutrient uptake by the plants and algae. As a result, their growth becomes stunted and, eventually, they die.

pH and Eutrophication

Eutrophication is the process of aging or increasing productivity of a lake. **Eutrophic** means "adequate food", or nutrient-rich. As a lake ages, it accumulates nutrients from runoff. It may also get nutrients from pollution such as sewage. These nutrients increase the amount of life in the lake, or its **productivity**.

A young clean lake in the early stage of eutrophication is **oligotrophic**, or "lacking food". This kind of lake will likely be basic if it is in an area with basic bedrock such as limestone or dolomite. The pH of such a lake normally drops as the lake ages. That is, the water becomes more acidic with time. This is because the decay of organic matter releases acids into the water. Among these acids is carbonic acid. This acid forms when the carbon dioxide from respiration reacts with water. The lake at this more acidic stage is called **mesotrophic** ("middle amount of food").

In time, a mesotrophic lake ages further and becomes an eutrophic lake. As this process occurs, the pH usually rises again and the lake becomes more basic (less acidic). You will see why in Section 5.6.

YOUNG LAKE	→	MIDDLE-AGED LAKE	→	OLD LAKE
basic		more acidic		more basic
OLIGOTROPHIC		MESOTROPHIC		EUTROPHIC

A young clean lake in an area with acidic bedrock such as quartz or granite, will likely be slightly acidic. But, like the lake just discussed, it will probably turn more acidic and, later, more basic as it ages.

Factors Affecting pH

You have seen how the life in a lake and the bedrock can affect the pH of water. Many other factors can also affect pH. Acid spills by industries lower the pH. Also, smelters and coal-burning power plants put sulfur dioxide into the air. The sulfur dioxide reacts with water vapour in the air to form sulfuric acid. When it rains or snows, this acid gets into lakes and rivers. Such snow or rain is called **acid precipitation** or, sometimes, **acid rain**. The pH of acid precipitation is usually below 4.0. The low pH of the Adirondack Lakes and of precipitation in Toronto is due mainly to acid precipitation.

Sewage usually raises the pH of water. Household sewage has many bases in it. Also, the decay of sewage by bacteria produces bases (see Section 5.6).

Section Review

1. What is pH?
2. Describe the pH scale.
3. Why is it important to remember that the pH scale is logarithmic?
4. Make a summary of the effects of pH on life.

5. **a)** What is eutrophication?
   b) Describe the changes in pH which occur as a young clean lake in a limestone region ages.
6. List five factors which can affect the pH of water.
7. What is acid precipitation?
8. Why does sewage raise the pH of water?

Measuring the pH of Water Samples

5.5   *ACTIVITY*

You learned in Section 5.4 that pH is an important measure of water quality. In this activity you will measure the pH of several water samples. Then you will decide how the pH of each sample might affect animal life in the water.

Problem

How does the pH of the water vary with the nature of the water sample?

Materials

test tube	water samples prepared or collected
pH paper	by students and teacher

Procedure

a. Copy Table 5-3 into your notebook.
b. Wash the test tube well.
c. Put 1-2 mL of distilled water (from the bottle labelled "Sample 1") in the test tube.
d. Find the pH of Sample 1 using the pH paper (Fig. 5-5). Record your results.
e. Repeat steps (b) to (d) using tap water (Sample 2).
f. Repeat steps (b) to (d) for a weak acid (Sample 3) and a weak base (Sample 4).
g. Repeat steps (b) to (d) for other samples provided. Your teacher may ask you to provide some samples. It will be interesting to test water from a local river or lake, from a swimming pool, and from an aquarium. You could also test water containing detergents, water containing decaying organic matter like fish food, dishwater, rainwater, and melted snow.
h. Read the part on pH in Section 5.4 again. Now complete the last column in your table.

Fig. 5-5 Finding the pH of water using pH paper. Match the colours as quickly as you can. The colour can change in the air.

Table 5-3   The pH of Water Samples

Sample number	Nature of sample	pH of sample	Effect on living things
1	Distilled water		
2	Tap water		
3	Carbonic acid (a weak acid)		
4	Limewater (a weak base)		
5			

Discussion

1. What is the pH of distilled water? Why?
2. Did tap water have a different pH than distilled water? Why?
3. Which has the higher pH, carbonic acid or limewater? Why?
4. Try to give a reason for the pH of each sample from number 5 on.

5.6   Alkalinity

What Is Alkalinity?

Alkalinity is the ability of water to neutralize acids. Therefore, the alkalinity of water can also be described as the sum of all the bases in water. (Bases neutralize acids.) In natural waters, the alkalinity is due mainly to carbonates and bicarbonates. But hydroxides may also contribute to the alkalinity if domestic or industrial pollution are present. These three substances—carbonates, bicarbonates, and hydroxides—are used in many antacid pills that people take to neutralize excess stomach acid.

Sources of Alkalinity

Respiration in the Water   When organisms in the water (including decomposers) respire, they release carbon dioxide into the water. The carbon dioxide dissolves in the water to form carbonic acid. Almost as fast as it forms some of this carbonic acid breaks up into carbon dioxide and water. You have likely seen this happen. Carbonic acid is present in the soda water used to make most soft drinks. The fizz that occurs when you take the top off a bottle of "pop" is due to the escape of some of the carbon dioxide.

Some of the carbonic acid that is left breaks down to form bicarbonates and carbonates:

Carbon dioxide + Water $\rightleftharpoons$ Carbonic Acid $\rightleftharpoons$ Bicarbonate + Carbonate
                                                                    ALKALINITY

The arrows indicate that all reactions are reversible. In other words, the carbonates and bicarbonates can change back into carbonic acid. And the carbonic acid can change back into carbon dioxide and water. You will see later why this is important.

Rain and Groundwater You learned in Section 5.3 that rain dissolves carbon dioxide as it falls. More important, it dissolves still more carbon dioxide as it runs through the soil. Thus groundwater will usually contain carbonates and bicarbonates. Further, if the bedrock is a carbonate such as limestone, the now acidic groundwater reacts with that bedrock to form still more bicarbonate and carbonate.

Domestic and Industrial Sources Many household drain cleaners contain lye, which is a hydroxide. Baking soda is a bicarbonate. Both of these can raise the alkalinity of water if you put them down the drain. Water softeners also put carbonates into the water.

Domestic sewage also raises the alkalinity of water. Decomposers produce carbon dioxide as they feed on the sewage. The carbon dioxide, in turn, produces carbonates and bicarbonates. Many industries also discharge substances into rivers and lakes which raise the alkalinity. What might some of these substances be?

Importance of Alkalinity

The alkalinity is a fairly reliable measure of the productivity (ability to support life) of a lake. To show you why, we are going to write the chemical equations for the word equations you saw earlier. You need not learn the chemical equations unless your teacher asks you to. But they will help you see why alkalinity is a good measure of productivity.

CO_2 + H_2O $\rightleftharpoons$ H_2CO_3 $\rightleftharpoons$ H^{1+} + | START HERE
carbon   water   carbonic | HCO_3^{1-}
dioxide   acid |
                                                       | bicarbonate
                                                       | $\downarrow\uparrow$
                                                       | H^{1+} + CO_3^{2-}
                                                       | carbonate

photosynthesis

C C C C C   C C C C C   C C C C C   C C C C C
plant and   eaten zooplankton eaten minnows   eaten trout
C C C C C   ----→ C C C C C   ----→ C C C C C   ----→ C C C C C
algal tissue
C C C C C

A productive lake has a great deal of life in it. Thus a great deal of carbon dioxide forms. Carbon dioxide, in turn, forms high concentrations of bicarbonate and carbonate. In other words, a productive lake has a high alkalinity.

This high alkalinity helps keep the lake productive. During sunny days the free carbon dioxide (CO_2) is quickly used up. If the lake has no reservoir of carbonate and bicarbonate, photosynthesis would stop. But the carbonates and bicarbonates form carbon dioxide (by the reverse reactions) and keep photosynthesis going.

Follow the carbon atoms counterclockwise beginning with carbonate. See how those atoms eventually become part of the tissue of trout. (All the molecules in an organism have a "skeleton" of carbon atoms.) Thus the number of trout a lake can support depends directly on the alkalinity of the lake. Acid precipitation has reduced the alkalinity of some lakes in Northern Ontario and the north-east United States to almost zero. Thus these lakes support no fish, even though they may be otherwise quite suitable for fish.

A total alkalinity below 50 $\mu g/g$ is considered low. In fact, one might even say that such water is "too clean". It will contain little life and appear quite clear. It simply contains too little carbon (as carbonate and bicarbonate) to support much life. In contrast, an alkalinity of 200 $\mu g/g$ is becoming quite high. Such high values are not uncommon in sedimentary areas such as the prairies. If you can see no natural causes of high alkalinity suspect sewage pollution to be the cause.

Section Review

1. a) What is alkalinity?
   b) What three substances contribute to alkalinity?
2. Describe how respiration in the water increases the alkalinity of the water.
3. Why does the alkalinity of rainwater increase as it runs through soil?
4. Name two household products which can raise the alkalinity of water.
5. Why does domestic sewage increase the alkalinity of water?
6. Explain why alkalinity is a good measure of the productivity of a lake.
7. State the "low" and "high" levels of alkalinity for natural waters.

5.7   Hardness

Causes

Hardness in water is caused mainly by calcium and magnesium ions. The hardness is usually high in regions of sedimentary rock such as limestone (calcium carbonate) and dolomite (magnesium calcium carbonate). Calcium and magnesium ions are picked up by the water as it runs over these minerals. Runoff from cities is also often hard. Acidic rain dissolves calcium and magnesium from buildings and streets.

Table 5-4 shows the commonly accepted standards for degrees of hardness.

Table 5-5 shows some hardness values obtained by the authors when they tested water from various places.

Table 5-4   Degrees of Hardness

Degree of hardness	Total hardness ($\mu g/g$)
Soft	0-60
Moderately hard	61-120
Hard	121-180
Very hard	over 180

Table 5-5   Some Hardness Values

Water sample	Total hardness ($\mu g/g$)
Distilled water	0
Rainwater	0
Lake on igneous rock	20
Lake Ontario	100
Lake on limestone rock	250
Deep well in limestone area	350
Small city creek	520
Well in prairies	600

Importance

Supports Life   Some hardness is necessary for all living things. All living things need calcium and magnesium in order for their cells to function. Vertebrates like fish need calcium to build bones. Every chlorophyll molecule has a magnesium atom in it. If all other changes are favourable, then the productivity of a lake will likely be higher if the hardness is higher.

Human Health   Water with a total hardness around 250 $\mu g/g$ is best for drinking. People who drink soft water for long periods of time are more likely to get cardiovascular diseases (diseases of the heart and circulatory system).

Water with a total hardness above 500 $\mu g/g$ can make you very ill if you are not accustomed to it. It often causes diarrhea. In your large intestine are billions of coliform bacteria. They help the lining of the intestine remove water from the waste food material. This water is then put back into the bloodstream. (This is an excellent example of mutualism — see Section 2.4, page 24.) However, a sudden change in the hardness of drinking water causes the coliform bacteria to stop functioning. Thus the water stays in the waste food material, and you get diarrhea.

Economics Very hard water is undesirable for many economic reasons. First, the calcium and magnesium ions react with soap to form curds. These make it difficult to wash properly. Synthetic detergents have been developed that do not form curds. Nonetheless, if you want to use soap and the water is hard, you must soften the water. This process is expensive.

The calcium and magnesium ions also precipitate out in household plumbing. If the water is very hard, the pipes can become clogged unless the water is softened. These ions also cause the familiar tea kettle scale and the costly boiler scale that torments industry.

Section Review

1. What causes hardness in water?
2. Copy the table for degrees of hardness into your notebook.
3. Explain why hard water tends to be more productive than soft water.
4. Describe two effects of hardness on human health.
5. Explain why very hard water can be costly to some people.

5.8   *ACTIVITY* Measuring the Hardness of Water Samples

You learned in Section 5.7 that hardness is important for ecological, health, and economic reasons. In this activity you will measure the hardness of several water samples. Then you will consider the implications of your results.

Problem

How does hardness vary with the nature of the water sample? What do your results mean?

Materials

test tube   water samples collected by
hardness testing kit (Hach   students and teacher
   kit) or hardness testing paper

Procedure

a. Copy Table 5-6 into your notebook.

Table 5-6   The Hardness of Water Samples

Sample number	Nature of sample	Hardness of sample	Implication
1	Distilled water		
2	Tap water		
3	Rainwater		
4			

b. Wash the test tube well.

c. Put about 5 mL of distilled water (from the bottle labelled Sample 1) in the test tube.

d. Find the hardness of Sample 1 using the Hach kit or hardness paper (Fig. 5-6). Record your result.

e. Repeat steps (b) to (d) using tap water (Sample 2).

f. Repeat steps (b) to (d) using rainwater or melted snow (Sample 3).

g. Repeat steps (b) to (d) for the other samples provided. Your teacher may ask you to provide some samples. It will be interesting to test water from these sources: local rivers and lakes, aquariums, home drinking water, and street runoff.

h. Read Section 5.7 again. Then complete the last column of Table 5-6. Your implication could be: "too soft for drinking water" or "should support abundant life" or "bedrock must be limestone".

Fig. 5-6   Finding the hardness of a water sample.

Discussion

1. What is the hardness of distilled water? Why?
2. What is the hardness of rainwater? Why?
3. What is the hardness of tap water? Why?
4. Try to give a reason for the hardness of all other water samples.

Main Ideas

1. Oxygen is an important limiting factor in aquatic ecosystems.
2. Excess carbon dioxide can be harmful to aquatic life.
3. Excessively high or low pH values can harm organisms.
4. Alkalinity is a fairly reliable measure of the productivity of water.
5. Water hardness is important to organisms (including humans).

Key Terms

acid precipitation
algal bloom
alkalinity
eutrophic

eutrophication
hardness
limiting factor
mesotrophic

metabolic rate
metabolism
oligotrophic
pH

poikilothermic
productivity
solubility
thermal pollution

Chapter Review

A. True or False

Decide whether each of the following statements is true or false. If the sentence is false, rewrite it to make it true. (Do not write in this book.)
1. Fish need more oxygen as the water gets warmer.
2. Lakes get most of their carbon dioxide from the air.
3. A pH of 5 is ten times as acidic as a pH of 4.
4. Aquatic plants will likely grow better in soft water than in hard water.

B. Completion

Complete each of the following sentences with a word or phrase that will make the sentence correct. (Do not write in this book.)
1. Warm water holds ▨▨▨▨▨ oxygen than cool water.
2. Lakes lose most of their carbon dioxide through ▨▨▨▨▨ .
3. Alkalinity in natural waters is due mainly to ▨▨▨▨▨ and ▨▨▨▨▨ .

C. Multiple Choice

Each of the following statements or questions is followed by four responses. Choose the correct response in each case. (Do not write in this book.)
1. A lake has 2 $\mu g/g$ of oxygen and 55 $\mu g/g$ of carbon dioxide. This lake could support
   a) trout   b) chub   c) little animal life   d) most types of animal life
2. An industry put warm water into a stream. The water temperature changed from 10°C to 20°C. The oxygen level would likely
   a) increase by about 2 $\mu g/g$ c) drop by over 5 $\mu g/g$
   b) drop by about 2 $\mu g/g$ d) remain unchanged
3. The pH of a lake was 6.0 in 1930. It dropped to 3.0 in 1985. This lake has become
   a) 1000 times more acidic   c) twice as acidic
   b) 100 times more acidic   d) half as acidic
4. Ecologists often measure alkalinity of a lake because alkalinity is
   a) a reliable measure of the hardness of the lake
   b) an easy way to get the pH of the lake
   c) an indicator of the safety of the water for drinking purposes
   d) a reliable measure of the productivity of the lake

Using Your Knowledge

1. The temperature of a fast turbulent river is 20° C. Its oxygen level is 3 μg/g. What do you conclude from the data?
2. The data in Table 5-7 were obtained during a field trip to a pond on a bright sunny day. The water was a pale green colour. Account for the data.
3. Imagine a pond with considerable vegetation on a sunny day. Table 5-8 shows data obtained where the water enters and leaves the pond. Account for the changes in each factor.
4. Suppose you found a cold, clean-looking lake with no trout in it. Its alkalinity is 15 μg/g. Would you stock it with trout? Why?
5. Figure 5-4 shows that "clean rain" (rain without human pollution in it) has a pH of 5.6. Why is "clean rain" acidic?

Table 5-7 Pond Field Trip

Time	Oxygen (μg/g)	Carbon dioxide (μg/g)
9:00	6	35
11:00	9	15
13:00	14	5
15:00	11	10

Table 5-8 Chemical Factors in a Pond

Factor	Water entering pond (μg/g)	Water leaving pond (μg/g)
Oxygen	7	13
Carbon dioxide	20	5

Investigations

1. Monitor the temperature and oxygen concentration in a classroom or home aquarium that does not have a thermostatically controlled heater. Measure these factors two or three times a day for about 2 weeks. Summarize your data in tabular form. Then present a case for or against the need for a thermostatically controlled heater.
2. Find out how hard water helps prevent cardiovascular diseases. Write a report of about 200 words on your findings.
3. Find out how a water softener works. Write a report of about 150 words on your findings.

6

Chemical Properties: Further Factors

In Chapter 5 you studied some of the important chemical factors affecting aquatic ecosystems. This chapter explores the sources and importance of four other chemical factors: nitrogen, phosphorus, chloride, and total dissolved solids. These four things are present in all natural aquatic ecosystems. As well, they are important to the functioning of those ecosystems. But sometimes the concentrations are increased too much by human activities, which can cause problems.

6.1   Nitrogen

The element nitrogen is present in all proteins. Thus it occurs in all living things and is an essential part of all ecosystems. Too much of this element, however, can cause some problems. Nitrogen exists in two common forms in ecosystems: ammonia and nitrate.

Ammonia (NH_3)

As the formula shows, nitrogen occurs in the compound ammonia, NH_3. You have likely smelled ammonia from household cleaning products, baby diapers, an outhouse on a hot day, or a washroom that hasn't been kept clean.

% nitrogen
% phosphorus
% potassium

4-9-15 NUTRITE

winterguard

Fig 6-1 Most fertilizer bags show three numbers. The first number on a fertilizer bag is the percent nitrogen. North Americans used 25 000 000 t of fertilizer on their lawns last year. Much of this washes off into rivers and lakes.

Ammonia comes from the following sources.

- The natural decay of organic matter (dead plants and animals, fecal matter, urine).
- The decay of human sewage (fecal matter and urine).
- The decay of wastes from farm feedlots.
- Fertilizer runoff from farms and lawns (Fig. 6-1).

We can expect, then, to find ammonia in pond and marsh water, since decaying matter is always present in the bottom ooze. However, we would not expect to find it in a fast river. If we find ammonia there, we should suspect sewage input or farm runoff.

In many areas beef cattle are raised in feedlots. Hundreds of cattle are placed in a very small area. They are force-fed until they are ready for market. The large quantities of cattle urine and fecal matter produced can create a serious nitrogen pollution problem for nearby waters. Corn-growing areas often have ammonia-polluted streams. Corn is a heavy nitrogen user. Thus the farmers fertilize their cornfields heavily with ammonia and other nitrogen compounds. Heavy rains can wash these compounds into streams.

Nitrate (NO_3^{1-})

The diagram of the nitrogen cycle (Fig. 2-28, page 41) shows you that ammonia is changed to nitrite then nitrate. Thus the presence of nitrate in water could indicate input of nitrogen from any of the sources listed for ammonia. Also, nitrates themselves are present in many fertilizers. Thus the presence of nitrate could also mean that nitrate-bearing fertilizers are leaching from farm soil and lawns.

Importance

Nitrogen is a key nutrient for all living things. Thus it must be present in all ecosystems. Too much, however, causes problems such as excessive algal and plant growth. Ecologists generally agree that, on the average, a lake should not have over 0.30 μg/g of total nitrogen in it. If it does, an **algal bloom** could result. (Of course, other nutrients must be present in adequate amounts before this can occur.)

Concentrations of ammonia over 0.5 μg/g can be directly harmful to many aquatic animals. Fortunately, ammonia is usually quickly changed to nitrate. However, the nitrate is absorbed by plants and algae—hence the algal blooms.

Most experts agree that drinking water should have less than 10 μg/g of nitrate in it. In fact, 45 μg/g is hazardous to humans, particularly infants. In infants this concentration can cause methemoglobinemia (a "blue baby" condition). Many infant deaths occur every year as the result of nitrate poisoning. Most of these deaths take place on farms, particularly on corn-producing farms. Nitrates from fertilizer and animal wastes have reached the groundwater and have entered the drinking water supply.

1. Why is nitrogen an essential part of all ecosystems?
2. List our main sources of ammonia in water.
3. List two ways that nitrates get into water.
4. How much nitrogen is needed to cause an algal bloom?
5. Discuss the relationship between nitrates and human health.

6.2 Phosphorus

Phosphorus, like nitrogen, is an important nutrient element (see Fig. 6-1). Many important molecules within cells contain phosphorus atoms. For example, adenosine triphosphate (ATP) is a phosphorus-bearing compound. It occurs in every living cell where it plays a key role in energy storage.

Sources

The inorganic form of phosphorus (P) in water is the phosphate ion (PO_4^{3-}). But phosphorus also occurs in water in dissolved organic compounds (see Phosphorus Cycle, Figure 2-29, page 42). These 2 forms of phosphorus enter the water system through much the same sources as nitrogen. (There are, however, some differences.)

- The natural decay of organic matter (dead plants and animals, and fecal matter).
- The decay of human sewage (fecal matter).
- The decay of fecal matter from feedlots.
- Detergents.

As you can see, the main source is the decay of organic matter from natural sources, human sewage, and feedlots. Detergents are also a major contributor to phosphate pollution. Many provinces and states have put total or partial bans on phosphates in detergents. However, far too much still goes into the waterways. Most dishwasher detergents, for example, are about 45% phosphate—just to prevent those "ugly spots"!

Note that fertilizer runoff is not listed as a major source of phosphorus pollution. Most fertilizers contain a great deal of phosphate. But many soil particles such as clay can "fix" or hold on to phosphate ions (Fig. 6-2). The phosphate ions are attracted to the surfaces of the soil particles. Therefore, unless soil erosion occurs, the phosphate ions do not wash away into streams.

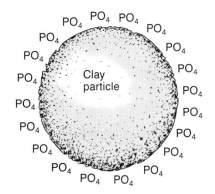

Fig. 6-2 Clay is one type of soil particle that "fixes" phosphate ions.

Importance

Phosphorus is a key nutrient for all living things. Thus it must be present in all ecosystems. Too much, however, can cause problems such as algal blooms. Ecologists generally agree that, on the average, a lake should not have over 0.015 $\mu g/g$ of phosphorus in it. If it does, an algal bloom could result.

Many ecologists feel that phosphorus is a limiting factor in the production of algal blooms in lakes. If this is so, algal blooms can be stopped by keeping most of the phosphorus out of the water. It doesn't matter how much nitrogen and other nutrients are present. As a result, special units have been placed on many sewage treatment plants. These remove up to 95% of the phosphorus at a cost of 1-2¢ for 1000 L of water.

Section Review

1. Why is phosphorus an essential part of all ecosystems?
2. List the four main sources of phosphorus in water.
3. Explain why fertilizer runoff usually does not contribute to phosphorus pollution.
4. How much phosphorus is needed to cause an algal bloom?
5. Why do many sewage treatment plants remove most of the phosphorus from the sewage water before they release it?

6.3 Chloride

Sources

The most common chloride in water is sodium chloride, or common salt. Sea water contains about 27 000 $\mu g/g$ of chloride. Even fresh water generally contains some chloride. In fact, it is not uncommon for clean rivers and lakes to contain 20-50 $\mu g/g$. Much of this comes from natural deposits of salt in the ground.

In areas with heavy snowfalls, salt is often used to melt snow and ice from roads. Street runoff from such areas adds salt to rivers and lakes. Sewage also contributes to chloride pollution. Before sewage is released into rivers or lakes, it is chlorinated to kill bacteria. The chlorine used for this purpose becomes chloride. Sewage and street runoff often raise chloride levels in city rivers to 300-1500 $\mu g/g$ (Fig. 6-3).

Importance

All organisms need chloride in their protoplasm. Thus some chloride is essential to all ecosystems. But high concentrations can be harmful. Marine (saltwater) organisms are adapted to high chloride levels, while freshwater organisms are not. Therefore high chloride levels in fresh water can kill many forms of life.

Most authorities suggest that drinking water should have no more than 250 $\mu g/g$ of salt in it. At that concentration, most people can taste salt. Also, high salt levels can contribute to hypertension (high blood pressure) in some people.

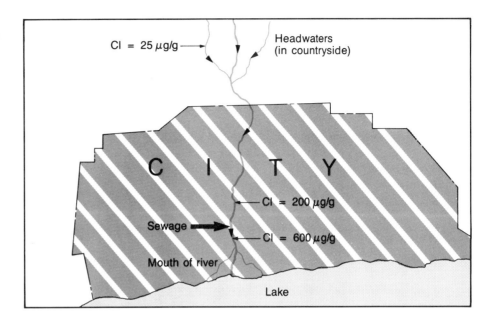

Many large cities are located on Lake Ontario. As a result, scientists have been concerned about the amount of salt entering the lake. At this time, about one million tonnes go into the lake every year. But only 20% of this is from road salt. Most of the rest comes from a natural salt deposit near the Detroit River. In spite of this input, the concentration is only 26 $\mu g/g$. This is far from the level needed to harm aquatic life.

Section Review

1. Compare the amount of chloride in sea water and clean fresh water.
2. Describe two causes of chloride pollution of urban rivers.
3. What is the acceptable level of salt in drinking water?

6.4 Total Dissolved Solids (T.D.S.)

In Section 4.7, page 79, you investigated the total *suspended* solids in water. In this section and the following activity, you will study the total *dissolved* solids. Suspended solids make water cloudy and can be filtered out. Dissolved solids, however, leave the water clear, though it may be coloured. They cannot be filtered out.

The total dissolved solids in water include phosphates, nitrates, chlorides, hardness (calcium and magnesium), and many other nutrients. Thus some ecologists say that the T.D.S. is the best *single* measure of the productivity of water.

When the T.D.S. is below 100 μg/g, a lake is considered oligotrophic. Lakes with a T.D.S. below 50 μg/g are considered "salt-poor". They contain too few nutrients to support a reasonable community of living things. Values above 100 μg/g are generally considered to represent eutrophic conditions. If you live along or near the Great Lakes, you might find the data in Table 6-1 interesting. Can you account for the increase from Lake Superior to Lake Ontario? (Treated sewage often has a T.D.S. of 300-400 μg/g.)

Table 6-1   Total Dissolved Solids in the Great Lakes

Lake	T.D.S. (μg/g)
Superior	60
Huron	110
Michigan	150
Erie	180
Ontario	185

Section Review

1. Distinguish between total suspended solids and total dissolved solids.
2. Why might a T.D.S. value be the best single measure of the productivity of a lake?
3. Define oligotrophic and eutrophic in terms of T.D.S.
4. Explain why the T.D.S. increases along the Great Lakes.

6.5   ACTIVITY Total Dissolved Solids (T.D.S.)

Scientists use a conductivity meter to find the T.D.S. of water. Here, though, you will find the T.D.S. by evaporation. You cannot filter dissolved solids out of water. Therefore you have to find out how much dissolved solid is in the water by evaporating the water from the solid.

Problem

What is the T.D.S. of a water sample?

Materials

250 mL beaker
analytical balance ($\pm$0.1 mg)

100 mL of filtered water
hot plate

Procedure

a. Weigh the beaker to the nearest 0.1 mg.

b. Add 100 mL of filtered water to the beaker. (Filtration removes the suspended solids.)

c. Slowly and carefully evaporate all the water from the beaker. Do not let the beaker get hot to the touch. Excess heat may vaporize or decompose some of the solids.

d. Weigh the beaker plus dissolved solids to the nearest 0.1 mg. (You will see the dissolved solids as a fine film on the glass.)

Sample Calculation

Mass of beaker + T.D.S.	=	105.0250 g
Mass of beaker	=	105.0030 g
Mass of T.D.S.	=	0.0220 g

Thus 0.0220 g of solids were dissolved in 100 mL of water
or, 0.220 g of solids were dissolved in 1 L (1000 mL) of water
or, 220 mg of solids were dissolved in 1 L of water.
Therefore the T.D.S. = 220 mg/L = 220 $\mu g/g$.

Discussion

1. Is the water sample more likely from an oligotrophic or an eutrophic body of water?

2. List five nutrients which could be in this water.

6.6 ACTIVITY Analyzing an Unknown Water Sample

The aquarium for this activity contains water with certain chemical properties. It also has certain forms of life in it. As you know, the chemical factors (non-living) interact with the organisms. That is, the chemical factors and the organisms affect one another. Can you find out how?

Problem

How do chemical and biological factors interact in the aquarium?

Materials

selection of Hach water testing kits (oxygen, carbon dioxide, pH, alkalinity, hardness, ammonia, nitrate, phosphate, chloride)

an aquarium with enriched water, organisms, and a light
thermometer ($-10°$ C to $110°$ C)

Table 6-2 Water Analysis

Factor	Value			
	Trial 1	Trial 2	Trial 3	Average
Oxygen				
Carbon dioxide				
pH				
Alkalinity				
Hardness				
Ammonia				
Nitrate				
Phosphate				
Chloride				

Fig. 6-4 Don't stir up any sediment as you get your sample.

Procedure

a. Copy Table 6-2 into your notebook.

b. Get one of the water testing kits from your teacher. Carry out the test on the water in the aquarium (Fig. 6-4). Enter your data in the table that your teacher has prepared on the chalkboard.

c. Return the kit, obtain another, and repeat step (b).

d. Continue tests until the teacher announces that time is up. Your teacher will see that each test is performed at least 3 times so that accuracy can be checked.

e. Take the temperature of the water.

f. Record all the data in your table.

g. Make careful notes on other non-living properties of the aquarium ecosystem. These should include light intensity, clarity of the water, presence or absence of aeration, and the nature of any debris on the bottom.

h. Make careful notes on the biological properties of the aquarium ecosystem. These should include a description of the types and abundance of organisms present (fish, snails, plants, algae and small animals).

Discussion

1. Account for the results of each test. For example, if you obtained an oxygen concentration of 8 μg/g, explain why it was that value.

2. Explain the effects of each result on living organisms. For example, if you obtained a pH of 9, what effect will that pH have on living organisms? Can the aquarium support a wide range of fish species?

3. Make an overall judgment on the quality of the water in the aquarium. Will it support a wide range of species of organisms? Is it polluted?

Effects of Organic Matter on Water Quality

6.7   *ACTIVITY*

Organic matter is matter that contains carbon. Matter that is or was once part of a living organism is organic. Therefore, it contains carbon. It also contains nitrogen, phosphorus, and other elements. Many of these are nutrients. What do you think will happen if this kind of organic matter breaks down in water?

Problem

How does organic matter affect water quality?

Materials

small aquariums or pails of
   at least 5 L size (2)
several sprigs of an
   aquatic plant
100 W lamps (2)

organic matter (for example,
   fish food)
Hach water testing kits
thermometer (-10°C to 100°C)

Procedure

a. Fill both containers to within 2 cm of the top with water.
b. Add about 10 sprigs of aquatic plant to each container.
c. Place the containers side by side. Then mount a 100 W lamp over each one (Fig. 6-5).

Fig. 6-5 How will organic matter affect water quality?

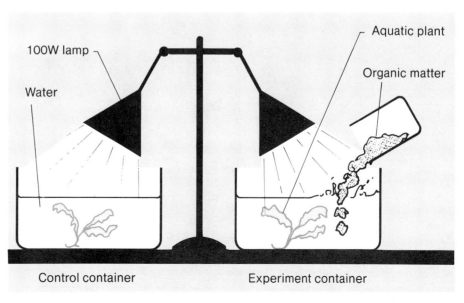

100W lamp

Water

Aquatic plant

Organic matter

Control container   Experiment container

d. Dump a can of fish food (or other organic matter) into one container.

e. Wait at least 2 or 3 d. Then test the water in each container. If possible, test for oxygen, carbon dioxide, pH, alkalinity, ammonia, nitrate, phosphate, and chloride. Record your results in a table. Also record the water temperature.

f. Note any changes in the appearance of the water and plants.

g. If time permits, repeat the tests two weeks later. Also, note any changes in the appearance of the water and plants.

Discussion

1. No organic matter was added to one container. Why?
2. Explain any differences between the tests for the two containers.
3. Explain any differences in appearance between the two containers.
4. What difference did two weeks make? Why?

Main Ideas

1. Excess nitrogen or phosphorus can cause algal blooms in lakes.
2. Chlorides often enter city rivers from sewage and street runoff.
3. The total dissolved solids is the best single measure of the productivity of water.
4. When organic matter decomposes, it adds nutrients to the water.

Key Terms

dissolved solids	organic matter	phosphorus cycle
fertilizer runoff	phosphate	suspended solids
nitrogen cycle		

Chapter Review

A. True or False

Decide whether each of the following statements is true or false. If the sentence is false, rewrite it to make it true. (Do not write in this book.)

1. Nitrogen is needed by organisms to make proteins.
2. If you find ammonia in water, you can be sure the water has been polluted by farms or industries.
3. Animal feedlots are a major source of phosphorus in many streams.
4. The high chloride levels in many urban rivers are often due to sewage.

B. Completion

Complete each of the following sentences with a word or phrase that will make the sentence correct. (Do not write in this book.)
1. Extra phosphate in a lake can cause an ▓▓▓▓▓▓▓▓ .
2. Chloride levels in a river can be raised by ▓▓▓▓▓ and ▓▓▓▓ .
3. Many detergents add ▓▓▓▓▓ to rivers and lakes.

C. Multiple Choice

Each of the following statements or questions is followed by four responses. Choose the correct response in each case. (Do not write in this book.)
1. The presence of ammonia in water indicates that the water may contain
    a) decaying plant and animal matter, fertilizer runoff, and domestic pollution, or any combination of these
    b) decaying plant and animal matter, fertilizer runoff, but *not* domestic pollution
    c) decaying plant and animal matter, domestic pollution, but *not* fertilizer runoff
    d) decaying plant and animal matter, but *neither* domestic pollution or fertilizer runoff
2. Effluent from a sewage treatment plant contains a high concentration of chloride ion because
    a) street runoff commonly goes through the sewage treatment plant
    b) common salt (sodium chloride) is added to sewage effluent in order to sterilize it
    c) groundwater, and hence household water, contains a high concentration of chloride ion
    d) the effluent is treated with chlorine before it is released
3. Which one of the following is *not* a major source of phosphate pollution in the Great Lakes?
    a) fertilizer runoff from cropland   c) detergents
    b) beef feedlots   d) human fecal matter
4. A river contains 6 μg/g of ammonia, 4 μg/g of phosphate, and 900 μg/g of chloride. The river is most likely polluted with
    a) street runoff   c) sewage
    b) fertilizer runoff   d) animal wastes

Using Your Knowledge

1. Imagine a pond with considerable vegetation on a sunny day. Table 6-3 shows data obtained where the water enters and leaves the pond. Account for the changes in each factor.

Table 6-3 Chemical Factors in a Pond

Factor	Water entering pond (μg/g)	Water leaving pond (μg/g)
Nitrate	1.2	0.1
Phosphate	1.0	0.4

2. Biologists consider Lake Erie to be more eutrophic than Lake Ontario. Yet its T.D.S. value is lower. Why is this so?
3. Use the nitrogen cycle to answer these questions.
   a) What might happen to a lake if the nitrate concentration doubled through pollution over a short period of time?
   b) What would happen to a lake if an industry released a large quantity of nitrite-bearing effluent into the water?
   c) Agricultural runoff from fields and manure piles often contains ammonia and ammonium compounds. What effects will this runoff have on lakes that it eventually enters?
4. If you are doing a pollution study on a lake, ammonia and nitrate levels should be determined when spring overturn is complete but before any significant growth occurs. Why?

Investigations

1. Find out what branch of your provincial or state government is responsible for water quality standards. Get a copy of those standards from the government. What levels of nitrates, chlorides, sulfates, and mercury are recommended for drinking water?
2. Laws in many states and provinces limit phosphates in laundry detergents to less than 5%. This has helped reduce pollution of lakes. However, dishwasher detergents are allowed to have up to 45% phosphate. The main reason for this is that the phosphate makes the dishes dry spotless. Discuss this matter with 2 or 3 people who have dishwashers. Then write a report with the title "Are Spotless Dishes More Important than Clean Lakes?"
3. Design and conduct an experiment to see how the chloride level in a river changes with the seasons. Check your design with your teacher before you begin.
4. Find out what kind of sewage treatment facilities exist in your community. Does your community have tertiary treatment that removes phosphates? If not, is it planning to install this in the near future? What are the immediate and long-term plans of your local, provincial or state, and federal governments with respect to phosphate removal through tertiary treatment?

UNIT THREE

Freshwater ecosystems like this pond contain many large species that you can easily see. But they also contain many smaller species that you will not see until you look for them.

Freshwater Ecosystems: Biotic Factors

A freshwater ecosystem, small or large, contains a wide variety of organisms. These organisms range in size from microscopic plankton to animals as large as beavers, and plants as large as cattails. All these organisms interact with one another and with their abiotic environment to form the freshwater ecosystem.

This unit describes the common organisms of freshwater ecosystems. It begins in Chapter 7 with plankton, the smallest organisms. Then each of Chapters 8 to 10 deals with organisms that are more complex. Chapter 11 discusses organisms adapted to the stream environment. Chapter 12 shows you how to use organisms to judge water quality.

7 Standing Waters: The Plankton Community

In Chapter 4 you investigated the **geophysical properties** of freshwater ecosystems. Then in Chapters 5 and 6 you investigated **chemical properties**. Therefore only the **biological properties** need to be studied before you can understand the ecology of freshwater ecosystems.

This chapter begins your study of biological properties by looking at the plankton community of standing waters. In this chapter you will read about and examine many planktonic organisms. Always think about how they interact with geophysical and chemical factors.

7.1 What Are Plankton?

A Classification of Plankton

Plankton means "small drifting organisms". They spend most of their time drifting in open water. Most plankton can be classified into two groups, phytoplankton and zooplankton. Examples of both groups are shown in Figure 7-1. **Phytoplankton** ("plant" plankton) are those which photosynthesize—like plants. **Zooplankton** ("animal" plankton) are those which move —like animals.

Though they can move, zooplankton have limited swimming ability. In fact, their horizontal movement in a lake is determined largely by the currents. However, some do migrate vertically (up and down) in a lake. As you will see later, this movement is largely a response to changes in light intensity.

Fig. 7-1 The two types of plankton.

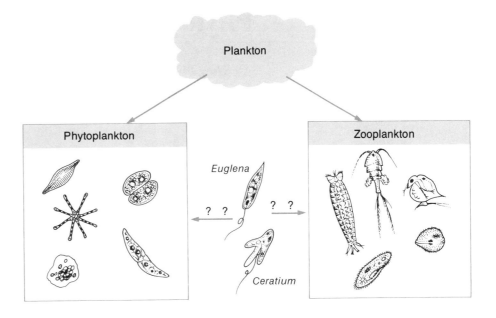

Another Classification of Plankton

This classification system, though widely used, has some problems. *Euglena* and *Ceratium*, the two organisms in the centre of Figure 7-1, photosynthesize. They also move. Thus they fit into both groups of plankton. Many bacteria and fungi are plankton. But they neither photosynthesize or move like animals. Thus they do not fit into this classification system.

To overcome these problems, plankton are also classified according to their trophic levels as follows.

- **Producers** All phytoplankton are producers. That is, they produce food by photosynthesis. In fact, they form the base of most food chains in lakes. Lakes also contain producers which move, like the two in Figure 7-1.
- **Consumers** The zooplankton are consumers. That is, they feed on phytoplankton, bacteria, or detritus. *Euglena* feeds on such things. Therefore *Euglena* can be classified as a consumer. Remember, though, that *Euglena* also photosynthesizes. Therefore it can also be classified as a producer.
- **Decomposers** This group includes bacteria and small fungi such as yeasts.

Section Review

1. What are plankton?
2. How do phytoplankton and zooplankton differ?
3. Describe two types of organisms which are not easily classified as either phytoplankton or zooplankton.
4. Describe how plankton are classified according to their trophic levels.

7.2 Phytoplankton

All living things can be classified into five kingdoms:

- kingdom Monera
- kingdom Protista
- kingdom Fungi
- kingdom Plantae
- kingdom Animalia

Phytoplankton occur in three of these kingdoms: Monera, Protista, and Plantae. (However, all organisms in these three kingdoms are not phytoplankton.) This section looks at some typical phytoplankton in each kingdom.

Phytoplankton are often called algae (singular: alga). However, not all algae are phytoplankton. Some algae, like pond scum, occur in large "globs". Others, like the giant ocean kelp (a "seaweed"), are up to 45 m long and may be attached to the bottom. Such algae are not "small drifting things".

Kingdom Monera

Description All monerans are either bacteria or blue-green algae. They live almost everywhere. They have been found in the arctic and in hot springs. They live in fresh water and in salt water. They have been found at the tops of mountains and at the bottoms of oceans. They even live on rocks.

Monerans are the simplest of organisms. They are one-celled, though the cells may occur in chains or groups. Also, the cells lack a true nucleus. As well, they have no organelles as chloroplasts do.

Of the monerans, many of the blue-green algae are phytoplankton. That is, they photosynthesize and drift freely in the open water. Figure 7-2 shows some common blue-green algae. As you might suspect, *Chroococcus* and *Anacystis* are usually planktonic. The others, because they occur in chains, do not float as freely. Thus, though they may be planktonic, they are more often found attached to rocks and plants.

Importance Blue-green algae are important for four reasons.
1. *They are producers.* Like other chlorophyll-bearing organisms, blue-green algae photosynthesize. That is, they produce food using carbon dioxide, water, and light. As a result, they form the start of some food chains in ponds and lakes. In fact, humans can be at the end of many food chains that start with blue-green algae. Here is an example.

Blue-green algae ⟶ Tiny animals ⟶ Minnows ⟶ Trout ⟶ Humans

2. *They make oxygen.* Since blue-green algae photosynthesize, they add oxygen to water and air. This helps many other organisms to respire.

Fig. 7-2 Some blue-green algae. Note that some occur as single cells. Others occur as chains or colonies.

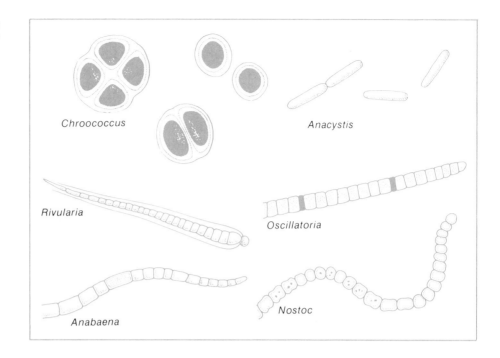

Chroococcus

Anacystis

Rivularia

Oscillatoria

Anabaena

Nostoc

3. *Some of them fix nitrogen.* All living things need nitrogen. They use it to make proteins. There's lots of nitrogen in the air. But few living things are able to use it in that form. The nitrogen must be *fixed* first. This means that nitrogen must be changed into nitrates which are a form of nitrogen that plants and other producers can use. *Anabaena* is one of several blue-green alga that can fix nitrogen.

4. *They are often found in polluted water.* Many species of blue-green alga grow well in enriched or eutrophic water. For example, *Anabaena* is among the dominant phytoplankton of Lake Erie. Such algae often undergo a rapid increase in numbers, resulting in an algal bloom (see Section 6.1). Algal blooms often ruin swimming beaches. They also clog filters in water purification plants. They can give water a bad taste and odour. Some species like *Anabaena* and *Anacystis* give off toxins (poisons). These can kill fish and mammals such as cattle that drink the water.

Kingdom Protista

Description Protists are of two types: protozoan protists and algal protists. The former are zooplankton and the latter are phytoplankton.

The algal protists are one-celled. All the cells have nuclei. They also have organelles such as chloroplasts. There are about 11 000 species of algal protists. Of these, about 500 species are coloured flagellates. About 1000 species are dinoflagellates. Most of the rest are diatoms.

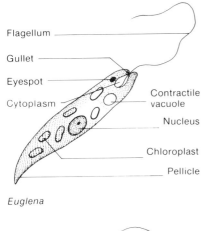

Flagellum
Gullet
Eyespot
Cytoplasm
Contractile vacuole
Nucleus
Chloroplast
Pellicle

Euglena

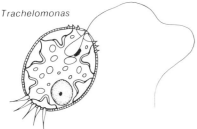

Trachelomonas

Fig. 7-3   Two typical coloured flagellates. Why might they also be classified as zooplankton?

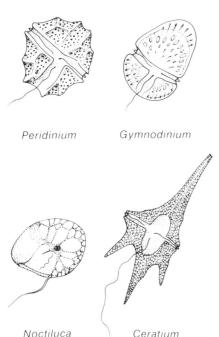

Peridinium   *Gymnodinium*

Noctiluca   *Ceratium*

Fig. 7-4   Four typical dinoflagellates.

Importance   Let's take a brief look at the importance of these three groups of algal protists.

1. *Diatoms*   Diatoms are beautiful cells to study. They come in all kinds of interesting shapes (Fig. 7-3). They have cell walls which are made of silica (the glassy substance in sand). Their surfaces are often wrinkled in appearance. They are also called golden algae because the cells are golden, brown, or amber in colour.

Diatoms are the most important of all algae. In fact, they are among the most important of all living things. They are the first step in many food chains in the oceans and in lakes. As a result, they help produce much of our food. They also make much of the world's oxygen.

Next to bacteria, there are probably more diatoms on earth than any other type of organism. They are particularly abundant in oligotrophic (clean) water. In lakes, ponds, and streams many diatoms are planktonic. Others live attached to plants, logs, rocks, and bottom sediment. They often form a thick brown layer on the rocks in the bottom of a river or stream.

2. *Dinoflagellates*   These organisms use *two* flagella to move about (Fig. 7-4). They have true cell walls which, like plant cells, are made of cellulose. The cell wall is made of overlapping plates. This often makes the cell look like a suit of armour. It also places dinoflagellates among the most beautiful organisms to observe under the microscope.

Dinoflagellates are the second most important algae in the world. They are the first step in many ocean and lake food chains. As a result, they help produce many of the fish we eat. They also add oxygen to the water and atmosphere.

Many species form algal blooms easily. In some blooms there are 20 000 000 dinoflagellates in just one litre of water! The water often turns reddish during such blooms. As a result, these blooms are called "red tides". They are common along all the ocean shores of North America, but not very common in fresh water.

3. *Coloured Flagellates*   These organisms move themselves with one or two flagella (whip-like "tails"). That's why they are called flagellates. They are called *coloured* flagellates because they are green. Figure 7-5 shows two common coloured flagellates, *Euglena* and *Trachelomonas*.

When water is rich in nutrients, *Euglena* may bloom. Sometimes this turns the water bright green because of all the *Euglena*. But at other times the water turns red or brown. This is caused by *Euglena*'s red eyespots.

Coloured flagellates are often the first step in food chains in polluted water. Therefore, without the flagellates, the water would contain few fish. The flagellates also add oxygen to the water.

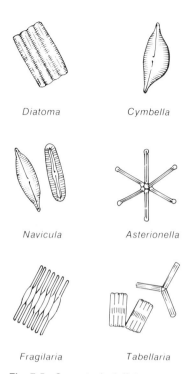

Diatoma   Cymbella

Navicula   Asterionella

Fragilaria   Tabellaria

Fig. 7-5 Some typical diatoms.

Kingdom Plantae

Description   Among the numerous plants on earth are a group of about 6000 organisms called **green algae**. Not all green algae are phytoplankton; but many are. The **desmids**, for example, are nearly all planktonic (Fig. 7-6). Figure 7-7 shows some green algae which are not desmids but are also planktonic. As the name suggests, green algae are green. They impart a green colour to the water when they bloom.

Importance   The desmids tend to prefer oligotrophic water. They are often quite common in soft, slightly acid water. *Chlorella* is widespread throughout Canada and the United States. It is found in nearly all waters that contain organic matter such as sewage. It gives the water a musty odour.

Green algae are, in general, more abundant in ponds and *small* lakes than all the other algal groups combined. As a result, they support many of the food chains in such bodies of water. As well, they are important suppliers of oxygen.

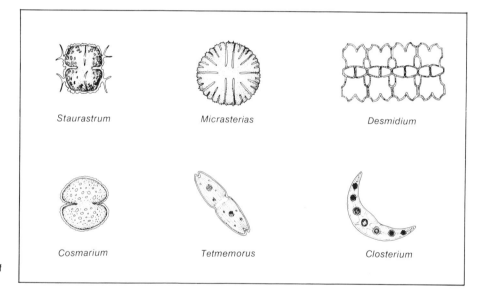

Staurastrum   Micrasterias   Desmidium

Cosmarium   Tetmemorus   Closterium

Fig. 7-6   Some typical desmids, a type of green alga.

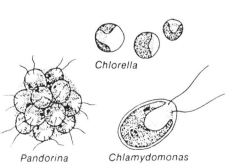

Chlorella

Pandorina   Chlamydomonas

Fig. 7-7   Some planktonic green algae which are not desmids.

Section Review

1.   Name the three kingdoms which contain phytoplankton.
2.   **a)** Give a general description of monerans.
     b) Describe the importance of blue-green algae.
3.   **a)** Give a general description of algal protists.
     b) Name three groups of algal protists.
     c) Describe the importance of diatoms.
     d) Describe the importance of dinoflagellates.
     e) Describe the importance of coloured flagellates.
4.   **a)** In what kingdom do green algae occur?
     b) Describe the importance of the green algae.

7.3 Zooplankton

Zooplankton occur in two kingdoms, Protista and Animalia. They are microscopic and near-microscopic aquatic protozoans and animals. They play key roles in most aquatic food chains. Some are scavengers which feed on dead organic matter. Others are consumers, feeding on algae and bacteria. Still others feed on smaller zooplankton. Zooplankton, in turn, become food for higher-order consumers such as mayflies and caddisflies.

Kingdom Protista

Like the algal protists (see Section 7.2), the protozoan protists are one-celled. Protozoans, as they are often called, are by far the most abundant zooplankton in water. They feed mainly on algae, bacteria, and particles of dead organic matter. There are three main phyla of protozoans that contain planktonic organisms (Fig. 7-8).

Phylum Sarcodina (Group A)   The sarcodinans, represented by the famous *Amoeba*, have no definite shape. They move by flowing into extensions of the cytoplasm called pseudopods ("false feet"). As you can see in Figure 7-8, some have shells. Most of the sarcodinans with shells live in the oceans. But the rest live in ponds, lakes, puddles, and wetlands.

Many sarcodinans live on vegetation and on the bottom, where they feed on bacteria, detritus, algae, and smaller protozoans. But, from time to time, they drift through the water as plankton.

Phylum Ciliophora (Group B)   The ciliates, represented by *Paramecium*, are covered with hair-like projections called cilia. These beat in a rhythmic manner to move the organism. Like *Paramecium*, most ciliates move through the water as plankton. Some, like *Vorticella*, live attached to plants, wood, stones, and leaves. Though most ciliates are microscopic, *Spirostomum* is easily visible to the unaided eye. It is usually located near the surface of calm, well-shaded water and gives the water a white colour.

Ciliates feed on dead organic matter, bacteria, algae, and smaller protozoans. They are usually most abundant in stagnant pools along the edges of ponds.

Phylum Zoomastigina (Group C)   The organisms in this phylum are called animal flagellates or colourless flagellates. These names distinguish them from coloured flagellates and dinoflagellates (see Section 7.2). These organisms lack chlorophyll and move with a whip-like lashing of their flagella.

Most animal flagellates are planktonic. Many species occur in fresh water. Some species feed on dead organic matter. Others feed on bacteria, algae, and smaller protozoans.

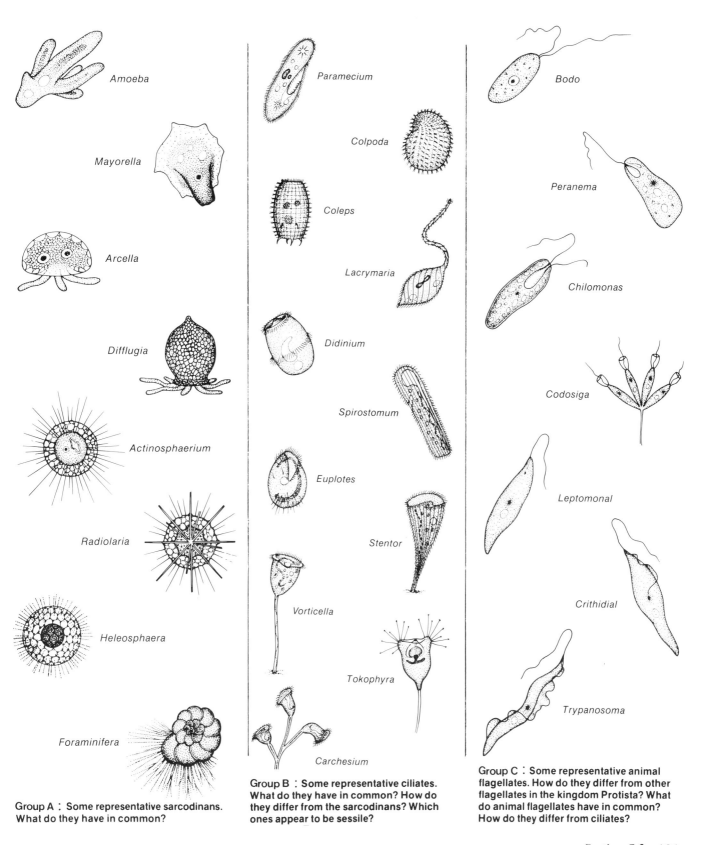

Amoeba

Mayorella

Arcella

Difflugia

Actinosphaerium

Radiolaria

Heleosphaera

Foraminifera

Group A ： Some representative sarcodinans. What do they have in common?

Paramecium

Colpoda

Coleps

Lacrymaria

Didinium

Spirostomum

Euplotes

Stentor

Vorticella

Tokophyra

Carchesium

Group B ： Some representative ciliates. What do they have in common? How do they differ from the sarcodinans? Which ones appear to be sessile?

Bodo

Peranema

Chilomonas

Codosiga

Leptomonal

Crithidial

Trypanosoma

Group C ： Some representative animal flagellates. How do they differ from other flagellates in the kingdom Protista? What do animal flagellates have in common? How do they differ from ciliates?

Kingdom Animalia

Two groups of animals contain important zooplankton of fresh water ecosystems. These are the **rotifers** (phylum Rotatoria) and **crustaceans** (class Crustacea of the phylum Arthropoda).

Rotifers

These small animals are often mistaken for single-celled organisms (Fig. 7-9). Actually they are many-celled animals and are not closely related to protozoans. Most species are barely visible to the naked eye. Over 95% of rotifier species occur in fresh water. Of those, about 75% occur in the littoral (shore) zone of ponds and lakes. There you can find up to 500 rotifers in one litre of water. They prefer clean water and are generally intolerant of pollution.

Most species of rotifers have cilia that appear to rotate like wheels as they sweep food into their mouths. They feed mainly on protozoans and algae. That's why you find rotifers in the littoral zone. Protozoans and algae are most common there. Some species of rotifers live attached to plants, but many are planktonic.

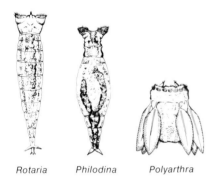

Rotaria   *Philodina*   *Polyarthra*

Fig. 7-9   Some typical planktonic rotifers.

Crustaceans

You have likely seen some of the larger crustaceans—crayfish, crabs, and lobsters. The planktonic crustaceans, however, are barely visible to the unaided eye. They are a little larger than rotifers. Like rotifers, these crustaceans are usually numerous in ponds and lakes. As well, they are an important trophic level in aquatic food chains. Figure 7-10 shows three common groups of planktonic crustaceans.

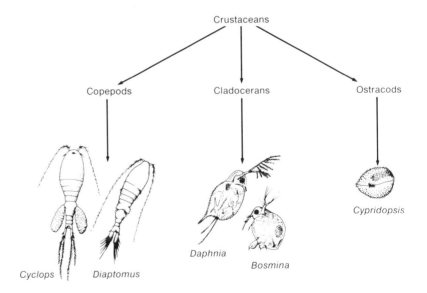

Fig. 7-10   Some common planktonic crustaceans.

Cladocerans *Daphnia* is the best known cladoceran. It occurs in most lakes and ponds, but is uncommon in fast water. *Bosmina* is generally most abundant in larger lakes. Because of their appearance, cladocerans are called water fleas. Usually, a population of cladocerans is mostly females. In fact, in some species males are unknown.

Cladocerans are filter feeders. That is, they filter their food from the water. They feed mainly on algae (phytoplankton) and protozoa. They may also feed on bacteria and detritus. Cladocerans are often the most important herbivore in ponds and lakes:

Algae ⟶ Cladocerans ⟶ Small fish ⟶ Large fish

Cladocerans undergo a diurnal (daily) vertical migration in ponds and lakes. They move to the top when it is dark and they move down when the day is at peak brightness.

Copepods *Cyclops* is the best known copepod. Like all copepods, it swims with a jerky forward motion. Egg sacs are often prominent on the females. Copepods often dominate the zooplankton of the oceans. They are generally not as common as cladocerans in ponds and lakes. They still occur, however, in the littoral zone of most ponds and lakes. There they feed as filter feeders on algae, protozoans, and bacteria. Some species also feed on detritus.

Like cladocerans, copepods undergo a diurnal vertical migration in the water. At night, water near the surface can have a thousand copepods and cladocerans per litre!

Ostracods *Cypridopsis* is a common ostracod or, as ostracods are often called, seed shrimp. These often occur in large numbers just above the bottom sediment in lakes and ponds. There they feed as filter feeders on bacteria, algae, and fungi such as yeasts. Under the microscope they look like tiny clams. Often you can see them open up and extend their appendages. Since they are adapted to life near detritus, they are also adapted to low oxygen conditions. How do you know this is true?

Section Review

1. What kingdoms contain zooplankton?
2. **a)** What are the three main phyla of protozoans?
   b) Describe each of these phyla.
   c) List the main foods of each of these phyla.
3. **a)** Give a general description of rotifers.
   b) Where are rotifers usually found?
   c) What do rotifers eat?
4. **a)** What are the three main groups of planktonic crustaceans?
   b) Describe a member of each of these groups.
   c) List the main foods of each group.

7.4 ACTIVITY **Investigating Planktonic Organisms**

In the preceding three sections you read about planktonic organisms. In this activity you will get a chance to see some of these organisms.

Problem

What do plankton have in common? How do they differ?

Materials

microscope
microscope slides (2)
cover slips (2)
paper towel
lens paper

dropper
1.5% methyl cellulose solution
identification guide e.g. Needham & Needham,
    A Guide to the Study of Fresh-Water Biology
    (Holden-Day Publishers).

prepared slides of:

a) phytoplankton $\left\{\begin{array}{l} \text{blue-green algae} \\ \text{algal protists (flagellates, dinoflagellates, diatoms)} \\ \text{desmids and other green algae} \end{array}\right.$

b) zooplankton $\left\{\begin{array}{l} \text{protozoan protists (sarcodinans, ciliates, flagellates)} \\ \text{rotifers} \\ \text{crustaceans} \end{array}\right.$

living culture of mixed plankton (phyto- and zoo-)

Procedure A   Study of Prepared Slides

a. Copy Table 7-1 into your notebook. Make it a full page in size, with the right column largest. Don't copy the example in the table.

Table 7-1 Some Plankton

Name of organism	Phyto- or zooplankton	Group	Sketch
Asterionella	Phytoplankton	Diatom	

b. Look at as many slides of plankton as possible. Observe them first under low power. Then switch to medium and finally to high power.

For each slide enter the following information in the table:

- The name on the slide.
- Whether the organism is phytoplankton or zooplankton.
- The group to which the organism belongs (blue-green algae, dinoflagellate, diatom, rotifer, etc.).
- A sketch of the organism.

Procedure B   Study of Living Plankton

For this part of the activity, your teacher has purchased or collected a culture which contains a wide variety of phytoplankton and zooplankton. The slimy brown "globs" which one often sees on plants, logs, and rocks in ponds and lakes is a good source.

a.   Copy Table 7-2 into your notebook. Make it a full page in size.

Table 7-2   Plankton Data Sheet

Phytoplankton

Blue-green algae	Diatoms	Desmids	Others

Zooplankton

Protozoans	Rotifers	Crustaceans	Others

b.   Use the dropper to get a drop of the culture.

c.   Prepare a wet mount of the culture. But do not add a cover slip.

d.   Look at the culture under low power. If the zooplankton are moving too quickly, add a drop of 1.5% methyl cellulose solution. It will slow them down without killing them.

e.   Now add a cover slip.

f.   Single out *one species* and study it closely as follows.

- Examine it under low, medium, then high power.
- Decide the group to which it belongs (blue-green algae, diatoms, etc.).
- Turn to the page in the identification guide which shows that group.
- Locate the drawing of the organism and put its name in your table.
- If you cannot find the organism in a book, make a sketch in your table instead.

Your tables are your write-up for this activity. Make sure they are complete.

7.5 ACTIVITY Ecology of the Water Flea, *Daphnia*

In nature all organisms interact with abiotic factors in their environments. In this activity you will find out how *Daphnia* respond to two factors, light and carbon dioxide levels.

Problem

How do *Daphnia* respond to light and carbon dioxide levels? What advantage is gained from this response?

Materials

Daphnia culture	cylinder of carbon dioxide
1000 mL beakers (2)	lamp
dechlorinated water	

Procedure

a. Fill the two beakers with well-aerated dechlorinated water. (Let tap water stand overnight, preferably with aeration.)
b. Place the beakers in a location where the light is dim and uniform.
c. Bubble carbon dioxide into one beaker for 5-10 min.
d. Place equal numbers of *Daphnia* (about 20) in each beaker.
e. Observe the locations of the *Daphnia* for about 5 min. Do they go to the top, bottom, or sides? Or are they distributed equally throughout the water?
f. Shine a bright light on the beakers from above. Observe the locations of the *Daphnia* for about 5 min.
g. Move the light so that it shines on the sides of the beakers. Again, observe the locations of the *Daphnia* for about 5 min.

Discussion

1. **a)** How do *Daphnia* respond to high carbon dioxide levels?
    b) What advantage do they get from this response?
2. **a)** How do *Daphnia* respond to bright light?
    b) What advantage do they get from this response?

Main Ideas

1. Phytoplankton occur in the kingdoms Monera, Protista, and Plantae.
2. Zooplankton occur in the kingdoms of Protista and Animalia.
3. Phytoplankton are at the start of many aquatic food chains.
4. Zooplankton play key roles in most aquatic food chains.

Key Terms

algal bloom	oligotrophic	protist
eutrophic	phytoplankton	toxin
moneran	plankton	zooplankton
nitrogen fixation		

Chapter Review

A. True or False

Decide whether each of the following statements is true or false. If the sentence is false, rewrite it to make it true. (Do not write in this book.)

1. All zooplankton are in the kingdom Animalia.
2. All algae are phytoplankton.
3. Some blue-green algae give off toxins.
4. The most abundant algae in ponds and small lakes are usually green algae.
5. Rotifers thrive in polluted water.

B. Completion

Complete each of the following sentences with a word or phrase that will make the sentence correct. (Do not write in this book.)

1. Some blue-green algae can fix _____ .
2. Cladocerans are _____ feeders.
3. _____ dominate the zooplankton of the oceans.
4. The most numerous algae on earth are _____ .

C. Multiple Choice

Each of the following statements or questions is followed by four responses. Choose the correct response in each case. (Do not write in this book.)

1. The most important algae on earth are
   a) diatoms   b) dinoflagellates   c) blue-green algae   d) desmids
2. Sarcodinans, ciliates, and colourless flagellates are all
   a) crustaceans   b) protozoans   c) rotifers   d) phytoplankton

3. The organism most likely to be found just above the detritus of a pond is the
   a) copepod   b) cladoceran   c) rotifer   d) ostracod
4. Which of the following feed on detritus (decaying organic matter)?
   a) sarcodinans, ciliates, and animal flagellates
   b) rotifers, copepods, and cladocerans
   c) coloured flagellates, animal flagellates, and rotifers
   d) blue-green algae, coloured flagellates, and diatoms

Using Your Knowledge

1. Construct 5 food chains involving organisms discussed in this chapter. Begin each food chain with a producer or with detritus.
2. Make one food web using some of the food chains you constructed in question 1.
3. What conditions in a pond will likely produce high numbers of rotifers and cladocerans? Why?
4. In what way are cladocerans like *Daphnia* important to humans?
5. a) In what ways are diatoms important to humans?
   b) What must we do to ensure that diatoms remain abundant?

Investigations

1. Find out how cladoceran species which have no males produce young.
2. Find out from your local water purification plant which algae most frequently clog the filters of the plant. How do the plant operators deal with this problem?
3. Isolate and culture one planktonic organism (either phytoplankton or zooplankton). Your teacher will recommend a suitable reference book.
4. Bring on an algal bloom in a large container of pond water by using fertilizer. Carefully monitor all other changes which occur in this ecosystem over a period of 2-3 months.

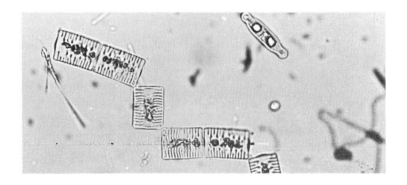

8 Standing Waters: From Sponges to Crustaceans

You have likely seen many of the large animals that live in and around standing waters—fish, birds, mammals, amphibians, and reptiles. As well, you have likely seen the large plants that live in and around standing waters. Now that you have finished Chapter 7, you have also seen the smallest organisms that live in standing waters, phytoplankton and zooplankton. But in between the plankton and large organisms is a wide variety of animal species that you probably have not seen. They are visible to the unaided eye. But, unless you look carefully, you will not see them.

This chapter surveys nine groups of these important animals: sponges, hydras, flatworms, rotifers, moss animals, roundworms, segmented worms, water mites, and crustaceans. As you read about them, pay particular attention to their habitats and ecology. Then you will be able to find them on a field trip. Even more important, you will see how vital they are to the balance of life in standing waters.

8.1 From Sponges to Nematodes

This section describes the ecology of the simplest animals in ponds and lakes. They occur in six phyla:
- phylum Porifera—the sponges
- phylum Cnidaria—the hydras
- phylum Platyhelminthes—the flatworms
- phylum Rotatoria—the rotifers
- phylum Bryozoa—the moss animals
- phylum Nematoda—the roundworms

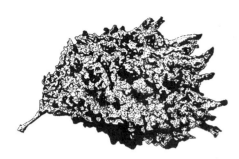

Fig. 8-1 A typical freshwater sponge, growing on a submerged twig.

The Sponges (Phylum Porifera)

Almost all sponge species are marine (salt water) dwellers. In fact, of 4500 species of sponge, only 25 have been discovered in the fresh waters of the United States and Canada.

Freshwater sponges occur in standing or flowing clean water. They often go unseen because they are usually brown, green, or gray. Further, they live attached to twigs, rocks, pebbles, and submerged vegetation (Fig. 8-1). They vary widely in size. Some may be nothing more than a thin slimy coating the size of a quarter. Others grow as thick as 3-4 mm and cover an area of 30-40 m².

Sponges occur most commonly in clean shallow water (less than 2 m deep). Most species prefer soft water, and most like slightly acidic water. They feed by filtering bacteria, algae, and detritus from the water.

The Hydras (Phylum Cnidaria)

Over 9000 species belong to the phylum Cnidaria. Among them are the jellyfish, corals, and sea anemones of the oceans. Only about 20 species occur in fresh water habitats in Canada and the United States. These include 14 hydras. The familiar *Hydra* is one of these (Fig. 8-2).

Hydras are not easily seen, though they are common animals in ponds, the littoral zone of lakes, and unpolluted streams. They are only a few millimetres long, and they live attached to stones, twigs, and vegetation. If you put a handful of submerged plants in an aquarium, you can often see the hydra on the glass a few days later.

Hydras are strictly carnivores. They feed largely on crustaceans (copepods and cladocerans), small insects, and small worms. They, in turn, become food for larger crustaceans, insects, and fish.

Hydras prefer moderately hard water with a pH between 7.6 and 8.4. They do best in well-oxygenated water. In fact, most species die when oxygen levels drop to 3 μg/g. You can tell when hydra are "unhappy" with their environment. They contract (pull in) their tentacles. Also, they will not bud (produce young on their bodies).

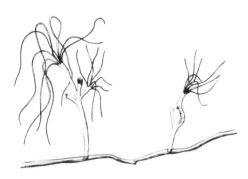

Fig. 8-2 Two *Hydra* attached to a stalk of aquatic plant. The one on the left is budding.

The Flatworms (Phylum Platyhelminthes)

Freshwater flatworms are found in almost all aquatic habitats—streams, ponds, lakes, marshes, and even ditches. They are usually associated with the bottom material. For example, they abound in the aquatic mosses and algae which often cover submerged rocks. Most flatworms are easily visible once they come out of the bottom material. They are up to 4 or 5 mm long. They can be mistaken for small leeches, since they resemble them in shape and colour (Fig. 8-3).

Flatworms feed on living zooplankton, dead animal matter, and, less commonly, on other decaying organic matter such as dead plants. They feed by sucking the food in through a long pharynx which is extended from the

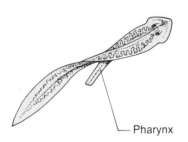

— Pharynx

Fig. 8-3 The planarian, one of the flatworms.

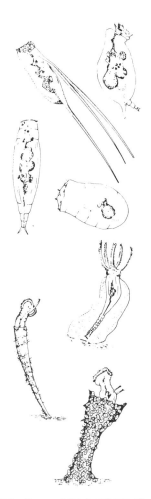

Fig. 8-4 Some of the hundreds of species of rotifers which live in fresh waters. The top four species are planktonic. The others are attached to plants or bottom debris.

Fig. 8-5 A typical moss animal, or bryozoan.

ventral (lower) surface. Flatworms, in turn, are food for dragonfly nymphs and other aquatic insects.

Flatworms prefer shallow water. They don't like bright light. As a result, they are found under bottom debris or deep in an algal mat. Most species thrive in the low oxygen conditions of the bottoms of ponds and lakes.

Rotifers (Phylum Rotatoria)

You have already learned that rotifers are an important part of the zooplankton of ponds and lakes. Many species live, however, attached to plants and, occasionally, to debris in the water (Fig. 8-4).

Rotifers are barely visible to the unaided eye, being about 0.1 mm to 0.5 mm long. They feed by sweeping food into their mouths using cilia (hairs) which seem to rotate like wheels. They eat mainly protozoans, smaller rotifers, and algae.

Of the 1800 species of rotifers, almost all live in fresh water. Most of these occur in the littoral zone of lakes and ponds. Only about 100 species live fully in the limnetic zone. These are, of course, the ones which are zooplankton. Rotifers generally prefer water that is fairly clean and above $20°C$. They are most common among submerged plants. In general, basic water has few species of rotifers but large numbers of individuals. In contrast, acidic water has large numbers of species and low numbers of individuals.

Moss Animals (Phylum Bryozoa)

Of the 4000 or so species of bryozoans, only about 20 occur in freshwater ecosystems in the United States and Canada. They exist in colonies of thousands of individuals. A colony may cover an area as large as a square metre. The colonies often look like a carpet of moss—hence the name "moss animals" (Fig. 8-5). Some species form gelatinous balls the size of a large softball.

Bryozoans occur in clean ponds and the shallow areas of lakes and slow streams. They are particularly common where there are submerged rocks, twigs, logs, and vegetation. They don't like bright light and, as a result, live on the underside or shady side of their selected habitat. They are most abundant in summer when the water temperature is $19°C$ to $23°C$. They may be found in stagnant water but are never found in badly polluted water. They need at least 4 μg/g of oxygen.

Bryozoans have tentacles with cilia on them. These wave phytoplankton, zooplankton, and small particles of detritus to the mouth region.

Roundworms (Phylum Nematoda)

Roundworms, or nematodes, occur in the detritus, mud, sand, and vegetation at the edge and bottom of lakes, ponds, rivers, and streams. They are usually less than 1 cm long. They move with an S-shaped motion. This motion is often called serpentine, since it is like a snake's motion. As the

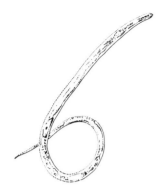

Fig. 8-6 A typical nematode from the bottom of a pond or lake.

name suggests, these worms are circular (round) in cross-section and their bodies are not segmented (Fig. 8-6).

Among the species of freshwater nematodes one finds all types of feeding habits.

- Some eat only dead animal material.
- Some eat only dead plant material.
- Some eat any form of detritus.
- Some are herbivores, feeding on living plants.
- Some are carnivores, feeding on living animals.

Regardless of the food eaten, each species shows special adaptations for eating that food. For example, herbivores may be specialized for biting and chewing or they may have a hollow stylet which pierces plant cells and sucks the protoplasm out. The carnivores may show either of the same adaptations. The prey of the carnivores are largely protozoans, rotifers, and small worms, including other nematodes.

Nematodes can withstand oxygen levels as low as 1 μg/g. They help recycle nutrients in ponds and lakes by stirring up the bottom material. The eggs of nematodes can remain viable after months without oxygen and after many successive freezings and thawings. These kind of conditions often occur in the mud at the edges of lakes and ponds.

Section Review

1. Copy Table 8-1 into your notebook. Then complete it as you read this section again.

Table 8-1 A Summary

Group of organisms	Description	Habitat	Food	Ecology
Sponges				
Hydras				
Flatworms				
Rotifers				
Bryozoans				
Nematodes				

8.2   The Segmented Worms

The segmented worms make up the phylum Annelida. This section deals with two main classes of annelids. These are the aquatic earthworms (class Oligochaeta) and the leeches (class Hirudinea).

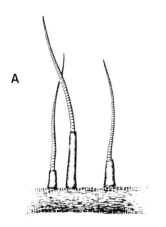

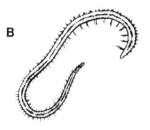

Fig. 8-7 Two common aquatic earthworms: the sludgeworm *Tubifex* (A) and the bristleworm *Nais* (B).

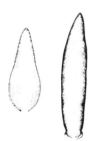

Fig. 8-8 Two of the approximately 50 species of leeches that live in the fresh waters of Canada and the United States.

Aquatic Earthworms

Aquatic earthworms are similar in structure to their familiar terrestrial relatives. They are segmented and usually pink to red in colour. They range in size from 1 mm to 30 mm in length. They are common in the mud and detritus of stagnant pools. They also occur in just about all ponds, lakes, streams, and rivers.

Most aquatic earthworms feed just like the earthworms in your garden. They ingest large quantities of the mud or detritus. This material passes through the intestine, where the organic matter is digested. As they feed, they mix the bottom material and release nutrients from it.

Two common aquatic earthworms are the bristleworm, *Nais*, and the sludgeworm, *Tubifex* (Fig. 8-7). The bristleworm crawls through the detritus and dense vegetation. The sludgeworm constructs a tube, above a burrow, extending down into the bottom material. It feeds, mouth down, on the bottom material. Its "tail" sticks out of the tube and sways back and forth, exchanging oxygen and carbon dioxide with the water. As the oxygen concentration drops, the "tail" moves more rapidly. Why is this so?

Sludgeworms have been found in numbers as high as 10 000/m² in deep lakes. But they are many times more abundant than this in slow mud-bottomed rivers polluted with sewage. One study found a writhing mass of 600 000/m² near the mouth of such a river! The species *Tubifex tubifex* commonly dominates such environments. These organisms, and most other aquatic earthworms, can tolerate oxygen concentrations as low as 1 μg/g.

Leeches

You likely call leeches "bloodsuckers" (Fig. 8-8). However, very few species actually suck blood from warm-blooded animals like you. Many are carnivores, feeding on snails, insects, worms, and small crustaceans. Others are scavengers, feeding mainly on dead animal matter. Those that are bloodsuckers feed only occasionally. A full meal, however, often increases the worms mass by four times! The stored blood is digested slowly. Leeches have been kept alive for two years without eating.

Leeches vary in colour. Many, though, are brightly coloured with beautiful patterns. They range in length from 0.5 cm to 45 cm. Leeches are graceful and rapid swimmers. They usually occur on plants and bottom material in warm sheltered shallow waters. They conceal themselves among debris, stones, and plants. The margin of a pond, lake, or slow river can have numbers as high as 700/m². You may see few in the daytime—unless you stand barefoot in the water for several minutes! That's because leeches are nocturnal and seek dark areas in the daytime.

Leeches need a firm material to which they can attach themselves. Thus they are uncommon in areas with a pure sand, mud, or clay bottom. They require cleaner water and higher oxygen levels than the aquatic earthworms.

Section Review

1. Describe the habitat, food, and ecology of the aquatic earthworm, *Tubifex*.
2. Describe the habitat, food, and ecology of the leech.

8.3   The Water Mites

Fig. 8-9   A typical water mite.

Over 1 000 000 species of animals are arthropods (phylum Arthropoda). In fact, most animals are arthropods. Among them are insects, crustaceans, millipeds, centipedes, and arachnids. In the group called arachnids are spiders, scorpions, ticks, and mites. The water mite belongs to this group (Fig. 8-9).

Water mites are most abundant amongst the dense submerged vegetation of ponds, the littoral zone of lakes, and quiet regions of streams and rivers. You can't miss them if you put some of the vegetation and water in a white tray. Their globular shape and bright colours (red, yellow, green, and blue) make them easy to spot. They are small, however. The length ranges from 0.4 mm to 3 mm. At first glance they look like their close relatives, spiders. But closer examination shows that the head, thorax, and abdomen are joined into a single mass. A spider, in contrast, has the head and thorax joined into a single mass which is separate from the abdomen.

Many water mites are carnivorous. They feed on worms and small insects. Others are parasites. In both cases they pierce the prey with their mandibles and suck fluids from it. Some species feed on dead animals. A few may even feed on plants and detritus.

Unlike most aquatic invertebrates, water mites remain active in the winter. They are most common, however, in the late spring and early autumn. In dense submerged vegetation one can find as many as 2000/m² at those times of the year. Mites are active only during daylight hours.

Section Review

1. Describe the appearance of water mites.
2. What do water mites eat?
3. Describe the preferred habitat of water mites.

8.4   The Crustaceans

Crustaceans belong to the phylum Arthropoda. Most of the 35 000 species are marine. Just 1100 or so species live in the fresh waters of Canada and the United States. All crustaceans breathe through gills or the body surface. All have two pairs of antennas. As well, all body segments normally have a pair of jointed appendages.

The crustaceans can be divided into seven groups as follows:

Mainly Planktonic	*Not Planktonic*
cladocerans	isopods
copepods	amphipods
ostracods	decapods
	fairy shrimps

You studied the planktonic groups in Section 7.3. Read that section again. Then read the following information on the remaining four groups.

Isopods

Ascellus is a common genus of isopod. Like all aquatic isopods, it is commonly called an **aquatic sow bug**. *Iso-* means "equal" and *-pod* means "foot". Look at Figure 8-10. You can see why this animal is called an isopod. All legs, except the first pair, are similar.

You have likely seen terrestrial sow bugs, or pill bugs. They are the gray animals you find under logs, rocks, and in other moist dark habitats. They roll up into a ball when you touch them. Aquatic sow bugs also seek out shelter under rocks, logs, and detritus. They seldom come out into the open.

Isopods are about 0.5 cm to 1 cm long. They are flattened dorsoventrally (top to bottom) and they are black, brown, or rusty in colour. They are scavengers, and crawl over the detritus, eating dead animals and decaying plants. They rarely exist in water deeper than 1 m. Also, the water must not be polluted, though it can contain some organic matter. They require moderate amounts of oxygen.

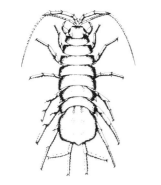

Fig. 8-10 *Ascellus*, a common isopod.

Amphipods

Gammarus is a common genus of amphipod (Fig. 8-11). Like all amphipods, it is also called a **sideswimmer** or **scud**. It does, in fact, swim on its side. Amphipods are from 5 mm to 20 mm long. They are flattened laterally (from side to side) and they are usually brown, gray, or green.

One species of amphipod is planktonic. But the rest live on the bottom or amongst dense vegetation. When the vegetation is disturbed, the amphipods quickly move into the bottom detritus. They occur in unpolluted lakes and ponds, and along the margins of rivers and streams.

Amphipods seem to be eating all the time. They feed on all kinds of dead plant and animal matter. Those which live amongst vegetation graze on the film of algae, zooplankton and detritus that covers leaves and stems. In short, amphipods are omnivorous scavengers.

Amphipods don't like bright light. Therefore they spend the day in vegetation or under stones and debris. Unbelievable numbers sometimes collect in

Fig. 8-11 *Gammarus*, a common amphipod.

vegetation. One study discovered over 10 000/m² among submerged plants! Amphipods generally need abundant oxygen. Most species are found in water of low to medium hardness.

Decapods

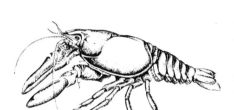

Fig. 8-12   The crayfish, a freshwater decapod.

Crayfish are our common fresh water decapods (Fig. 8-12). They are found in the littoral zone of lakes and in ponds, sloughs, swamps, and even wet meadows. They also abound in rivers and streams. As the name decapod suggests, they have ten legs. The anterior (front) pair have pincers which are used for feeding and defence. Crayfish range from 10 mm to 150 mm in length, not including antennas.

Crayfish are omnivores. They eat all kinds of thick juicy vegetation, living and dead. And they occasionally eat dead animals. Since they seldom are predaceous (feeding on live animals), they are often classed as scavengers. They feed mainly at dawn and dusk. During the day they hide in burrows and under stones or debris. They seldom live in water deeper than 1 m.

Fairy Shrimps

Fig. 8-13   The fairy shrimp, a crustacean found in temporary ponds.

These crustaceans are never found in running waters. In fact, because they are fairly large (15-20 mm long) and slow, predators make life difficult for them in ponds and lakes. As a result, they are most common in temporary pools and ponds. These bodies of water dry up in the summer. This eliminates predators like fish. But the fairy shrimps have a life cycle that lets them survive the dry period. They lay eggs in the bottom ooze. The eggs can be dried out in the summer and frozen in the winter, yet still hatch. They usually hatch just after the ice has melted in the spring.

Fairy shrimps are beautiful animals and graceful swimmers (Fig. 8-13). They swim upside down with a wavelike motion of the legs. Their food consists mainly of bacteria, zooplankton, algae, and small pieces of detritus.

Section Review

1. **a)** Name seven groups of crustaceans.
   b) Name the three groups which are mainly zooplankton.
2. Copy Table 8-2 into your notebook. Complete it as you read this section again.

Table 8-2   A Summary

Group of organisms	Description	Habitat	Food	Ecology
Isopods				
Amphipods				
Decapods				
Fairy Shrimps				

8.5   *Activity* **Detailed Study of an Invertebrate**

You are to select one organism from the following list and study its ecology in detail. You will need to work in both the library and laboratory.

- copepods
- ostracods
- flatworms
- roundworms
- sludgeworms
- isopods
- amphipods

The specimens will have to be collected from a pond. Thus the list may have to be changed if all organisms cannot be found.

Problem

How does the chosen organism interact with its environment, biotic and abiotic?

Materials

1000 mL beakers (2)	reference books
culture of an invertebrate	other supplies as needed

Procedure

a. Select the organism you wish to study. Read what this book has to say about this organism.

b. Visit your school library and other libraries and research the following information on the organism:

- General description
- Locomotion
- Food and feeding
- Reproduction
- Life cycle
- Habitat and general ecology
- Response to specific abiotic factors

c. Select two environmental factors and design and do an experiment to see how your organism responds to those factors. Activity 7.5 will give you some ideas.

- The effects of variation in temperature, light, pH, oxygen, and carbon dioxide are interesting to study.
- Changes in the availability and type of food also create interesting responses.
- Changes in the physical environment (more and less cover, deep or shallow detritus, and so on) will affect the organisms.

Discussion

Write a report of about 800-1000 words, using the headings listed in step (b). Then, under the heading "The Experiments", describe the two experiments you did. Also, give the results and your interpretation of them.

Main Ideas

1. A wide variety of simple animals occur in standing waters: sponges, hydras, flatworms, rotifers, moss animals, roundworms, segmented worms, mites, and crustaceans. Each species has a unique ecology.
2. Each type of animal has specific habitat requirements.
3. Each type of animal occupies a unique niche.
4. A wide variety of planktonic and non-planktonic crustaceans live in standing waters.

Key Terms

bryozoan	hydra	roundworm
crustacean	mite	segmented worm
detritus feeder	moss animal	sponge
flatworm	rotifer	

Chapter Review

A. True or False

Decide whether each of the following statements is true or false. If the sentence is false, rewrite it to make it true. (Do not write in this book.)

1. Most sponges are marine organisms.
2. Flatworms are omnivores.
3. Rotifers thrive in polluted waters.
4. *Tubifex* worms need fairly high oxygen levels.
5. All leeches are "bloodsuckers".
6. Isopods are bottom scavengers.
7. Crayfish normally occur in shallow water.

B. Completion

Complete each of the following sentences with a word or phrase that will make the sentence correct. (Do not write in this book.)

1. Freshwater sponges commonly occur in clean ▢▢▢▢ water.
2. Hydra ▢▢▢▢ their tentacles when their environmental conditions are unfavourable.
3. A good place to look for flatworms is under ▢▢▢▢ in a pond or lake.
4. Nematodes can be easily identified because they swim with a ▢▢▢▢ motion.
5. Sludgeworms can tolerate very ▢▢▢▢ oxygen conditions.
6. Water mites are most abundant among ▢▢▢▢ .

C. Multiple Choice

Each of the following statements or questions is followed by four responses. Choose the correct response in each case. (Do not write in this book.)

1. Hydras are
   a) omnivores   b) scavengers   c) carnivores   d) herbivores
2. Amphipods are best described as
   a) carnivores   b) omnivorous scavengers   c) herbivores   d) predators
3. Which one of the following animal communities is most likely to occur in clean standing waters? Assume that high numbers of individuals of each population will be present.
   a) sponges, rotifers, bryozoans, amphipods
   b) sponges, flatworms, roundworms, and sludgeworms
   c) sludgeworms, rotifers, leeches, sow bugs
   d) bristleworms, flatworms, roundworms, bryozoans

Using Your Knowledge

1. a) Why are sludgeworms usually abundant in slow rivers which receive sewage effluent?
   b) What useful function do sludgeworms perform in this habitat?
2. Amphipods are abundant in the grass and other vegetation that dangle into a pond or stream from the banks. Why is this so?
3. The littoral zone of a certain lake has abundant flatworms, few rotifers, no sponges, abundant nematodes, and abundant aquatic earthworms. What would you expect the abiotic environment to be like? Give your reasons.
4. Sludgeworms, nematodes, and flatworms are often found in the same habitat. Why is this so?

Investigations

1. Design and conduct an experiment to determine the optimum environmental requirements of one of the animals described in this chapter. Write a report of your findings. It should describe your purpose, procedure, results, and conclusions.
2. Find out how the sludgeworm has adapted physiologically to live in water with little oxygen in it.
3. With your teacher's permission, investigate the diversity of life in a local pond or lake. Write a report on your findings. Include in your report your judgment of the water quality of the pond or lake.
4. Set up and maintain a culture of rotifers, copepods, or cladocerans. Your teacher will recommend a reference book to get you started. Describe and analyze any problems you encountered.

9 Standing Waters: Insects and Molluscs

Chapter 8 described the simpler animals that live in ponds and lakes. This chapter deals with the more complex animals in those ecosystems, the insects and molluscs.

9.1 Aquatic Insects

What Are Insects?

Insects belong to the class Insecta of the phylum Arthropoda. They are the most successful group of animals on earth. Over 1 000 000 species have been identified. In fact, most arthropods are insects.

Adult insects have distinct head, thorax, and abdomen regions. The thorax consists of three segments. Each segment bears a pair of legs. Insects usually have two pair of wings. However, some have only one pair and others have none. The wings are on the thorax.

The class Insecta is divided into about 30 orders. Of those, 11 have members that are aquatic or semi-aquatic. In this chapter we will take a look at animals in 9 of those orders. Table 9-1 gives an overview of those orders.

How Do Aquatic Insects Breathe?

You likely know that insects have a **tracheal breathing system**. Air travels

Table 9-1   Main Orders of Aquatic Insects

Name of Order	Examples
Diptera	midge flies, mosquitoes
Odonata	dragonflies, damselflies
Plecoptera	stoneflies
Ephemeroptera	mayflies
Trichoptera	caddisflies
Megaloptera	dobsonflies, alderflies, fishflies
Hemiptera	true bugs
Coleoptera	beetles
Collembola	springtails

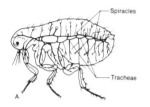

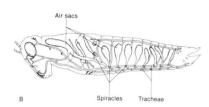

Fig. 9-1   The tracheal system of insects: flea (A) and grasshopper (B).

through tubes called tracheae (singular: trachea) to each cell. In adult terrestrial insects the tracheae are connected to pores in the body wall called spiracles (Fig. 9-1). Air enters the spiracles and travels through the tracheae to the cells. Aquatic insects have a problem, then. How does air enter the spiracles when the insect is under water? There are four ways that insects have adapted to breathe in an aquatic environment.

1. Some adult beetles and bugs simply come to the surface from time to time to exchange gases through their spiracles.

2. Some adult beetles and bugs form an air bubble under the wings or among hairs on the body. Such bubbles are placed over spiracles. Each bubble acts like a lung. Oxygen diffuses from the water into the bubble. From there it enters the spiracles. Carbon dioxide leaves the spiracles, enters the bubble, and diffuses out into the water. The bubble, then, exchanges gases between the insect and water just as your lungs exchange gases between your body and the air.

   If the insect is inactive, the bubble need not be replaced for hours or even days. But in some cases it is replaced at the surface every few seconds.

3. The larvas of some diptera like the mosquito use a siphon. They come to the surface, put the siphon above the water, and breathe (see Figure 9-3).

4. Many larvas have no spiracles. Gas exchange with the water occurs through the body surface. These larvas need not come to the surface of the water.

5. Many larvas have gills. These are just thin extensions of the body surface to make the gas exchange described in 4 easier.

1. List four characteristics of insects.
2. Copy Table 9-1 into your notebook. Look ahead through this chapter for drawings of these insects.
3. Describe five ways that aquatic insects are adapted to breathing.

9.2 Insects: The True Flies

The true flies make up the order Diptera. These insects have just two wings. Among the true flies are houseflies, mosquitoes, horseflies, and midges. Of the 16 500 species of flies in Canada and the United States, 2000 have larval stages that are aquatic. The adults are never aquatic. This section looks at the larval stages of seven families of Diptera commonly found in ponds and lakes.

Midge Flies (Family Chironomidae)

This family contains about 2000 species. The adults are tiny (about 5 mm long), delicate flies that look like mosquitoes. They do not bite. However, they can be very annoying! They commonly occur in swarms, especially near water. You may have had such a swarm accompany you on a walk.

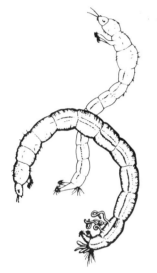

Fig. 9-2   The bloodworm, *Chironomus*, is the larva of the midge fly.

The larva are 2 mm to 30 mm long. They have a pair of prolegs (a simple type of leg) on the first segment of the thorax and on the last segment of the abdomen (Fig. 9-2). They vary in colour from white, yellow, and pink to a deep red. The one shown in Figure 9-2 is a deep red. That's why it is called a bloodworm. Of course, it is not a worm, even though it looks somewhat like one. (Can you see two differences?) The red species contain hemoglobin which assists with absorption of oxygen from the water. They need this because they live in a low oxygen environment. Midge larvas (chironomids) occur in aquatic vegetation and in the detritus of ponds, lakes, and streams. Some species make tubes out of algae, silt, and sand. Others simply crawl around in the detritus.

Midge larvas are mainly herbivores; they eat plants and algae. They are also scavengers, feeding on detritus. Midge larvas are, in turn, food for fish. In fact, many lakes would be without fish if they didn't have midge larvas.

Chironomids can be spotted by the way they move. On the bottom they move with a looping action. Those that swim wriggle back and forth as they move up and down in the water.

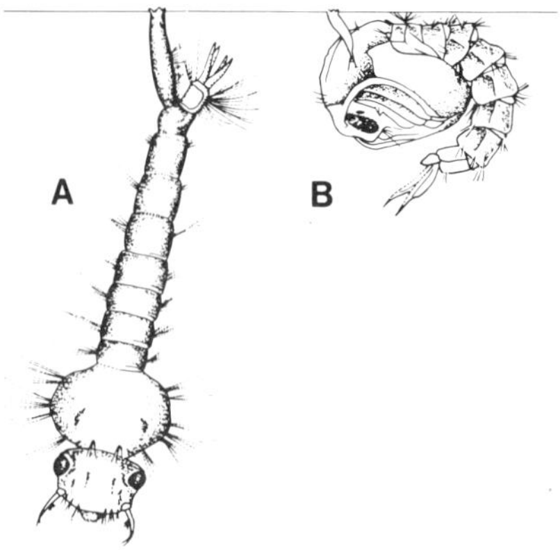

Mosquitoes (Family Culicidae)

Fig. 9-3   The larva (A) and pupa (B) of the mosquito, *Culex*. Note that both breathe with a siphon.

You all know this family of biting flies! But you may not have seen the larva or pupa (Fig. 9-3). As you can see, both the larva and pupa breathe with siphons. The larvas usually hang from the surface as shown in the drawing. However, if they are disturbed they move to the bottom and, eventually, back to the top with a wriggling action. Thus they are called "wrigglers". The pupas move by tumbling "head over heels". They are, as a result, called "tumblers".

Since mosquito larvas do not depend on dissolved oxygen, they can live in stagnant water with no oxygen in it at all. In fact, they abound in such water, since most predators such as fish will be absent.

Mosquito larvas feed on protozoans, algae, and tiny pieces of detritus.

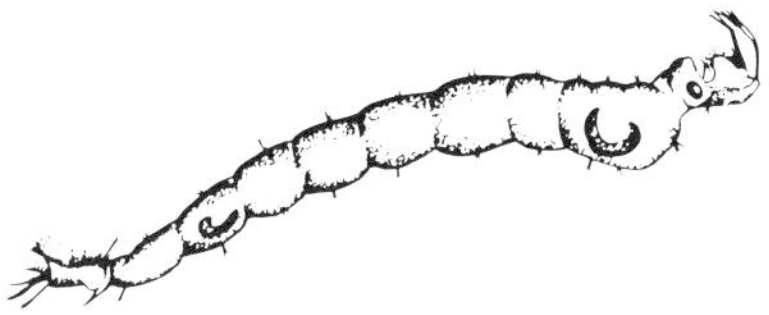

Phantom Midges (Family Culicidae)

The phantom midge, *Chaoborus*, is quite common in most lakes and large ponds. They are a real delight to observe (Fig. 9-4)! Except for two silvery air sacs that help them move up and down in the water, they are transparent. Hence the name "phantom". The air sacs also take oxygen from the water at times.

Phantom midges swim with a jerky, lashing movement. They are carnivores. They prey on small insect larvas and small crustaceans, using their antennas to catch them.

Crane Flies (Family Tipulidae)

You have probably seen adult crane flies. They look like giant mosquitoes. They are often found fluttering helplessly on windows at dusk, particularly on homes near water (Fig. 9-5).

Crane fly larvas look like fat worms. They range in colour from white to brown. They are found in most types of aquatic habitats, including standing waters. *Tipula* is found in most habitats. The finger-like projections on the anal end are gills. The anal end also bears a pair of spiracles (breathing pores). These are pushed up into the air when dissolved oxygen supplies are low. Some crane fly larvas are herbivores; others are carnivores.

Biting Midges (Family Heleidae)

Adult biting midges are tiny flies, usually under 4 mm long. You can feel them bite you, although you are not able to see them. As a result, they are often called "no-see-ums". They are also called "punkies" or "sand flies". Campers know that these flies can crawl through the netting on the doors and windows of tents, unless you have special "no-see-um" netting.

The larvas are present in most aquatic ecosystems (Fig. 9-6). But they are most abundant in the floating masses of algae we see on some ponds and lakes. These larvas are from 3 to 12 mm long. Some species are carnivores and, in fact, are even cannibalistic (eat their own species). Other species are herbivores.

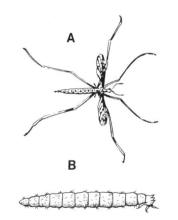

Fig. 9-4 Larva of the phantom midge, *Chaoborus*.

A

B

Fig. 9-5 The crane fly, *Tipula*: the adult (A) and the larva (B).

Fig. 9-6 The larva of the biting midge, *Dasyhelea*.

Moth Flies (Family Psychodidae)

Moth flies often gather by the thousands around lights at night. The adult flies are tiny (less than 4 mm long) and their bodies are hairy. One common genus in North America is *Psychoda*.

The larvas of *Psychoda* are very common in stagnant water (Fig. 9-7). They even occur in sewage water. These larvas are from 3 to 10 mm long and are grayish in colour. They can inhabit stagnant water because they move to the top and breathe with siphons.

Moth fly larvas feed mainly on algae and decaying plant material.

Fig. 9-7   The larva of the moth fly, *Psychoda*.

Horseflies (Family Tabanidae)

The adult horsefly is a serious pest. This large fly (10 to 25 mm long) inflicts painful bites on horses, cattle, and other domestic animals. It plagues wild mammals such as deer. It will take a hunk out of you too, if it gets a chance!

The larvas are large, from 15 to 40 mm long (Fig. 9-8). Fortunately, they don't bite! You can find them on the bottoms of ponds, the shallow lakes, swamps, and pools. Some species also live in flowing waters. The larvas are white, green, brown, or yellow. They are tapered at both ends. The head is quite tiny. The anal end bears a short siphon. Some species feed on detritus. *Tabanus*, the one shown in Figure 9-8, is predaceous. It eats sludgeworms, bristleworms, insect larvas, and even snails.

Fig. 9-8   The larva of the horsefly, *Tabanus*.

Hover Flies (Family Syrphidae)

Hover flies are also called flower flies and bee flies. These colourful flies are often found around flowers. They often hover in one place in the air for many seconds. Hence the name hover flies. Since they feed on nectar and pollen, they are also called bee flies. You may have had a toe nipped by a hover fly as you sat outside barefooted on a hot sunny day.

Figure 9-9 shows the larva of one hover fly, *Eristalsis*. Note the long siphon. It is in three segments, and can telescope out, just like a radio antenna, from two to four times the length of the body. (The body alone is from 5 to 25 mm long.) *Eristalsis* larvas are fairly inactive. They feed on detritus in shallow water. They usually select water shallow enough that the siphon can be extended to the surface for breathing. Because of their appearance, *Eristalsis* larvas are called "rat-tailed maggots".

Fig. 9-9   The larva of the hover fly, *Eristalsis*.

Section Review

1. What is the distinguishing feature of the true flies (Diptera)?
2. Copy Table 9-2 into your notebook. Then complete it as you read this section again.

Table 9-2   A Summary of Diptera

Family	Description of larva	Habitat	Food	Other comments
Midge flies				
Mosquitoes				
Phantom midges				
Crane flies				
Biting midges				
Moth flies				
Horseflies				
Hover flies				

9.3   Insects: The "Other Flies"

Several orders of insects bear the name "fly", but are not true flies (2-winged, or Diptera). Four of these orders have members which live in standing waters:

- Mayflies (order Ephemeroptera)
- Caddisflies (order Trichoptera)
- Dragonflies and Damselflies (order Odonata)
- Alderflies, Dobsonflies, Fishflies (order Megaloptera)

Mayflies (Order Ephemeroptera)

Adult mayflies are seldom seen when the wind is blowing. They cling to vegetation in sheltered locations (Fig. 9-10). But when it is calm, countless thousands of males form hovering swarms. Then females enter the swarm, one at a time, to pick their mates. Mating occurs during flight. The adults don't eat, and they often live for just a few hours or days. Most of the mayfly life cycle is spent in the water as a nymph. This time varies from half a year to three years.

Mayfly nymphs occur in all types of freshwater ecosystems, if they have abundant oxygen. Some species can exist at levels as low as 2 μg/g. But most need at least 5 μg/g.

Ecologists classify mayfly nymphs of ponds and lakes according to their habitats. This creates three groups:

- Bottom sprawlers
- Vegetation dwellers
- Burrowers

Fig. 9-10 Adult mayflies of most species look like this one.

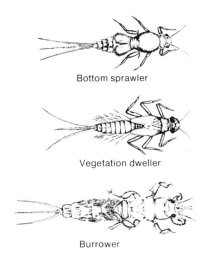

Bottom sprawler

Vegetation dweller

Burrower

Fig. 9-11 Examples of the three groups of mayflies found in ponds and lakes. How is each adapted to its habitat?

Each group shows unique adaptations to its habitat (Fig. 9-11). Let's see what some of these are.

1. ***Bottom Sprawlers*** Mayfly nymphs of this group crawl about slowly on the bottom. They are often covered with detritus. Look at the adomen and note how the first pair of gills covers much of the others. This helps prevent the gills from getting clogged up with silt and other debris. Note, too, that these animals tend to be flattened, and their legs are spread out to the sides.

2. ***Vegetation Dwellers*** Mayfly nymphs of this group are adapted for climbing, running, and swimming amongst submerged vegetation. The plate-like gills and "tails" move strongly and suddenly to propel the animal quickly through the water.

3. ***Burrowers*** These nymphs show the most striking adaptations to their habitat. They spend their time burrowing like moles through the bottom material. Thus they live in an oxygen-poor environment. As a result, they have large gills which they flutter in the water to get extra oxygen. Note, too, the specially adapted jaw. The tusk-like projections help the animal dig its burrow, as do the muscular legs.

Mayfly nymphs are best called **opportunistic feeders**. That is, they will eat whatever the opportunity provides. However, all species are mainly herbivores. They graze on plants and algae. But, if the opportunity provides, they will feed on detritus and even live animals.

Caddisflies (Order Trichoptera)

Adult caddisflies look like small moths (Fig. 9-12). They can be seen near water, usually from May to September. But you may have to look at night; they are nocturnal. They are black, gray, brown, or tan in colour. The adults live no more than one month. The larvas, on the other hand, live from six months to a year before they change to adults.

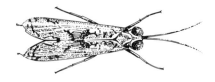

Fig. 9-12 An adult caddisfly.

Caddisfly larvas occur in most freshwater habitats. Several species are adapted to life in ponds and lakes. The first time you see them on the bottom of a lake or pond, you will be quite surprised. You will see "sticks" walking around on the bottom! These larvas build cases from leaves, gravel, sand, bark, twigs, grass, or other debris (Fig. 9-13). The larva, often called a **caddis-worm**, lives in its case. Its head, thorax, and legs come out when it wants to move. The caddis-worm drags its home with it!

Caddisfly larvas need moderately high levels of oxygen. Most species require at least 4 μg/g. Those which live in cases use a waving action of their abdomens to pump water through their cases. This provides them with the oxygen they need.

Fig. 9-13 Two types of cases built by caddisfly larvas.

Caddisfly larvas feed on a wide variety of food. Some species are classified as **grazers**. They feed on detritus, fungi, algae, and even small invertebrates. Others are **carnivores**, feeding mainly on worms, small insect larvas, and small crustaceans. Still others are **suspension feeders**. They filter algae, zooplankton, and small pieces of detritus from the water, using hairs around the mouth and on the legs. As well, some are scrapers. These eat the same food as grazers, but have mouthparts adapted for scraping the food off the bottom material. Some stream species are net filter feeders. They build nets to filter algae, zooplankton, and detritus from the water.

Dragonflies and Damselflies (Order Odonata)

Almost everyone has seen these colourful insects flying around ponds, lakes, and streams. You may have seen them darting quickly in various directions as they catch mosquitoes and other small flies.

Dragonfly and damselfly adults are easy to tell apart. Damselflies are smaller and more delicate. They fly more slowly. When they land, they fold their wings along the abdomen or tilt them upward. Dragonflies, on the other hand, hold their wings in a horizontal position when they land (Fig. 9-14). Also, the hind wings of the dragonfly are broader than the front wings where they join the body.

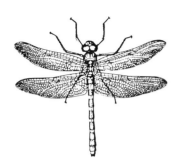

Fig. 9-14 A dragonfly adult holds the wings in a horizontal position when it lands.

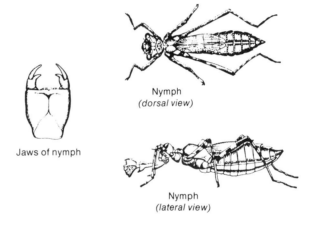

Jaws of nymph

Nymph
(dorsal view)

Nymph
(lateral view)

Fig. 9-15 One of the many species of dragonfly nymphs. ➤

Mature dragonfly nymphs are from 15 to 45 mm long (Fig. 9-15). Mature damselfly nymphs are from 10-20 mm long, not counting the gills at the rear end (Fig. 9-16). Most Odonata spend about a year in the nymph stage before the adult emerges.

Like mayflies, Odonata nymphs can be classified as vegetation dwellers, bottom sprawlers, and burrowers. If you get a chance to capture nymphs from the three different habitats, be sure to look for their special adaptations.

All Odonata nymphs are carnivores. Some sit motionless for hours, covered with debris or lurking in vegetation, until food comes nearby. Then the special mouthpart unfolds, shoots forward, and traps the prey with two spikes (Fig. 9-17). The prey is now brought back to the mouth to be eaten. The food is mainly insects such as mosquito larvas and pupas, worms, snails, and small crustaceans.

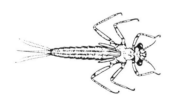

Fig. 9-16 A typical damselfly nymph.

Fig. 9-17 A dragonfly uses its extendable mouthparts to catch a mosquito pupa.

A dragonfly nymph has a large chamber in its abdomen. The abdomen pulses up and down, forcing water in and out of this chamber through the anus. The chamber contains gills which extract oxygen from the water. You can easily see the breathing pulsations of the abdomen. In contrast, a damselfly nymph breathes by means of the three gill filaments that look like tails. Odonata nymphs require water with moderate amounts of oxygen.

Dobsonflies, Alderflies, and Fishflies (Order Megaloptera)

This order of insects is divided into two families. Table 9-3 compares them.

Table 9-3 The Two Families of Megaloptera

Factor	Alderflies	Dobsonflies and fishflies
Colour	black, brown, or orange	black, gray, or brown
Length of adult	10-15 mm	40-75 mm
Time of activity	diurnal	nocturnal
Length of larva	up to 25 mm	up to 65 mm

Figure 9-18 shows the adult and larva of the dobsonfly, *Corydalus*. Most other megalopterans are similar in shape and structure. The larvas exist for two or three years before an adult is formed. During that time they live along the margins of ponds and lakes, and between stones in streams. They are predators, and actively pursue their prey. Insect larvas are their favourite food. The large dobsonfly larvas, called hellgrammites, are used as live bait by fishermen.

Section Review

1. Copy Table 9-4 into your notebook. Then complete it as you read this section again.

Table 9-4 Summary of "Other Flies"

Order	Description of larva or nymph	Habitat	Food	Other comments
Mayflies				
Caddisflies				
Dragonflies & Damselflies				
Dobsonflies, Fishflies, & Alderflies				

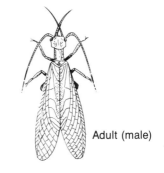
Adult (male)

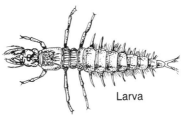
Larva

Fig. 9-18 The adult and larval forms of the dobsonfly. The larva is called a hellgrammite. Note the large mandibles on the adult.

9.4 Insects: Bugs, Beetles, and Springtails

This section briefly describes some common members of three orders of insects:

- The True Bugs (order Hemiptera)
- The Beetles (order Coleoptera)
- The Springtails (order Collembola)

The True Bugs (Order Hemiptera)

The "bugs" differ from other insects in two obvious ways.
1. The mouthparts form a "beak" which is used to pierce the prey and suck out body fluids.
2. The forewings are thick at the base instead of being membranous throughout (as other insect wings are).

In addition, almost all the bugs are predators, feeding mainly on aquatic insect larvas. Also, most have forelegs which are specialized for grabbing and holding the prey while its body fluids are sucked out.

The water strider is a well-known bug (Fig. 9-19). It skates and jumps about on the surface of the water. Its legs have waxy hairs on their tips. These make it possible for the insect to walk on the water. The water strider eats aquatic insects.

Two other bugs, which look somewhat alike at first glance, are the water boatman and the backswimmer (Fig. 9-20). They can be told apart because the backswimmer swims (you guessed it) on its back. The backswimmer also has a habit of hanging upside down from the surface of the water. The backswimmer carries air with it when it dives. The air is in two troughs on the lower side of the abdomen. Backswimmers may bite you if you swim among them or handle them. They fly easily from one swimming hole to another. They feed mainly on aquatic insects.

Water boatmen are the most common aquatic bugs. They spend most of their time on the submerged vegetation and on the bottom. When they dive, they take with them a film of air that covers the entire body. Air is also held beneath the wings. This bubble of air acts as a lung as described in Section 9.1. Water boatmen, if inactive, need not come to the surface for air. They feed on small crustaceans, rotifers, and protozoans. They even suck the juices from filamentous algae. Also, they often swim over the bottom ooze, sweeping plankton into their mouths with their front feet. Most water boatmen are strong fliers.

The most striking bug, by far, is the giant water bug (Fig.9-21). One genus, *Lethocerus*, reaches a length of 70 mm and a width of 25 mm. It is the largest of the bugs. These bugs live on the bottom of shallow ponds and in the

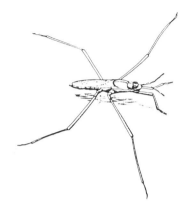

Fig. 9-19 *Gerris*, a common water strider of ponds and lakes.

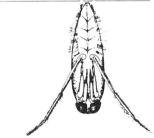

Fig. 9-20 A water boatman (on the vegetation) and a backswimmer (hanging from the surface).

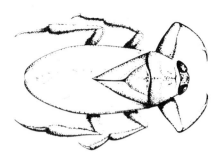

Fig. 9-21 The giant water bug, *Lethocerus.*

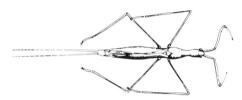

Fig. 9-22 The water scorpion, *Ranatra.*

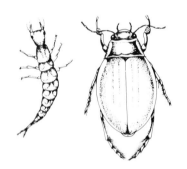

Fig. 9-23 The larval and adult forms of *Dytiscus*, a predaceous diving beetle.

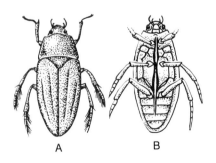

A   B

Fig. 9-24 *Hydrophilus*, a water scavenger beetle, showing a dorsal view (A) and a ventral view (B). Note the spiny projection between the legs in the ventral view.

littoral zone of lakes. When they dive, they take a bubble of air with them. They are fierce predators and feed on insect larvas, tadpoles, small frogs, and even fish. They fly, too. Therefore you may find them out of the water. If you decide to pick one up, be careful! It secretes a toxin (poison) through its beak as it bites.

Another interesting bug is the **water scorpion** (Fig. 9-22). This insect hangs upside down in vegetation, close to the surface. The two filaments that look like tails are brought together to form a breathing tube. This tube is stuck out of the water so air can enter. Note how this bug's front legs are adapted for grabbing prey. They are held "in the ready", and quickly lash out to grab insect larvas. Water scorpions seldom fly. Also, they are hard to find in the water. Their stick-like shape and colour help them blend in with grasses and other aquatic plants.

The Beetles (Order Coleoptera)

The beetles make up the largest order of insects. Over 250 000 species have been identified world-wide. About 30 000 of these live in the United States and Canada. But very few of those are aquatic. Three of the common families are discussed here. All beetles have two pair of wings. But the forewings are hard instead of membranous. They cover and protect the other pair of wings.

The **predaceous diving beetle** is a very active predator, both as an adult and as a larva (Fig. 9-23). In some individuals the jaws of the larva are larger than the rest of the head! If you put some of these in a tray with other organisms, they will often attack everything in sight ... including one another. The beetles live on submergent vegetation in clean ponds and small lakes. They feed on insect larvas, tadpoles, and fish.

The **water scavenger beetle** looks much like the predaceous diving beetle from above (Fig. 9-24). But if you turn it over, you will see a long spine between its legs. These beetles are common in shallow ponds where there is abundant submerged vegetation. Some species can swim, but most crawl. All adults can fly, however. Like all beetles, they take an air bubble with them when they dive. These beetles feed mainly on decaying vegetation, hence the name "scavenger". Sometimes they eat living plants, dead animals, and even the occasional live insect larva.

If you have ever observed a pond closely, you have probably seen **whirligig beetles** (Fig. 9-25). They glide around on the surface like little motorboats. Part B of Figure 9-25 shows one interesting adaptation to this unusual mode of life. The beetle's eyes are divided. One half of each eye looks up into the air, while the other half looks down into the water. Whirligig beetles often occur in large colonies. They scatter in all directions and dive when they are alarmed. They often sparkle because of the air bubble they carry. These beetles can fly, but must crawl out of the water before they can take off. They feed mainly on live insects that fall upon the surface of the water. They also feed as scavengers on dead plant and animal matter.

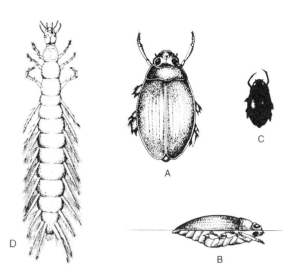

Fig. 9-25 The whirligig beetle, *Gyrinus*, showing a dorsal view (A), a side view so you can see the divided set of eyes (B), the natural size (C), and the larva (D).

The Springtails (Order Collembola)

The springtail is only 3 or 4 mm long. But, by thrusting its tail downward, it can jump over 30 cm through the air (Fig. 9-26)! Strictly speaking, these interesting insects, are not aquatic. The springtails live on the surface of quiet areas in lakes, ponds, and marshes. They are most common in the early spring or late autumn. The springtails feed on algae, fungi, plants, and plant detritus. On occasion, they also feed on dead crustaceans, worms, snails, and protozoans. They are most abundant where this type of food is located, amongst the debris and plants near the shore.

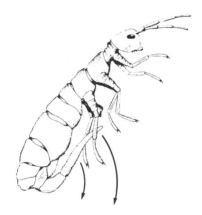

Fig. 9-26 The springtail snaps its tail down to propel itself through the air.

Section Review

1. State two identifying features of true bugs.
2. Describe the habitat and food of each of these bugs: water strider, water boatman, backswimmer, giant water bug, water scorpion.
3. How do a beetle's wings differ from those of other insects?
4. Describe the habitat and food of each of these beetles: predaceous diving beetle, water scavenger beetle, whirligig beetle.
5. Describe the habitat and food of the springtail.

9.5   The Molluscs

The phylum Mollusca has 75 000 species. It is the second largest phylum of animals. Among the molluscs are clams, snails, whelks, conchs, oysters, and octopuses. All molluscs have a soft body which is often enclosed in a shell. The shell is very small or missing in some species like the octopus. As well, all have a "foot" on the underside, that is used for crawling, burrowing, or swimming.

Most molluscs occur in salt water habitats. Two classes, however, have important fresh water members:

- Snails and Limpets (class Gastropoda)
- Clams and Mussels (class Plecypoda)

Snails and Limpets

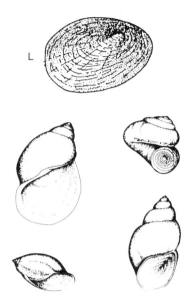

These animals are univalve molluscs. Snails have *one* spiral or coiled shell. Limpets have *one* shell in the form of a low cone (Fig. 9-27). Almost every type of freshwater ecosystem, standing and flowing, contains snails. Many also contain limpets. Only badly polluted water, very cold mountain lakes, and very salty prairie sloughs contain no snails or limpets.

These animals are mainly herbivores. They feed on the coating of living algae which covers rocks, logs, plants, and bottom detritus. They also act as scavengers, feeding mainly on dead vegetation. Some species even feed on dead animals.

Since snails and limpets need calcium to build shells, very few of these animals are found in soft water. In contrast, hard water contains both many individuals and many species. These animals also prefer basic water. This could be largely because hard water is normally basic. Snails and limpets are never found in true sphagnum bogs, because bogs are acidic.

Snails require moderately high levels of oxygen. That's the main reason they avoid polluted water. Limpets need even more oxygen, and are seldom found in water that isn't saturated with oxygen. Almost all snails and limpets occur in water less than 3 m deep.

Fig. 9-27 A limpet (L) and some of the many types of snails you will find in ponds and lakes.

Clams and Mussels

These animals are bivalve molluscs. They have *two* shells, or valves, hinged together (Fig. 9-28). Like snails and limpets, they occur in almost every type of freshwater ecosystem. They are most abundant, both in species and number of individuals, in large rivers. They are also common in wave-swept sections of lakes. Unlike the other molluscs, clams and mussels have no head.

Clams and mussels are omnivores. They feed mainly on phytoplankton (algae), zooplankton, and small pieces of detritus, all of which they filter from the water.

Though bivalves occur in almost every type of freshwater ecosystem, the water must not be polluted. Also, these animals prefer water less than 2 m deep. They tend to choose a stable bottom material such as mud in a lake or gravel in a stream. Sand is generally a poor habitat because it shifts. Like the univalves, the bivalves are most common in basic water which is relatively hard. They, too, need these conditions for shell building.

Fig. 9-28 A typical bivalve.

Section Review

1. What is a univalve mollusc?
2. Describe the trophic level of snails and limpets.
3. Describe the type of water in which snails and limpets are most likely to occur.
4. What is a bivalve mollusc?
5. Describe the trophic level of clams and mussels.
6. Describe the habitat in which clams and mussels are most likely to occur.

9.6   *ACTIVITY*   Classifying Aquatic Invertebrates

Suppose you have found an aquatic invertebrate. You don't know what it is, but you would like to know. If you compare it to pictures in this book and others, you might be able to find out what it is. But that takes a long time. Therefore, biologists usually identify organisms with a **classification key**. That's what you are going to try here.

Your teacher will provide you with living or preserved invertebrates, or good drawings of them. Your teacher will then help you identify one organism so you can see how the key works. This key lets you identify some organisms only as far as phylum. Most, however, are identified to class and some as far as order. To identify them to family, genus, or species requires a much more complex key.

Key to Aquatic Invertebrates

1a	Legs present	go to 2
1b	Legs absent	go to 5
2a	3 pairs of legs	class Insecta (insects) (except Diptera)
2b	More than 3 pairs of legs	go to 3
3a	4 pairs of legs	class Arachnida (spiders and mites)
3b	More than 4 pairs of legs	class Crustacea: go to 4
4a	Body flattened top to bottom .	order Isopoda (sow bugs)
4b	Body flattened sideways; swims on its side	order Ampipoda (scuds)
5a	Has a head	order Diptera (flies)
5b	Does not have a head	go to 6
6a	Does not have body segments .	go to 7
6b	Has body segments	go to 8
7a	Body round	phylum Nematoda (roundworms)
7b	Body flat	phylum Platyhelminthes (flatworms)
8a	Has suckers at both ends	clas Hirudinea (leeches)
8b	Has no suckers	class Oligochaeta (bristleworms, sludgeworms)

9.7   _ACTIVITY_ Classifying Aquatic Insects

If the classification key in Activity 9.6 tells you an organism is an insect, you can use this key to find out what order it is in. In other words, you can find out if it is a fly, bug, beetle, caddisfly, etc. This key contains the order Plecoptera (stoneflies). You haven't met these insects yet, since they live only in running water.

Key to Aquatic Insects (to Order)

1a	Legs absent........................	Diptera (true flies)
1b	Legs present........................	go to 2
2a	Wings present.......................	go to 3
2b	Wings absent........................	go to 4
3a	Sucking mouthparts (look like a beak)....	Hemiptera (true bugs)
3b	Chewing mouthparts..................	Coleoptera adult (beetles)
4a	Mouthparts can be extended.............	Odonata; go to 5
4b	Mouthparts cannot be extended.........	go to 6
5a	3 plate-like gills at tip of abdomen........	damselflies
5b	Without plate-like gills.................	dragonflies
6a	2 or 3 "tails" (cerci) present; wing pads present.............................	go to 7
6b	"Tails" absent; wing pads absent..........	go to 8
7a	2 tails; 2 tarsal claws; gills on thorax......	Plecoptera (stoneflies)
7b	2 or 3 tails; 1 tarsal claw; gills on abdomen...........................	Ephemeroptera (mayflies)
8a	Anal prolegs usually absent; if present, no hooks..............................	Coleoptera larva (beetles)
8b	Anal prolegs present; with hooks.........	go to 9
9a	2 anal prolegs; 1 hook per proleg........	order Trichoptera (caddisflies)
9b	2 anal prolegs; 2 hooks per proleg (or above may be replaced by a central tail)...	order Megaloptera (dobsonflies, fishflies, alderflies)

9.8   _ACTIVITY_ Adaptations of Pond Invertebrates

All organisms show adaptations to their habitats. You read about many of these in this and the last chapter. Some adaptations are structural. For example, one type of mayfly nymph has strong legs and large gills. These adaptations benefit the mayfly nymph since it digs into the detritus and lives there. Other adaptations are behavioural. For example, the sludgeworm builds a tube in the bottom ooze and twirls its tail through the water. This behaviour assists with gas exchange. In this activity you will study the adaptations of some pond invertebrates.

Notes
1. All of you cannot crowd around the aquarium at once. Therefore all of you won't be doing this activity at the same time.
2. The aquarium contains submergent plants, bottom detritus, invertebrates, and plankton collected from a pond.

Problem

How are pond invertebrates adapted to their habitat?

Materials

large aquarium containing   probe
   pond invertebrates   small beaker
hand lens   dip net

Procedure

a. Copy Table 9-5 into your notebook.

Table 9-5   Adaptations of Pond Organisms

| Organism | Habitat | Adaptations | | Advantages to organism |
		Structural	Behavioural	

b. Capture an invertebrate with the small beaker or dip net (Fig. 9-29).
c. Identify it using the keys in Activities 9.6 and 9.7. Put its name in your table.
d. Look for other invertebrates of the same species in the aquarium. Note their habitat (bottom ooze, vegetation, open water, sides of aquarium, etc.). Record the habitat in your table.
e. Look at the invertebrate in the beaker with a hand lens. Note and record structural adaptations.
f. Observe the behaviour of this invertebrate and similar ones in the aquarium. Note and record behavioural adaptations.
g. What advantages do these adaptations appear to give the organism? Record these in your table.
h. Repeat steps (b) to (g) for the number of invertebrates suggested by your teacher.

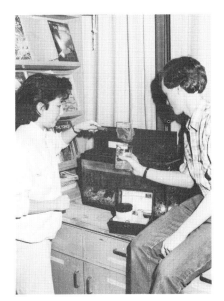

Fig. 9-29 Most invertebrates are easy to capture. Don't handle them. Return them promptly to the aquarium. The light keeps the plants growing. Also, slow aeration at one end helps keep the oxygen level up.

Discussion

A completed table is your write-up for this activity.

Main Ideas

1. Several orders of insects have members that are aquatic.
2. Aquatic insects have unique adaptations to their habitats.
3. Freshwater ecosystems contain a variety of molluscs that have unique adaptations to their habitats.

Key Terms

bivalve	opportunistic feeder	suspension feeder
grazer	proleg	trachea
net filter feeder	spiracle	univalve

Chapter Review

A. True or False

Decide whether each of the following statements is true or false. If the sentence is false, rewrite it to make it true. (Do not write in this book.)

1. All insects that live in water have gills.
2. Most mayfly nymphs need high levels of oxygen.
3. Almost all bugs are predators.
4. All molluscs are bivalves.

B. Completion

Complete each of the following sentences with a word or phrase that will make the sentence correct. (Do not write in this book.)

1. The true flies (order Diptera) have _____ pair of wings.
2. Midge larvas (chironomids) need _____ levels of oxygen.
3. True bugs have their mouth parts formed into a _____ .

C. Multiple Choice

Each of the following statements or questions is followed by four responses. Choose the correct response in each case. (Do not write in this book.)

1. Which one of the following best shows four aquatic organisms, in order, from the one that needs the least oxygen to the one that needs the most?
   a) hover fly, sludgeworm, dragonfly, mayfly
   b) mayfly, dragonfly, sludgeworm, hover fly
   c) sludgeworm, hover fly, dragonfly, mayfly
   d) sludgeworm, mayfly, dragonfly, hover fly

2. Which one of the following groups contains only true flies?
   a) mayfly, caddisfly, damselfly   c) damselfly, dragonfly, mayfly
   b) mosquito, damselfly, mayfly   d) mosquito, midge, crane fly
3. Clams are most likely to be found in
   a) polluted water with a gravel bottom
   b) clean water with a gravel bottom
   c) clean soft water
   d) clean water with a sandy bottom

Using Your Knowledge

1. Construct 10 food chains involving organisms discussed in this chapter. You may use organisms from Chapters 7 and 8 if you wish. Begin each food chain with a producer or detritus.
2. Make one food web using at least 5 of the food chains you constructed in question 1.
3. Why do molluscs require hard water? (Hint: You may wish to review the causes of hardness in Chapter 5.)
4. Midge larvas (chironomids) and sludgeworms (tubificids) are commonly found in the same habitat. Describe that habitat.
5. Why do burrowing mayflies generally have larger gills than vegetation dwellers?
6. Why is it an advantage to an organism to be an opportunistic feeder?
7. Compare the methods by which dragonfly nymphs and dobsonfly larvas catch their food.
8. a) What do all bugs (true bugs) have in common?
   b) Why is it an advantage to a bug to have strong forelegs?

Investigations

1. Find out how mosquitoes are controlled with insecticides. What insecticides are used? What other species do they kill? How persistent are these insecticides? That is, how long do these insecticides remain in the environment before they break down into less harmful chemicals?
2. Find out how one family of caddisfly builds its cases. What materials are used? How are they put together? What holds them together?
3. Set up and maintain a population of sludgeworms. Investigate their response to changes in oxygen concentration and/or temperature.
4. Collect some mosquito larvas and set up a habitat for them in the classroom. Investigate the completion of the metamorphosis of this insect through the pupal and adult stages.
5. Prepare a demonstration which shows that clam and snail shells will break down in acidic water. Use shells from dead animals.

10 Standing Waters: Plants and Vertebrates

In Chapters 8 and 9 you looked at the invertebrate animals that live in standing waters. Many of these animals depend on plants for their habitat, food, and/or oxygen. In other words, plants are very important in maintaining an ecological balance. This chapter describes the ecology of the most common aquatic plants.

Plants also provide habitat, food, and oxygen for a wide range of vertebrate animals: reptiles, amphibians, birds, mammals, and fish. These vertebrates are dealt with briefly in this chapter.

10.1 Submergent Plants

The submergent plants on a pond or lake are of great importance to those ecosystems.

- They provide a habitat for a wide range of organisms.
- They are food for many organisms.
- They add oxygen to the water.

Three phyla in the plant kingdom have members in the submergent plant community. These are the stoneworts (phylum Charophyta), the flowering plants (phylum Anthophyta), and the green algae (phylum Chlorophyta).

Stoneworts

Chara, a common stonewort, is shown in Figure 10-1. This plant grows on the bottom of a pond or lake and reaches a height of 30-40 cm. It is a simple plant. It has no roots; nor does it produce flowers. *Chara* grows well in hard water. Its stem and branches are often hard and brittle because calcium carbonate from the hardness in the water deposits on them. In fact, this is how the name "stonewort" came to be. ("Wort" means plant.) *Chara* is also called muskgrass. It gives water an unpleasant musky odour.

Few animals will eat *Chara*. However, algae stick to the *Chara*, often growing there as colonies. Thus many animals move through the *Chara*, feeding on the algae.

Fig. 10-1   Some common submergent plants.

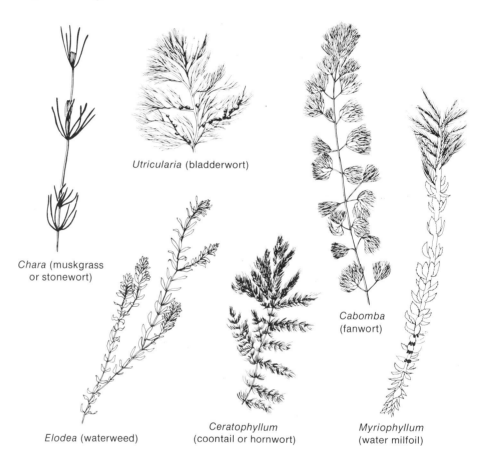

Utricularia (bladderwort)

Chara (muskgrass or stonewort)

Cabomba (fanwort)

Elodea (waterweed)

Ceratophyllum (coontail or hornwort)

Myriophyllum (water milfoil)

Flowering Plants

Figure 10-1 also shows several flowering plants. These plants normally follow stoneworts in succession. Decaying of stoneworts form the soil that these flowering plants need for rooting.

The most interesting of these plants is the bladderwort, *Utricularia*. Like some bog plants described in Chapter 3, this plant is a carnivore. As its name suggests, it has bladder-like traps (Fig. 10-2). Each bladder has a valve at one end. This valve is usually closed. Small glands in the bladder "pump" water out of the bladder. This creates a partial vacuum in the bladder. Some of the hairs around the trap are sensitive to touch. When a small animal swims against one of these, the trap opens. Water rushes in, sucking the prey with it. Then the valve closes, and the animal is digested.

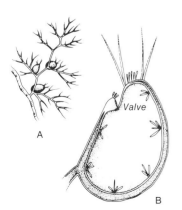

Valve

A

B

Fig. 10-2   The bladderwort, showing bladders on a leaf (A) and a single bladder (B).

Green Algae

Many green algae live among the other submerged plants. These algae rise to the surface of the water from time to time. This is because the oxygen they produce during photosynthesis makes them buoyant. You may have seen these algae on the top of ponds. They are usually present in large "globs" and are called "pond scum".

Up close, these algae look like masses of fine green threads, or filaments. Figure 10-3 shows what two of these algae, *Spirogyra* and *Zygnema*, look like under a microscope.

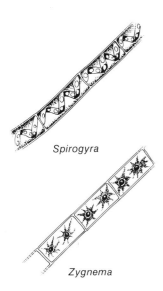

Fig. 10-3 Two common green algae of ponds.

Section Review

1. List three important functions of submerged plants in lakes and ponds.
2. Describe the stonewort *Chara*.
3. Make a list of the scientific and common names of six common submerged flowering plants.
4. Describe how bladderworts capture animals.
5. Describe the green algae which make up pond scum.

10.2 Emergent Plants

All emergent plants are flowering plants. Figure 10-4 shows two emergent plants which just manage to reach the surface. Wild celery, *Vallesneria*, has leaves which stretch up for a metre or more toward the surface. The female flowers float on the surface. Male flowers are submerged until they are mature. Then they break off and float to the top. The male flowers float among the female flowers fertilizing them with their pollen. After they are fertilized, the female flowers are pulled beneath the surface by their stems. The seeds develop in this protected environment.

The *Potamogeton* shown in Figure 10-4 is just one of many species of potamogetons, or pondweeds. Generally, this group of plants is the most important to waterfowl. The leaves and seeds of some species are eaten by ducks, geese, swans, coots, woodcocks, and other birds. These plants also provide food for mammals such as moose and muskrats.

Some potamogetons have broad leaves which float on the surface (Fig.10-5). They normally occur among other floating-leafed plants such as white water lilies (*Nymphaea*), yellow water lilies (*Nuphar*), and water shield (*Brasenia*). These plants provide a unique habitat for a wide variety of animals.

In calm stagnant areas of ponds and small lakes, an interesting group of plants, the duckweeds, can be found. Figure 10-6 shows two species of duckweed. *Spirodela* is one of the larger species. Yet, it is still only about 5 mm across. *Wolffia* is even smaller. It is less than 1 mm across. The

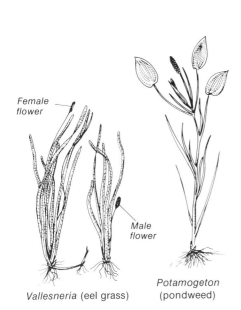

Female flower

Male flower

Vallesneria (eel grass)

Potamogeton (pondweed)

Fig. 10-4 These two plants scarely make the surface.

Fig. 10-5 Four common floating-leafed plants. ➤

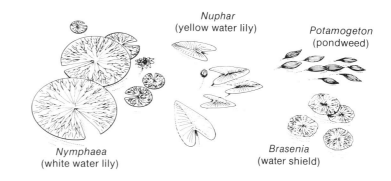

Nuphar (yellow water lily)

Potamogeton (pondweed)

Nymphaea (white water lily)

Brasenia (water shield)

Spirodela

Wolffia

Fig. 10-6 Two duckweeds, small floating plants of stagnant areas of ponds and lakes.

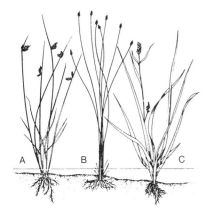

Fig. 10-7 Three common plants found near the shores of ponds and lakes. These are the bulrush, *Spirpus* (A), the spike rush, *Eleocharis* (B), and the sedge, *Carex* (C).

duckweeds, though small, are true flowering plants. They float on the surface and produce tiny flowers. Their roots hang below the surface. Duckweeds often form a mat on a pond which is so thick that birds can walk on it.

Figure 10-7 shows three common plants, the bulrush, the spike rush, and the sedge, that grow near the shore of ponds and lakes. From a distance, all three plants look similar. They look just like tall grasses. However, the sedges, like *Carex*, have solid triangular stems. The rushes have round stems. All three plants are food for a wide variety of wildlife including moose, beaver, muskrat, elk, deer, bobwhite, grouse, and waterfowl.

Figures 10-8 and 10-9 show four common plants, *Pontedaria, Calla, Sagittaria,* and *Alsima,* which can live in water just a few centimetres deep. Figure 10-10 shows the cattail, *Typha,* which can live in waterlogged soil. All these plants form a habitat for a wide variety of amphibians and reptiles. Also, they are food for many species of wildlife.

Fig. 10-8 Pickerel weed, *Pontedaria*, is one of the most beautiful emergent plants. It can live in water a few centimetres deep.

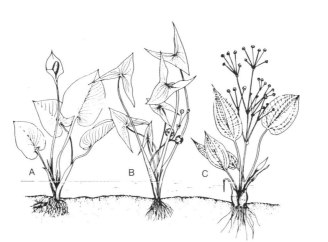

Fig. 10-9 *Calla* (A), *Sagittaria* (B), and *Alisma* (C) are white-flowered plants which grow in water just a few centimetres deep.

Fig 10-10 The cattail, *Typha*, is usually an emergent plant. However, sometimes it grows in waterlogged soil.

Section Review

1. Suppose you were in a canoe and could see *Vallesneria* next to you. Then you paddled slowly toward shore. Make a list of the emergent plants you would likely see along the way (in order).
2. Describe the importance of potamogetons (pondweeds) to animals.
3. Describe the importance of rushes and sedges to animals.

10.3   *ACTIVITY* **Duckweed Ecology**

In this activity you will study how duckweed interacts with some abiotic and biotic factors in its environment.

Problem

How does duckweed interact with these abiotic factors: light, aeration, nutrients? How does duckweed interact with invertebrates?

Materials

1 L beakers or wide-mouthed jars (5)
1-2 L of duckweed in a bucket of pond water
aerator
lamps, if required
liquid plant fertilizer (such as 20-20-20)

Procedure

a. Visit a pond and collect 1-2 L of duckweed in a bucket of water.
b. Set up a control as follows. Fill one beaker with pond water. Cover the surface with duckweed. Place this beaker where it will get daylight but not direct sunlight.
c. Study the effect of light as follows. Prepare 2 more beakers as in (b). Place one in direct sunlight and one in dim light.
d. Study the effect of aeration as follows. Prepare a beaker as in (b). Expose it to the same conditions as the control, but add an aerator.
e. Study the effect of nutrients as follows. Prepare a beaker as in (b). Expose it to the same conditions as the control, but add several drops of plant fertilizer.
f. Shortly after the control has been set up, observe it carefully. Find out what invertebrates use duckweed as a habitat.
g. Observe each of the experimental beakers closely from time to time for several weeks. Find out how the changed abiotic conditions affected the invertebrates.
h. Continue the experiment for several weeks.

1. How does light affect the duckweed? How does light affect invertebrates in the duckweed?
2. How does aeration affect the duckweed and the invertebrates in it?
3. How do extra nutrients affect the duckweed and the invertebrates in it?

10.4 Vertebrates

Green sunfish

Horned dace (creek chub)

Yellow perch

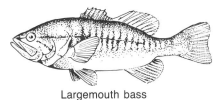

Largemouth bass

Fig. 10-11 A few of the fish which commonly live in small lakes and ponds.

Vertebrates are divided into five classes: reptiles, amphibians, birds, mammals, and fish. All five classes are represented in ponds and lakes. Among the reptiles are turtles. Turtles generally live in emergent vegetation. Most turtles are omnivores, feeding mainly on living and dead plants and dead animals. Frogs are the most common amphibians in most ponds and lakes. As tadpoles they are vegetarians; as adults they are carnivores. Muskrats and beavers are among the most common mammals. Geese, ducks, and other waterfowl also inhabit these waters. Most of these large animals are very secretive. You don't get much of a chance to study their ecology on field trips.

Fish, of course, are the first vertebrates we think of in connection with ponds and lakes. They are 100% aquatic. Thus they usually have more influence on the ecology of a pond or lake than any other vertebrate. They feed almost exclusively on other aquatic organisms. In fact, they are top carnivores in many food chains. Figure 10-11 shows some of the fish that commonly live in many small lakes and ponds.

Section Review

1. Name the five classes of vertebrates.
2. Name one common animal in each of these classes.

Main Ideas

1. Submergent plants provide habitat, food, and oxygen for a wide variety of aquatic animals.
2. Emergent plants provide habitat and food for aquatic animals and many semi-aquatic animals.
3. Duckweed populations are affected by light, aeration, and nutrients.
4. All five classes of vertebrates are represented in standing waters. All these animals play important roles in the ecology of standing waters.

Key Terms

emergent plant   green algae   submergent plant
flowering plant   stonewort   vertebrate

Chapter Review

A. True or False

Decide whether each of the following statements is true or false. If the sentence is false, rewrite it to make it true. (Do not write in this book.)
1. Submergent plants are the habitat of many animals.
2. The stonewort, *Chara*, must have stones on which to grow.
3. Potamogetons, or pondweeds, are important in the diets of many ducks and geese.

B. Completion

Complete each of the following sentences with a word or phrase that will make the sentence correct. (Do not write in this book.)
1. The stonewort, *Chara*, grows well in ▨▨▨ water.
2. The ▨▨▨ is a carnivorous aquatic plant.
3. Sedges can be identified by their solid ▨▨▨ stems.

C. Multiple Choice

Each of the following statements or questions is followed by four responses. Choose the correct response in each case. (Do not write in this book.)
1. The globs of pond scum that often appear on the surface of a pond are most likely
    a) stoneworts   c) floating-leafed emergent plants
    b) green algae   d) duckweed
2. Which one of the following is the most important group of plants for waterfowl?
    a) green algae   c) pondweeds (potamogetons)
    b) stoneworts   d) duckweed

Using Your Knowledge

1. A small lake had few fish in it, yet the water appeared clean. Therefore, the government stocked it with trout. The growth of these fish was stunted. Make a list of possible reasons for this.

2. A city parks department tried to keep a pond looking clean by raking out all the submergent vegetation they could reach. How might this affect the pond's ecology?
3. Why are cattails a good habitat for amphibians and reptiles?

Investigations

1. Obtain several strands of a submergent plant such as *Elodea* or coontail. Conduct an experiment to investigate the plant's optimum environmental conditions. You may get some ideas for your experiment from Section 10.3, Duckweed Ecology.
2. Design and conduct an experiment to study interspecific competition between two submergent plant species such as *Elodea* and coontail.
3. Select any one plant discussed in Section 10.2, Emergent Plants. Research its life cycle and ecological importance.

11 The Biology of Flowing Waters

Streams contain mayflies, caddisflies, midge flies, crane flies, and many other organisms also found in ponds and lakes. The species, however, are usually different. For example, the mayflies of a pond are those species which are adapted to standing water. In contrast, the mayflies of a stream are those species which are adapted to flowing water. This chapter looks at the organisms which are found in a wide variety of stream types. As well, it describes how these organisms are adapted to their habitats.

11.1 Adaptations of Stream Organisms

Each stream is made unique by its speed. The speed of the water determines, to a large extent, the nature of the bottom (see Section 4.6, page 77). It also helps determine the water temperature, oxygen content, and food supply. As we just said, organisms adapt to the conditions present in the stream in which they live. Let's see what some of those adaptations are.

Adaptations to Speed and Bottom Material

Organisms which live in very fast water must have adaptations for holding on to the bottom material. Otherwise they would be swept away. Stoneflies and mayflies have flattened streamlined bodies (Fig. 11-1). They also have muscular legs, and hooks on their "feet". Many caddisflies glue their homes to the bottom material. Others build nets in which they live. Blackflies and water pennies have suckers on their ventral (lower) surfaces. Most organisms live under cobble and gravel in fast streams for protection against the current. Slower streams have a sandy or muddy bottom. Dragonflies and mayflies make burrows in such bottoms to prevent being swept away.

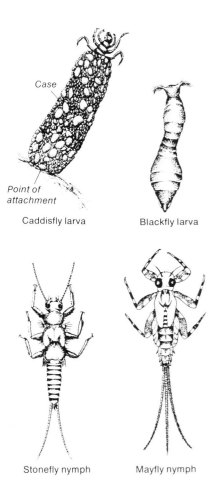

Case

Point of attachment

Caddisfly larva

Blackfly larva

Stonefly nymph

Mayfly nymph

Fig. 11-1 Note the adaptations of these organisms to fast water.

Few plants live in fast streams. But those which do have strong roots and thin flexible stems and leaves. Phytoplankton are rare in fast streams. However, many species of microscopic algae live in such streams. They remain attached to rocks and other submerged material.

Adaptations to Oxygen Levels and Temperature

The headwaters of rivers and streams tend to be fast and cool. Fast water evaporates more rapidly than slow water. Evaporation causes cooling. The headwaters are usually quite narrow. As a result, they are often well-shaded by shrubs, trees, and other plants. This shading also helps keep the water cool. You learned in Section 5.1, page 84, that cool water contains more oxygen than warm water. The headwaters, then, will commonly be inhabited by organisms which are adapted to fast, cool, highly oxygenated water. Stoneflies, mayflies, and many caddisflies are adapted to such conditions.

In contrast, the lower sections of rivers and streams tend to be slower, warmer, and lower in oxygen. Thus they will be inhabited by organisms which are adapted to those conditions, such as midge flies and sludgeworms.

Adaptations to Food Supply

Fish and other predators are usually numerous in streams that have overhanging vegetation. They get much of their food from terrestrial animals that fall into the stream from the vegetation. They also feed on stoneflies which are usually abundant in such waters. The stoneflies, in turn, lie under rocks, waiting for a meal of mayflies, caddisflies, and worms. Some stoneflies also feed on plant and algal material.

Many caddisflies are adapted for scraping algae from rocks. Others have hairs on their legs, heads, and mouthparts for filtering algae from the water. Still others build nets between the rocks to strain food from the water (Fig. 11-2).

These few examples should convince you to always note the behaviour and structure of stream organisms. All organisms show adaptations, either behavioural or structural, for feeding.

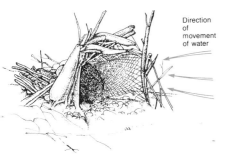

Direction of movement of water

Fig. 11-2 This net serves as a home and food-catching device for a caddisfly larva.

Section Review

1. Name four abiotic factors which are affected by the speed of a stream.
2. List eight ways in which animals have adapted to fast water.
3. List two ways in which plants have adapted to fast water.
4. Where are most algae found in fast streams? Why?
5. **a)** Describe the physical conditions of many headwaters.
   b) Name three organisms which are adapted to these conditions.
6. List five adaptations of stream organisms for feeding.

11.2 ACTIVITY Adaptations of Stream Invertebrates

Fig. 11-3 How is this stonefly nymph adapted to fast water?

The stonefly lives in fast water. As Figure 11-3 shows, it is well-adapted to that habitat. The stonefly's body is streamlined. Its legs are muscular and it has claws on its feet. Without those adaptations the stonefly would be swept away by the current.

All stream invertebrates show adaptations to their environments. Can you find them?

Note

All invertebrates in this activity live in riffle (fast) regions of streams.

Problem

How are stream invertebrates adapted to their environments?

Materials

several species of preserved   hand lens
  stream invertebrates in petri dishes   probe

Procedure

a. Copy Table 11-1 into your notebook. Don't copy the stonefly example. It simply shows you the detail required.

Table 11-1   Adaptations of Stream Invertebrates

Number of organisms	Name of organism	Adaptations
1	stonefly	flattened streamlined body; muscular legs; hooks on feet; short protected gills
2		
3		
4		

b. Get a specimen from the front bench. Write its number in your table.
c. Use the keys in Sections 9.6 and 9.7 (pages 153 to 154) to identify the organism. Write its name in your table.

d. Study the animal closely using the hand lens. Move the animal about, when necessary, with the probe. Be careful; do not damage it. Record its adaptations in your table.

e. Repeat steps (b) to (d) for the other organisms.

Discussion

1. In general, how are stream invertebrates adapted in structure to fast water?

2. How do these adaptations benefit the organisms?

3. Which of these organisms might have trouble living in slow water? Why?

11.3 Life in Bedrock Bottom Streams

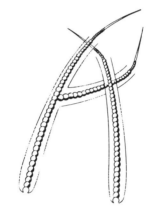

Fig. 11-4 *Rivularia*, a blue-green alga found on bedrock stream beds.

A bedrock bottom stream is a hostile environment for most organisms. The bottom consists of large expanses of solid rock. It provides little shelter for animals and few places for plants to become established.

The blue-green alga, *Rivularia*, is one organism which can live in this environment. It often coats the rock in a brown, jelly-like, slippery mass (Fig. 11-4). Like many blue-green algae, the cells of *Rivularia* are held together in chains by a gelatinous sheath. This is what makes *Rivularia* slippery.

Few plants live on the bedrock. However, fountain moss, an aquatic moss, is often found along cracks and crevices (Fig. 11-5). It sometimes covers much of the bottom with a dark green carpet. Its stems are about 10 cm long when mature.

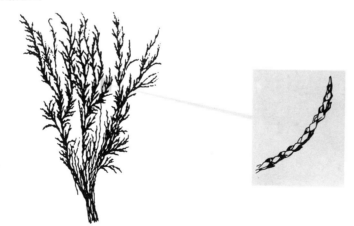

Fig. 11-5 Fountain moss, one of the few plants found on bedrock.

Nematodes (see Fig. 8-6) are common in the fountain moss. If you swish some fountain moss through water in a tray, the nematodes will come out. You will see them swimming with a lashing S-shaped motion. These non-segmented worms feed on living and dead fountain moss, detritus, bacteria, and small animals.

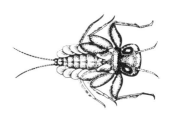

Fig. 11-6 A mayfly nymph which is commonly found on bedrock bottoms.

One species of mayfly is especially adapted to bedrock bottoms (Fig. 11-6). Unlike other mayflies, it has only two tail filaments. Note how slender the filaments are. Also, its body is quite flat. Among its adaptations for gripping the bedrock are strong claws, muscular legs, and a suction disc, formed by its plate-like gills.

Other organisms are often found in bedrock stream beds. They usually live in special environments within the stream bed such as pools, weed-beds near the banks, and crevices.

Section Review

1. Describe a common blue-green alga of bedrock stream beds.
2. Why are nematodes common in fountain moss?
3. Describe the adaptations of one mayfly to the bedrock bottom.

Life in Cobble and Pebble Bottom Streams

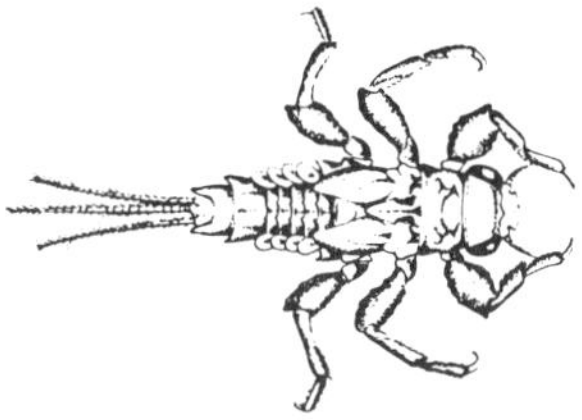

11.4

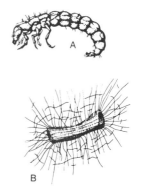

Fig. 11-7 Note the adaptations of this mayfly nymph commonly found in cobble stream beds.

Fig. 11-8 Two caddisflies. *Rhyacophila* (A) crawls freely under the rocks. *Polycentropus* lives in a net which you see here (B).

Streams with a cobble or pebble bottom are usually fast and highly oxygenated. They also have many places for organisms to escape from the current and to lie in wait for prey. Therefore these streams contain a wide variety of species. This section describes some of the more common species.

Blue-green algae, such as *Rivularia*, and fountain moss are common in these streams. Diatoms (see Fig. 7-5) often cover the cobble and pebbles with a crusty brown coating. Rooted aquatic plants such as *Elodea* and *Ceratophyllum* (see Fig. 10-1) may find enough protection among the larger rocks to become established.

As you can see, the tops of the rocks are covered with algae and plants while the bottoms are covered with animals. Sponges and bryozoans (Figs. 8-1 and 8-5) often cover large patches of the rocks. Both filter microscopic life and detritus from the water. On the sides and bottoms of the rocks you can find a wide variety of insect larvas and nymphs. Some of these are true flies such as the midge larva, crane fly, soldier fly, blackfly, and horsefly (see Section 9.2).

Among the "other flies" (those that are not true flies) are the stonefly, mayfly, caddisfly, alderfly, dobsonfly, dragonfly, and damselfly (see Section 9.3). Of course, the species present in streams are often different from those found in ponds. Note, for example, the muscular legs and long front claws of the mayfly in Figure 11-7. The caddisflies of cobble and pebble bottoms are adapted in three ways. Some, like *Rhyacophila*, crawl freely about on the protected bottoms of rocks (Fig. 11-8). Others, like *Polycentropus*, build nets. Still others build homes of pebbles cemented to the rocks (see Fig. 11-1).

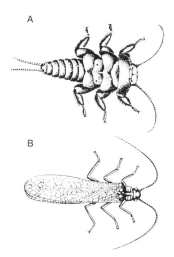

Fig. 11-9 The stonefly nymph (A) and adult (B).

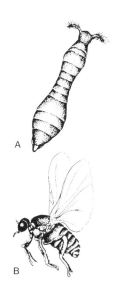

Fig. 11-10 The blackfly larva (A) and adult (B).

Fig. 11-11 Some common fish of cobble and gravel bottom streams.

Stoneflies are found only in streams and rivers (Fig. 11-9). They do not live in ponds. They are often found in association with mayflies and caddisflies in cobble bottom areas. Their bodies are quite flattened and streamlined. They differ from mayflies in three clearly visible ways. First, all species of stoneflies have just two tail filaments. Most mayflies have three. Second, stoneflies have two claws on each foot. Mayflies have just one. And third, the gills of the stonefly are on the ventral (lower) surface. Those of the mayfly are on the dorsal (upper) surface or along the sides of the abdomen.

The blackfly larva is also well adapted to a life in fast water (Fig. 11-10). Many of us wish that this insect would stay in the water! The adult is a common biting insect of the northern woods. It makes camping and canoe tripping almost impossible in May and June. The larva has a suction disc at the rear end. It fastens this to a rock and dangles head down in the current. Hairs around the mouth filter algae from the water. This larva spins out a silken thread as it moves from rock to rock. This thread prevents the larva from being swept away. Blackfly larvas often cover the bottoms of rocks in cold streams so thickly they appear as a dark green coating.

Many other invertebrates also live in cobble and pebble bottom streams. Among them are clams, snails, amphipods, leeches, and crayfish. Of course, the most famous occupants in these streams are fish. The wide variety of invertebrates attracts a wide variety of fish. Types of fish range from minnows which are just a few centimetres long to trout (Fig. 11-11).

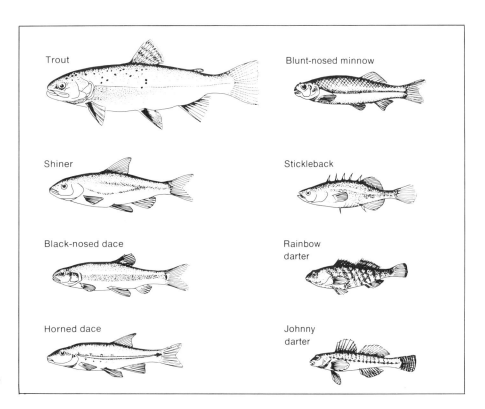

Trout

Blunt-nosed minnow

Shiner

Stickleback

Black-nosed dace

Rainbow darter

Horned dace

Johnny darter

Section Review

1. Why do cobble and gravel bottom streams contain a wide variety of species?
2. Name two common algae of cobble bottom streams.
3. Name four true flies found in these streams.
4. List three ways in which caddisflies are adapted to these streams.
5. List three differences between stoneflies and mayflies.
6. Describe the adaptations of the blackfly to fast water.

11.5   Life in Sandy Bottom Streams

Large stretches of sandy bottom are uncommon. However, sandy bottom sections do occur in other types of streams such as cobble and gravel bottom streams.

Little life is normally found in sandy bottom areas. The bottom is constantly shifting. Thus it does not provide a firm rooting medium for plants. Nor does it provide solid surface to which blue-green algae, diatoms, and mosses can attach themselves. Finally, it offers little food or protection to animals.

If a sandy bottom area occurs in the midst of a cobble or gravel bottom area, some animal life may wander into the sandy area. Nematodes, planaria, caddisflies, and mayflies can sometimes be sieved from the sand. Generally, though, these sections of streams are the least productive of all flowing waters.

Section Review

1. Why is little life found in sandy bottom streams?
2. What kind of a sandy bottom area would you select if you wanted to find animal life in the sand?

11.6   Life in Mud or Silt Bottom Streams

Slow streams and rivers generally have a mud or silt bottom. This condition frequently occurs near the mouths of rivers and streams. The slow water allows small particles to settle out and accumulate. Such streams and rivers are much like ponds. They contain a wide variety of organisms. As well, they

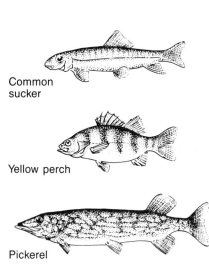

Common
sucker

Yellow perch

Pickerel

Miller's thumb

Catfish

Fig. 11-12 Common fish of mud or silt bottom streams.

are high in productivity. Of course, the organisms will be adapted to the slow water and mud bottom. Look back to Chapters 7 to 9 for descriptions and drawings of the organisms mentioned in this section.

Phytoplankton such as diatoms and desmids are common in this water. So, too, are zooplankton. Stream rotifers, unlike most pond rotifers, are attached to plant material or submerged objects like sticks. Protozoans of all types abound, as do crustaceans such as copepods. The mud bottom is home to a wide variety of worms: nematodes (roundworms), flatworms, bristleworms, and sludgeworms. The latter two, in particular, thrive in the low oxygen conditions of many mud bottom streams.

Mayflies, dragonflies, and caddisflies also inhabit these streams. They are generally different species than those found in faster streams. They show special adaptations to their environment. For example, their gills are protected to prevent them from getting clogged up with mud, silt, and other bottom material.

The midge larva, leech, crayfish, and amphipod are also common in these waters. In the slower sections of mud or silt bottom streams, rooted plants grow along the edges. Among these are familiar pond plants such as arrowhead, coontail, pickerelweed, and burreed.

Mud or silt bottom streams contain a wide variety of fish including pickerel, catfish, and the common sucker (Fig. 11-12). These are adapted to the low oxygen conditions present in such streams. Many of these are scavengers, feeding on dead plant material.

Section Review

1. Why do slow streams often have a mud or silt bottom?
2. List five common types of plankton in mud bottom streams.
3. Why are the mayflies of slow streams usually different species than those of fast streams?
4. Name five fish species found in many mud bottom streams.

11.7   _ACTIVITY_   **Stream Improvement**

This is a "thought activity". You don't actually do an experiment. Instead you are to imagine what is happening in Figure 11-13 and then figure out why these changes were made to the stream.

Problem

How will a stream and the life in it benefit from the changes shown in Figure 11-13?

Fig. 11-13 Some stream improvements.

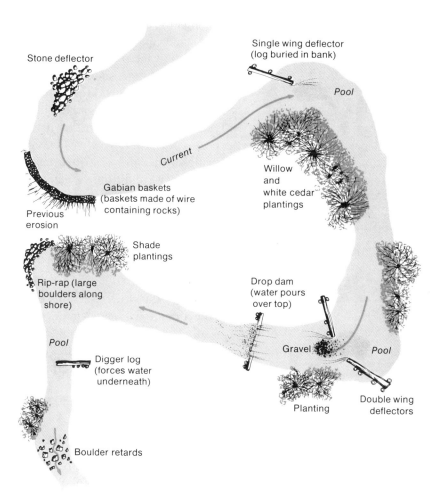

Stone deflector

Single wing deflector
(log buried in bank)

Pool

Current

Willow
and
white cedar
plantings

Gabian baskets
(baskets made of wire
containing rocks)

Previous
erosion

Shade
plantings

Rip-rap (large
boulders along
shore)

Drop dam
(water pours
over top)

Gravel

Pool

Pool

Digger log
(forces water
underneath)

Double wing
deflectors

Planting

Boulder retards

Questions

1. **a)** What will the stone deflector do to the water?
   b) How will this affect the bottom?
   c) Name three organisms which will benefit from this change. Why will they benefit?
2. Why were the Gabian baskets placed in the stream?
3. **a)** Why does the single wing deflector make a pool?
   b) Why were shrubs and trees planted over the pool?
   c) What organisms may select this habitat (shaded pool)?
4. **a)** Why do double wing deflectors create a gravel bottom?
   b) Name three organisms, not previously in this area, which may now move into it.
5. List two functions of the drop dam.
6. What is the function of the rip-rap?

7. Why was a digger log installed in the stream?
8. What do the boulder retards accomplish?
9. Most of these changes were done to make the stream more suitable for trout. List four ways in which the stream is now more suitable for trout.
10. Trout are highly prized by people who like to fish. That's why these changes are called improvements by many people. Name ten organisms for whom these changes are not improvements.
11. Do you think that it is acceptable for humans to manage a stream in this fashion? In other words, is it proper to make changes which benefit a species we want, even though other species suffer? Defend your position.

Main Ideas

1. Stream organisms show adaptations to water speed, bottom material, oxygen level, temperature, and food supply.
2. Bedrock bottom streams contain organisms which can cling to rock in fast water.
3. Cobble and gravel bottom streams are highly oxygenated and contain a wide diversity of life.
4. Sandy bottom streams contain little life.
5. Mud or silt bottom streams are highly productive and contain pond-like organisms.
6. Streams can be managed to favour certain species such as trout.

Key Terms

bedrock
cobble

Gabian basket
pebble

Chapter Review

A. True or False

Decide whether each of the following statements is true or false. If the sentence is false, rewrite it to make it true. (Do not write in this book.)
1. Mud bottom streams are generally faster than cobble bottom streams.
2. All mayfly nymphs have two tails.
3. Fast water tends to be cooler than slow water in the same stream.
4. The blackfly larva feeds on the blood of fish.

B. Completion

Complete each of the following sentences with a word or phrase that will make the sentence correct. (Do not write in this book.)
1. Plants in fast streams have ▨▨▨▨ roots and ▨▨▨▨ stems.
2. The lowest diversity of life is usually found in a ▨▨▨▨ bottom stream.
3. A gravel bottom can be created in the centre of a stream by building ▨▨▨▨ .

C. Multiple Choice

Each of the following statements or questions is followed by four responses. Choose the correct response in each case. (Do not write in this book.)
1. Which one of the following organisms requires the highest oxygen level?
   a) stonefly **b)** midge larva **c)** crayfish **d)** amphipod
2. An organism found in cobble bottom streams but never in ponds is the
   a) caddisfly **b)** mayfly **c)** stonefly **d)** sludgeworm
3. Suckers, catfish, and perch are most likely to be found in a
   a) bedrock bottom stream **c)** sand bottom stream
   b) cobble bottom stream **d)** mud bottom stream

Using Your Knowledge

1. Why is a mud or silt bottom stream usually high in productivity?
2. Why will a cobble bottom stream usually have more life in it than a bedrock bottom stream?
3. Suppose a dam was constructed in a stream. When this is done, silting often occurs above the dam. Name five organisms which could be negatively affected by the silting. Explain why each one would be affected.
4. List four reasons why trout are most common in cobble bottom streams.

Investigations

1. Build a stream table. (A geography teacher could give you some directions.) Now set up a demonstration of three or four of the stream improvements shown in Figure 11-13.
2. Find out how suckers and catfish are adapted to mud bottom streams.
3. Walk along a stretch of a stream. Make a sketch map of the stream. Mark on your sketch map the "improvements" you would make if you wanted to create more trout habitat in this stream.

12

Biological Indicators of Water Quality

You know that biotic and abiotic factors interact in an aquatic ecosystem. For example, you learned in Chapters 5 and 6 that the chemical properties of water play a major role in determining the types of organisms that live in the water. Water quality can be judged by doing chemical tests on the water. It follows, therefore, that water quality can also be judged by studying the organisms in the water.

Here is an example. Suppose chemical tests show that a pond has little oxygen, a high pH, and abundant organic matter on the bottom. You could conclude that the water is of low quality. But you could draw the same conclusion if an abundance of sludgeworms and midge larvas lived on the bottom. Of course, the most valid conclusion is one that is based on both biotic and abiotic data. You have learned the necessary abiotic information in Chapters 4 to 6. This chapter, combined with Chapters 7 to 11, provide the biotic information. Sections 12.7 to 12.11 give you an opportunity to make judgments using both biotic and abiotic data.

Freshwater ecologists look at both biotic and abiotic data before they draw conclusions about water quality. By the time you have finished this chapter you should be able to do this, too.

12.1   Index Species

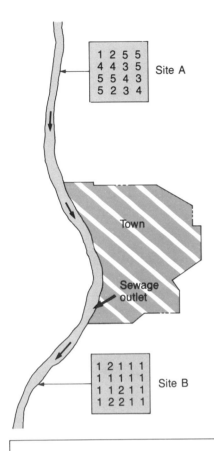

1 – Sludgeworm
2 – Midge larva
3 – Leech, clam, or snail
4 – Caddisfly larva
5 – Mayfly or stonefly nymph

Fig. 12-1 **Effect of domestic sewage on the kinds and abundance of bottom fauna. The numerals in the boxes represent the species present (see the key above). The abundance of each species is represented by the number of times its numeral is repeated in the box.**

A pollutant can kill all the living things in an aquatic ecosystem. More commonly, though, the pollutant kills certain species and does not harm others. Then the few species that are not killed increase in numbers (Fig. 12-1). This is because competition for space, food, oxygen, and other necessities is reduced when some species die. As well, some predators may die. Therefore the surviving species surge in numbers.

Therefore, two things happen as water becomes more polluted:

- Species diversity (the number of species) decreases.
- The population density (number of individuals per unit area) of the surviving species increases.

A decrease in the diversity of species is probably the best biological indicator of pollution. The species present in the highest population density are called the index species or indicator species of water quality. The presence of species is a better indicator of water quality than their absence. For example, trout and stoneflies require clean oxygenated water. Therefore their presence in a stream is an indicator of high water quality. However, their absence does not necessarily mean that the water is of poor quality. It may simply mean that the trout have been eliminated by fishing and that the stream lacks the bottom material stoneflies need.

Biologists use five groups of organisms as indicators of water quality. These are fish, bottom fauna (animals that live on, in, and near the bottom), algae, bacteria, and zooplankton. In later sections of this chapter you will look at the first four of these. We will not discuss zooplankton because they are very difficult to use as an index species unless you are a specialist in that field.

Section Review

1. **a)** What two things happen to populations of organisms as pollution increases?
    b) What causes these changes?
2. What is the best indicator of pollution?
3. What are index (indicator) species?
4. The presence of trout and stoneflies indicates that the water is clean and well-oxygenated. However, their absence does not mean the water is polluted or poorly oxygenated. Why?
5. What five groups of organisms do biologists use as indicators of water quality?

12.2   Eutrophication

What Is Eutrophication?

All lakes and ponds will eventually fill up and disappear due to a natural aging process called eutrophication. (See also Section 5.4, page 90). To see how this works, let us consider the history of a lake that was formed in the last ice age. When the glaciers retreated, they left behind a basin that filled with water and became a lake. The lake was a cold, clear body of relatively clean water. Such a body of water contains little life and is called a oligotrophic ("little nourishment") lake. However, over the years, the rivers that fed this lake brought nutrients like nitrogen and phosphorus to it. In addition, these rivers carried silt and organic materials to the lake. As a result, the lake became more shallow. Further, the added nutrients increased the productivity of the lake. More life appeared, resulting in still more organic material on the bottom. The combination of warmer water, decreased depth, and added nutrients greatly increased the amount of life in the lake. When this stage is well advanced, the lake is called a eutrophic ("adequate nourishment") lake. The process of aging or increasing productivity is called eutrophication. In between the oligotrophic and eutrophic stages, a lake is usually called mesotrophic ("middle amount of food").

When natural eutrophication is well advanced, the water may appear polluted to an untrained observer. The diversity of species is usually low, while the population density of the few remaining species is high. Natural eutrophication is generally a slow process. However, pollution with organic material such as sewage or the addition of nutrients such as nitrogen and phosphorus can greatly speed up the rate of eutrophication.

Characteristics of Eutrophic Waters

Eutrophic waters can normally be identified by some or all of these characteristics.
- They are often warm and shallow.
- The total dissolved solids is high, often greater than 100 μg/g.
- They are of high productivity. That is, they support abundant life.
- They often support phytoplankton (algal) blooms.
- They contain "warm water" fish (those in the lower half of Figure 12-2, page 180).
- They have a low diversity of species, while the population density of the few remaining species is high.
- They have a reduced stability. For example, an algal bloom may occur then collapse. The oxygen level drops markedly as the dead algae decay.
- They usually have a high pH.

Section Review

1. Give the meanings of the following terms: oligotrophic, eutrophic, eutrophication, mesotrophic.
2. Distinguish between natural eutrophication and eutrophication caused by humans.
3. Make a point-form summary of the characteristics of eutrophic waters.

12.3 Fish as Indicators of Water Quality

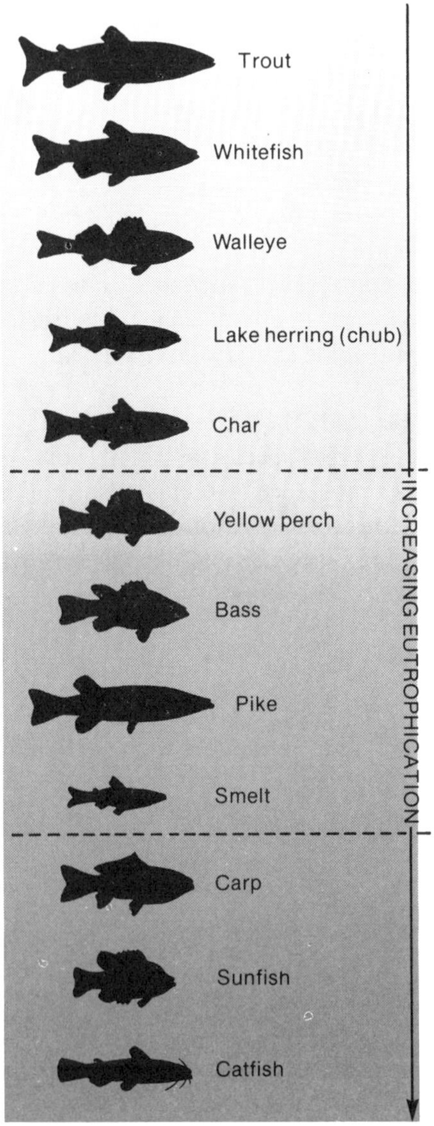

The dominant fish in oligotrophic lakes are those that need clean, cool water. These include lake trout, whitefish, walleye, lake herring, and char (Fig. 12-2). At the mesotrophic stage, most of these species remain, but in decreased numbers (Fig. 12-3). Perch, black bass, pike, and smelt become the dominant species. After further eutrophication, carp, sunfish, and catfish dominate.

The presence of perch, carp, and sunfish does not mean that the water is polluted. It may simply mean that the water is eutrophic. More specifically, it

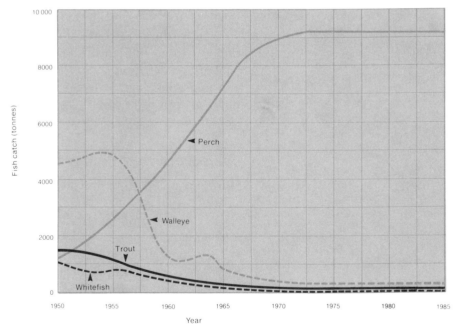

Fig. 12-3 Changes in fish population numbers in Lake Erie from 1950 to 1985.

What do the trends shown on this graph tell you about the lake?

Trout

Whitefish

Walleye

Lake herring (chub)

Char

INCREASING EUTROPHICATION

Yellow perch

Bass

Pike

Smelt

Carp

Sunfish

Catfish

Fig. 12-2 Fish species in a lake change as eutrophication proceeds.

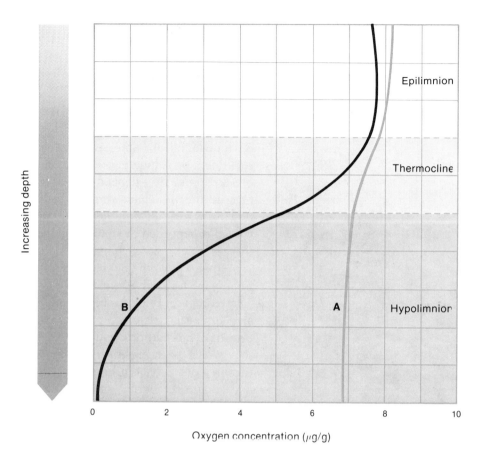

Fig. 12-4 Oxygen concentration versus depth for an oligotrophic lake (A) and an eutrophic lake (B), in mid-summer. Epilimnion means "upper lake". Hypolimnion means "lower lake". The thermocline is a region where temperature changes rapidly with depth. (See also Section 4.5, page 75.)

means that the oxygen concentration in the deep, cool water is low (Fig. 12-4). The decomposition of organic material in the bottom sediment uses up oxygen. This makes survival impossible for trout and other fish that require the cool water near the lake bottom. However, fish like carp that can live in the warm upper water thrive.

In like manner, the presence of carp and sunfish in a stream may simply mean that the water is generally too warm for trout and similar species. The water could be quite free of pollution. However, should you find a cool, deep stream that contains trout at its headwaters but mainly carp in the waters below a town, you should suspect the town of polluting the water.

Section Review

1. Name five fish species that dominate oligotrophic lakes.
2. Name four fish species that dominate mesotrophic lakes.
3. Name three fish species that dominate eutrophic lakes.
4. Explain why trout are uncommon in eutrophic lakes.
5. Why can a stream be free of pollution but still not have a trout population?

12.4 Bottom Fauna as Indicators of Water Quality

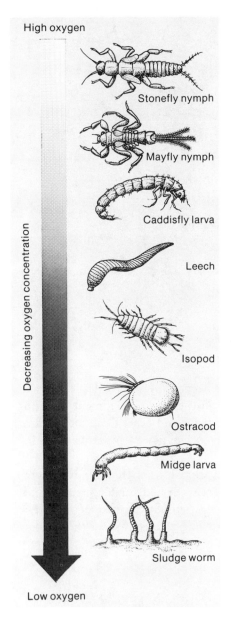

High oxygen

Stonefly nymph

Mayfly nymph

Caddisfly larva

Leech

Isopod

Ostracod

Midge larva

Sludge worm

Decreasing oxygen concentration

Low oxygen

Fig. 12-5 Bottom fauna and their oxygen requirements.

Fauna in Water with Abundant Oxygen

Bottom fauna are animals that live on or in the bottom sediment, under rocks, and on submerged vegetation. The types of fauna found on the bottom of a stream or river depend to a large extent on the nature of the bed. This, in turn, is directly related to the speed of the water (see Table 12-1). In rapidly flowing water, all but the larger rocks are gradually carried downstream. Gravel is deposited in slower regions and sand in still slower regions. Where there is little or no current, silt and mud are deposited on the bed.

As you know, the oxygen concentration plays an important role in determining the fauna in a stream. The water in a fast stream is usually turbulent. Therefore, as a rule, it is highly oxygenated. Thus the bottom fauna in a fast area of a stream are those that require high oxygen conditions. They must also have adaptations that enable them to cling to the bottom. Otherwise, they would be swept downstream. Some of the dominant bottom fauna of this area of a stream are insects such as stoneflies, some species of mayflies, and some species of caddisflies (Fig. 12-5). All three are generally found under and around rocks and coarse gravel. If the stream is polluted to the point where its oxygen concentration drops greatly, these animals will not be found in the stream.

Fauna in Water with Little Oxygen

At the bottom of Figure 12-5 are organisms that live in mud-silt bottoms. There the oxygen concentration is usually very low. The sludgeworm is a segmented worm like the earthworm. It feeds on the muddy bottom just like an earthworm feeds on the soil in a garden. It builds a tube above a burrow extending down into the bottom ooze. While it feeds in the stream bottom, its tail sticks out of the tube. The tail sways back and forth. This aids the exchange of carbon dioxide and oxygen with the water. Blood vessels close to the body surface also help the sludgeworm to get even the smallest traces of oxygen from the water.

The midge larva is another common bottom burrower that can tolerate low oxygen conditions. This larva occupies a tube that it makes from sludge material. Some species are red in colour and are called bloodworms. However, they are not worms. They are insect larvas. You have likely seen the adult midge fly. It is an annoying little creature that looks like a small mosquito without piercing mouthparts. Clouds of midge flies often gather around your head on a humid, windless day.

Table 12-1   Speed and Nature of the Bed

Speed	Nature of the Bed
over 100 cm/s	boulder
60-100 cm/s	cobble
30-60 cm/s	gravel
20-30 cm/s	sand
10-20 cm/s	silt
under 10 cm/s	mud

Leeches, isopods (aquatic sowbugs), and ostracods generally live in muddy areas with slightly higher oxygen levels than those in which sludgeworms and midge larvas live. Note that the fauna which live in mud-silt bottoms of streams are also among those that you will find on the bottoms of many lakes and ponds. Why is this so?

Summary

As Figure 12-5 shows, the bottom fauna found in a stream depend, in part, on the oxygen level. The oxygen level, in turn, depends on the water quality. In particular, it depends on the amount of organic matter such as sewage in the water. When such matter decays, it uses up oxygen.

Remember, though, that the presence of certain species is a better indicator of water quality than the absence of certain species. Remember, too, that species diversity is the best indicator of water quality.

Section Review

1. Name three types of bottom fauna that generally prefer clean oxygenated water.
2. Name two types of bottom fauna that thrive in the low oxygen environment of mud-silt bottoms.
3. Name three types of organisms that prefer oxygen conditions between those of the organisms named in 1 and 2.
4. Describe how the sludgeworm has adapted in behaviour and structure to low oxygen conditions.

Algae as Indicators of Water Quality

12.5

If you have not already done so, you should read Section 7.2, page 116, before you proceed with this section.

Algal Diversity and Eutrophication

As is the case for other organisms, the best indicator of water quality is the diversity of species. Clean water usually has a wide diversity of species, while eutrophic water usually has a narrow diversity of species. This is true both for natural eutrophic water and water made eutrophic by pollution. Thus, in clean water you can expect to find moderate numbers of many species of algae, including species of desmids (a form of green alga), other green algae, diatoms, and blue-green algae. However, in eutrophic water many species will be missing. The species that remain will be present in high population numbers.

Types of Algae and Eutrophication

As eutrophication proceeds, algal diversity decreases. Also, a shift in the structure of the algal community usually occurs as shown in Figure 12-6. Diatoms and desmids dominate oligotrophic water. But as eutrophication proceeds, green algae (other than desmids) and blue-green algae become dominant.

Oligotrophic water has, therefore, a wide diversity of diatom and desmid species. A few species of green algae and blue-green algae may also be present. In contrast, eutrophic water has a wide diversity of green and blue-green algae. A few species of diatoms and desmids may also be present.

When conditions are just right, the algae in eutrophic water often reproduce at a rapid rate. This phenomenon is called an algal bloom. You may have seen a pond or lake in which the water is green from such a bloom. (See also Sections 6.1, 6.2, 7.2, and 12.2.)

Section Review

1. Describe how algal diversity can be an indicator of water quality.
2. Write a short paragraph which gives the meaning of Figure 12-6.
3. What is an algal bloom?

12.6 Bacteria as Indicators of Water Quality

Many types of bacteria live in freshwater ecosystems. Some of these are useful indicators of water quality. They are especially useful when the water is used for swimming or drinking.

Bacteria are classified into four groups according to their feeding habits. These are autotrophic bacteria, saprophytic bacteria, parasitic bacteria, and mutualistic bacteria (Fig. 12-7). Let us see what each group can tell us about water quality.

Autotrophic Bacteria

Autotrophic bacteria are bacteria which can make their own food from simple inorganic compounds. Some autotrophic bacteria, like plants, can carry out photosynthesis. Others make their food by chemosynthesis. This process does not require chlorophyll.

Autotrophic bacteria are often abundant in the effluent (waste) from mining operations. For example, certain species favour mining effluents which are rich in iron and sulfates. These bacteria break down iron and sulfur compounds to obtain needed nutrients for the synthesis of food. The by-products they form often have a low pH. This low pH can affect plant and animal life in the water (see Section 5.4, page 90).

Oligotrophic

↑ Increasing eutrophication

Diatoms
(golden algae)

Desmids
(green algae)

Other green algae

Blue-green algae

Eutrophic

Fig. 12-6 Algae and water quality.

Fig. 12-7 The four groups of bacteria, classified by feeding habits.

Saprophytic Bacteria

Saprophytic bacteria are bacteria which feed on non-living organic matter (see "Trophic Levels", Section 2.4, page 24). They occupy the niche of decomposer in an ecosystem. As such, they play a key role in the maintenance of nutrient cycles (see Section 2.5, page 34). They feed on non-living organic matter to get the energy they need for life processes. As they do so, they release nutrients into the ecosystem.

Saprophytic bacteria, or decomposers, are abundant in the detritus (decaying organic matter) on the bottoms of ponds, lakes, and slow streams. They are especially common in the detritus of waters polluted with organic wastes such as domestic sewage. Their abundance can cause serious problems. As the bacteria feed on the organic matter, they respire. This uses up oxygen. In fact, the bottoms of some lakes have no oxygen at all at certain times of the year (see Section 4.3, page 71). As you know, lower oxygen concentrations can make it impossible for certain animals to live in the water.

Parasitic and Mutualistic Bacteria

Parasitic bacteria get the energy they need by feeding on living hosts (see Section 2.4, page 24). Among the parasitic bacteria are disease-producing bacteria called **pathogens**. These bacteria are of particular interest to people who test water to see if it is fit for drinking or swimming.

Pathogens in Human Wastes   Human wastes in the effluents from sewage treatment plants are the greatest source of pathogens in rivers and lakes. Pathogens can also enter the water from other sources such as leaching from septic tank systems and outhouses. These sources are common in areas where homes are built on shallow soil with no communal sewage system. Such a situation often occurs when summer cottages are built around lakes in remote rocky areas.

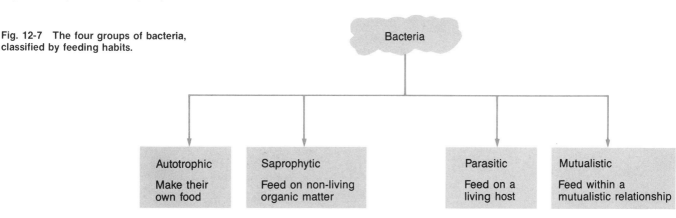

Bacteria

Autotrophic	Saprophytic	Parasitic	Mutualistic
Make their own food	Feed on non-living organic matter	Feed on a living host	Feed within a mutualistic relationship

It is important to know if there are pathogens in water before you drink it or swim in it. However, it is not easy to detect pathogens in water. Most of them do not live long outside human hosts. They need the moisture and temperature conditions of the human body. However, a few do survive. The best methods of detection are expensive and take a long time to give results. Further, some pathogens may escape detection. Yet they are still in the water and could infect humans. For these reasons, scientists usually do not try to detect pathogens. Instead, they use another method to indicate the presence of pathogens.

Coliforms as Indicators of Pathogens   Coliforms are bacteria that are grouped together because of certain similarities. Some coliforms live in plants and in soil. Others live in the large intestines of humans and many other animals. These latter coliforms are called fecal coliforms.

Fecal coliforms have a mutualistic relationship with the animal in which they live. These mutualistic bacteria get the energy they need through a co-operative relationship with the animal. The animal provides water, food, warmth, and other environmental necessities for the coliforms. The coliforms, in turn, help the animal make nutrients like certain vitamins. Coliforms also help the animal recycle water from the waste material back into the bloodstream. Each day billions of coliforms leave a human in the feces. In fact, over half of dry feces is dead coliforms. From 80 to 95% of these coliforms are of the species *Escherichia coli*, commonly called *E. coli*.

Clearly, then, the presence of *E. coli* in water indicates that the water has likely been polluted by human sewage. The feces of diseased people could contain pathogens. Therefore the presence of *E. coli* in water indicates that pathogens may be present. Pathogens are hard to detect; coliforms are not. Therefore public health officials test for coliforms and not pathogens when they are assessing the safety of water for swimming and drinking. Coliforms live much longer outside the human body than do most pathogens. Therefore, if water is found to contain no coliforms, it is likely also free of pathogens and is safe to drink.

Remember, then, that coliforms themselves are generally not harmful. They are index organisms of the fecal pollution of water. Or, if you like, they are index organisms of possible contamination of the water by pathogens such as cholera, typhoid fever, and hepatitis.

Public health associations throughout North America have set standards that they feel are acceptable for drinking water and swimming areas. These standards vary from place to place. Generally, though, the commonly accepted standards are close to the following.

- Drinking water: The *total coliform* count must not exceed 5 in a sample of 100 mL of water. The *fecal coliform* count must be 0.
- Swimming areas: The *total coliform* count must not exceed 1000 in a sample of 100 mL. The *fecal coliform* count must not exceed 100 in a sample of 100 mL.

Two procedures for testing for coliforms are outlined in *Investigating Environmental Issues*. Investigation 6 at the end of this chapter suggests an experiment you may wish to do (Fig. 12-8). It describes how to test a swimming beach or river.

Section Review

1. **a)** What are parasitic bacteria?
   b) What are pathogens?
2. How do pathogens get into streams and lakes?
3. What factors make pathogens hard to detect?
4. **a)** What are coliforms?
   b) What are fecal coliforms?
5. Describe the mutualistic relationship which exists between coliforms and animals.
6. **a)** What does the presence of *E. coli* in water indicate?
   b) Explain why coliforms are a good indicator organism of water quality.
7. **a)** State the commonly accepted standards for total and fecal coliforms in drinking water.
   b) State the commonly accepted standards for total and fecal coliforms in swimming areas.

Fig. 12-8 Millipore Coli-count tabs provide a simple yet effective way of monitoring the coliform count of a body of water.

12.7 *FIELD TRIP* **Investigating Pond Ecology**

The purpose of this field trip is for you to learn all you can about the ecology of a pond. Clearly, the more sites you study, the more you will learn. However, the number of sites you can study depends on the size of your class, the size of the pond, and the time available.

Five sites arranged as shown in Figure 12-9 give good coverage of the pond. These sites are at:
- A—the inlet
- B—the outlet
- C—an area dominated by submergent plants
- D—an area dominated by emergent plants
- E—the open water

If the pond is large, if your class is small, and if time is limited, it may be impractical to try to study all these sites. A good alternative is to compare two sites such as the inlet and a site well down the pond, like C. Your objective could be to determine how and why the water and organisms differ between the inlet stream and the body of the pond. You will work at one site with a group of other students to help achieve the class objective.

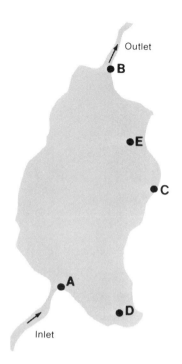

Fig. 12-9 Site selection for a pond study.

Fig. 12-10 Bottom fauna show up well against the white background of the tray.

Problem

What ecological relationships exist in the pond?

Materials

Note: This list is for a class of 30. Your group may have to share some items with other groups.

set of Hach water testing kits (preferably oxygen, carbon dioxide, pH, alkalinity, hardness, ammonia, nitrate, phosphate, chloride)
white tray (8)
sieve (8)
hand lens (8)
probe (8)
thermometer (2)
plankton net (1)

dip net (2)
collecting bucket (2)
Coli-count tab (2)
Pond Life or other identification guides (8)
compass (1)
binoculars (5) (optional)
identification books for birds, mammals, fish, reptiles, and amphibians (optional)

Procedure

(to be carried out by a group of 5 or 6 students)

a. Prepare a full-page copy of each of Tables 12-2, 12-3, and 12-4. (Do not copy the example.)

b. Make two more full-page copies of Table 12-3. On one copy replace "Invertebrates" by "Vertebrates". On the other copy replace "Invertebrates" by "Plants".

c. Complete your copy of Table 12-2. That is, do the geophysical and chemical tests listed. Each chemical test should normally be done three times. If one value differs greatly from the other two, ignore it. Otherwise average the three trials.

d. Sample the site (except site E) for bottom fauna as follows. Put 3 or 4 cm of water in the white tray. Then sit it on a level place on the ground (Fig. 12-10). Now draw the sieve back and forth through submergent vegetation (Fig. 12-11). Then tap the sieve, upside down, on the side of the tray to make the organisms fall into the water. Also, scoop up some bottom material with the sieve. Wash away as much of the earth as you can by swishing the sieve back and forth in the water. Then add the organisms to the tray. Repeat this procedure several times. If you cannot reach the submergent vegetation with the sieve, use the dip net (Fig. 12-12). Examine each type of bottom fauna with the hand lens. Identify the bottom fauna using *Pond Life* or another identification guide and Chapters 8 and 9 of this book. Put their names in your copy of Table 12-3. Note their relative abundance (a = abundance, f = frequent, o = occasional, r = rate) in your table. Look closely for adaptations and add these to your table.

Fig. 12-11 A kitchen sieve can be used to capture bottom fauna and other organisms.

Fig. 12-12 A dip net can be used to catch bottom fauna.

Table 12-2 Lake or Pond Survey (Abiotic Factors)

Name of lake or pond＿＿＿＿＿＿＿＿＿ Date＿＿＿＿＿＿＿＿＿＿＿＿＿
Site No.＿＿＿＿＿＿＿＿＿＿＿＿＿＿＿＿ Time＿＿＿＿＿＿＿＿＿＿＿＿＿＿
Description of site＿＿＿＿＿＿＿＿＿＿ Weather—wind speed＿＿＿＿＿＿
＿＿＿＿＿＿＿＿＿＿＿＿＿＿＿＿＿＿ wind dir.＿＿＿＿＿＿
＿＿＿＿＿＿＿＿＿＿＿＿＿＿＿＿＿＿ sky＿＿＿＿＿＿＿＿

Nature of shore＿＿＿＿＿＿＿＿＿＿＿
Nature of watershed＿＿＿＿＿＿＿＿＿
Nature of bottom＿＿＿＿＿＿＿＿＿＿
Appearance of water＿＿＿＿＿＿＿＿
＿＿＿＿＿＿＿＿＿＿＿＿＿＿＿＿＿＿

Temp. (air) ＿＿＿＿＿°C
Temp. (water) ＿＿＿＿＿°C

Sketch map showing prominent features (inlets; outlets; emergent plants; logs; etc.)

	Trial 1	Trial 2	Trial 3	Average
Oxygen				
Carbon dioxide				
pH				
Alkalinity				
Hardness				
Ammonia				
Nitrate				
Phosphate				
Chloride				

Table 12-3 Lake or Pond Survey (Invertebrates)

Organism	Relative abundance (a,f,o,r)	Adaptations	Advantages to organism
Damselfly nymph	f	3 feathery flexible gills on the tail end; hinged mouthparts; greenish-brown colour; sharp points on feet	gas exchange is speeded up by moving gills; prey easily captured; well-camouflaged; assists climbing in vegetation

Table 12-4   Lake or Pond Survey (Plankton)

Phytoplankton		Zooplankton	
Organism	Relative abundance (a,f,o,r)	Organism	Relative abundance (a,f,o,r)

Include both structural and behavioural adaptations. You can complete the final column of the table at home or at school. You may wish to dump the contents of your tray into a bucket so you can take organisms back to the classroom for closer study. If you do this, someone should be prepared to return the organisms to the pond after you have studied them.

e. Most vertebrates will have left the study site when you arrived. However, do your best to complete your vertebrate table. Use binoculars to search for birds and mammals. Use close observation and the dip net to search for fish, reptiles, and amphibians. Do not keep any of these vertebrates in captivity. Look at them and release them unharmed.

f. Complete your plant table. You may collect specimens of submergent plants to take back to the classroom. Put them in the bucket with the bottom fauna. Emergent plants should be examined but not collected.

g. Use the plankton net to collect a plankton sample from the open water (site E). Throw the net out as far as you can, holding the rope in your other hand (Fig. 12-13). Then draw the net in. Do not let it scoop up debris from the pond bottom. Do this several times. Then dump the contents of the collecting tube into a jar full of pond water. As soon as possible, dump this jar of water into a white tray. The larger surface area is needed to ensure an adequate oxygen supply for the organisms. Take your plankton collection back to the classroom. Complete your copy of Table 12-4. You will find Activity 7.4, page 124 and the information in Chapter 7 helpful.

h. Perform a coliform test at your site. Follow the directions that came with the Millipore Coli-count tab.

Fig. 12-13   This plankton net has pores small enough to stop both phytoplankton and zooplankton.

Discussion

1. Write as many food chains as you can for the pond.
2. Draw one food web that involves at least four food chains.
3. Is the pond oligotrophic, mesotrophic, or eutrophic? Refer to data to support your conclusion.
4. If the pond is eutrophic, what do you think is the cause of this condition?
5. Propose a management program that would enhance the ecology of the pond.

12.8

Pond Ecology

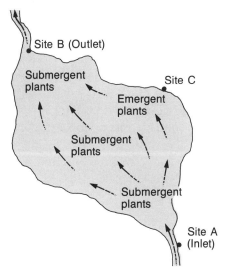

Fig. 12-14 How do the living things in a pond affect the water quality as the water flows from the inlet to the outlet?

A class of students studied the ecology of a pond as described in Section 12.7. Some of the data from that field trip are recorded in Table 12-5. The data were obtained at the sites shown in Figure 12-14. Study the data closely. Then answer the questions that follow. The following conditions were also noted on the field trip.

- The day was sunny and the tests were done around mid-day.
- The air temperature was 22°C on this late spring day.
- The water moved very slowly through the pond, from inlet to outlet.
- The emergent plants were growing in a stagnant bay.
- Most of the bottom of the pond was covered with submergent plants.
- The water was pale green in colour due to an algal bloom.
- The incoming stream (inlet) drains an urban area.

Table 12-5   Pond Ecology Data

	Site A	Site B	Site C
Oxygen (μg/g)	6.0	15	7.5
Carbon dioxide (μg/g)	45	5.0	30
pH	9.0	8.6	8.9
Alkalinity (μg/g)	340	185	290
Hardness (μg/g)	510	270	350
Ammonia (μg/g)	2.5	1.0	2.0
Nitrate (μg/g)	0.5	0.2	1.5
Phosphate (μg/g)	2.8	0.0	1.8
Chloride (μg/g)	650	490	500
Total coliforms/100 mL	12 050	52	47
Water temperature (°C)	18	20	21
Number of types of bottom fauna	3	17	7
Number of types of diatoms	0	7	5
Number of types of blue-green algae	4	7	4

Questions

1. a) What is responsible for the change in oxygen concentration from site A to site B?
    b) What evidence supports your conclusion?
    c) Why is the oxygen concentration lower at site C than at site B?
2. What is your opinion of the water quality of the incoming water? Refer to the data to support your answer. Use as much of the data as possible.
3. Is either the stream or pond fit for swimming? Give your reason(s).
4. The algal bloom in the pond will probably not get much worse in the near future. Why is this so?
5. Account for the decrease in each of the following between sites A and B: alkalinity, hardness, ammonia, nitrate, phosphate, chloride.
6. a) What does the high chloride concentration at the inlet suggest?
    b) What data support this conclusion?
7. Why does site C have higher concentrations of ammonia, nitrate, and phosphate than site B?
8. Eventually the algae in the bloom will die. If they die suddenly, many changes will likely occur in the chemical tests. Identify those changes.
9. a) In your view, what single action could greatly increase the water quality of the pond?
    b) Many urban ponds are in the condition of this pond. What do you feel is the main reason why steps are not taken to improve the water quality?

12.9   *FIELD TRIP*   Investigating Stream Ecology

This field trip compares two contrasting sites in a stream. Site A is a fast water zone (Fig. 12-15). The fast water has washed away small particles, leaving largely gravel and cobble on the bottom. Site B is a slow water zone and, as a result, has a sand and mud bottom.

The principles of ecology tell us that, because of these differing geophysical factors, most other factors will also differ between the two sites. This includes both abiotic and biotic factors. Your objective is to investigate those differences and deduce reasons for them.

Your class will be divided into two teams, one for each site. If time permits, your team will investigate both sites. Choose the sites far enough apart that the activities of one group will not influence the tests of the other group.

CAUTION: For safety reasons, you must not enter the stream without your teacher's permission.

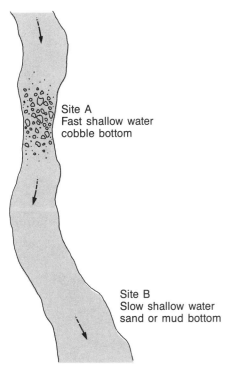

Site A
Fast shallow water
cobble bottom

Site B
Slow shallow water
sand or mud bottom

Fig. 12-15   Site selection for a stream study.

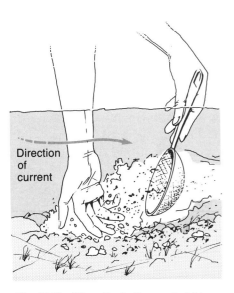

Direction
of
current

Fig. 12-16   When the bottom material is disturbed, organisms will leave it. The current will carry them into your sieve.

Problem

How and why do the ecological aspects of two sites on a stream differ?

Materials

Note: This list is for a class of 30. Your group may have to share some items with other groups.

set of Hach water testing kits (preferably oxygen, carbon dioxide, pH, alkalinity, hardness, ammonia, nitrate, phosphate, chloride)

white tray (8)   dip net (2)
sieve (8)   collecting bucket (2)
hand lens (8)   Coli-count tab (2)
probe (8)   *Pond Life* or other identification guide (8)
thermometer (2)   compass (1)

Procedure

a. Prepare a full-page copy of Tables 12-6 and 12-7.

b. Make another copy of Table 12-7 but replace "Invertebrates" in the title by "Plants and Algae".

c. Complete your copy of Table 12-6. That is, do the geophysical and chemical tests listed. Each chemical test should normally be done three times. If one value differs greatly from the others, ignore it. Otherwise average the three trials. The procedure for finding the speed of the water is outlined in Section 4.6.

d. Sample the site for bottom fauna as follows. Put 3 or 4 cm of water in the white tray. Then sit it on a level place on the ground (see Figure 12-10). Draw the sieve back and forth through submergent and emergent vegetation along the stream banks. Do this also through grasses and other terrestrial plants that dangle into the water. Tap the sieve, upside down, on the side of the tray to make the organisms fall into the water.

If the stream has a mud, silt, or sand bottom, scoop up some of this bottom material with the sieve. Wash away as much of the material as you can by swishing the sieve back and forth in the water. Then add the organisms to the tray.

If the stream has a gravel bottom, catch the bottom fauna as shown in Figure 12-16. If the stream has a cobble bottom, catch the bottom fauna as follows. Hold a piece of cobble over the tray. Then carefully dislodge the organisms with a probe. You can also dislodge many organisms by swishing the cobble back and forth in the water of the tray. Return each piece of cobble to where you found it. Also, place it the same way up. Why is this important?

Examine each type of bottom fauna with the hand lens. Identify the bottom fauna using *Pond Life* or another identification guide and Chapters 8, 9, and 11 of this book. Put their names in your copy of Table 12-7. Note their relative abundance (a = abundant, f = frequent, o = occasional,

Table 12-6   Stream Survey (Abiotic Factors)

Name of stream_____   Date_____
Site No._____   Time_____
Description of site_____   Weather—wind speed_____
_____   wind dir._____
_____   sky_____

Nature of shore_____
Nature of watershed_____
Nature of bottom_____
Appearance of water_____
_____

Temp. (air) _____°C
Temp. (water) _____°C
Speed _____m/s

Sketch map showing prominent
features (shoreline;
obstructions; riffles, rocks; etc.)

	Trial 1	Trial 2	Trial 3	Average
Oxygen				
Carbon dioxide				
pH				
Alkalinity				
Hardness				
Ammonia				
Nitrate				
Phosphate				
Chloride				

r = rare) in your table. Look closely for both behavioural and structural adaptations. Add these to your table. You may complete the final column of the table at home or at school. Do not take any organisms back to the classroom. Many of them will die if they are not put back into the stream promptly. They are not adapted for living in anything but running water.

e. Complete your table titled "Stream Survey (Plants and Algae)". Include in your survey submergent plants and the emergent plants along the banks. Examine the cobble closely for plants and algae. If necessary, take small pieces back to the classroom for identification. Do not collect plants, however. Most stream plants will not live long in an aquarium.

f. Perform a coliform test at each site. Follow the directions that came with the Millipore Coli-count tab.

Table 12-7 Stream Survey (Invertebrates)

Organism	Relative abundance (a,f,o,r)	Adaptations	Advantages to organism
Stonefly nymph	o	streamlined; muscular legs; 2 hooks on each foot; flattened dorso-ventrally; brownish colour; crawls under objects	able to hold on to cobble in fast water; camouflaged; conceals itself from predators

Discussion

1. Write as many food chains as you can for the stream. Remember that some of them are detritus food chains which begin outside the stream.
2. Draw one food web that involves at least four food chains.
3. Make a general conclusion regarding the water quality of the stream. Refer to data to support your conclusion.
4. Propose a management program and/or a cleanup program which would improve the water quality and overall ecology of the stream.

12.10 CASE STUDY Effects of Domestic Sewage on Water Quality

The stream in this study is about 20 km long. It drains into a lake that is about 5 km long at its longest place. A town of about 10 000 people is located near the headwaters of the stream. A biological and chemical survey was done to find out how sewage from the town affects the water quality of the stream. The tests were performed on a sunny, warm day in the late spring.

Six stations were set up, five along the stream and one in the lake (Fig. 12-17). The dimensions of the stream and the speed of the water were about the same at all five sites. The town has a sewage treatment plant. However, the plant was built when the town had a population of about 8000 people and it has not been updated since.

The results of the survey are summarized in Tables 12-8 and 12-9. Study them carefully then answer the discussion questions.

Table 12-8 Chemical Analysis

	A	B	C	D	E	F
Water temperature (°C)	18.0	18.9	18.2	18.0	18.1	18.0
Oxygen (μg/g)	9.5	2.2	3.0	5.8	7.1	9.0
Alkalinity (μg/g)	110	320	312	300	280	160
Ammonia (μg/g)	0.10	3.20	3.00	2.51	2.05	1.04
Nitrate (μg/g)	0.00	1.10	1.15	1.61	2.05	0.22
Phosphate (μg/g)	0.02	2.20	2.15	1.74	1.45	0.31
Chloride (μg/g)	20.0	195.0	192.4	190.5	190.1	135.0
T.D.S. (μg/g)	255	690	652	648	615	380

Table 12-9 Biological Data

	A	B	C	D	E	F
Stoneflies per m²	31	0	2	8	17	0
Mayflies per m²	78	4	21	35	54	3
Caddisflies per m²	58	4	18	28	42	2
Midge flies per m²	7	85	72	54	31	24
Sludgeworms per m²	4	154	138	122	118	65
Coliforms per 100 mL	11	6500	6200	6050	5900	22
Diatom species	7	0	0	0	2	4
Blue-green algal species	1	5	5	4	4	2

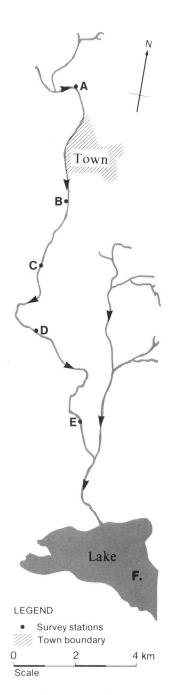

Fig. 12-17 How are this stream and lake affected by sewage from the town?

LEGEND

• Survey stations
/// Town boundary

0   2   4 km
Scale

Discussion

1. Is the stream of high water quality at station A? How do you know?
2. a) Account for the changes in oxygen concentrations from station A to station E.
   b) The lake receives water from the stream which contains only 7.1 μg/g of oxygen. The lake has 9.0 μg/g of oxygen. How can this be?
3. a) What components of the sewage may be responsible for the increase in alkalinity at station B?
   b) Why does the alkalinity gradually decrease from station B to station E?
   c) The lake receives water with an alkalinity of 280 μg/g. Its alkalinity is only 160 μg/g. Why is this so?

4. **a)** What components of the sewage are likely responsible for the increase in ammonia at Station B?

   b) Account for the gradual drop in the ammonia concentrations from station B to station F.

5. Account for the changes in the nitrate concentrations from station A to station F.

6. Account for the changes in the phosphate concentrations from station A to station F.

7. Account for the changes in the chloride concentrations from station A to station F.

8. Is the lake likely to be oligotrophic or eutrophic? Cite the chemical data which support your conclusion.

9. Five types of bottom fauna were studied: stoneflies, mayflies, caddisflies, midge flies, and sludgeworms. Account for the changes in the densities of each type from station A to station F.

10. At which sites could one swim with little or no danger of ingesting pathogenic bacteria? Explain your choices.

11. Account for the changes in the numbers of diatom and blue-green algal species from station A to station F.

12. Prepare a one-page statement that you would present to the mayor of the town to encourage the mayor to study the data and then take action to upgrade the sewage treatment plant.

Effects of Agriculture on Water Quality

12.11   *CASE STUDY*

The stream in this study passes through a large agricultural area. The main crop grown in the area is corn. Several farmers in the area also raise livestock. Four of these farmers have large beef feedlots. A scientific study was done in late May to find out what effects, if any, agriculture had on the water quality of the stream.

Six stations were set up, five along the stream and one in the lake (Fig. 12-18). Geophysical, chemical, and biological tests were conducted. The results are listed in Tables 12-10, 12-11, 12-12, and 12-13. Study the results carefully then answer the discussion questions.

Questions

1. What is the overall quality of the water at A? Cite evidence to support your answer.

2. **a)** Is the water saturated with oxygen at A?

   b) Account for the change in oxygen concentration from station A to station E.

   c) Account for the increase in oxygen at station F.

LEGEND

- - - Swamp
- Sampling stations
Agricultural area

0   2   4 km
Scale

Fig. 12-18 How does agriculture affect water quality in a stream and lake?

3. **a)** What is the likely cause of the increase in total suspended solids (T.S.S.) from station A to station E?
   b) Are the suspended solids at F likely to be similar to those at the stream stations? Explain.
4. **a)** What factors are likely responsible for the increase in ammonia from station A to station E?
   b) The lake receives water with an ammonia concentration of 0.7 μg/g. Its ammonia concentration is only 0.1 μg/g. Why is this so?
5. **a)** Account for the changes in nitrate concentrations from station A to station E.
   b) Why does the nitrate concentration drop so much when the water enters the lake?
6. **a)** At which station does the impact of soil erosion first appear? Give your reasoning.
   b) Which nutrient, nitrate or phosphate, is often carried into water by eroded soil?
   c) What evidence does this study offer to show that your answer to (b) is likely true?
7. Station B receives some farm runoff. Yet station B has more stoneflies, mayflies, and caddisflies than station A which receives no farm runoff. What is a possible reason for this?
8. Why are there no stoneflies at Station F?
9. Use the bottom fauna data (Table 12-12) to support a discussion of the effect of agriculture on water quality.
10. Where are the feedlots likely located on the stream system? How do you know?
11. Use the algal data (Table 12-13) to support a discussion of the effect of agriculture on water quality.
12. Is the lake oligotrophic or eutrophic? Cite chemical and biological data to support your conclusion.
13. What do you feel should be done to improve the water quality of the stream and lake?

Table 12-10   Chemical Analysis

	A	B	C	D	E	F
Oxygen (μg/g)	9.1	9.0	8.8	8.2	8.2	10.5
Ammonia (μg/g)	0.0	0.1	0.4	0.6	0.7	0.1
Nitrate (μg/g)	0.0	0.1	0.2	0.5	0.8	0.2
Phosphate (μg/g)	0.0	0.0	0.3	0.4	0.4	0.0
T.D.S. (μg.g)	225	234	261	275	279	205

Table 12-11 Geophysical Factors

	A	B	C	D	E	F
Temperature (°C)	20.0	19.8	19.8	19.2	19.0	16.5
Speed (m/s)	1.1	1.0	0.8	0.8	0.3	—
Width (m)	5.4	5.2	6.0	7.1	9.0	—
Average depth (m)	0.4	0.4	0.6	0.7	1.1	4.2
T.S.S. (μg/g)	15	18	78	98	104	77

Table 12-12 Bottom Fauna per Square Metre

	A	B	C	D	E	F
Stoneflies	15	28	31	12	6	0
Mayflies	51	60	42	31	17	5
Caddisflies	44	54	47	35	18	6
Midge flies	8	19	54	71	111	72
Sludgeworms	3	14	28	34	71	84

Table 12-13 Bacteria and Algae

	A	B	C	D	E	F
Coliforms per 100 mL	o	o	o	640	672	6
Cladophora	ab	ab	o	f	a	ab
Chlorella	ab	ab	ab	ab	o	a
Ulotrix	ab	ab	ab	ab	o	ab
Spirogyra	ab	ab	ab	o	f	a
Microcystis	ab	ab	ab	ab	ab	a
Anabaena	ab	ab	ab	ab	ab	a
Nostoc	ab	ab	ab	ab	ab	f
Rivularia	r	r	o	f	a	ab

a = abundant
f = frequent
o = occasional
r = rare
ab = absent

Main Ideas

1. A decrease in species diversity is the best biological indicator of pollution.
2. Eutrophication is the process of aging or increasing productivity in a lake.
3. Eutrophic waters often support algal blooms.
4. Fish, bottom fauna, algae and bacteria can be used as indicators of water quality.

Key Terms

algal bloom	eutrophic	mutualistic bacteria
autotrophic bacteria	eutrophication	oligotrophic
bottom fauna	fecal coliform	parasitic bacteria
coliform	index (indicator) species	pathogen
E. coli	mesotrophic	saprophytic bacteria

Chapter Review

A. True or False

Decide whether each of the following statements is true or false. If the sentence is false, rewrite it to make it true. (Do not write in this book.)
1. Species diversity is the best biological indicator of water quality.
2. Eutrophication is a natural process for most lakes.
3. An abundance of midge larvas is an indication of good water quality.
4. Clean water usually has a high diversity of algal species.
5. Autotrophic bacteria require a host organism.
6. *E. coli* bacteria are essential to the human body.
7. Public health officials close swimming beaches if fecal coliforms are found in the water.

B. Completion

Complete each of the following sentences with a word or phrase that will make the sentence correct. (Do not write in this book.)
1. Polluted water usually has a ▨▨▨▨ diversity of species than clean water.
2. Eutrophic water often has a total dissolved solids concentration greater than ▨▨▨▨ .
3. An eutrophic lake often has an ▨▨▨▨ bloom.
4. Saprophytic bacteria are also called ▨▨▨▨ .
5. Disease-producing bacteria are called ▨▨▨▨ .
6. Fecal coliforms live in the ▨▨▨▨ .

C. Multiple Choice

Each of the following statements or questions is followed by four responses. Choose the correct response in each case. (Do not write in this book.)

1. Which one of the following best describes an eutrophic lake?
   a) warm, low productivity, algal bloom, high diversity of species
   b) cold, high productivity, no algal bloom, low diversity of species
   c) cold, high productivity, algal bloom, high diversity of species
   d) warm, high productivity, algal bloom, low diversity of species
2. Which one of the following groups of fish would most likely occur in an oligotrophic lake?
   a) perch, whitefish, bass, smelt
   b) perch, black bass, pike, smelt
   c) carp, sunfish, catfish, perch
   d) walleye, whitefish, lake trout, char
3. Which one of the following groups of bottom fauna would most likely occur on the bottom of a fast clean stream?
   a) stoneflies, mayflies, and caddisflies
   b) stoneflies, leeches, and ostracods
   c) mayflies, caddisflies, and midge flies
   d) sludgeworms, midge flies, and mayflies
4. What word best describes the relationship between *E. coli* and the human body?
   a) mutualism   b) parasitism   c) symbiosis   d) commensalism

Using Your Knowledge

1. Midge larvas and sludgeworms thrive in water polluted with sewage. A stream was found to have few of these organisms in it. Does this mean that the stream is not polluted? Explain your answer.
2. Distinguish between an oligotrophic lake and an eutrophic lake.
3. A small lake is found to contain mainly sunfish, catfish, and other fish that can tolerate low oxygen conditions. Is the lake polluted? Explain your answer.
4. Look back to Figure 12-4. Account for the difference in the shapes of the two curves.
5. Four decades ago mayflies were so abundant in some towns and cities along Lake Erie that shovels were used to remove their bodies from streets and sidewalks. This problem no longer exists. Why?
6. Sludgeworms and midge larvas are usually more abundant at the mouth of a river than at the headwaters of the same river. Why?
7. Figure 12-19 shows the effects of sewage effluent on some stream organisms. Interpret the graph. In other words, explain the relationship between distance downstream and the number of organisms for each curve.

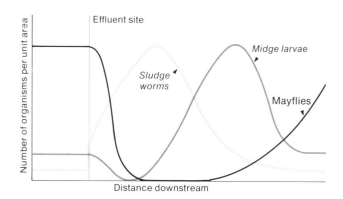

Fig. 12-19 Effect of organic pollution from domestic sewage on three kinds of bottom fauna.

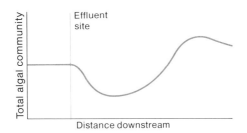

Fig. 12-20 Effect of sewage on the algal community of a stream.

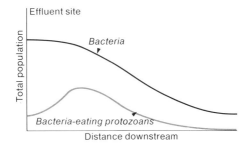

Fig. 12-21 Effect of domestic sewage (organic matter) on bacteria and protozoan populations.

8. Figure 12-20 is a graph which shows how effluent from a sewage plant affects the total algal community of a stream. Account for the shape of the graph.

9. Interpret the graphs in Figure 12-21.

10. Suppose you were on a camping trip and had to get your drinking water from a stream. What two things could you do to make sure the water is free from pathogens?

11. One large city on Lake Ontario often has its swimming beaches closed during the summer because the coliform count is too high. The main cause is an outdated system of sewer pipes. The mayor says that many years will be needed to replace the pipes. The reason the mayor gives is that the city must spread the cost over many years. Studies show that the cost is about $80 for each person living in the city. Write a one page letter to the mayor in which you either support the mayor or demand immediate action.

Investigations

1. Find out from your local public health department the standards for total coliform and *E. coli* for drinking water and swimming areas.

2. Find out if your municipal sewage is free of pathogenic bacteria before it is released into a stream or lake.

3. Find out what level of government sets the standards for coliform counts in your area.

4. **a)** Find out how a citizen can get drinking water and water from a swimming area tested for coliforms.
   b) Send in a suspect sample of water to be tested.

5. Find out from your local water purification plant which algae commonly clog the filters of the plant. Learn the significance of the presence of these algae, and how the plant operators deal with this problem.

6. Monitor the bacterial count of a local swimming beach or river for two weeks. Interpret your results. (See *Investigating Environmental Issues* for procedures.)

UNIT FOUR

Introduction to Marine Ecosystems

Oceans ... seas ... rocky shores ... sandy shores ... salt marshes ... mud flats ... estuaries ... Marine ecosystems like these cover about 71% of the earth's surface. In fact, 97% of the world's water is salt water. Only 3% is fresh water.

The main purpose of this unit is to introduce you to the marine ecosystems, and the basic ecological principles that govern them. The main abiotic factors in marine ecosystems and an explanation of their importance and effects on living things are also discussed in this unit. In Unit 5 you will learn more about the biotic properties of each type of marine ecosystem.

13 Types of Marine Ecosystems

14 The Ecology of Marine Ecosystems: Basic Principles

15 Marine Ecosystems: Abiotic Factors

The ocean is a marine ecosystem. Like all marine ecosystems it supports a variety of marine life. Marine ecosystems are a valuable resource which we must protect.

13 Types of Marine Ecosystems

Marine ecology is the study of the relationships among the organisms of the sea and relationships between those organisms and their environments. Many of the abiotic and biotic factors that interact in the various types of marine ecosystems are unique to marine (salt water) environments. However, the basic ecological concepts you studied earlier for freshwater ecosystems still apply.

In this chapter you will study the characteristic features of the open ocean and of shore ecosystems. Let's begin by finding out how marine ecosystems differ from freshwater ecosystems.

13.1 What Is a Marine Ecosystem?

The oceans and seas of the world are marine ecosystems. Rocky and sandy shores, salt marshes, mud flats, and estuaries are all marine ecosystems. Even the tiny tidal pools that dot a rocky coast are marine ecosystems. Each **marine ecosystem** is an interacting system that consists of marine organisms and their non-living environment (Fig. 13-1).

Fig. 13-1 Marine ecosystems.

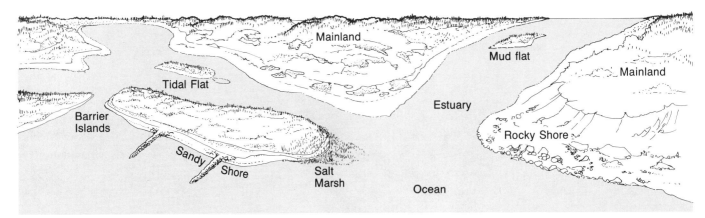

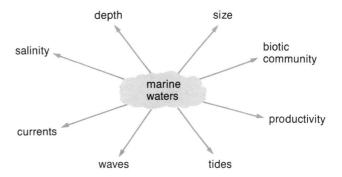

Fig. 13-2 Marine ecosystems differ from freshwater ecosystems in several ways.

Characteristic Properties

Big or small, marine ecosystems differ from freshwater ecosystems in several ways (Fig. 13-2). The most significant differences are:

- size
- depth
- salinity
- currents
- waves
- tides
- productivity
- biotic community

Size   The ocean ecosystem is very large. It occupies about 71% of the earth's surface. In fact, 97% of the world's water is salt water. Other marine ecosystems, such as estuaries and marshes are quite small in comparison.

Depth   The ocean ecosystem is also deep. The deepest parts are over 10 km deep. The average depth of the sea is about 3.8 km. However, the average depth of land is only 0.75 km. In other words, there is about 300 times more living space in the ocean than what is available for life on land. If our earth had a smooth surface, the waters of the sea would cover it to a uniform depth of about 2.5 km.

Salinity   The salinity or concentration of dissolved minerals in sea water is very high. In the open sea it averages about 3.5% or 35 000 μg/g. In fact, most sea water is about 2.7% common salt. Sodium chloride, or common salt, gives sea water its salty taste. For this reason, sea water is also called salt water.

Currents   The oceans and seas are interconnected by currents. These mighty rivers of moving water occur at both the surface and ocean bottom. The Gulf Stream in the North Atlantic is perhaps one of the best known of the surface currents. Ocean currents are of great importance. For example, in many parts of the world, they influence the climate. Ocean currents transport food and oxygen to marine organisms. They also move waste products away from the organisms. They even move the organisms themselves.

Fig. 13-3 This rocky shore along the North Atlantic coast, north of Cape Cod, supports marine life of many kinds. Marine organisms live in distinct zones, each at a depth suited to its needs.

Waves Oceans and seas are dominated by waves. These vary in size and speed. The most destructive of all wave types is the tidal wave. Tidal waves are quite harmless in the open sea. However, when they enter shallow water, they become large and destructive. You can read more about waves in Section 15.1.

Tides All shores—rocky, muddy, sandy, and marshy—have one thing in common. They are exposed to the tides. A tide is the rhythmic rise and fall of the ocean's water. This slow change in sea level has resulted in distinct zones of organisms along these shores. Figure 13-3 shows the zonation on one rocky shore. Depending on the type and location of the shore, the organisms making up the zones differ. Zonation is discussed in more detail in Unit 5.

Productivity Productivity is the ability to support life. Within an ecosystem productivity is controlled by several factors. These include the availability of light, water, and nutrients. In the ocean ecosystem, productivity is limited. This is due to the dilution of nutrients in the vast waters. Also, the surface area receiving sunlight is small in comparison to the total volume of water involved. Thus in the open ocean, productivity is low. However, it is higher in regions where nutrients are brought up to the surface layers by ocean currents. It is also higher in the shallow waters of the continental shelf. Coral reefs and salt marshes are among the most productive ecosystems on earth.

Biotic Community Each marine ecosystem has its own characteristic biotic community. This is determined by the geophysical and chemical properties of each ecosystem. You will study this fascinating array of life in Unit 5.

There are many other differences between marine and freshwater ecosystems. These are discussed in the following chapters.

1. Define the term marine ecosystem.
2. Name 7 types of marine ecosystems.
3. List the 8 main differences between marine and freshwater ecosystems.
4. **a)** What percentage of the earth's crust is occupied by marine ecosystems?
   b) What is the average depth of the sea?
5. **a)** What is meant by the term salinity?
   b) What is the average salinity of the oceans?
6. What is the most destructive of all wave types?
7. State 2 reasons why productivity is limited in the ocean ecosystem.

Biozones: The Life Zones of the Ocean

13.2

The oceans and seas are subdivided into two main environments: the pelagic, or water environment, and the benthic, or bottom environment. Within each of these, there is a variety of environments (Fig. 13-4).

Fig. 13-4 Classification of marine environments.

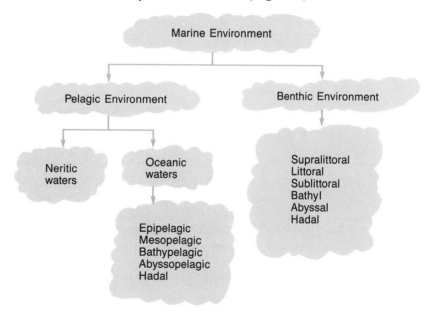

Pelagic Environment

Horizontal Zonation   The term pelagic refers to the water of the oceans. The pelagic environment is divided into two provinces, the neritic and oceanic (Fig. 13-5). The neritic province or near-shore zone is the water

Fig. 13-5 Biozones in the marine ecosystem (not to scale).

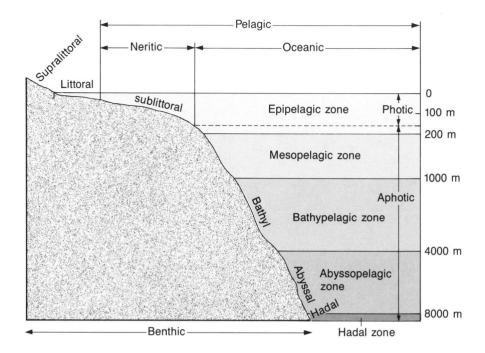

which covers the continental shelves. The oceanic province, or open ocean, is the water beyond the shelves.

The neritic environment is distinct from the oceanic environment. Neritic waters represent less than 10% of the total ocean area. Yet these waters contain 90% of all ocean life. In fact, most of the world's fisheries occur here.

Neritic waters tend to be richer in plant nutrients. One reason is that nutrients are not continually lost to deeper water through the sinking of organic matter before its decomposition is complete. As well, there is more mixing of the water. This is the result of turbulence, wave action, and upwelling caused by offshore currents and winds. In addition, nutrients leached from the land are washed into the ocean by rivers and streams.

Unlike neritic waters, the salinity and temperature do not vary a great deal in the oceanic province. Light penetration is somewhat greater here. There are also distinct differences between the organisms in the two provinces.

Vertical Zonation   The oceanic province is divided into five vertical layers or zones (see Figures 13-4 and 13-5). These divisions are based on depth and light penetration. The boundaries between them vary somewhat. However, each zone has its own distinctive characteristics.

Extending from the surface to a depth of about 200 m is the epipelagic zone. In this zone, light is generally sufficient to support photosynthesis.

However, most photosynthesis takes place in the upper part which is called the photic zone. Sharp gradients in illumination, temperature, and salinity occur in the epipelagic zone. This zone contains most of the life of the pelagic environment.

Below the epipelagic zone is the mesopelagic zone. This zone extends down to about 600 to 1000 m. Here, light penetration is too brief and too little to support photosynthesis. Below the mesopelagic zone are, in order, the bathypelagic zone, abyssopelagic zone, and hadal zone. These along with the mesopelagic zone occur in the aphotic zone where, for all practical purposes, no light penetrates. It is always pitch-black. The bathypelagic zone extends from about 1000 m to 4000 m. Many of the larger organisms such as tuna and whales live here. Below this zone is the abyssopelagic zone. Animals at these depths are adapted to the great pressures.

Finally, in the deepest parts of the oceans, below 8000 m, is the hadal zone. It is located in the deep-sea trenches.

Benthic Environment

Regardless of depth, the benthic environment is found at the bottom of the ocean. It is divided into six zones: supralittoral, littoral, sublittoral, bathyl, abyssal, and hadal zones (see Fig. 13-5). Each zone has a characteristic array of organisms. These are discussed in more detail in Unit 5.

Supralittoral Zone   The supralittoral zone is the area above high tide level. Most of the time this region is dry. However, during times of intense wave action it becomes wet. Thus it is also called the spray zone. A few algae and plants have adapted to these conditions.

Littoral Zone   As you walk from the supralittoral zone toward the ocean, you will have little trouble telling the littoral or tidal zone. This region is covered and uncovered daily by tides. It is further divided into subzones. Each subzone is inhabited by specific species of organisms.

Sublittoral Zone   Next is the sublittoral zone. It is also known as the continental shelf. This zone extends from below the littoral zone to the outer edge of the continental shelf. It is here that the densest population of bottom-dwelling organisms live.

Bathyl, Abyssal, and Hadal Zones   Beyond the continental shelf, the benthic environment is generally stable and uniform. It is divided into three zones. The bathyl zone, at depths of between 2000 and 4000 m, includes the slope, and at times some of the ocean floor. The abyssal zone includes the abyssal plains. This is the ocean floor environment at a depth of 4000 and 8000 m. Below this is the hadal zone. It includes the deep-sea trenches.

1. Distinguish between pelagic and benthic environments.
2. **a)** Name the two provinces into which the pelagic environment is divided.

    b) What part of the marine ecosystem do they represent?
3. State three differences between neritic and oceanic waters.
4. **a)** List in order from surface to ocean bottom the five zones of the pelagic environment.

    b) State the approximate depths at which these zones occur.
5. Distinguish between photic and aphotic zones.
6. **a)** List the six zones of the benthic environment.

    b) Briefly describe their locations and their distinguishing features.

13.3   The Ocean

What Is the Ocean?

The oceans cover nearly 71% of the earth's surface or about 361 000 000 km². Coastal waters represent 7% of the ocean area. The remainder is **open ocean**.

If you look at a map of the world, you can find the five great oceans: the Atlantic, Pacific, Indian, Arctic and Antarctic (Fig. 13-6). Because they are all interconnected by currents and tides, only one **world ocean** actually extends over the earth's surface. The seven continents are islands in this one huge body of water.

Fig. 13-6 The major oceans of the world are interconnected to form one world ocean.

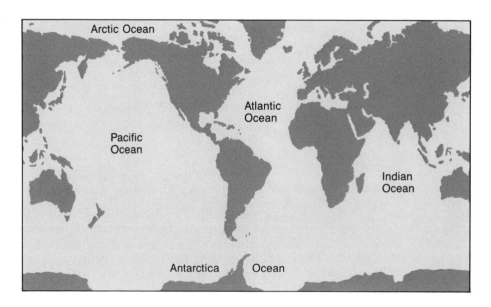

The open ocean is vast and complex. The deepest parts are over 10 km deep. It is divided into five vertical zones: the epipelagic, the mesopelagic, the bathypelagic, the abyssopelagic, and the hadal zones. Each zone is inhabited by marine species adapted to the physical and chemical conditions of that depth.

The dominant producers of the open ocean are phytoplankton. The chief consumers are zooplankton. The physical, chemical, and biological properties of the open ocean are discussed in detail in Chapters 15 and 16.

Importance of the Ocean

From the beginning of recorded time, the ocean has been a highway for ships. It has also served as a source of foods and other products for coastal populations. Modern technology has made possible the exploration and extraction of resources from all depths of the ocean. Food, chemicals, minerals, energy—the ocean indeed holds great treasures (Fig. 13-7). It is up to us to manage these resources wisely.

Fig. 13-7 The importance of the world ocean.

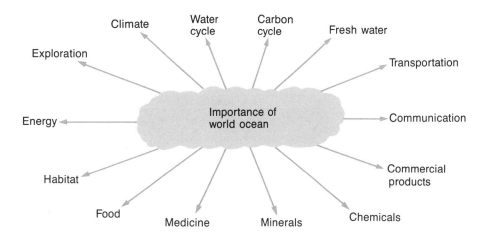

World Regulator   The ocean regulates several major processes occurring on the earth's surface. It supplies most of the water vapour that falls as precipitation on the continents. As well, it contains the largest reservoir of carbon within the carbon cycle.

The ocean is also an important regulator of climate. This is especially true of coastal and maritime areas. Warm currents carry tropical warmth into higher latitudes. Cold currents often bring bitter temperatures to adjacent lands. As well, the ocean stores up vast quantities of heat from the sun. This heat helps to prevent the temperature of the earth from rising or falling extremely.

Food Source   At present, the ocean contributes less than 2% of the world's food supply. It provides about 5% of the current intake of protein. In many

Fig. 13-8 Seaweeds are a nutritious food source.

developing countries, fish is virtually the only source of high-quality animal protein.

Molluscs, crustaceans, fishes, whales, and seaweed are major food resources for many areas of the world. Large modern fishing fleets, floating factory ships, sonar, and helicopters have helped to make annual large-scale catches possible. Attempts are even being made to seek new marine food sources. Most of the fish occur in coastal areas. In fact, more than 90% of all fishing is done in coastal areas. For centuries, seaweeds have been used for animal feed and as a food supplement for humans. Today they are recognized as a healthy vitamin and mineral rich "sea vegetable" (Fig. 13-8). Chief consumers of seaweeds are Japan, China, Korea, and the Philippines.

The ocean is being looked to as a major source of food for the future. It is hoped that the ocean may help solve the problem of feeding the world's hungry. Will it be able to? Presently, most of the fish catch is being channeled to people already well-fed. These are the people who can afford to buy seafood. Trash fish is ground to make fish meal and fish oil. These in turn are used to make high-protein animal foods for poultry, hogs, and pets.

Until recently the number of fish and other animals we could catch from the ocean seemed unlimited. The decline of the whale population in recent years is a strong case against rapid and unwise exploitation of ocean food resources. In order to meet the future needs of an ever-increasing world population, we must manage this marine resource wisely.

Commercial Products   In addition to being a valuable food source, marine animals and plants provide many other useful products. For example, pearls, shells, and shark teeth are collected for jewellery and ornaments. Oil from whale blubber is used for making lubricants and soaps. The blades of the eelgrass *Zostera* are often used by the Seri Indians of Sonora Mexico for constructing roofs and mats. For centuries seaweeds have been used as fertilizer for crops. They still provide such chemicals as soda, potash, and iodine.

Today seaweeds also provide several commercial extracts. Agar is used as a stabilizer in food processing. It also serves as a solidifying agent in microbial culture media used in many laboratories. The substance algin is used as a thickener in chocolate milk, ice cream, cheeses, jellies, and jams. It is a key substance in many cosmetics, drugs, textiles, paints, and explosives. In the future seaweeds may be fermented to provide alcohols for use as fuels. Seaweeds may even be used in the treatment of sewage waste.

Medicine   Various marine algae have long been used in the treatment of many diseases, including worms, goiter, and kidney disease. Some algae are able to reduce blood cholesterol. Still others are used in treating hypertension and ulcers.

Goiter is caused by a lack of iodine in the diet. However, this disease is rare in seacoast populations. Seafoods, especially seaweeds, contain high levels of iodine. Seaweeds are also rich in vitamins, minerals, and trace elements. Thus a number of widespread human diseases such as malnutrition could be prevented by the use of seaweeds and their products.

Many beneficial drugs have been developed using chemicals isolated from marine animals and plants. Antibiotics occur in some marine fungi. The powerful nerve drug tetrodatoxin comes from the puffer fish. It is used to relax muscle spasms. Many other chemicals are used to treat various viral, fungal, and yeast infections. Others are used to help treat tumors.

Marine animals and plants have also proven useful in testing new drugs. As well, certain algae are capable of absorbing heavy metals and radioactive elements. This ability has been used to medical advantage.

Chemicals and Minerals   The ocean is a vast storehouse of chemicals and minerals. Much of this valuable material is still untouched. Much is present in too low a concentration to be recovered. Others are located too deep in the ocean sediment or water to be mined.

For centuries sodium chloride, or common salt, has been obtained by evaporating ocean water. Today potassium and magnesium salts are also being extracted in large quantities. Bromine and iodine are produced commercially from seawater salts.

Many valuable minerals are found on or under the ocean floor. Most of the minerals mined lie in the shallow waters of the continental shelves. Many are seaward extensions of valuable land deposits.

Among the minerals recovered are diamonds. These are mined off the southwest coast of Africa. Gold is mined off Alaska. Tin deposits are found off the coasts of England and Southeast Asia.

The ocean floor also yields sulfur, iron, platinum, and coal. Offshore wells supply increasing amounts of the world's petroleum and natural gas. Sand, gravel, and oyster shells are collected from the ocean bottom for construction purposes.

Phosphorite is a phosphorus mineral known to be available on the ocean floor. It may one day prove to be a valuable agricultural fertilizer.

Manganese nodules may also be important economically one day. These are round, flat, or odd-shaped pieces of minerals found on the deep-ocean floor (Fig. 13-9). Each nodule has a mass of about one kilogram. These nodules consist chiefly of manganese and iron. They also contain smaller amounts of nickel, cobalt, copper, aluminum and 30 or 40 other minerals. These are all valuable minerals that have not been obtained yet to any great extent from the ocean floor. It is estimated that there are over 1 000 000 000 000 t of these nodules on the ocean floor. They are especially abundant in the Pacific Ocean. Recovery of these nodules is currently in the experimental stage. Most promising is a method of sucking the nodules off the ocean floor with a great "vacuum cleaner" (Fig. 13-10). What disadvantages might this method have?

Fig. 13-9   Manganese nodules.

Fig. 13-10 Mining the ocean floor for manganese nodules.

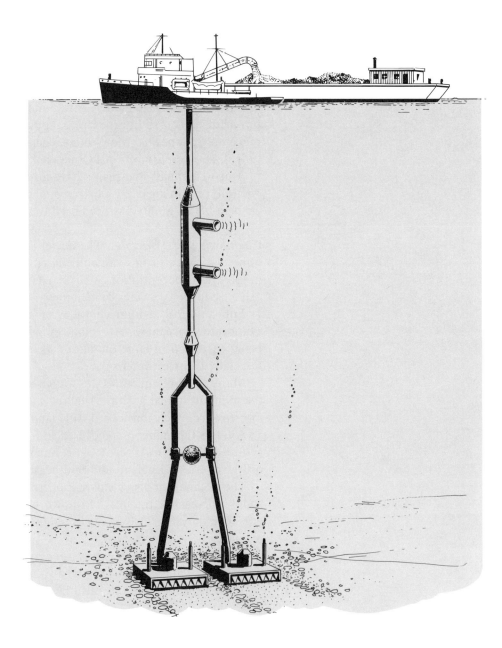

Water Perhaps one of the most important future resources from the ocean will be fresh water. Increased population growth and pollution have placed more pressure on our fresh water supply. Consequently, the ocean may have to provide a source of fresh water for irrigation, industry, and domestic use.

Desalination is the process of removing salts and other chemicals from sea water. This process is very expensive. However, desalination plants are common in arid areas. They are also being built in several major coastal cities.

Energy Some scientists believe that the ocean could one day provide us with considerable energy. Potential sources of energy include tides, waves, ocean currents, and thermal gradients.

At present energy is being harnessed from the flow of tides in and out of bays and estuaries. Since the 16th century, numerous devices have been built to harness the energy in waves and currents. However, as of 1986, there are no large scale wave or current energy generators in use.

Thermal power takes advantage of the temperature differences between sunwarmed surface waters and the cold ocean depths. However its efficiency is low. As well, it is very costly. It may be decades before thermal power is economically feasible on a large scale.

Section Review

1. What percent of the earth's surface is covered by ocean?
2. Explain why there is only one world ocean and not five as shown on maps of the world.
3. List ten major importances of the ocean to life on earth.
4. What major food resources are found in the ocean?
5. Briefly discuss the many uses of seaweed.
6. Why is the disease goiter rare in seacoast populations?
7. What minerals are found on or under the ocean floor?
8. a) What are manganese nodules?
   b) Where are they found?
   c) Why are attempts being made to recover them in large quantities?
9. Briefly discuss the importance of the ocean as a major food, water, and energy source to future generations.

13.4   Shore Ecosystems

Rocky Shores

The rocky shore is one of the most fascinating intertidal (shore) areas to visit and study. Waves slowly erode cliffs, leaving unusual forms and shapes. Distinct zones of plants and animals cover the rocks in parallel bands. Tide pools, or water-filled depressions, dot the rocky surface when the tide recedes. These, too, are inhabited by an array of organisms adapted to the ever-changing conditions.

The rocky coast has three main zones. The intertidal zone, or littoral zone, is alternately covered and exposed by tides (Fig. 13-11). Above it is the supralittoral zone, or spray zone. Below it is the sublittoral zone or the area above the continental shelf.

Fig. 13-11 Zonation in the littoral zone. Note the parallel bands of organisms.

Sandy Shores

For many people, the most familiar part of the coastal ocean is the sandy shore or sand beach (Fig. 13-12). Sandy shores are found in most parts of the world. They are continually being reshaped by waves, currents, tides, and winds. For this reason a sandy beach is often described as a "sediment deposit in motion". The harsh conditions on the sandy shore force most life to exist beneath the sand.

Fig. 13-12   The sandy beach is a popular place to spend a holiday.

Estuaries, Salt Marshes, and Mud Flats

Waters of all rivers and streams eventually drain into the ocean. The semi-enclosed parts of the coastal ocean where fresh water from the land mixes with salt water is called an estuary (Fig. 13-13). Estuaries vary in size, shape, water flow, and salinity. But common to all types is the increase in salinity from river entrance to open ocean. Almost all large estuaries are the site of a major city.

Fig. 13-13   A salt marsh on the Atlantic coast. The plants in this marsh are able to live in salty water.

Salt marshes are low-lying nearly flat marine wetlands. They form in intertidal areas. They border most estuarine and well-protected areas in temperate regions. In fact, many marshes mark the locations of former, small, shallow estuaries. But unlike other coastal habitats, their shallow waters are generally overgrown by salt-tolerant vegetation (Fig. 13-14).

Fig. 13-14 A mud flat at low tide looks like a barren environment (A). Many species live in the mud, while many others inhabit the areas at high tide (B).

A

B

Most of the marsh area consists of mud and sand flats. **Mud flats** are also common in many estuaries. These flats are intertidal habitats. They are covered by shallow water at high tide. They are usually exposed to air at low tide (Fig. 13-15). Sometimes these **tidal flats** are covered with grasses and mats of green and blue-green algae. If they are exposed to waves and winds, the flats may be barren of plants.

Fig. 13-15 This fiord receives fresh water from a river that is fed by meltwater from glaciers. The fiord dumps this fresh water into the ocean. Because of this mixing of fresh water and salt water the fiord can be called an estuary.

Summary

All shores—rocky, sandy, muddy, marshy, and estuaries—have one thing in common. They are exposed daily to tides. Therefore, organisms that live here must be adapted biologically to the harsh conditions that accompany the changing water levels. You will learn about these adaptations in Unit 5.

1. Name two characteristic features of the rocky shore.
2. **a)** Name the three main zones of the rocky shore.
    b) What is zonation on a rocky shore based on?
3. What is a tide pool?
4. What feature is characteristic of the sandy shore?
5. List four physical forces which are responsible for the continuous reshaping of the sandy shore.
6. **a)** What is an estuary?
    b) What feature is common to all estuaries?
7. **a)** What is a salt marsh?
    b) Where are salt marshes commonly found?
8. **a)** What is a mud flat?
    b) Where are mud flats commonly found?

Main Ideas

1. A marine ecosystem is an interacting system that consists of marine organisms and their non-living environment.
2. Oceans, rocky and sandy shores, salt marshes, mud flats, estuaries, and tide pools are all marine ecosystems.
3. Marine ecosystems differ from freshwater ecosystems in several ways: size, depth, salinity, currents, waves, tides, productivity, biotic community.
4. The ocean consists of two environments: pelagic and benthic.
5. The ocean is divided into five vertical zones: epipelagic, mesopelagic, bathypelagic, abyssopelagic, and hadal zones.
6. The world ocean influences almost every aspect of our lives.
7. Rocky shores are characterized by a zonation of organisms.
8. Rocky, sandy, marshy, muddy, and estuarine shores are exposed daily to tides.
9. Organisms of the rocky and sandy shores, salt marsh, mud flat, and estuary have adapted biologically to the harsh conditions in their environment.

Key Terms

abyssal zone	intertidal zone	rocky shore
abyssopelagic zone	littoral zone	salinity
aphotic zone	marine ecosystem	salt marsh
bathyal zone	mesopelagic zone	sandy shore
bathypelagic zone	mud flat	spray zone
benthic	neritic province	sublittoral zone

desalination   oceanic province   supralittoral zone
epipelagic zone   pelagic   tidal flat
estuary   photic zone   tide pool
hadal zone

Chapter Review

A. True or False

Decide whether each of the following statements is true or false. If the sentence is false, rewrite it to make it true. (Do not write in this book.)
1. The average salinity of seawater is 35%.
2. Productivity is high in the open ocean.
3. Seaweed is a nutritious seafood.
4. Most life on a sandy shore is hidden beneath the surface.
5. All shore ecosystems are exposed daily to tides.

B. Completion

Complete each of the following sentences with a word or phrase that will make the sentence correct. (Do not write in this book.)
1. The average depth of the sea is ▨▨▨▨▨ m.
2. The pelagic environment is divided into two provinces called ▨▨▨▨▨ and ▨▨▨▨▨ .
3. The process of removing salts and other chemicals from sea water is called ▨▨▨▨▨ .
4. When the tide recedes, water filled depressions called ▨▨▨▨▨ often cover the rocky shore.
5. In an estuary, salinity ▨▨▨▨▨ from river entrance to open ocean.

C. Multiple Choice

Each of the following statements or questions is followed by four responses. Choose the correct response in each case. (Do not write in this book.)
1. What percent of the earth's surface is covered by marine ecosystems?
    a) 31%   **b)** 50%   **c)** 71%   **d)** 97%
2. The zone which is covered and uncovered daily by tides is called the
    a) sublittoral zone   **c)** supralittoral zone
    b) littoral zone   **d)** bathyal zone
3. In which zone of the open ocean does most photosynthesis occur?
    a) photic zone   **c)** bathypelagic zone
    b) mesopelagic zone   **d)** abyssopelagic zone
4. In which of the following zones are mud flats found?
    a) supralittoral   **b)** intertidal   **c)** sublittoral   **d)** land
5. The place where fresh water mixes with salt water is called a(n)
    a) salt marsh   **b)** tidal flat   **c)** estuary   **d)** mud flat

Using Your Knowledge

1. What is the basic difference between a marine ecosystem and a freshwater ecosystem?
2. Why is it important that we manage our ocean resources wisely?
3. What are the disadvantages of sucking up manganese nodules off the ocean floor?
4. List two differences and two similarities between sandy and rocky shores.
5. a) What effect would a decrease of 15 cm in the present average world ocean level have on the various shore ecosystems? What human activities would also be affected?
   b) Repeat part (a) for a 15 cm increase.
6. Explain why salt water cannot be used directly for irrigation purposes.

Investigations

1. Choose one valuable resource from the ocean. Research its importance, abundance, and possible exploitation as a resource. Write a 200 word paper on your findings.
2. Research modern fishing methods in the open ocean. How are fish located? How are they caught? Write a 200 word paper on your findings.
3. "Farming the sea" is a term used to refer to attempts to raise fish in large quantities in bays, beach ponds, and other marine environments. Find out about one such attempt. What was done? Did it work? Write a 150 word report on your findings.
4. The next time you go to the grocery store, visit the frozen fish section and the canned fish section. How many different products of the ocean are there? Which countries export fish to our country? Which fish are processed in our own country?
5. During World War II little fishing took place in the North Sea (between Britain and Norway). As a result, fish catches were exceptional after the war. This encouraged more fishing boats to operate in the North Sea. With their new fishing methods, these boats reduced the numbers of some species to dangerous levels. For example, about 250 000 t of herring were caught in 1948 but hardly any herring could be found by 1980. Many European countries fish for herring. Propose a solution to the herring shortage that will ensure a reasonable supply of herring for several countries. Your solution should also ensure that the basic stock remains constant.
6. Choose an estuary which is the site of a major city. Research its importance to the city. Write a brief paper (about 100 words) on your findings.

14 The Ecology of Marine Ecosystems: Basic Principles

The basic ecological concepts you studied earlier for freshwater ecosystems also apply to marine ecosystems. The only differences are the types of organisms involved and their environment. This chapter describes the basic principles of ecology as they apply to marine ecosystems. From your studies you will realize that all parts of a marine ecosystem are interrelated. Each marine organism is dependent upon other marine organisms and upon the environment in which it lives. Therefore, if one part of the ecosystem is changed in any way, all the other parts will also be changed.

14.1 Marine Habitat and Niche

Habitat

Life is found throughout the marine environment. It is as varied as the physical and chemical conditions that prevail. For this reason, each marine ecosystem offers a variety of habitats or "homes". These include the substrate (bottom material), water, and numerous living organisms. You will learn more about the habitats of specific marine organisms in Unit 5.

Depending on their habitat and swimming ability, marine organisms are classified into three categories: plankton nekton, and benthos (Fig. 14-1). Many animals can be planktonic at one stage of their lives and yet be nektonic or benthic at another stage.

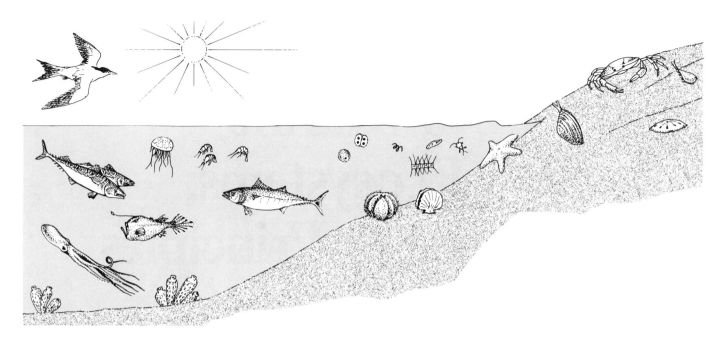

Fig. 14-1 Marine organisms are classified as plankton, nekton, and benthos. Can you name their habitats?

Plankton   These are organisms that drift or float with the currents. Some of these organisms can swim weakly and migrate vertically. The term plankton comes from the Greek word *planktos* meaning "to wander".

Plankton includes both plant-like and animal-like organisms. Drifting plant-like organisms such as diatoms and dinoflagellates are called phytoplankton. Drifting animal-like organisms are called zooplankton. These include small crustaceans, swimming molluscs, and jellyfish.

Nekton   These are larger animals which can control the direction and speed of their own movement. Among the nekton are adult squids, larger crustaceans, fishes, and marine mammals.

The term nekton implies complete freedom of movement. Nekton are found in all parts of the marine environment. However, some organisms are restricted to certain geographical locations and depths. As well, physical and chemical properties can limit their distribution. These include changes in temperature, salinity, oxygen, and nutrient supply.

Benthos   These are plants and animals that live on or in the sea bottom. For example, sponges, barnacles, corals, oysters, and sea anemones attach themselves to the bottom substrate. Clams and worms burrow into the substrate. Starfish, crabs, lobsters, and snails creep over the substrate.

Some benthos are the habitat for other marine life. For example, the small swimming crab *Lissocarcinus orbicularis* is often found living in the mouth, anus, or on the body of large species of sea cucumber. Coral reefs provide shelter for numerous marine organisms. Another interesting example is the hermit crab (Fig. 14-2).

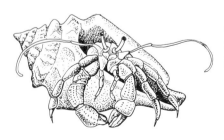

Fig. 14-2 The hermit crab lives in an abandoned snail shell.

As in freshwater ecosystems, habitats may overlap. However, as long as the animals do not occupy the same niche, no problems should result from this overlap of habitats.

Niche

The niche of an organism is its total role in the community (Fig. 14-3). For example, the niche of a clam is to feed on plankton, to become food for starfish, crabs and some fish, to return nutrients to the ecosystem, and so on.

If two species have the same habitat and similar niches, they will compete with one another. For example, song sparrows and clapper rails often live in the same salt marsh. That is, they have the same habitat. Both species feed on small crustaceans. Both are preyed upon by the short-eared owl and attacked by many of the same parasites. That is, they have similar niches. Clearly they will compete for available space and food in the salt marsh. How do you suppose this competition is resolved so that both species of bird can still live in the same marsh?

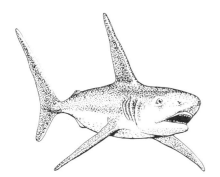

Fig. 14-3 What is the habitat and niche of this marine organism?

Section Review

1. Distinguish between habitat and niche.
2. **a)** Name the three major habitats of marine life.
   b) Give one example of marine life found in each type of habitat.
3. **a)** Distinguish among plankton, nekton, and benthos.
   b) Distinguish between phytoplankton and zooplankton.
4. What happens if two species have similar niches in the same habitat?

14.2   Feeding Relationships

Trophic Levels, Food Chains, and Food Webs

All ecosystems have trophic (feeding) levels called producers, consumers, and decomposers. Together they interact to form food chains and food webs (Fig. 14-4). These terms are explained in Chapter 2. Read that material if you do not know the meanings of these terms.

As you might expect, the species dominating each trophic level vary according to the marine ecosystem. In the open ocean, for example, the dominant producers are diatoms and dinoflagellates. The herbivores that feed on these producers are mainly copepods and other small crustaceans (Fig. 14-5). Herring, other small fish, squid, and many other animals feed on the crustaceans. These are examples of carnivores. Then tuna and other larger fish feed on the smaller fish. If you eat a tuna sandwich, you get some of the sun's energy that was passed along this food chain. Decomposers break down non-living organic matter and return valuable nutrients to the ecosystem.

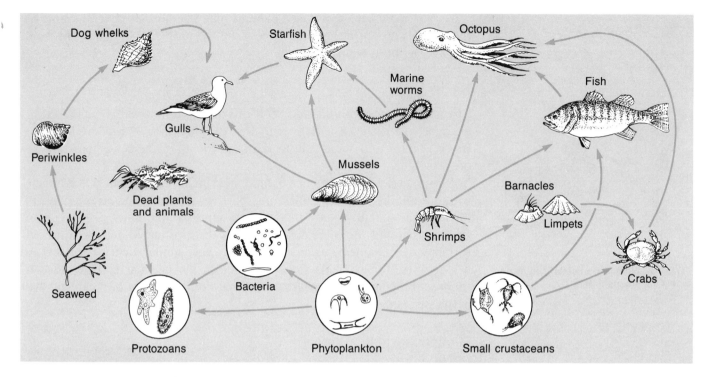

Fig. 14-4 A food web on a rocky
seashore.

Ecological Pyramids

Before continuing, review the concepts of pyramids of numbers, biomass,
and energy in Chapter 2.

Pyramid of Numbers The concepts of ecological pyramids also apply to
marine ecosystems. Marine food chains tend to proceed from very small
organisms to progressively larger ones. Also, as the size of the organisms
increases, the number of individuals involved in the food chain decreases. As
shown in Figure 14-6, such numerical relationships can be represented by a
pyramid of numbers.

Pyramid of Biomass In general, the biomass decreases as we move along
the food chain. This decrease is often represented by a pyramid of biomass
(Fig. 14-7).

Pyramid of Energy The efficiency with which energy is passed along a food
chain is more important than either the numbers of organisms or their
biomasses. As Figure 14-8 shows, the amount of energy remaining at each
trophic level decreases rapidly along a food chain. You will see why in
Section 14.3.

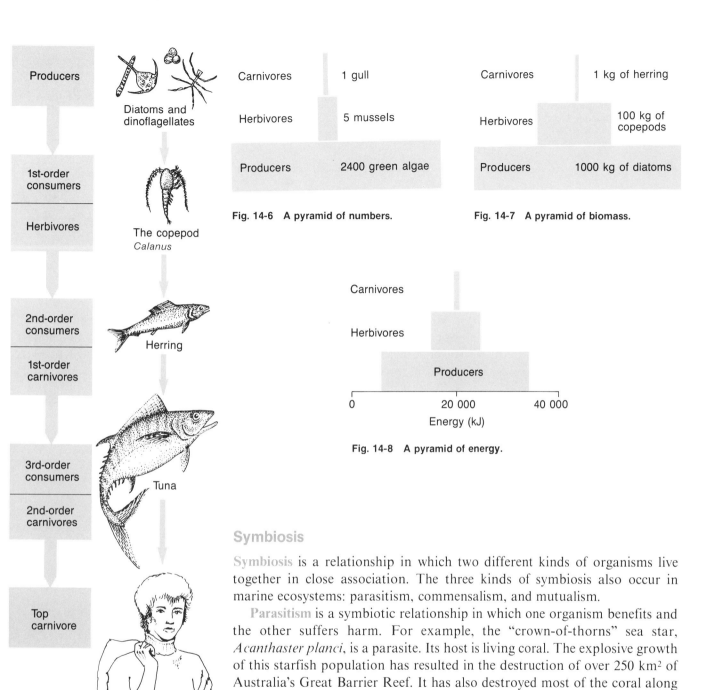

Producers	Diatoms and dinoflagellates
1st-order consumers	
Herbivores	The copepod *Calanus*
2nd-order consumers	Herring
1st-order carnivores	
3rd-order consumers	Tuna
2nd-order carnivores	
Top carnivore	Humans

Fig. 14-5   A typical food chain of the open ocean.

Carnivores	1 gull
Herbivores	5 mussels
Producers	2400 green algae

Fig. 14-6   A pyramid of numbers.

Carnivores	1 kg of herring
Herbivores	100 kg of copepods
Producers	1000 kg of diatoms

Fig. 14-7   A pyramid of biomass.

Carnivores

Herbivores

Producers

0   20 000   40 000

Energy (kJ)

Fig. 14-8   A pyramid of energy.

Symbiosis

Symbiosis is a relationship in which two different kinds of organisms live together in close association. The three kinds of symbiosis also occur in marine ecosystems: parasitism, commensalism, and mutualism.

Parasitism is a symbiotic relationship in which one organism benefits and the other suffers harm. For example, the "crown-of-thorns" sea star, *Acanthaster planci*, is a parasite. Its host is living coral. The explosive growth of this starfish population has resulted in the destruction of over 250 km² of Australia's Great Barrier Reef. It has also destroyed most of the coral along a 40 km stretch of the coast of Guam.

Commensalism is a symbiotic relationship in which one organism benefits and the other neither benefits nor suffers harm. Barnacles and whales have a commensal relationship. In the open sea, certain barnacles live on the jawbones of whales. The barnacles benefit by having a safe place of attachment and a steady food supply. Yet the whale receives neither harm nor benefit from this relationship (Fig. 14-9).

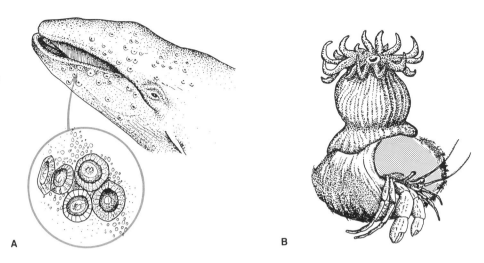

Fig. 14-9 A commensal relationship exists between the barnacles and the whale. (A)

Fig. 14-10 Mutualism. Both the hermit crab and sea anemone benefit from this relationship. (B)

A   B

Mutualism is a symbiotic relationship in which both organisms benefit. For example, hermit crabs often share their shell homes with sea anemones. The crab benefits by the sea anemone protecting it with its stinging tentacles. In return, the sea anemone profits by picking up bits of the crab's meal (Fig. 14-10).

Section Review

1. Complete the following food chains:
   a) In an open ocean: diatoms ⟶ krill
   b) In a salt marsh: grass ⟶ grasshopper
   c) In a rocky shore: seaweed ⟶ periwinkles
   d) In a coral reef: plankton ⟶ coral
2. Name and describe the three main trophic levels that occur in all ecosystems.
3. Define each of the following terms:
   a) pyramid of numbers
   b) pyramid of biomass
   c) pyramid of energy
4. What is symbiosis?
5. **a)** Distinguish among parasitism, mutualism, and commensalism.
   b) Give one example of each form of symbiosis.

14.3   Energy Flow and Nutrient Cycling

If you spent a few hours walking along coastal waters, you would likely be surprised by the constant activity around you. Fish are always searching for food. Crabs, lobsters, clams, and starfish crawl over the ocean bottom. Jellyfish and squid dart everywhere. Zooplankton drift with the current.

Total energy
production
by salt marsh
grasses

Energy to other
consumers,
decomposers,
etc.

Energy lost
through
respiration
of grasses

Energy used
by grasshopper

Energy to other
consumers,
decomposers,
etc.

Energy lost
through
respiration
of grasshopper

Energy used
by shrew

Energy to other
consumers,
decomposers,
etc.

Energy lost
through
respiration
of shrew

Fig. 14-11 Energy flow along a simple salt marsh food chain.

Activity is the essence of life. In order to have activity, energy and nutrients are required. Ecologists measure the functioning of an ecosystem by the rates of energy flow and nutrient cycling.

Energy Flow

The ultimate source of energy is the sun. Producers store some of the sun's energy in the foods they make by photosynthesis. They use some of this food for their own life processes. The rest is stored. Herbivores get their energy by eating producers and carnivores get their energy by eating herbivores or other carnivores.

As Figure 14-11 shows, the passing of energy along a food chain is not very efficient. A great deal is lost at each trophic level. Energy is lost through respiration. Energy is lost to other feeding levels. As well, some is lost through undigested remains.

The energy lost at each trophic level cannot be recaptured by any organisms in the food chain. It is lost forever to that ecosystem. Thus energy flow is one-way along a food chain. For an ecosystem to keep operating, energy must always enter it from the sun.

Nutrient Cycling

An ecosystem needs more than energy in order to function. It needs over 20 different elements. The main ones are carbon, hydrogen, oxygen, nitrogen, phosphorus, and sulfur. Ecologists call these elements nutrients.

Unlike energy, nutrients cycle continuously through an ecosystem. Producers pass the nutrients on to consumers. Then decomposers break down animal wastes and dead organisms. This releases nutrients so producers can use them again.

The water, carbon and nitrogen cycles in the marine ecosystem are basically the same as those in the freshwater ecosystems (see Section 2.5, page 34). More prominent in the marine carbon cycle are the aquatic animals which absorb carbon dioxide and convert it to insoluble calcium carbonate ($CaCO_3$). This is used to build their hard protective shells. When the animals die, the seashells accumulate as bottom sediments. Eventually, they may turn into sedimentary rocks such as limestone. After millions of years, these rocks may be lifted above sea level. When these rocks erode, carbon is released as carbonates and bicarbonate.

Availability of Nutrients The availability of nutrients varies within the marine ecosystem. Availability depends on the growth of plants and animals throughout the year. It is also controlled by ocean circulation. For example, nutrient reserves are limited in the upper surface water of the open ocean. Here nutrients are continuously lost to deeper waters through sinking of organic matter before its decomposition is complete. But some nutrients are returned to the surface by a process called upwelling (Fig. 14-12).

Fig. 14-12 Cycling of nutrients in the open ocean.

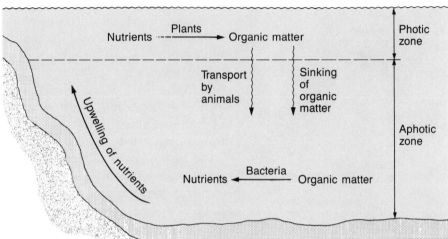

Coastal waters, on the other hand, tend to be richer in plant nutrients. Upwellings bring the nutrient-rich deep waters to the surface coastal waters. Turbulence and wave action stir up and circulate nutrients from coastal bottom sediments. Additional nutrients are leached from the land and washed into coastal areas by rivers and streams. Tidal and longshore currents (currents parallel to shore) then transport these nutrients along the coasts. Together these help to make the shallow coastal waters highly productive areas.

Section Review

1. Describe the path of energy from the sun to carnivores.
2. Describe how energy is lost along a food chain.
3. What is meant by "energy flow is one-way"?
4. Name six main nutrients.
5. How does nutrient flow differ from energy flow in an ecosystem?
6. Account for the differences in availability of nutrients in the marine ecosystem.

14.4

ACTIVITY

A Marine Aquarium for Your Classroom

A marine aquarium provides an exciting way to study the chemical and biological properties of a marine ecosystem. In this activity you will set up and maintain a marine aquarium. Certain basic requirements must be followed to ensure a high degree of success (Fig. 14-13). Those requirements are outlined here. In a later activity (Section 15.11) you will analyze the chemical and biological properties of the aquarium.

Problem

Can you set up and maintain a successful marine aquarium?

Fig. 14-13 A successful marine aquarium needs daily attention.

Materials

all-glass 90 L aquarium	thermometer-hydrometer
aquarium cover with fixture	10 kg of marine gravel
air pump and tubing	4.5 kg of marine salt mixture
undergravel filter	marine organisms
power filter	marine fish food
100 W heater	

Note: Complete marine aquarium kits and animals may be obtained from a biological supply house. Detailed instructions for aquarium set up and maintenance are included with these kits.

Procedure A   Setting Up the Aquarium

a. Obtain a 90 L aquarium. Be sure the aquarium is all glass. Metal ions are toxic to many marine organisms.

b. Place the aquarium in a location away from windows, radiators, air conditioners, and other places where light and temperature conditions change greatly during the day.

c. Wipe the aquarium tank and lid with a wet paper towel to remove any dust. Only use baking soda to clean the aquarium. Never use glass cleaners or detergents. These could contaminate the water.

d. Place the assembled underground filter in the bottom of the aquarium.

e. Completely cover the undergravel filter with clean marine gravel to an average depth of 2 to 3 cm.

f. Add about 80 L of tap water or deionized water to the aquarium (Fig. 14-14). Carefully add the 4.5 kg of synthetic salt mixture. Plug in the air pump and allow it to run for about 14 d before adding any animals.

Fig. 14-14 When adding water to the tank, break the fall of the water so that it doesn't stir up the bottom sediment.

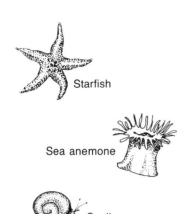

Starfish

Sea anemone

Snail

Sea urchin

Bannerfish

Fig. 14-15 Some common marine aquarium fish and invertebrates.

g. Using a hydrometer, check that the salt concentration produces a specific gravity of 1.025. A reading of 1.020 to 1.030 will be tolerated by most marine organisms. Add water or salt mixture as required to reach this level.

h. The temperature will depend on the type and origin of marine life. For example, most tropical marine organisms can live in a temperature range of 20°C to 27°C.

i. The exact number and types of marine fish and invertebrates in the aquarium will depend on several factors (Fig. 14-15). In general, allow 2-3 cm of fish or invertebrates for every 5 L of water. Also consider their niche and position in the food chain. Sea urchins, hermit crabs, spider crabs, and lobsters are very aggressive animals. These species should not be kept with marine fish or filter feeders.

j. Specific feeding instructions are included with each organism you purchase. Most fish and invertebrates prefer some type of animal food.

Procedure B   Maintenance of the Aquarium

a. Most marine animals are not adapted to tolerate sudden changes in temperature, pH, or salinity. To maintain a successful aquarium, check daily the temperature, salinity, pH (7.5 to 8.4), and filter system. Also observe the tank's general appearance and remove uneaten food after 24 h.

b. The water can be buffered with sodium bicarbonate (baking soda) or calcium carbonate to return it to a slightly basic solution. Crushed limestone rock, oyster shell, coral sand, and dolomite are commonly used as pH buffers.

c. Once a month draw off one-fourth of the aquarium's water and replace it with fresh artificial sea water. This will help to prevent any nitrogen products from building up to a toxic level.

Discussion

1. Why is it important that an all-glass aquarium be used?
2. Why is artificial sea water used rather than natural sea water?
3. State the trophic level of each species of organism in the aquarium ecosystem.
4. **a)** List any food chains that exist in your ecosystem.
   b) Construct a food web using the organisms within your ecosystem.
5. What nutrient cycles are taking place in your ecosystem? How do you know?
6. **a)** What is the pH range of marine waters?
   b) Name 3 substrates used to buffer aquarium water.
7. **a)** Is your aquarium a closed or open ecosystem?
   b) In what basic way does it differ from a natural ecosystem?

Main Ideas

1. The basic principles of ecology apply to both freshwater and marine ecosystems.
2. Marine organisms are classified as plankton, nekton, or benthos.
3. Ecosystems have three main feeding levels.
4. Parasitism, commensalism, and mutualism are close relationships between two different species of organism.
5. Energy flow in ecosystems is one-way. Energy is not recycled.
6. Nutrients are recycled in ecosystems.

Key Terms

benthos	herbivore	plankton
carnivore	mutualism	producer
commensalism	nekton	pyramid of biomass
consumer	niche	pyramid of energy
decomposer	nutrients	pyramid of numbers
food chain	parasitism	symbiosis
food web	phytoplankton	zooplankton
habitat		

Chapter Review

A. True or False

Decide whether each of the following statements is true or false. If the sentence is false, rewrite it to make it true. (Do not write in this book.)

1. Benthos are organisms that live on or in the sea bottom.
2. Energy is recycled in ecosystems.
3. Nutrients are recycled in ecosystems.
4. The habitat of an animal is the place where it lives.

B. Completion

Complete each of the following sentences with a word or phrase that will make the sentence correct. (Do not write in this book.)

1. Organisms that drift or float with the current are called ▨▨▨▨ .
2. The total role or "job" of an organism in the community is called its ▨▨▨▨ .
3. Diatoms are called ▨▨▨▨ because they produce their own food.
4. A symbiotic relationship in which one organism benefits and the other suffers harm is called ▨▨▨▨ .

C. Multiple Choice

Each of the following statements or questions is followed by four responses. Choose the correct response in each case. (Do not write in this book.)

1. Consider this food chain:

   salt marsh plants ⟶ grasshoppers ⟶ shrews ⟶ marsh hawks

   The shrews in this food chain are
   - **a)** second-order carnivores
   - **b)** first-order carnivores
   - **c)** top carnivores
   - **d)** third-order carnivores

2. Which of the following organisms is an example of a zooplankton?
   - **a)** octopi   **b)** dinoflagellates   **c)** oysters   **d)** copepods

3. Consider this food chain:

   diatoms ⟶ copepods ⟶ herring ⟶ tuna ⟶ humans

   At which level is energy most available?
   - **a)** producer
   - **b)** first-order consumer
   - **c)** second-order consumer
   - **d)** top carnivore

Using Your Knowledge

1. Complete the following food chains:
   - **a)** in an open ocean: diatoms ⟶ copepods ⟶
   - **b)** in a rocky shore: green algae ⟶ mussels ⟶
   - **c)** in a sandy shore: seaweed ⟶ sand hopper ⟶
2. Draw pyramids of numbers for these food chains:
   - **a)** plankton ⟶ shrimp ⟶ sting ray
   - **b)** dead fish ⟶ bacteria
3. Explain how ocean bottom nutrients are returned to the surface coastal and open ocean waters.
4. Explain why decomposers are important to all ecosystems.
5. What effect will overharvesting of krill have on the open ocean food web?

Investigations

1. Choose a particular marine ecosystem and find out what effect pollution has had on its feeding levels and food chains. Write a paper of about 250 words on the effects and possible solutions to this problem.
2. Choose three marine organisms. Write a short paper (about 150 words) describing the habitat and niche of each organism.
3. Construct a food web of the open ocean that includes at least one marine mammal. Be sure to identify the trophic level of each organism. List the sources from which you got your information.
4. Scientists are now discovering plants and algae in the deep-ocean bottom. Find out how plants and algae are able to grow at these depths with so little light available.

15 Marine Ecosystems: Abiotic Factors

The abiotic factors that operate in marine ecosystems can be divided into two groups, geophysical and chemical. Among the geophysical factors are waves, tides, and temperature. Among the chemical factors are salinity, oxygen, and carbon dioxide. Some of these abiotic factors are characteristic of only marine ecosystems. Many change from one type of marine ecosystem to the next. All of these factors interact with one another and with biological factors.

This chapter looks at the main geophysical and chemical factors that affect marine ecosystems. In Unit 5 you will learn how all these abiotic factors interact with biological or biotic factors.

15.1 Waves

What Are Waves?

One of the most prominent features of the ocean is waves. A **wave** is defined as a disturbance which moves through or over the surface of a fluid medium.

Any disturbance, such as a pebble dropped into the water or an underwater landslide, can generate a wave. Most waves in the ocean are caused by the wind. If you blow on the surface of still water, tiny ripples form. When you stop blowing, the ripples soon stop. But the wind on the ocean blows for a much longer time, and the ripples soon grow into waves.

A wave is also a form of energy. If you have ever been thrown up onto the beach by a wave, you have experienced its great energy (Fig. 15-1). Waves obtain their energy from such disturbances as the wind. Large waves often contain enough energy to continue travelling for many hundreds of kilometres across the ocean. This explains why you may see waves at the shore on a windless day.

Wind, earthquakes, and the gravitational attraction of the moon and sun are the three most important wave generators. Waves are also caused by undersea landslides, volcanoes, changes in atmospheric pressure, and the movement of ships.

Fig. 15-1 The ocean surface is rarely still. The waves continuously cross its surface carrying energy.

Characteristics of an Ocean Wave

Parts of a Wave A wave has two basic parts. The highest point of the wave is called the crest. The lowest part of the wave is called the trough (Fig. 15-2).

Fig. 15-2 Parts of a wave.

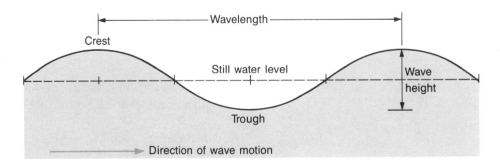

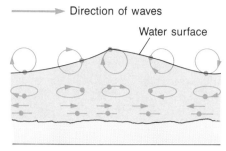

A. Shallow water

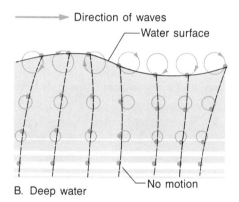

B. Deep water

Fig. 15-3 Movement of water particles caused by the passage of waves in shallow water (A) and deep water (B).

Any wave can be described by three characteristics: height, wavelength, and period. The **wave height** is the vertical distance from a crest to a trough. One crest and one trough form one **wavelength**. The time required for two wave crests or troughs to pass a fixed point is called the **wave period**.

Size of Waves The size of waves (their height and wavelength) depends on three factors: wind speed, length of time the wind blows, and the extent of open water across which the wind can blow. In an ocean, the waves are large. However, in a sheltered harbour, the same wind will create small waves. These waves will also be closer together. Generally, waves that are close together will not become very large.

Waves can range in size from ripples less than a centimetre high to giant waves more than 30 m high. About half the waves in the ocean are 2 m or less in height. Only about 10 to 15% of the ocean waves exceed 6 m in height. The sailors' rule of thumb says that the height of the wave in metres will usually be no more than one-tenth of the wind's speed in kilometres per hour. For example, a 40 km/h wind will usually not generate waves higher than 4 m.

Water Motion in Waves The actual movement of water particles is not as it appears to the casual observer. That is, water particles do not travel across the ocean with the wave motion. Instead, the water particles travel in vertical circular orbits (Fig. 15-3).

As the wave passes a given point, the water particles at the surface trace one complete circle. The diameter of the circle at the surface is equal to the height of the wave. At the crest of the wave, the water particles move in the direction of wave travel. The direction is reversed in the trough. The water particles return and advance only a few centimetres from their original position. This occurs because the water particles move slightly faster in wave crests than in wave troughs. Thus, the surface water remains in place. Only the crests and troughs move across the ocean.

You can see how this works by placing a cork or ping pong ball on the water's surface. As a wave approaches, the cork will move forward to the crest. Then it will move backward to the trough. The cork will have moved only a few centimetres from its starting point (Fig. 15-4).

You can also experience the opposed movement of the crest and trough of a wave the next time you are at the beach. Float in the ocean just beyond the breakers. As the waves pass, you will feel a gentle rocking motion.

As shown in Figure 15-3, water particles move differently in shallow and deep water. In shallow water, the circular motion of water particles becomes flattened as the waves reach to the bottom and move sediment. In deep water, the diameter of the orbits of the water particles decreases as the depth increases. At a depth of approximately one-half the wavelength, the diameter of the circular path is less than one-twentieth of that at the surface. Here, the motion of water is negligible. This explains why submarines can avoid stormy seas by diving beneath the surface.

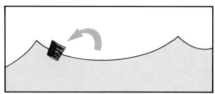
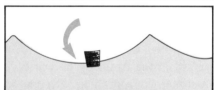

Fig. 15-4 The position of the cork shows how a wave travels. Water particles do not travel across the ocean with the wave.

Waves as Energy It is important to remember that waves transport energy, not water. Energy is passed on continuously from water particle to water particle within a given wave. But there is a continuous loss of energy downward from the water surface at which energy is received. In general, larger waves contain more energy than smaller waves.

Importance of Waves

Shaping of Coastlines Waves are an important force in shaping the coastlines. They erode cliffs. They grind rocks into fine sand. They also make and remake ocean beaches each year.

Ecology Waves are also important ecologically. Rock surfaces exposed directly to wave action are usually sparsely populated. Organisms that colonize these areas are usually adapted to withstand constant wave action. Many organisms have specific mechanisms for attachments. Others have reduced surface area. Extreme wave action may prevent some organisms from attaching to the substrate. It may even prevent others from feeding.

The splashing of water into tidal pools allows marine organisms to live there. The splashing also keeps the upper part of the intertidal area above the position of highest tide wet. This allows organisms such as barnacles and snails to live higher in the intertidal zone.

Wave action returns oxygen to surface water. It also mixes the sediments which contain organic matter. This mixing makes food available for filter feeders.

Section Review

1. **a)** What is a wave?
   b) What causes the majority of waves in the ocean?
   c) Explain why you can see waves on the shore on a windless day.
   d) List six other ways in which waves can be generated.
2. **a)** Draw a wave and label the following parts: crest, trough, wavelength, wave height.
   b) List the three characteristics by which any wave may be described.
   c) Explain each of these characteristics.
3. List the three factors that determine the size of waves.
4. Describe the movement of water particles in shallow and deep water. A diagram may be useful.
5. Discuss the importance of waves under the following headings:
   a) erosion of coastlines
   b) ecology

15.2 *ACTIVITY* A Study of Wave Motion

In Section 15.1 you learned that water particles do not travel across the ocean with the wave motion. Instead, energy is carried in the waves. In this activity you will demonstrate this fact by generating waves in a rope.

Problem

Do the particles in the wave move in the direction of the wave?

Materials

rope 2 m long

Fig. 15-5   Generating waves in a rope.

Procedure

a. Tie a knot in the middle of the rope.
b. Tie one end of the rope to a doorknob.
c. Extend the rope to its full length.
d. Using the free end, move the rope in an up and down motion (Fig. 15-5).
e. Observe and record the motion of the rope and the knot.
f. Vary the size of the waves. Which size of wave requires the most energy?

Discussion

1. Describe the motion of the rope.
2. What is required in order to generate waves?
3. a) Describe the motion of the knot.
   b) How does the motion of the knot compare to the motion of the water particles in an ocean wave?
4. What size of wave requires the most energy?

15.3 Currents

What Are Currents?

Currents are another characteristic feature of oceans. These great wide "rivers" of water circle slowly between the continents. They cross all the world's oceans (Fig. 15-6). They occur at both the surface and ocean bottom. The Gulf Stream in the North Atlantic is perhaps the best known of the surface currents. Currents are caused by three main forces. These are wind, rotation of the earth, and changes in the density of the water.

Fig. 15-6   Major surface currents of the oceans.

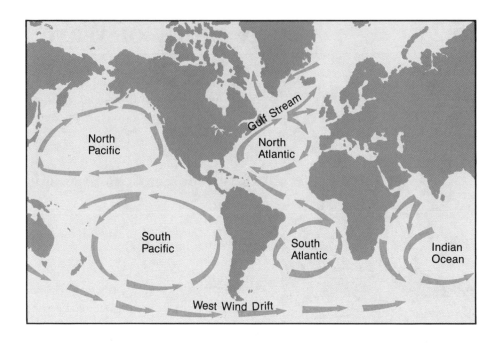

Surface-ocean Currents

Surface-ocean currents are broad, slow drifts of surface water. They move in large, almost circular paths north and south of the equator.

Wind-generated   These currents are set in motion by the prevailing surface winds. Thus the patterns displayed by surface currents reflect the prevailing wind patterns of the globe (Fig. 15-7). For example, the warm steady Trade Winds from the east blow the ocean waters on either side of the equator westward. In contrast, the cold Westerlies blow from west to east. Thus the ocean waters between latitudes of 30° and 60° move eastward. As the currents approach a continent, they swing around in a circular motion.

Fig. 15-7   Major wind patterns of the earth.

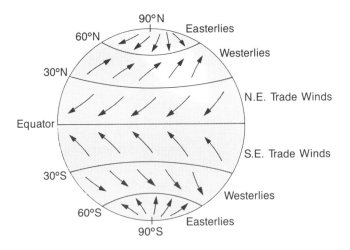

Coriolis Effect   In the Northern Hemisphere, currents flow clockwise. In the Southern Hemisphere, currents flow counterclockwise. This is called the Coriolis Effect. It is caused by the earth's rotation to the east. The Coriolis Effect is zero at the equator. It is at a maximum at the poles. Therefore, the Coriolis Effect has a direct influence on the currents of the ocean.

West Wind Drift   There is another major difference between circulations north and south of the equator. Below the tip of South America, the water flows freely from one ocean to another. The West Wind Drift makes possible a major globe-circling movement of water.

Longshore Currents   Longshore currents flow parallel to the shore. They are located within the surf zone (Fig. 15-8). These currents move fine suspended sand along the shoreline.

Fig. 15-8   Longshore currents move sand along the shoreline.

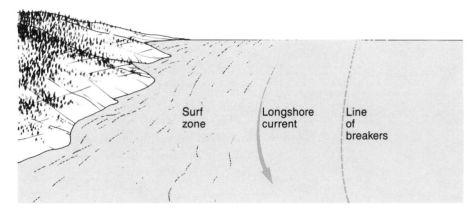

Deep-ocean Currents

Deep-ocean currents flow deep beneath the ocean surface. They generally move north-south. Unlike surface currents, they cross the equator. They circulate at much slower rates. However, they are equally powerful. Unfortunately, they are rather difficult to study. Therefore they are not as well-known as the surface currents.

Density-generated   Deep-ocean currents are caused by density differences within the water. These differences arise from varying water temperature and salinity. Hence circulation based on these factors is called thermohaline (thermo- means "heat" and -haline means "salt").
   Water becomes more dense with increased salinity, or decreased temperature, or both. In the polar regions, the dense cold water sinks. It flows slowly

along the ocean bottom to the equator. This may take between 300-1500 years. As it flows, it displaces the bottom water already there upward. The cold polar water gradually is warmed. As it becomes less dense, it too will be displaced upward to the surface. Thus deep-ocean currents move both vertically and horizontally. Surface currents only move horizontally.

Importance of Currents

Climate   In many parts of the world, ocean currents influence the climate. Currents flowing away from the equator carry warm tropical water to higher latitudes. Currents flowing toward the equator carry cold water from higher to lower latitudes. Precipitation and temperature may both be affected.

Ecology   Ocean currents are of great importance to the life of the ocean. Currents transport food and oxygen to marine organisms. They also remove waste products. As well, they transport floating organisms and their larvas. Currents help determine water temperature. This in turn controls the distribution of marine organisms.

In regions where the prevailing winds blow offshore (from land to ocean), surface waters move away from the continents. This water is replaced by colder, deeper water from as much as 300 m down. Such movements are called upwelling. It is common along the west coast of Mexico. It also occurs along the coasts of Peru and Chile.

The deep water is rich in nutrients. Upon reaching the surface, it causes increased phytoplankton growth. Some of the world's most important fisheries are found in areas of upwelling. Thus areas of upwelling have high biological productivity.

Section Review

1. **a)** What are currents?
    b) Where do currents occur?
2. **a)** What is a surface current?
    b) What causes surface currents?
    c) In which direction do surface currents flow in the Northern and Southern Hemisphere?
    d) Account for these differences in direction of flow.
3. What are longshore currents?
4. **a)** State four differences between surface and deep-ocean currents.
    b) What causes deep-ocean currents?
5. Discuss the importance of currents under the following headings:
    a) Climate
    b) Ecology
6. **a)** Define the term upwelling.
    b) How does upwelling benefit the ocean ecosystem?

15.4   Tides

A

B

Fig. 15-9   High tide (A) and low tide (B) in a Baffin Island fiord.

What Are Tides?

If you have ever spent a few hours at the ocean beach, you would have observed the slow change in water level. The rhythmic rise and fall of the ocean's water is called the tide. The rising or incoming tide is called the high tide. The receding or outgoing tide is called the low tide (Fig. 15-9).

Tides are very long slow waves. They have a period of more than 12 h. Their wavelength is almost 22 000 km. Their wave height ranges from a few centimetres to more than 15 m. Tides occur once or twice daily in all water bodies, fresh and marine. However, they are most prominent in marine waters. Why is this so?

What Causes Tides?

Tides are caused by interactions between gravity and centrifugal forces. The sun and moon exert gravitational pulls on the ocean waters. Their pull acts like enormous magnets. It draws the ocean waters slightly away from the earth's surface. Because the moon is closer to the earth than is the sun, it exerts a greater gravitational force. The moon's gravitational attraction is greatest on the side of the earth nearest the moon. It is least on the opposite side of the earth.

The forces of gravity, however, are opposed by centrifugal forces. Centrifugal forces are produced by the motions of the earth, moon, and sun. Such forces are equal on the earth's surface. On the side nearest the moon, the attraction of the moon exceeds the centrifugal force. This causes the water to be pulled towards the moon. A tidal bulge results. On the opposite side of the earth, the centrifugal force exceeds the moon's attraction. A tidal bulge is produced here too. This bulge on the side facing the moon is called the direct tide. The bulge on the other side is called the opposite tide. These two tidal bulges follow the moon as it moves around the earth. They represent the high tides. The low areas between the bulges are the low tides.

Types of Tides

The position of the moon and sun in relation to the earth has a great effect on the tidal range. The tidal range is the height of the bulge. This is equivalent to the vertical distance between high and low tides.

Spring and Neap Tides   When the moon and sun are in direct line with the earth, their pulls are added together. This results in an unusually high tidal range. These tides are called spring tides (Fig. 15-10A). They do not occur with the season as the name might suggest. Instead, they take place twice each month, a few days after the full and new moons (Fig. 15-11).

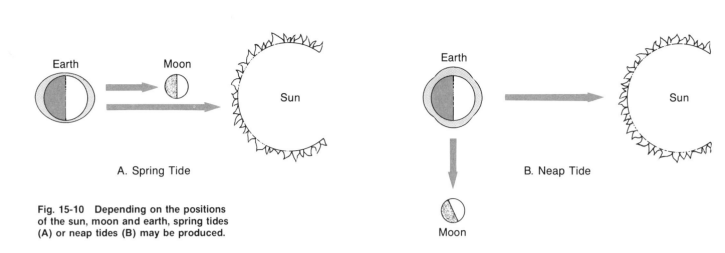

A. Spring Tide

B. Neap Tide

Fig. 15-10 Depending on the positions of the sun, moon and earth, spring tides (A) or neap tides (B) may be produced.

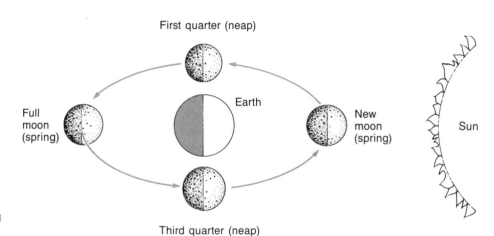

Fig. 15-11 Sun and moon pull with and against each other at the four phases of the moon. This results in two spring and two neap tides in each lunar month.

In the first and last quarter phases of the moon, the sun and moon are at right angles to each other. Consequently, their pulls partly cancel each other. At this time, the pull on the ocean waters is weakest. This results in an unusually low tidal range. These tides are called neap tides (Fig. 15-10B). They occur approximately one week after spring tides.

Perigee and Apogee Tides   The distance between the moon and earth also affects the tidal range. When the moon is closest to the earth, it produces exceptionally high tides. These are called perigee tides. During perigee spring tides, coastal areas may experience flooding. When the moon is farthest from the earth, exceptionally low tides are produced. These are called apogee tides.

Diurnal, Semidiurnal, and Mixed Tides   A few ocean areas have one high and one low tide each day. These once daily tides are called diurnal tides.

They occur along parts of the Gulf of Mexico and Southeast Asia. They have a tidal period of 24 h and 50 min. Tidal period is the time between high (or low) tides. The moon passes over any given location on earth approximately every 24 h and 50 min.

On the Atlantic coasts of North America and Europe, there are two high and two low tides each day. These twice daily tides are called semidiurnal tides. The successive high water and low water levels are about equal. Their tidal period is 12 h and 25 min.

Along the Pacific coast of North America, mixed tides occur. These tides occur twice daily. However, the height of the two high tides varies. The low tides also vary in height.

Tidal Range

The tidal range varies in different parts of the world. In the open ocean, the height of the tide is about 1 m. Nearer land, the tidal range may vary from a few centimetres to more than 15 m. The tidal range depends on local conditions. These include coastal configurations, distribution of land, latitude, wind, currents, and the nature of the ocean bottom.

For example, the tidal range in the Gulf of Mexico is only a few centimetres. The Gulf is very large and has a gently sloping bottom. Thus the incoming water can easily spread out over a large area. The water in the Bay of Fundy, however, can rise over 15 m. This is the greatest tidal range known. This bay is located between New Brunswick and Nova Scotia. It consists of a very narrow channel between high steep walls. Thus the incoming water has no room to spread out. Instead, the water rapidly accumulates.

Tidal Currents

The rise and fall of tides often produces very strong currents. These are called tidal currents. Tidal currents flowing shoreward are called flood currents. Seaward currents are called ebb currents. When the currents change direction, there is a period of little or no current. This is called slack water.

Importance of Tides

Industry   Tides are important to seaports. They determine when large ships can enter or leave the harbour. Tides also affect ocean fishing. On high tide, fish swim inshore into the bays. Here they find an abundance of food churned up by the tide. Fishermen often have their best catch about one hour before to one hour after full tide.

Tidal Power   Tides can be a source of energy. To tap this energy, water is trapped behind a dam at high tide and released at low tide. As the water flows through the dam, it turns turbines to generate electricity.

Ecology   A distinct community of living things lives in the intertidal zone. Tides provide circulation of food, nutrient elements, dissolved gases, and waste materials for these organisms. During low tide, many organisms are exposed to hot sunlight, rain, wind, and predation. These organisms must be adapted to the harsh conditions that accompany the changes in water levels. You can read about such adaptations in Unit 5.

Section Review

1. **a)** Define the term tide.
    b) State the period, wavelength, and height range of tides.
2. **a)** Summarize the causes of tides.
    b) What is a tidal bulge?
3. Distinguish between the following types of tides:
    a) spring and neap tides
    b) perigee and opogee tides
    c) diurnal, semidiurnal, and mixed tides
4. Define the term tidal period.
5. **a)** Define the term tidal range.
    b) List six factors which affect tidal range.
    c) Where does the greatest tidal range known occur?
6. **a)** What are tidal currents?
    b) Distinguish between flood currents and ebb currents.
7. Discuss the importance of tides under the following headings:
    a) industry
    b) tidal power
    c) ecology

15.5   Temperature

Temperature Distribution

Surface Temperature   The surface temperature of ocean water ranges from above 27°C in the tropics to about -3°C in the polar regions. Temperatures as high as 36°C have been recorded in the shallow coastal waters in the Persian Gulf. Surface temperatures generally decrease with increasing latitude.

Unlike fresh water, sea water has no definite freezing point. However, for any given salinity, there is a temperature at which ice crystals form. The more salt there is, the lower the freezing point.

Daily and seasonal temperature variations rarely exceed 7°C. These variations are caused by wind, currents, and climatic conditions.

Deep-water Temperature   The ocean temperature decreases from the surface to the bottom (Fig. 15-12). In the upper 50 to 200 m, the water is as

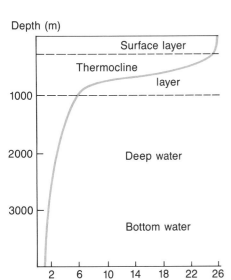

Depth (m)

Surface layer

Thermocline layer

Deep water

Bottom water

Temperature (°C)

Fig. 15-12 The temperature-depth profile for an ocean.

warm as at the surface. From there to depths of 500 to 1000 m, the temperature drops rapidly to about 5 or 6°C. This region of rapid temperature change is called the thermocline. Below this, the temperature gradually drops about another 4°C. At the ocean bottom, there is little temperature variation with latitude. It is always near 0°C.

Importance

Distribution of Organisms Temperature is one of the most important abiotic factors affecting the distribution of marine organisms. Some organisms can tolerate only a narrow range of temperatures. For example, reef-building species of coral are restricted to a temperature range of 18 to 20°C. Other organisms can live in a wide range of temperatures.

Areas of extremely cold water such as the polar regions, have low species diversity but high population numbers. Organisms that live in cold water generally grow larger. As well, they develop much more slowly than those in warm water. Fish tend to have more vertebrae, bony plates, and spines. They also have a smaller head. Fish in cold water reach sexual maturity later than members of the same species in warmer waters. In fact, this delay in reaching maturity may explain why these fish grow larger than those in warmer climates. More food reserves can be used for growth.

Warm waters are characterized by high species diversity and low population numbers. Organisms living in these waters tend to be smaller and have a shorter life span than those in cold water. This may be due, in part, to a reduced level of dissolved oxygen in warm water.

Survival A sudden change in water temperature can be lethal. Most species spawn within a narrow temperature range. Others reach sexual maturity at a certain temperature. At the poles, the minimum winter temperature will determine survival. The maximum summer temperature will control breeding. At the equator, the maximum summer temperature will determine survival and the winter minimum will control breeding.

Section Review

1. **a)** What is the temperature range at the ocean surface?
    b) Name three factors which cause daily and seasonal temperature changes at the ocean surface.
2. **a)** Summarize the temperature change from the surface to the bottom of the ocean.
    b) What is the thermocline region?
3. How do organisms in cold and warm ocean water differ according to the following:
    a) species diversity   **c)** size
    b) number of individuals of each species   **d)** life span

4. Account for the difference in size between fish living in cold and warm ocean water.
5. What effect will a sudden change in water temperature have on organisms living in the ocean?

15.6   Light Intensity

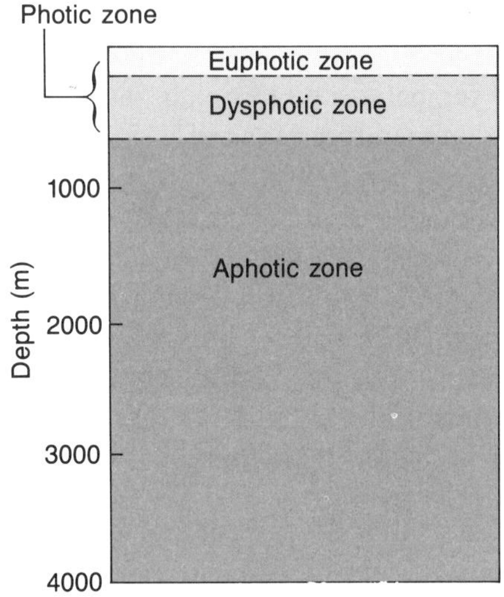

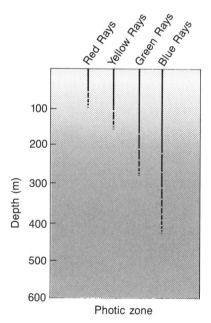

Fig. 15-13   **Light only penetrates the photic zone.**

The ocean can be divided vertically into zones based on the penetration of sunlight (Fig. 15-13). In the upper 100 m or so, light is generally sufficient for plant and algal growth. This surface zone is called the euphotic zone. Below this, the fading or dysphotic zone seldom extends deeper than 600 m. In this zone, light may penetrate dimly under ideal conditions. Together, these zones are called the photic zone. Below this is the aphotic zone. Here, for all practical purposes, no light penetrates. It is always pitch-black.

Approximately 65% of the incoming sunlight is absorbed in the first metre of water. About 80% is absorbed in the first 10 m of water. Even in particle-free water, less than 0.01% of the incoming sunlight remains as visible light at 200 m.

The rays making up light are absorbed and scattered at different rates in water (Fig. 15-14). The red and yellow rays are absorbed near the surface. The green and blue rays penetrate to greater depths.

Controlling Factors

The depth to which light penetrates in ocean water depends on several factors:
- elevation of the sun
- roughness of the water surface
- transparency of the water
- cloud cover
- ice cover

Maximum light penetration occurs when the sun is directly overhead. Only 2% of the incoming light is reflected. The other 98% enters the water. In the polar regions, where the sun is never very high, light strikes the surface at an angle. Thus a large percentage of light is reflected.

In rough waters as much as 60% of the sunlight is stopped or reflected in the upper few metres. Suspended and dissolved solids also limit the depth of light penetration. Coastal waters generally contain an abundance of floating marine organisms. They also contain lots of suspended sediment particles and dissolved substances. Thus the photic zone is shallower here than in the open ocean.

The transparency of ocean water can be measured with a Secchi disc. On clear bright days in the open ocean, the compensation depth may be approximately 85 m. (See Section 4.1, page 66 for the meaning of compensation

Fig. 15-14   **Light rays penetrate the photic zone to different depths.**

depth.) In more turbid ocean waters, the compensation depth is commonly between 25 and 85 m. In turbid coastal waters, it may be between 5 and 25 m. Polluted waters may have a Secchi disc reading as low as 25 cm.

Importance

Light intensity is one of the most important ecological factors in the ocean. Some reasons follow.

Photosynthesis   Light is required by plants and algae for photosynthesis. Photosynthesis only occurs in the euphotic zone. In the aphotic zone, all life depends on the supply of food from higher zones.

In the Arctic, photosynthesis only occurs for 3 months. In the tropics, light is adequate for photosynthesis to take place throughout the year.

Vision   Light enables many marine organisms to search for food and shelter. In some cases, it also helps them to spot predators.

Many organisms which live below the photic zone produce their own light. These are called luminiferous organisms. Among them are some dinoflagellates, jellyfish, shrimps, squids, and fishes. By emitting their own light, organisms can attract prey. They can also frighten enemies. As well, they can identify each other.

Distribution   Light controls the distribution of most marine organisms. Many green algae use the red rays for photosynthesis. Thus they exist in the upper portions of the intertidal zone. Brown and red algae often use the green and blue rays for photosynthesis. They occur in the lower portions of the intertidal zone.

Most zooplankton migrate vertically each day. This migration occurs in response to the changing light intensity. At sunset zooplankton rise toward the surface to feed on phytoplankton, and at dawn they swim or sink downward. How far up or down they move depends on the species and season. The ocean ecosystem receives several advantages from this behaviour. The dark provides safety for zooplankton from predators. Also, less energy is required by the zooplankton when they are resting in the cooler water. The zooplankton provide a source of food for those animals which remain below the photic zone.

Section Review

1. Draw a cross section of the ocean. Label the following zones of light intensity: euphotic zone, dysphotic zone, photic zone, aphotic zone.
2. **a)** What percent of incoming sunlight is absorbed in the first metre of water?
    b) What percent of incoming sunlight is absorbed in the first 10 m of water?

3. **a)** Which rays of light are absorbed near the surface?
   b) Which rays of light penetrate to greater depths?
4. Name five factors which determine the depth to which light can penetrate the ocean water.
5. In which area of the ocean does light generally penetrate the least? Explain why.
6. List three reasons why light intensity is considered one of the most important ecological factors in the ocean.
7. In which zone of the ocean does photosynthesis take place?
8. **a)** What are luminiferous organisms?
   b) Name three marine organisms which are luminiferous.
   c) State three advantages of being a luminiferous organism.
9. How does light intensity control the distribution of marine organisms.

15.7 Salinity

If you have ever swallowed a mouthful of sea water, you would have immediately noticed its salty taste. This salt content is the single most noticeable characteristic of sea water. Sodium chloride, or common salt, gives sea water its salty taste. For this reason, sea water is also called salt water.

What Is Salinity?

Sea water contains about 3.5% minerals. Expressed in micrograms per gram, the concentration of minerals in sea water is about 35 000 $\mu g/g$. The minerals in sea water are mainly salts. As a result, the concentration of minerals in sea water is usually called the salinity of the water. Thus the salinity of sea water is about 3.5% or 35 000 $\mu g/g$. Salinity is usually expressed as parts per thousand ($^0/_{00}$) and not as a percentage. Therefore sea water has a salinity of about 35 $^0/_{00}$. In other words, in every kilogram of sea water, there is about 35 g of dissolved salts (Fig. 15-15). The most abundant salt in sea water is sodium chloride, or common salt. Most sea water is about 2.7% common salt.

Fig. 15-15 Each kilogram of sea water contains about 35 g of dissolved salts.

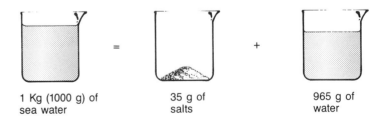

1 Kg (1000 g) of sea water = 35 g of salts + 965 g of water

Sea water contains enough salt to make it undrinkable. Nor can it be used to irrigate crops. Sea water destroys most metals in a short time if they are unprotected from it. There is enough salt in sea water that if it were precipitated, it would form a 56 m thick layer of solid salts over the entire sea floor.

Composition of Sea Salt

Sea water contains more than 70 elements. However, the ions of only six elements make up over 99% of the sea salts (Table 15-1). Sodium ions and chloride ions alone make up about 86% of sea salt.

About 78% of the sea's salt consists of sodium chloride (Table 15-2). There is also significant amounts of magnesium chloride, magnesium sulfate, calcium sulfate, sodium bromide, potassium sulfate, and calcium carbonate. Many other salts are also present but in very small amounts.

You can easily precipitate salts from water. All you have to do is fill a pan with salt water. Let it sit until it evaporates. You will be left with a gritty, bitter-tasting salt precipitate on the bottom of the pan.

Table 15-1   The Major Dissolved Substances in Sea Water

Ion	Percentage of Total Dissolved Solids
Chloride (Cl^{1-})	55.1
Sodium (Na^{1+})	30.6
Sulfate (SO_4^{2-})	7.7
Magnesium (Mg^{2+})	3.7
Calcium (Ca^{2+})	1.2
Potassium (K^{1+})	1.1
All others	0.6

Table 15-2   The Relative Amounts of Salts Precipitated by Evaporation of Sea Water

Salt	Percentage	Salt	Percentage
Sodium chloride (NaCl)	77.2	Sodium bromide (NaBr)	1.4
Magnesium chloride ($MgCl_2$)	8.6	Potassium chloride (KCl)	1.4
Magnesium sulfate ($MgSO_4$)	6.4	Calcium carbonate ($CaCO_3$)	0.3
Calcium sulfate ($CaSO_4 \bullet H_2O$)	4.6	Other	0.1

Constancy of Composition   The relative amounts of dissolved salts do not change significantly in the open ocean. That is, the amount of any of the major ions compared to another remains constant. This is due to the continuous mixing of all parts of the oceans. Thus each dissolved salt is found in about the same proportion everywhere in all oceans. However, the total concentration of salts may vary somewhat. This is a result of changes in the amount of water.

Sources   Each year rivers and streams carry several billion tonnes of new salts to the oceans. Salts are dissolved from rocks and soils as the water runs over them. Decaying marine organisms return dissolved nutrients to the oceans. Salts can enter the water from fertilizer runoff, sewage, and underwater volcanoes.

Factors Affecting Salinity

The salinity of a marine ecosystem varies from time to time and from place to place. Several factors determine the degree of salinity at any one time or place. Figure 15-16 shows those factors—evaporation, precipitation, freezing of ice, melting of ice, temperature, location, tidal cycle and stream and local runoff.

Fig. 15-16   Factors affecting salinity.

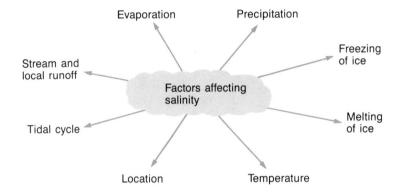

Oceans   In the open ocean, surface salinity ranges from about 32 $^0/_{00}$ to 38 $^0/_{00}$. It is lowest at the poles. This is due to dilution from rain, snow, and melting ice. Salinity is highest in the tropics where evaporation is greatest. Below a zone of a few hundred metres, salinity is constant in oceans. Here it usually ranges from about 34 $^0/_{00}$ to 35 $^0/_{00}$.

The Red Sea has the highest salinity of any open sea area. It is over 45 $^0/_{00}$. This is caused by high evaporation and little inflow of fresh water. Sea water with an abnormally high salinity (greater than 47 $^0/_{00}$) is called **hypersaline** water. Hypersaline conditions often occur in landlocked seas such as Great Salt Lake in Utah. They also exist in warm, shallow lagoons such as those found along the edges of the Gulf of Mexico. On a smaller scale, hypersaline conditions occur in tidal pools in the upper part of the littoral zone. Why is this so? The Baltic Sea has the lowest salinity. It is less than 10 $^0/_{00}$ in many places. It receives a large inflow of fresh water, and does not have open circulation with marine waters. As a result, the salts are greatly diluted. Sea water with an abnormally low salinity (less than 17 $^0/_{00}$) is called **brackish** water.

Tidal Pools   The salinity of nearshore waters can also range from very high to very low. For example, the salinity of a tidal pool may be only 5 $^0/_{00}$ after a rainfall. Yet it may be close to 35 $^0/_{00}$ after the tidal pool has been flushed with sea water by the tides. Also, the salinity of the surface water in a tidal pool is usually higher than the salinity of the water in the bottom. Evaporation of water by the sun concentrates the salts near the surface.

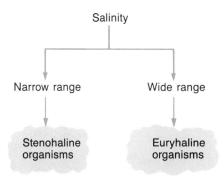

Salinity

Narrow range   Wide range

Stenohaline   Euryhaline
organisms   organisms

Fig. 15-17   How marine organisms are classified according to salinity.

Salinity and Marine Life

Salinity Barriers   Salinity is almost uniform in the open ocean. As a result, most marine organisms are adapted to living in water of constant salinity. They can tolerate only slight changes in salinity. Such organisms are called stenohaline (Fig. 15-17). Stenohaline organisms may also be adapted to low salinity (brackish) or high salinity (hypersaline) conditions.

In contrast, marine organisms living in waters of wide-ranging salinity must be able to tolerate such conditions. Such organisms are called euryhaline. They usually live in shallow isolated areas of coastal waters where runoff and evaporation can cause dramatic changes in salinity. What advantage might euryhaline organisms have over stenohaline organisms?

Response to Changing Salinity   The body and cell fluids of most marine invertebrates have a salt concentration that is the same as sea water. However, bony fish, crabs, and some worms maintain their salt concentration at a level higher or lower than that of sea water. When these organisms are placed in water with a salinity different from that of their internal fluids, they may respond in several ways:
- move to an area of optimum salinity
- reduce body contact with the surrounding water
- lower body metabolism
- control the movement of water in and out of their bodies

Organisms living in areas with frequent, often severe salinity changes of short duration, such as in intertidal areas, respond in the first three ways. Some move to an area of optimum salinity. Or they may protect themselves under rocks or in tidal pools. Others reduce body contact with the surrounding water. They do this by secreting a mucus or by withdrawing into burrows, tubes, or closed shells. This usually leads to a lowered metabolism.

Osmoregulation   Organisms that live constantly or for long periods of time in waters of different salinity have osmoregulatory organs. Gills, kidneys, and contractile vacuoles are all examples of osmoregulatory organs. They control the movement of water and salts in and out of the organism's body. Thus the proper salinity of the internal fluids are maintained.

Importance of Salinity   Salinity is important to plants and animals. The greater the salinity, the greater the buoyancy. Thus it is easier for marine organisms to float.

Section Review

1. **a)** What is meant by the term salinity?
    b) What is the average salinity of the oceans?
    c) What portion of the salinity of the oceans is common salt?

2. **a)** Name the ions of the six elements which make up over 99% of the sea salts.
   b) Account for the constancy of composition of sea water.
3. List eight factors which determine the degree of salinity.
4. **a)** Why is salinity lowest in the poles?
   b) Why is salinity highest in the tropics?
5. **a)** Distinguish between hypersaline and brackish water.
   b) Give an example of each of the above.
6. Distinguish between stenohaline and euryhaline organisms.
7. List four ways in which organisms may respond to changes in salinity.
8. **a)** What is the function of osmoregulatory organs?
   b) Name three osmoregulatory organs.
9. State the relationship between salinity and buoyancy.

15.8 Chemical Factors

Several chemical factors affect life in marine ecosystems. Their sources and importances are similar to those of freshwater ecosystems. Therefore you should review Chapters 5 and 6 before continuing. This section briefly describes some of the properties of these chemical factors that are unique to marine ecosystems.

Oxygen

Circulation In the ocean, all oxygen is introduced into the upper surface waters. However, oxygen is required by plants and animals living at all depths. How then do marine organisms living in the aphotic zone obtain their supply of oxygen? The answer is by vertical circulation. The cold, dense, oxygen-rich surface water in polar regions sinks. It spreads out over the ocean floor. The water already there is displaced upward. Thus a supply of oxygen can reach the deepest parts of the ocean.

Deficits Although oxygen is present in small amounts, it is not usually an important limiting factor in the distribution of organisms. There is usually more than enough oxygen for the organisms living in the ocean. However, in some environments its absence is important. One example is stagnant waters which lack good circulation. The Black Sea is a well-known example of a stagnant marine basin (Fig. 15-18). There is little mixing of top and bottom waters. Oxygen is found only in the top 150-200 m. Below this depth, hydrogen sulfide is found. Consequently, life is restricted to the surface layers. The deeper water is a "marine desert".

Only anaerobic sulfur bacteria can exist below 200 m. Anaerobes are organisms that can live without oxygen. Organisms that require oxygen are called aerobes.

Fig. 15-18 In the Black Sea, oxygen is only found in the top 150-200 m. Hydrogen sulfide occurs below.

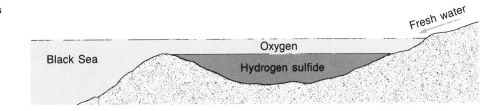

Table 15-3 Solubility of Oxygen in Salt Water (when air is the only source)

Temperature of water (°C)	Solubility (μg/g)
0	11.1
5	10.0
10	9.0
15	8.1
20	7.4
25	6.8
30	6.2

Periwinkle

Clam

Loggerhead turtle

Fig. 15-19 The skeletons and shells of many organisms contain calcium carbonate.

Solubility Table 15-3 gives the solubility of oxygen gas in salt water when air (21% oxygen) is in contact with the water. That is, air is the only source of the oxygen. In marine waters the amount of dissolved oxygen generally ranges from 0 to 9 $\mu g/g$. This is not as broad a range as is found in many freshwater ecosystems. The solubility of oxygen in salt water is determined by temperature and salinity: The colder the water, the greater the solubility; the higher the salinity, the lower the solubility. What determines the solubility of oxygen in fresh water?

Carbon Dioxide

As in most freshwater ecosystems, the major source of carbon dioxide is respiration by organisms, including decomposers. Organisms live at almost all depths in marine waters. Therefore carbon dioxide is introduced into marine waters at all depths. It is distributed in the ocean by diffusion and vertical circulation.

Solubility Carbon dioxide is highly soluble in salt water. Marine waters generally contain between 88 and 104 $\mu g/g$ carbon dioxide. This is a far greater value than is found in most freshwater ecosystems. As a result, there is no shortage of carbon dioxide for photosynthesis.

The solubility of carbon dioxide is determined by the temperature and salinity of the water. The higher the temperature and salinity, the lower the solubility is of carbon dioxide in the water.

Importance Carbon dioxide is required for photosynthesis. Also, carbon dioxide and calcium combine to form calcium carbonate. This is required by molluscs, brachiopods, and vertebrates to help form their skeletal materials (Fig. 15-19). Further, carbon dioxide acts as a buffer (neutralizing agent), helping to keep the pH constant.

pH

The pH of marine waters is rather constant. It normally varies from 7.6 to 8.3. The average pH value for all oceans is 7.8. Therefore, marine waters are slightly basic.

In marine ecosystems, pH is rarely a limiting factor. Most marine organisms can tolerate pH values ranging from 5.0 to 10.0.

Alkalinity and Hardness

Alkalinity   Alkalinity is the ability of water to neutralize acids. Or, it is the sum of all the bases in water (bases neutralize acids). In marine waters, the alkalinity is due mainly to carbonates and bicarbonates. Hydroxides may also contribute to the alkalinity if domestic or industrial pollution is present.

Hardness   Hardness in water is caused by calcium and magnesium ions. The source of these ions is the same as in fresh water. As well, when marine plants and animals die, their calcium carbonate containing "skeletal" material is a source of both ions. Marine waters are generally quite hard. They are usually saturated with calcium and may be supersaturated locally.

Nitrogen and Phosphorus

Nitrogen   A shortage of available nitrogen is one of the most important limiting factors in marine productivity. This is common in extensive tropical areas where there is little vertical mixing of water. Coastal waters, in general, are more productive than open oceanic waters. There is usually a continuous inflow of nitrogen from the land and from upwelling.

As in freshwater ecosystems, too much nitrogen can cause problems. Excessive algal and plant growth may result. Algal blooms often occur when the total nitrogen concentration is over 0.30 μg/g. Of course, other nutrients must be present in adequate amounts before this can happen.

Phosphorus   Like nitrogen, phosphorus affects life in marine ecosystems. If the total phosphorus is over 0.015 μg/g, an algal bloom may result. As in fresh water, many ecologists feel that phosphorus is a limiting factor in the production of algal blooms in marine waters.

Sulfur

Sulfur (S) is another important macronutrient. It is essential to all living organisms. It is present in many proteins. Thus it must be present in all ecosystems.

Sulfur occurs in two main forms in marine waters: sulfate (SO_4^{2-}) and hydrogen sulfide (H_2S). Most sulfur occurs as a sulfate. This is the third most abundant ion found in marine waters. Only chloride and sodium ions are present in greater amounts. Hydrogen sulfide is present in water only under special conditions.

Sources of Sulfate   Sulfate comes from the following sources:
- the oxidation of sulfur by bacteria
- the oxidation of hydrogen sulfide by bacteria
- the decay of human sewage (fecal matter and urine)
- the decay of wastes from farm feedlots
- fertilizer runoff from farms and lawns

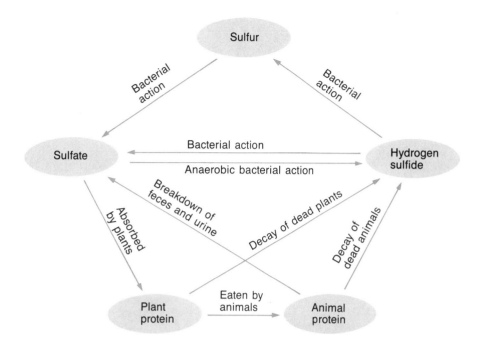

Fig. 15-20 The sulfur cycle.

Sources of Hydrogen Sulfide As shown in the sulfur cycle (Fig. 15-20), when organisms die, hydrogen sulfide can be produced. This is a poisonous gas which is quickly changed to sulfate. This in turn can be absorbed by plants.

Hydrogen sulfide is usually present in the stagnant, oxygen-starved, organic-rich areas of the ocean. As you learned earlier in this section, hydrogen sulfide is present in the deep waters of the Black Sea. It is also present in the deep waters of many fiords. It is also found in many stagnant, shallow, mud-bottom coastal waters.

The anaerobic sulfur bacteria obtain their oxygen by breaking down sulfate. In doing so, hydrogen sulfide is released. This often accumulates in the bottom sediments. If you have ever visited the coast, you may have smelled hydrogen sulfide. It has a distinct rotten-egg smell. This "aroma" escapes as the waves churn up the sediments or when the tide is especially low.

Section Review

1. How do marine organisms living in the aphotic zone obtain their supply of oxygen?
2. Why is oxygen *not* usually an important limiting factor in the distribution of organisms in the ocean?
3. **a)** What is the maximum amount of oxygen salt water can hold?
    b) What factors determine the solubility of oxygen in salt water?
    c) How do these factors affect the solubility of oxygen?

4. What range of carbon dioxide values would you expect to find in marine waters?
5. **a)** What factors determine the solubility of carbon dioxide in marine waters?
   b) How do these factors affect the solubility of carbon dioxide?
6. **a)** What is the pH range of marine waters?
   b) What is the average pH of all oceans?
7. **a)** What three substances contribute to alkalinity?
   b) In general, are marine waters hard or soft? Explain why.
8. **a)** How much nitrogen is needed to cause an algal bloom?
   b) How much phosphorus is needed to cause an algal bloom?
9. Why is sulfur an essential part of all ecosystems?
10. **a)** List five main sources of sulfate in water.
    b) List two ways hydrogen sulfide enters water.
11. How do sulfur bacteria living in the Black Sea obtain their oxygen?

15.9 ACTIVITY Analyzing the Water in a Marine Aquarium

In this activity you will analyze the chemical and biological properties of a marine aquarium ecosystem. As you know, the chemical factors interact with the organisms. That is, they affect one another. Can you find out how?

Problem

How do the chemical and biological factors interact in the marine aquarium?

Materials

selection of Hach water testing kits (oxygen, carbon dioxide, pH, alkalinity, hardness, phosphate, chloride, sulfate, silica)
a marine aquarium with enriched water, organisms, and a thermometer (-10°C to 110°C)
Note: The nitrogen tests are affected by salinity and, as a result, cannot be done.

Procedure

a. Copy Table 15-4 into your notebook.
b. Get one of the water testing kits from your teacher. Carry out the test on the water in the aquarium (Fig. 15-21). Enter your data in the table that your teacher has prepared on the chalkboard.

Table 15-4 Water Analysis

Factor	Value			
	Trial 1	Trial 2	Trial 3	Average
Oxygen				
Carbon dioxide				
pH				
Alkalinity				
Hardness				
Silica				
Sulfate				
Phosphate				
Chloride				

Fig. 15-21 Be careful not to stir up any sediment as you obtain your water samples.

c. Return the kit, obtain another, and repeat step (b).

d. Continue tests until the teacher announces that time is up. Your teacher will see that each test is performed at least three times so that accuracy can be checked.

e. Take the temperature of the water.

f. Record all the data in your table.

g. Make careful notes on other non-living properties of the aquarium ecosystem. These should include light intensity, clarity of the water, presence or absence of aeration, and the nature of any debris on the bottom.

h. Make careful notes on the biological properties of the aquarium ecosystem. These should include a description of the types and abundance of organisms present (fish, small animals, plants, and algae).

i. Monitor the marine aquarium ecosystem every two months. Make careful notes of any changes in the chemical and biological properties.

Discussion

1. Account for the results of each test. For example, if you obtained a pH of 8, why did you obtain that value?

2. Explain the effects of each result on living organisms. For example, if you obtained a sulfate concentration of 1.0 $\mu g/g$, what effect will this low value have on living organisms?

3. Describe and account for any chemical and biological changes with time.

Main Ideas

1. Waves, currents, and tides are characteristic features of oceans.
2. Waves transport energy, not water.
3. Deep-ocean currents are caused by differences in the density of water.
4. Tides are caused by the differences between gravitational and centrifugal forces of the sun, moon, and earth.
5. Temperature and light intensity are two of the most important abiotic factors affecting the distribution of marine organisms.
6. Most zooplankton migrate vertically each day in response to changing light intensity.
7. Sea water is a solution of salts of nearly constant proportions.
8. Marine organisms respond in several ways to changes in salinity.
9. Oxygen and carbon dioxide are not important limiting factors in marine ecosystems.
10. The pH of marine ecosystems is rather constant.
11. Nitrogen and phosphorus, when present in sufficient amounts, can cause an algal bloom.

Key Terms

anaerobic sulfur	euryhaline	spring tide
aphotic zone bacteria	hydrogen sulfide	stenohaline
apogee tide	hypersaline	sulfate
brackish water	mixed tide	thermocline
Coriolis Effect	neap tide	tidal current
diurnal tide	osmoregulatory organs	tidal period
dysophotic zone	perigee tide	upwelling
ebb current	photic zone	
euphotic zone	semidiurnal tide	

Chapter Review

A. True or False

Decide whether each of the following statements is true or false. If the sentence is false, rewrite it to make it true. (Do not write in this book.)

1. Water particles travel with the wave motion.
2. The currents in the Northern Hemisphere flow counterclockwise.
3. Spring tides occur a few days after the full and new moons.
4. Stenothermal organisms can tolerate a wide range of temperature.
5. The relative amounts of dissolved salts in the open ocean is constant.

B. Completion

Complete each of the following sentences with a word or phrase that will make the sentence correct. (Do not write in this book.)

1. Surface ocean currents are caused by ░░░░░ and ░░░░░ .
2. Polar regions are characterized by ░░░░░ species diversity and ░░░░░ numbers of individuals.
3. Zooplankton move ░░░░░ at sunset and ░░░░░ at dawn.
4. Salinity is lowest in the ░░░░░ and highest in the ░░░░░ .
5. In the Black Sea, anaerobic sulfur bacteria produce ░░░░░ .

C. Multiple Choice

Each of the following statements or questions is followed by four responses. Choose the correct response in each case. (Do not write in this book.)

1. As the ocean water cools, it tends to
   a) move upward
   b) move downward
   c) remain stationary
   d) spread out equally in all directions

2. Tides which occur daily are called
   a) perigee   b) apogee   c) diurnal   d) semidiurnal

3. An industry put warm water into the coastal ocean waters. The water temperature changed from $10°C$ to $20°C$. The oxygen level would likely
   a) increase by about 2 $\mu g/g$
   b) drop by about 2 $\mu g/g$
   c) drop by over 5$\mu g/g$
   d) remain unchanged

4. The average pH value for all oceans is
   a) 7.0   b) 7.8   c) 8.1   d) 8.3

5. Analysis of sea water shows that the substances that are found in greatest amounts are
   a) sodium and sulfate
   b) sodium and calcium
   c) sodium and magnesium
   d) sodium and chloride

Using Your Knowledge

1. Explain how you know that water particles do not travel across the ocean with the waves.
2. How much sea water must be evaporated to obtain 595 g of sea salts?
3. Explain why most freshwater fish are unable to live in marine waters.
4. What will happen to a plant cell if placed in a 15% salt solution?
5. a) Explain why oxygen is less soluble in warm water than in cold water.
   b) Why does oxygen become less soluble as the salinity increases?
   (*Hint*: For both parts (a) and (b), think about molecular theory.)

Table 15-5 Coastal Waters Field Trip

Factor	Concentration ($\mu g/g$)
Oxygen	8.8
Carbon dioxide	45.0
pH	8.6
Nitrate	1.1
Phosphate	1.0
Temperature	16° C

6. Figure 15-22 represents the oxygen-depth profile for an ocean. Account for the following observations.
   a) Below the first 100 m or so, the oxygen level decreases with depth until it reaches the minimum oxygen level (between 700 and 1000 m).
   b) Between 700 and 1000 m, the oxygen level begins to increase slightly with depth.
7. Scientists recorded the nitrate concentration every 500 m below the surface of the open ocean. They noted an unusually high nitrate concentration at the ocean bottom. No algal blooms or plants were observed floating in the surface waters. Account for the data.
8. The data in Table 15-5 were obtained during a field trip to the coastal waters of a major ocean on a bright sunny day. Account for the data.

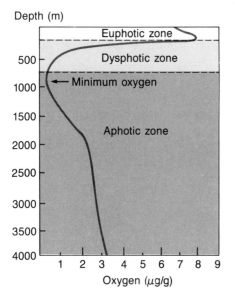

Fig. 15-22   The oxygen-depth profile for an ocean.

Investigations

1. Tsunamis, or seismic sea waves, are the most destructive of all ocean waves. Find out what causes tsunamis. How often do they occur? Which areas of the world are most susceptible? Why are they so destructive? How much damage do they cause? Set up a demonstration to show the cause(s) and effects of tsunamis.
2. Set up a ripple tank. Observe the various wave patterns. What effect does an obstruction have on the wave patterns? Why is this information useful to know when building long docks along the coastline?
3. Find out in what ways the working days of people in a coastal town are dependent on the tides.
4. Choose a marine organism. Write a short report on its adaptations to changes in salinity.
5. Find out what effect, if any, acid precipitation is having on marine ecosystems.
6. Find out how salt is commercially produced and used. Write a report of about 200 words on your findings.
7. Design an experiment to measure the salt content of sea water. After you have perfected your technique, use it to monitor the changes in salt concentrations in a local ecosystem (example: a tidal pool on a rocky shore).

UNIT FIVE

The Ecology of Marine Ecosystems

In this unit you will be introduced to the wide variety of marine life forms within each marine ecosystem. Also you will further explore the various abiotic factors of these marine ecosystems and see how they affect the life forms. With an understanding of marine ecology, you can help your generation to wisely manage this valuable resource.

This tidal pool is habitat for a variety of marine organisms. How many can you name?

16 Ocean Ecosystems

What types of organisms live in the ocean? Is there life in the deepest part of the ocean? What effect does pollution and overharvesting have on the ocean ecosystems? In this chapter you will seek answers to questions such as these. You will learn about the diverse life within the ocean. You will also learn how humans are affecting this life. This knowledge will help you do your part to keep the oceans "alive and well".

16.1 Mysteries of the Ocean

Fig. 16-1 The H.M.S. *Challenger* opened up the field of deep-ocean research.

Until 1858, it was commonly believed that few if any living organisms existed below a depth of 500 to 600 m. It was also assumed that about 90% of the ocean bottom had no life. Then in 1860 a change in attitude occurred. One of the first submarine telegraph cables was brought up from a depth of over 2000 m in the Mediterranean Sea. To many people's surprise, it was covered with living animals. These were obviously ocean bottom dwellers.

This discovery opened up the field of deep-ocean exploration. The most famous expedition was the three and a half year voyage of the British ship H.M.S. *Challenger* (Fig. 16-1). This was the first deep-ocean expedition formed to study the ocean. Starting in 1872, the *Challenger* expedition visited every ocean, travelling over 125 000 km. It observed currents, temperatures, and water chemistry at all depths. The shapes and depths of the ocean floors were established for the first time. Sediments and marine life were collected from all oceans. The *Challenger* discovered 715 new genera and 4417 species of living things. It proved beyond question that life exists at even the greatest depths in the ocean.

Today, direct observation of the ocean floor is made possible by underwater cameras and deep-water submarines. It is only in the last decade or so that people have obtained a clear understanding of the deep-ocean community.

1. What were the common beliefs of early oceanographers (before 1860) about life in the ocean ecosystem?
2. What event changed people's attitude about life in the deep ocean?
3. What discoveries did the H.M.S. *Challenger* expedition make about the abiotic and biotic properties of the ocean?

16.2 Phytoplankton

Phytoplankton are small free floating plant-like organisms. (*Phyto* means plant and *plankton* means to wander.) Because there is no dominant large plant life in the ocean, phytoplankton are the chief producers. Thus they form the basis for almost all food chains in the ocean.

Distribution

Photosynthesis can only occur when sunlight is available. Therefore, phytoplankton are restricted to the upper surface waters, or photic zone.

The type, number, and distribution of phytoplankton in the ocean changes with time and place. Several interacting factors including the seasonal, annual, and geographic variations in light control these changes. The temperature and salinity of the water also affect the distribution of species. Even the availability of nutrients and grazing by zooplankton are important factors.

In general, the distribution of phytoplankton is patchy and varies from season to season. Phytoplankton appear most abundant in surface waters high in phosphate. If nitrates, as well as other nutrients are present in adequate amounts, **algal blooms** may result.

Each ocean or region within an ocean has its own dominant forms. Some forms prefer the open ocean. Others occur only in neritic or coastal waters. Let's take a brief look at the five most common types of phytoplankton in the ocean ecosystem (Fig. 16-2).

Fig. 16-2 Important ocean phytoplankton.

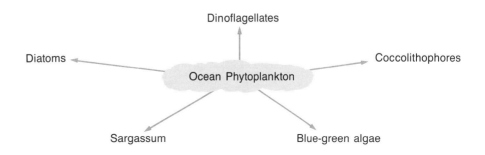

Chaetoceros

Asterionella

Rhizosolenia

Fig. 16-3   Some types of diatoms.

Fig. 16-4   Hairlike flagella help the dinoflagellate to move.

Diatoms

Characteristics   Diatoms are tiny one-celled algae. They come in many types and shapes. Some occur singly and others form chains. However, they are all beautiful to look at under the microscope (Fig. 16-3). Diatoms have cell walls. The walls are very hard since they contain silica (the glassy substance in sand).

Occurrence and Importance   Diatoms are the most abundant algae in the ocean. They are especially common in regions of upwelling and in cold waters. When diatoms die, everything decays except the silica cell walls. This material settles to the ocean bottom. Over the years it forms a deep layer of fine solid. This solid is called diatomaceous earth. This substance has many industrial and scientific uses. It is used for filtering sugar, gasoline, and water. It is also used as an abrasive in polishing preparations. It is even used in some types of insulation.

Diatoms are the most important of all algae. They are the first step in many food chains in the ocean. As well, they make much of the earth's oxygen.

Dinoflagellates

Characteristics   Dinoflagellates are one-celled algae that use two whiplike flagella to move about (Fig. 16-4). They contain chlorophyll as well as some orange colour. Therefore they usually look brown. These organisms are encased in a cellulose cell wall. The cell wall is made of overlapping plates. This often makes the cell wall look like a suit of armour.

Occurrence and Importance   Dinoflagellates are common in all oceans. They commonly outnumber the diatoms in the warm regions. In summer, especially in the tropics, high population densities of some kinds of dinoflagellates are responsible for producing "red tides" or "red water". The surface water takes on a red or brown colour. This occurs when the concentration of algal cells reaches 200 000 to 500 000 cells per litre. Sometimes concentrations rise to 1 000 000 to 6 000 000 cells per litre.

In large numbers, these algae are often toxic to other marine life. Dinoflagellates contain and secrete toxins (poisonous substances). In high concentrations, these toxins kill great numbers of fish and animals. This causes great economic losses to the fishing industry. Further, people and sea birds are sometimes poisoned by eating fish or shellfish contaminated with these toxins.

Dinoflagellates are the second most important algae in the ocean. They are the first step in many ocean food chains. As a result, they help to produce many of the fish we eat by providing food for them. They also add oxygen to the atmosphere.

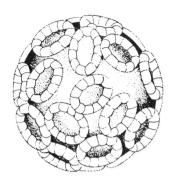

Fig. 16-5 Coccolithophores are protected by many tiny plates called coccoliths.

Coccolithophores

Characteristics Coccolithophores are among the smallest phytoplankton in the ocean. They have two flagella and are protected by a shell made of many tiny calcareous plates called coccoliths (Fig. 16-5). The coccoliths are embedded in a gelatinous sheath-like substance.

Occurrence and Importance Coccolithophores are most common in warm regions. They are an important source of food for filter-feeding zooplankton and animals. They also add oxygen to the atmosphere. After death, the coccolithophores quickly sink to the ocean floor. The coccoliths break apart. They accumulate with time and eventually become part of the calcareous ooze on certain parts of the ocean floor.

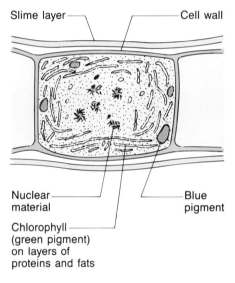

Slime layer — — Cell wall

Nuclear material

Blue pigment

Chlorophyll (green pigment) on layers of proteins and fats

Fig. 16-6 A blue-green algal cell.

Blue-Green Algae

Characteristics Blue-green algae are one-celled. They lack a true nucleus. As well, they do not have chloroplasts and other organelles. Each cell is surrounded by a stiff cell wall (Fig. 16-6).

Blue-green algae contain three pigments. The blue and green pigments give the algae a blue-green colour. That's how these algae got their name. They also contain a red pigment. Therefore these algae are sometimes purple or even black.

Occurrence and Importance Blue-green algae occur mainly inshore and in the warmer surface waters of the tropics. Some species grow well in polluted water. This often results in algal blooms.

Some species give off toxins. These can kill fish and the animals that drink the water.

Blue-green algae are producers. Humans are at the end of many food chains that start with these algae. They also make oxygen. Some species can fix nitrogen, thereby making this nutrient available to other algae and plants.

Sargassum

Fig. 16-7 The Sargasso Sea contains floating beds of the brown alga *Sargassum*.

Sargassum

Characteristics *Sargassum*, or rockweed, is a multi-cellular brown alga. It contains both chlorophyll and brown pigments. This seaweed consists of long branching stems and small stalked bladders. The bladders help the plant to float (Fig. 16-7).

Occurrence and Importance Most seaweeds are fixed algae. That is, they grow attached to something firm such as a rock. However, *Sargassum* is one exception. Waves detach it from shorelines. Then currents carry it into a calm region in the centre of the North Atlantic. This calm region is called the Sargasso Sea.

Sargassum is a producer. Thus it is an important first link in some food chains. Further, it produces oxygen. It is also habitat for some planktonic and nektonic organisms.

Section Review

1. What are the dominant producers of the ocean ecosystem?
2. **a)** Name five factors that affect the type, number, and distribution of phytoplankton.
   b) What conditions are required for algal blooms?
   c) In what area of the ocean do phytoplankton occur? Explain your answer.
3. In chart form, compare diatoms, dinoflagellates, coccolithophores, blue-green algae, and *Sargassum* under each of the following headings:

   a) characteristics
   b) occurrence
   c) importance
4. Why are red tides considered a major threat to marine life?

16.3   *ACTIVITY* **Investigating Marine Algae**

In this activity you will look at prepared slides of several types of marine algae. This will enable you to study the main characteristics of different types of algae. You will also make wet mounts of living algae.

Problem

What are the major characteristics of each type of algae?

Materials

microscope
prepared slides of diatoms, dinoflagellates, flagellates, blue-green algae
preserved sample of *Sargassum*
microscope slides (2)
cover slips (2)
paper towel
hand lens
lens paper
dropper
forceps
living algae (diatoms, dinoflagellates, and blue-green algae)
identification guides for algae

Procedure

Fig. 16-8 Never use the coarse adjustment on medium and high power. Focus only with the fine adjustment.

a. Your teacher will give you prepared slides of several types of diatoms, dinoflagellates, flagellates, and blue-green algae. Examine each type under low power. Then switch to medium, and finally high power (Fig. 16-8). Look at as many types as possible.

b. Make a sketch of at least two genera of diatoms, dinoflagellates, and blue-green algae.

c. Make a list of characteristics that all genera of a particular type of alga have in common.

d. Examine the *Sargassum* with the unaided eye and with a hand lens. Make a sketch of this brown alga. Also, make a list of its characteristic features.

e. Make a wet mount of a sample of living diatoms. Your teacher will show you how.

f. Study the wet mount under low power. Then switch to medium and, finally, to high power.

g. Make a sketch of each species you see. Note characteristic features.

h. Repeat steps (e) to (g) using dinoflagellates and blue-green algae.

Discussion

Your laboratory notes and sketches make up most of the write-up for this activity. Make sure that they are complete. Then answer these questions.

1. What were the advantages of prepared stained slides over your wet mount? What were the disadvantages?

2. What characteristics did all types of algae have in common?

16.4   Zooplankton

Zooplankton are free-floating animals and animal-like organisms. They range in size from about 0.01 mm to several metres. Because they are the main herbivores of the ocean, zooplankton are a vital link in almost all oceanic food chains.

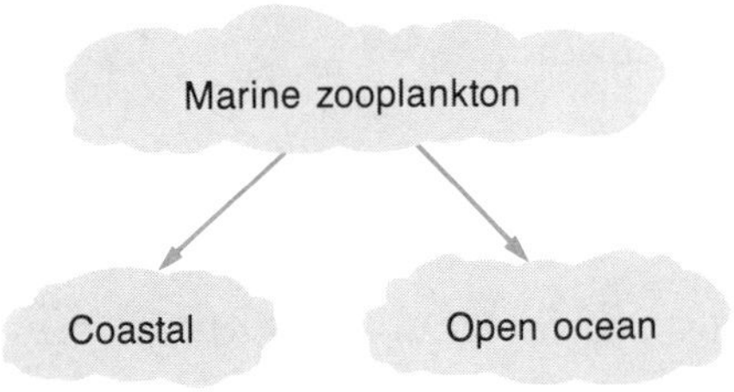

Distribution

Zooplankton are found throughout the ocean. Probably no other organisms of the ocean are as widely distributed. Their planktonic habitat enables them to be carried with the tides, currents, and upwellings. Many species migrate vertically each day in response to changing light intensities. Others live only in the deep, dark waters.

Zooplankton fall into two main groups. They are the coastal zooplankton and the open ocean zooplankton (Fig. 16-9).

Fig. 16-9 Classification of marine zooplankton.

Marine zooplankton

Coastal   Open ocean

Coastal Zooplankton A greater diversity of species live in the shallow coastal waters than in the open ocean. This reflects the greater diversity of environmental conditions that exists in the coastal waters. The temperature, salinity, turbidity and bottom substrate vary widely. They are influenced by waves, tides, and currents. In addition, coastal waters are rich in nutrients.

Many eggs and larvas of fish and benthic organisms live here. Zooplankton also tend to be larger in size in this region.

Open Ocean Zooplankton The zooplankton of the open ocean are less diverse. However, each species is present in higher numbers. The organisms tend to be smaller in size. These differences reflect the nutrient-poor and uniform conditions of the open ocean.

Temperature greatly affects the distribution and abundance of oceanic zooplankton. In general, warm waters contain a wider diversity of species than cold waters. Thus more species occur in tropical waters than in polar waters.

Abundance varies seasonally in polar waters. Zooplankton spend the winter in a dormant state in the deep cold waters. During short periods of diatom blooms, they rise to the surface to feed and reproduce. However, in the tropical regions the temperature is nearly uniform throughout the year. Therefore, zooplankton can reproduce throughout the year. Also, numbers tend to remain almost constant.

The maximum numbers of individuals and species also varies with depth from one area to another. For example, in the Northern Hemisphere the maximum number of individuals occur in waters above 500 m. The maximum number of species occurs between 1000 and 3000 m. What factors might account for this difference?

Vertical Migration

Most species of zooplankton migrate vertically each day. This enables them to remain at a preferred level of light intensity. At sunset they rise to the surface to feed on phytoplankton. At dawn, they swim back down to their preferred depths. The exact depth depends on the species and season.

There are several advantages to responding to changing light conditions. Zooplankton avoid heavy predation. They feed in the darkness of night, and hide in the darkened waters by day. Also, zooplankton conserve energy by resting in the cooler waters during the day. Both they and their by-products provide food for life in the deeper waters.

Diversity of Species

Compared to phytoplankton, the diversity of species of zooplankton is very great. Nearly all phyla of marine animals have representatives among the

Protozoa

Jellyfish

Combjellies

Segmented worms

Arrowworms

Pteropods (snails)

Sea urchin larvas

Fish larvas

Fig. 16-10 Some types of ocean zooplankton.

Table 16–1   Important Zooplankton Phyla

Phylum	Examples
Protozoa	single-celled animals: amoebas, foraminiferans, radiolarians
Cnidaria	jellyfish
Ctenophora	comb jellies
Annelida	segmented worms
Chaetognatha	arrow worms
Mollusca	oysters, clams, snails, octupus (mostly larval forms)
Arthropoda	insects, shrimp, lobsters, copepods, euphausids (larval and adult forms)
Echinodermata	starfish, sea urchins, sand dollars (mostly larval forms)
Chordata	fish (larval and juvenile forms)

zooplankton (Table 16-1). Either part or all of their life cycles are spent as plankton drifting or swimming freely.

Many bottom-dwelling species have planktonic larval stages. These include such organisms as oysters, clams, and starfish. Planktonic larvas serve to disperse the species.

As well, most nekton, or swimming animals, have planktonic eggs and young. Examples are the larval forms of comb jellies and arrow worms. Both of these are carnivorous zooplankton. They feed on the smaller herbivorous zooplankton.

Numerous other animals float and drift throughout their lives (Fig. 16-10). Among these are many kinds of one-celled animals. The foraminiferans and radiolarians are very common in warm waters. After death, their shells contribute to the deep-ocean sediments.

Probably the best known zooplankton is the jellyfish. It moves by expanding and contracting its umbrella-shaped structure. The tentacles of some jellyfish are like needles. If they touch you, they can sting very painfully. This stinging protects the jellyfish against its enemies. It also stuns or paralyzes the prey.

Arthropods (phylum Arthropoda) are perhaps the most important group of zooplankton. They are also the most numerous. About 70% of the ocean arthropods belong to the class Crustacea. Let us examine briefly two of the most important planktonic crustaceans.

Copepods

Foremost among planktonic ocean crustaceans are the copepods.

Characteristics   The bodies of copepods are elongate and segmented. They range in length from 0.2 to 20 mm. They have paired appendages and antennas. They occur in a wide variety of colours (Fig. 16-11).

Copepods are very efficient at sieving phytoplankton and detritus from the water. Many feathery bristles cover the larger appendages. These bristles form a filter chamber near the mouth. As the copepod swims, water is filtered trapping the food. The trapped food is then passed to the mouth.

Locomotion is jerky and rapid. Bursts of active swimming alternate with short periods of gliding or resting. Some species can glide backwards as well as forward.

Occurrence and Importance   Copepods are the most numerous zooplankton in the ocean. They are present throughout the oceans at all seasons.

Copepods are an important link in many marine food chains. They feed primarily on diatoms. As well, they serve as the main food source for many small carnivores, including fish. As a result, they help to produce much of our food.

Euphausids

Characteristics   Euphausids, commonly known as krill, are shrimplike in appearance (Fig. 16-12). They are from 1 to 6 cm in length. Luminescent spots, or light organs, occur along their sides. They have prominent compound stalk-eyes. Like the copepods, they are very efficient at sieving phytoplankton. Some have grinding jaws to accommodate larger food particles.

Like all other crustaceans, krill have an external skeleton (exoskeleton), jointed appendages, and segmented bodies. They also have two pairs of antennas. They grow by moulting. Krill propel themselves by beating their tiny swimming legs which are called swimmerets. The tail fin is used as a rudder. They swarm in schools. Sometimes they are so densely packed that they give a reddish hue to the water.

Occurrence and Importance   Krill are widely distributed. They live on or near the bottom as well as in surface waters. Like the copepods, they are basically herbivores, feeding mainly on diatoms. They are also carnivorous, preferring copepods to algae.

The name krill comes from an old Norwegian word "kril". Originally kril meant tiny creepy-crawly things and larval fish. Today krill means whale food.

Krill rival copepods as the most important of all zooplankton. They are the chief food for filtering-type whales such as the baleen whale. A large

Fig. 16-11   Copepods are the most numerous zooplankton of the ocean.

Fig. 16-12   Euphausids are the main food of many marine animals.

baleen whale will eat on average about 850 L of krill a day! Many of these whales feed in Antarctic waters. It is here that krill grow in enormous quantities. Because of the depletion of Antarctic whales, krill numbers are increasing yearly.

Krill are also the chief food for some species of seals and penguins. As well, many oceanic birds and fishes feed on them. Krill are also harvested by humans. They are processed into feed for livestock, poultry, and farmed fish. Their rather bland taste makes eating them rather unpleasant. However, they are a rich source of vitamins and protein. Because they are so plentiful, krill are the ocean's richest source of protein.

Section Review

1. Why are marine zooplankton so widely distributed?
2. Distinguish between coastal and open ocean zooplankton.
3. **a)** Explain why most species of zooplankton migrate vertically each day.
   b) State three advantages of vertical migration.
4. For each of the following, give two examples of marine zooplankton:
   a) bottom-dwelling species having planktonic larval stages
   b) nekton species having planktonic larval stages
   c) species drifting throughout their life
   d) herbivorous zooplankton
   e) carnivorous zooplankton
5. Name the phylum and class that contains the greatest number of marine zooplankton.
6. Make a summary of the characteristics, occurrence, and importance of copepods.
7. Make a summary of the characteristics, occurrence, and importance of euphausids.

16.5 ACTIVITY The Culture and Behaviour of Brine Shrimp

Brine shrimp, or *Artemia*, are tiny marine crustaceans. In this activity you will culture brine shrimps from eggs. Then you will observe their structure and response to light.

Problem

Can you culture brine shrimp? How do they respond to light? What is their structure?

Materials

3.5% non-iodized salt solution
dried brine shrimp eggs (can be
    bought in vials from aquarium
    stores and biological supply
    houses)
shallow rectangular dish with
    opaque cover
flashlight
compound microscope
microscope slides (2)

cover slips (2)
lens paper
paper towel
dropper
1.5% methyl cellulose solution

Procedure A   Culturing Brine Shrimp

a. Fill a shallow dish with 3.5% salt solution.
b. Sprinkle 5 to 10 dry brine shrimp eggs over the surface of the water. Use no more than 2.5 mL of eggs per 500 mL of solution.
c. Cover the dish, leaving an opening large enough for light to enter at one end (Fig. 16-13).
d. Place the dish in an area where it will not be disturbed. The culture should receive moderate light. After 2 d at a constant room temperature of about 21°C, the eggs will hatch.

Fig. 16-13   Do not completely cover the culture of brine shrimp.

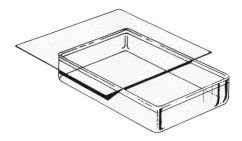

Procedure B   Response to Light

a. After 2 d, remove the lid. At which end of the dish are the brine shrimp located? Record this information in your notebook.
b. Replace the lid. This time leave the opening at the other end of the dish. Shine a flashlight for 2 min into the opening. What happens? Record this information in your notebook.
c. Remove the lid completely. Allow the dish to sit undisturbed for 20 min in a well lit area. In what direction are the brine shrimp oriented? Record this information in your notebook.

Procedure C   Structure

a. Use the dropper to get a drop of brine shrimp culture.
b. Make a wet mount of the sample. Do not add the cover slip.
c. Observe the brine shrimp under low power. Make notes on how they move.
d. Add a drop of methyl cellulose. It will slow down the brine shrimp without killing them.
e. Add a cover slip. Then switch to medium and high power. Study one brine shrimp closely.
f. Sketch the brine shrimp. Note any special adaptations of brine shrimp to an aquatic habitat.

Discussion

Your laboratory notes and sketches make up most of the write-up for this activity. Make sure that they are complete. Then answer these questions.

1. Why was it important that the lid not completely cover the brine shrimp culture?
2. **a)** How do brine shrimp respond to light intensity?
    b) How do you suppose brine shrimp orient themselves in the open ocean? Explain your answer.
3. How are brine shrimp adapted to an aquatic habitat?

16.6   Nekton

Nekton are free-swimming organisms. These include sharks, rays, bony fish, adult squids, octopi, and marine mammals. Even the sea turtles and some large crustaceans are able to swim (Fig. 16-14).

Distribution

Nekton are found in all parts of the ocean. However, some are restricted to specific geographical locations and depths. The boundary that limits the distribution of species need not be a physical one. In fact, most often it is environmental. Changes in temperature, salinity, and nutrient supply are common limiting factors. Cod, for example, swim only in waters cooler than 30°C. Some nekton can adjust easily to rapidly changing conditions, while others cannot. The result is often massive death.

This section takes a brief look at some of the characteristic features of nekton found in the major zones of the ocean.

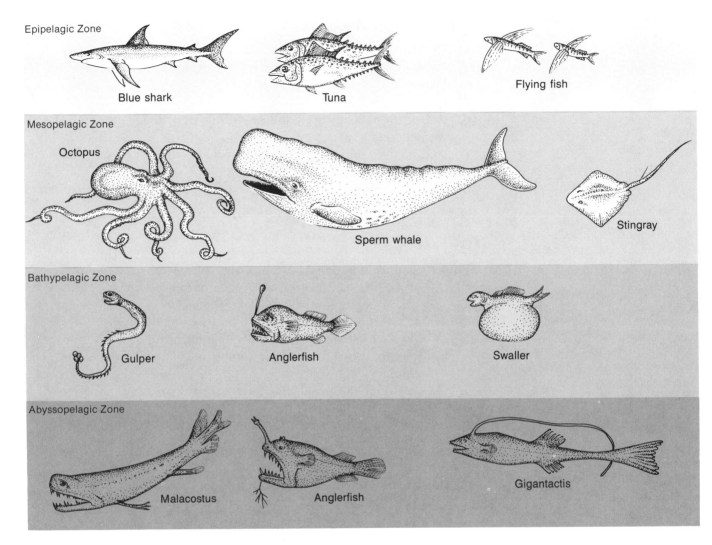

Epipelagic Zone

Blue shark

Tuna

Flying fish

Mesopelagic Zone

Octopus

Sperm whale

Stingray

Bathypelagic Zone

Gulper

Anglerfish

Swaller

Abyssopelagic Zone

Malacostus

Anglerfish

Gigantactis

Fig. 16-14 Distribution of some marine nekton.

Epipelagic Zone

The epipelagic zone has a wide diversity of nekton species. The species occur in high population numbers. This is due mainly to the great abundance of plankton which supports the food chains.

Of the nekton, fish are the most numerous. Neritic waters are rich in commercial schooling-type fish such as herring and mackerel. Others, like the speedy tuna, occur mainly in open waters. Their streamlined shape allows them to move very efficiently through the water.

Most of the animals that live in the ocean make use of body colours to hide from their enemies. The ocean from above looks blue or green. Therefore fish are generally blue or gray on top. The surface waters from below look silver or white. Fish are often these colours on their undersides. Some animals are even transparent.

Mesopelagic Zone

Below the epipelagic zone, life is less abundant than in the surface layers. Food is perhaps the most limiting factor in the mesopelagic zone. All life depends on food drifting down from the surface waters. With increasing depth, the food supply becomes more depleted. Therefore the numbers of species and individuals become fewer.

Some of the most bizarre looking creatures live below the epipelagic zone. Many are snake-like. Some are arrow-shaped with narrow fins running all around their bodies. And others, are almost as round as the sun.

Fish in the mesopelagic zone are more uniformly silver in colour than those at the surface. Some have huge telescopic eyes adapted to the dim light. Many have long needle-sharp teeth. Others have mouths that seem too big for the size of their bodies.

Some marine animals can produce light chemically without heat. This is called bioluminescence. It may serve to attract and illuminate prey, frighten or warn predators, identify species, and attract mates at spawning time. Many jellyfish, squids, deep-ocean shrimps and fishes are bioluminescent.

Bathypelagic and Abyssopelagic Zones

The deep-ocean dwellers live in a world of darkness, low temperature, and limited food. Therefore they have evolved many adaptations to assist them in food-gathering, protection, and reproduction.

Food-gathering   Some species have developed unusual methods of obtaining food. For example, the angler fish carries a long flexible stalk on its dorsal (upper) side. At the end of this stalk is a bioluminous lure. Fish, squids, and crustaceans are attracted to this lure. When the lure is dangled in front of the angler's large mouth, the curious victim is swallowed (Fig. 16-15).

Some fish have huge mouths and elastic stomachs. These allow the fish to eat an animal much larger than itself. This is important in an environment where food is scarce. In such an environment a fish has to take advantage of every possible meal.

Some species have large light-producing organs just before each eye. These might serve to illuminate food. Other species migrate vertically into higher waters in search of food.

Protection   Deep-ocean organisms are well camouflaged. They are usually black or dark in colour. As well, at least two-thirds are bioluminescent. Some fish can scare their enemies when they suddenly "light up". Many squids and shrimps emit a cloud of luminous ink when threatened. This confuses the enemy, giving the prey time to escape.

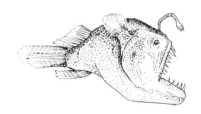

Fig. 16-15   The bioluminescent lure of the angler fish attracts prey.

Reproduction In an environment where generally the populations are dispersed, the locating of a mate can be a problem. However, the small male angler fish have overcome this problem. They live parasitically attached to the larger females. This symbiotic relationship assures the fertilization of the females' eggs. In return the males obtain nourishment from the females' bloodstreams.

Other Features In general, the fish are small, usually about 15 cm in length. They are scaleless and their skeletons are very fragile. They tend not to be streamlined. Many are blind. In place of vision, a few fish have developed specialized pectoral fins which are sensitive to touch.

Section Review

1. **a)** Give five examples of marine nekton.
   b) What factors influence the distribution of nekton?
   c) Which region of the ocean contains the widest diversity and greatest numbers of nekton? Explain why.
2. Briefly summarize the adaptations in food-gathering and protection for nekton living in the epipelagic zone.
3. Make a list of the characteristic features of nekton living in the mesopelagic zone.
4. **a)** What is bioluminescence?
   b) List four possible functions of bioluminescence.
   c) Name three bioluminescent marine nekton.
5. Briefly summarize the adaptations of deep-ocean dwellers (below 1000 m) in food-gathering, protection, and reproduction.

16.7   Benthos

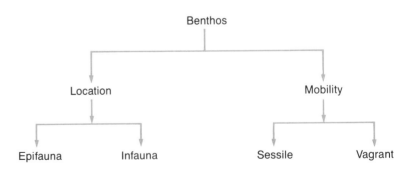

Fig. 16-16 Classification of benthos.

Organisms that live on the ocean floor are called benthos. There are two distinct subdivisions of benthic organisms, epifauna and infauna. Epifauna live on the surface of the bottom sediment. Infauna live within the bottom sediment. About four-fifths of all benthos are epifauna (Fig. 16-16).

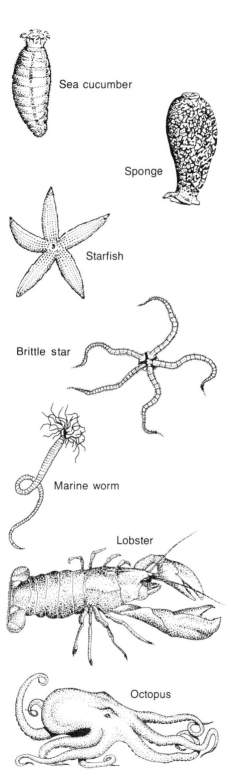

Sea cucumber

Sponge

Starfish

Brittle star

Marine worm

Lobster

Octopus

Fig. 16-17 Some types of ocean benthos.

Benthos can also be described in terms of their mobility. Plants and animals which are attached to the bottom are called sessile benthos. Those animals that can move about are called vagrant benthos. Some animals are both sessile and vagrant.

Distribution

Benthos occur at all depths of the ocean. Their diversity and abundance are influenced by several factors. The most important of these are the nature of the substrate, food availability, and temperature. Like nekton, benthos have a definite geographical distribution.

Continental-shelf Benthos   The most abundant and diverse benthic community occurs on the continental shelf or sublittoral zone. Here food is plentiful. Currents, upwellings, and coastal runoff provide a constant supply of nutrients. Also, this zone provides a wide variety of habitats and chemical conditions.

The substrate of the continental shelf is generally soft and sandy. Therefore most of the community consists of infaunal animals such as clams and worms. However, some epifaunal organisms also live here. Among them are starfish, crabs, and lobsters. Certain fish spend much of their lives associated with the bottom. Among the sessile animals are sea anemones, sponges, oysters, and coral (Fig. 16-17).

Plants are sometimes present if the bottom is stable and if light intensity is adequate. Eel grass, turtle grass, and calcareous algae are examples.

Deep-ocean Benthos   The numbers of deep-ocean benthos decrease rapidly with increasing depth. This is caused by the decreased availability of food. Diversity also decreases with increasing depth. This reflects the rather constant environmental conditions. The uniform soft, flat substrate permits the wide distribution of species. However, temperature differences and ridges can inhibit migrations.

Among the sessile organisms are glass sponges, sea lilies, and worms. Barnacles and some soft corals are also common.

Sea cucumbers, brittle stars, and crustaceans are common vagrants. As well, bottom-dwelling squids and octopi are among the deep-ocean benthos. Large populations of bacteria also live in the mud surface. They are the chief decomposers for the ocean system. They are also food for deposit and filter feeders.

Recently life has been found around hydrothermal vents. These vents in the ocean bottom shoot out hot water and sulfides. Various animals thrive on the heat, high pressure, and sulfur. Bacteria, for example, make their food from the hydrogen sulfide gas. Tube worms up to two metres long eat the bacteria.

Feeding Types

There are four major benthos feeding types. They are filter feeders, deposit feeders, scavengers, and predators (Fig. 16-18).

Fig. 16-18 Feeding methods common among marine benthos.

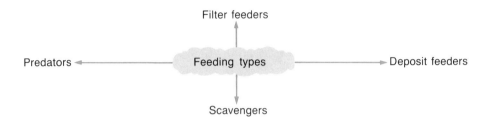

Fig. 16-18 Feeding methods common among marine benthos.

Fig. 16-19 The sea anemone catches suspended organisms and food particles by waving its tentacles in the water.

Filter Feeders Organisms that filter suspended material from the water are called filter feeders or suspension feeders. Clams, scallops, and mussels feed in this manner. So do many tube worms, sponges, and barnacles. Sea lilies and sea anemones trap their food by waving their tentacles about in the water (Fig. 16-19). Others, such as the clam, burrow into the substrate. They extend their siphons or feeding mechanisms above the substrate. Thus they can catch particulate matter.

Deposit Feeders This is the main method of feeding in the deep ocean. Deposit feeders, also called detritus feeders, feed on bottom deposits (detritus). Some of these animals are selective in their choice of food. Others are nonselective and feed on just about everything in their path. Almost all major groups of aquatic animals have deposit feeding members. Sea cucumbers and worms are examples of the deep-ocean benthos members.

Scavengers Animals that feed on dead organisms are called scavengers. These include snails, crabs, lobsters, and some fish. They eat dead plants and animals that sink to the bottom.

Predators Carnivores that feed on live animals are called predators. These include brittle stars, some fish, and some worms. Snails, squids, and octopi are also carnivorous.

Section Review

1. **a)** Distinguish between epifauna and infauna.
   b) Give two examples of each.
2. **a)** Distinguish between sessile and vagrant benthos.
   b) Give two examples of each.
3. **a)** Where is the most abundant and diverse benthic community located? Explain why.
   b) Where is the least abundant and diverse benthic community located? Explain why.
4. **a)** Name the four major benthos feeding types.
   b) Describe and give two examples of each feeding type.

Human Impact on the Ocean

The ocean is one of our most valuable and untapped resources. However, it is seriously threatened by overharvesting and pollution.

Overharvesting

For centuries humans have turned to the ocean in search of food. In recent years, improved fishing methods and expansion of fishing areas have greatly increased the annual catch. As a result, the fishing industry has become a large-scale operation in many countries. Now we are faced with the problem of overharvesting.

Overharvesting has resulted in the extinction of several species. Steller's sea cow, for example, was completely wiped out 27 years after its discovery. The entire British herring fishery was likewise eliminated within a few years in the late 1960s. As well, several species of seals are now extinct.

Many other once abundant species are now almost extinct. These include the blue whale, sea otter, and elephant seal. Stocks of salmon, tuna, cod, and sardines are being overharvested at similar rates. Even the swordfish, sailfish and tarpon are threatened.

Attempts are being made to save threatened and endangered species. The International Whaling Commission, for example, sets quotas for each species of whale every year. The most threatened whale species are now "fully protected". These include the blue, humpback, bowhead, and California gray whale. In 1982, the Whaling Commission declared a moratorium on all whaling as of 1986. Only time will tell whether some of the most threatened species can be saved.

Pollution

For a long time it was thought that the world ocean because of its vastness could not be polluted. We know now that this is not true. Even the deepest parts of the ocean are damaged by pollution. The effects could last for centuries.

Onshore winds and coastal configurations tend to keep many pollutants along the coast. Deep-ocean currents can also spread pollutants throughout the ocean. The pollutants that are a threat to the ocean ecosystem are summarized in Figure 16-20 and described in the following few pages.

Petroleum Petroleum (oil) is one of the most widespread forms of pollutants. It comes from many sources. Both oil refineries on land and ocean tankers have leaks or other accidents. Used oil dumped on land also finds its way into rivers and to the oceans.

Oil is toxic to most organisms. It floats on the surface of the water. Therefore, it prevents the diffusion of gases. It inhibits sunlight from entering

Fig. 16-20 Pollutants that threaten the ocean ecosystem.

Petroleum

Toxic chemicals

Thermal pollution

Pesticides

Ocean pollution

Dredged material

Radioactive material

Fertilizer

Sewage

for photosynthesis. Thus it kills the surface plankton. It fouls the gills of fish. It also prevents birds from flying, makes them sink in the water and sometimes poisons them.

Chemical Pollutants Chemical pollutants are found throughout the ocean. During the past two decades, their concentrations have increased greatly. Chemicals and heavy metals can kill or damage marine life. Copper, for example, is lethal to softshell clams in concentrations as low as 0.1 ppm. Lead is also poisonous to many organisms.

Other chemicals, like the pesticide DDT, become concentrated in living tissues throughout the food chain. DDT is even found in the fats of seals and penguins in the Antarctic. It also interferes with photosynthesis in diatoms and other marine algae. What effect might this have on the ocean ecosystem? You can read more about the effects of DDT and other toxic chemicals in this book's companion, *Investigating Environmental Issues*.

Sewage and Fertilizers Sewage, detergents, and fertilizers all have similar effects on the ocean ecosystem. They add great quantities of nutrients. Among these are phosphates and nitrates. In sufficient amounts, such nutrients can cause immense algal blooms. The increased bacterial decomposition which follows a bloom causes a depletion of oxygen in the water.

Thermal Pollution Thermal pollution is the release of heated water. It is discharged into coastal waters from industrial operations and power generating plants. Hot water usually causes changes in the local ecology. Occasionally it leads to a massive fish kill.

Control In 1972, representatives of 91 countries met and most signed an international ocean dumping agreement. They agreed to stop dumping substances known to cause harm to the marine environment. Among these substances are high-level radioactive wastes, oils, and durable plastics. Also included are mercury, cadmium, and some pesticides. However, some toxic substances can still be dumped with a permit. These include arsenic, lead, zinc, fluorides and cyanides. Progress is being made in controlling ocean dumping but the problem is far from solved. For example, materials dredged from harbours are often dumped in the ocean. This dredged material often contains toxic substances.

Section Review

1. What two human activities are a serious threat to the ocean ecosystem?
2. **a)** Make a short note on the effects of overharvesting on the ocean ecosystem.
   b) How are we trying to control overharvesting?
3. List four major pollutants that threaten the ocean ecosystem.
4. What effects does each of the following pollutants have on marine life?
   a) petroleum
   b) chemical pollutants
   c) sewage and fertilizers
5. Discuss briefly the 1972 international ocean dumping agreement.

Main Ideas

1. Life is found throughout the marine environment.
2. Diatoms and dinoflagellates form the base of most food chains in the ocean.
3. Copepods and krill are the most important marine zooplankton.
4. Life below the epipelagic zone depends on falling organic debris for its energy source.
5. Deep-ocean dwellers have evolved many adaptations to living in a world of darkness and limited food.
6. Below the epipelagic zone, the abundance and diversity of nekton and benthos decrease with increasing depth.
7. Overharvesting and pollution are serious threats to the ocean ecosystem.

Key Terms

benthos	epifauna	sessile benthos
bioluminescence	filter feeders	suspension feeders
deposit feeders	infauna	vagrant benthos
detritus feeders	nekton	

Chapter Review

A. True or False

Decide whether each of the following statements is true or false. If the sentence is false, rewrite it to make it true. (Do not write in this book.)

1. The H.M.S. *Challenger* expedition discovered marine life at all depths of the ocean.
2. Red tides are caused by large numbers of diatoms.
3. Copepods are also called krill.
4. Bacteria live in the ocean sediment.
5. Deep-ocean fish are brightly coloured and oversized.

B. Completion

Complete each of the following sentences with a word or phrase that will make the sentence correct. (Do not write in this book.)

1. The most abundant and important phytoplankton in the ocean are the ▨▨▨▨ .
2. Below the epipelagic zone, the diversity and abundance of nekton ▨▨▨▨ with increasing depth.
3. Marine animals that produce their own light are called ▨▨▨▨ organisms.
4. Filter feeding whales feed mainly on ▨▨▨▨ .
5. The ocean ecosystem is threatened by ▨▨▨▨ and ▨▨▨▨ .

C. Multiple Choice

Each of the following statements or questions is followed by four responses. Choose the correct response in each case. (Do not write in this book.)

1. Many ocean plankton migrate vertically each day. This is believed to be in response to
   - a) food availability
   - b) changing light intensities
   - c) oxygen availability
   - d) temperature differences
2. Benthos that live within the ocean sediment are called
   - a) epifauna
   - b) sessile
   - c) vagrant
   - d) infauna
3. Two examples of sessile epifauna are
   - a) lobsters and starfishes
   - b) sea lilies and sea cucumbers
   - c) sponges and sea anemones
   - d) worms and brittle stars
4. Clams are an example of a
   - a) filter feeder
   - b) deposit feeder
   - c) scavenger
   - d) predator

Using Your Knowledge

1. What factors influence the abundance and distribution of each of the following groups of ocean organisms?
    a) phytoplankton   c) nekton
    b) zooplankton   d) benthos
2. How have ocean nekton adapted to living in each of the following zones of the ocean?
    a) epipelagic zone   c) bathypelagic zone
    b) mesopelagic zone
3. The pesticide DDT interferes with photosynthesis in diatoms. What effect would this interference have on the ecology of the ocean ecosystem?
4. Write an ocean food chain with four trophic levels. What effect would overharvesting of the second-order consumer have on the remaining three levels of the food chain?

Investigations

1. Research the cause, occurrence, effects, and methods of cleanup of oil pollution in the marine environment. Write a report on your findings.
2. Find out your federal government's regulations regarding ocean fishing and ocean dumpings. Write a report on your findings.
3. Find out what causes bioluminescence in marine organisms.
4. Select one ocean benthos. Research its structure and methods of feeding, moving and reproduction.
5. Find out what commercial products are obtained from whales. Write a report on your findings.

17 Rocky Shores

A fascinating array of life exists on the shores where the ocean and land meet. All shores—rocky, sandy, muddy, and marshy—have one thing in common. They are exposed to the tides. This chapter explains how exposure to the tides creates the environment for a wide variety of living things. Then it describes the ecology of selected organisms that live on rocky shores.

17.1   Abiotic Factors and Zonation

Fig. 17-1 Zonation of organisms in the littoral zone of a rocky shore. Note the parallel bands of organisms.

Zonation

All ocean shores are exposed to the tides. Each has an intertidal zone, or littoral zone. This is the zone between the high tide and low tide marks. Within this zone, conditions are always changing. When the tide is in, the littoral zone is basically a sea water environment. However, when the tide is out this zone is a moist, salty, land environment. The organisms that live here must be adapted to the harsh conditions that accompany the changing water levels. The organisms in the upper region of the littoral zone experience the greatest changes. They are out of the water, exposed to the sun and drying winds, for the longest time each day. Those in the lower region are out of the water for only a short time each day.

The littoral zone has several zones within it. These zones are created by the different abiotic conditions that occur within the littoral zone. Since these zones have different abiotic conditions, they will also have different organisms. In fact, when the tide is out, a zonation of organisms can usually be seen within the littoral zone. Such zonation is most easily seen on a rocky shore (Fig. 17-1).

The Rocky Shore

Rocky shores show the greatest variation of all coastal environments. They range from steep cliffs to almost flat platforms. Their substrates may be smooth or they may be strewn with boulders. They usually have a wide variety of crevices and gullies. Waves slowly erode rocky shores, leaving unusual forms and shapes. Tide pools, or water-filled depressions, dot many rocky shores when the tide recedes.

The wide variety of environments on rocky shores provides a wide variety of habitats to which algae can attach and on which animals can feed, move and attach. The most striking feature of the rocky shore is, however, the zonation of life. Different levels of the shore have different groups of organisms. These groups of organisms usually show up clearly as parallel bands, or zones, along the rock.

A rocky shore has three main zones. You have already read about the intertidal zone, or littoral zone. It is the one that is alternately covered and exposed by the tide. Above it is the supralittoral zone or spray zone. Below it is the sublittoral zone or open ocean. These three main zones are themselves made up of zones. These smaller zones show up best in the littoral zone.

The species making up the zones in the littoral zone may differ from place to place. These differences depend on the type of coast, wave and tide action, light intensity and climate. However, the zones are quite similar throughout the world where these geophysical factors are similar. Even where the geophysical factors differ, the general patterns of the zones are similar. Each zone is characterized by certain dominant plants and animals that live there. The zonation discussed in the remainder of this chapter is typical of that found in temperate regions exposed to moderate wave action. The dominant organisms of each zone are discussed. Special attention is given to the adaptations that permit these organisms to live in a certain zone. We will look particularly at how the organisms have adapted for moisture retention, holding on, and feeding. The organisms may not be exactly the same where you live. However, the general principles described will be the same.

Section Review

1. What is the intertidal or littoral zone?
2. Which organisms in the littoral zone experience the greatest changes in abiotic factors? Why?
3. What causes the zonation within the littoral zone?
4. Describe the variation that can occur on rocky shores.
5. What is a tide pool?
6. Name the three main zones on a rocky shore.
7. List five abiotic factors that determine the nature of the zonation in the littoral zone.

Life in the Supralittoral Zone

Fig. 17-2 Zonation on a rocky shore along the North Atlantic coast, north of Cape Cod. Even in this region, the zonation varies in detail from place to place. However, the general pattern remains much the same.

A rocky shore has three main zones: supralittoral, littoral, and sublittoral. We will study these zones by taking an imaginary walk from the supralittoral zone on the right of Figure 17-2 to the water's edge. Let us begin by taking a close look at the supralittoral zone.

The supralittoral zone is also called the spray zone. It is made up of two zones, the land zone and the bare rock zone.

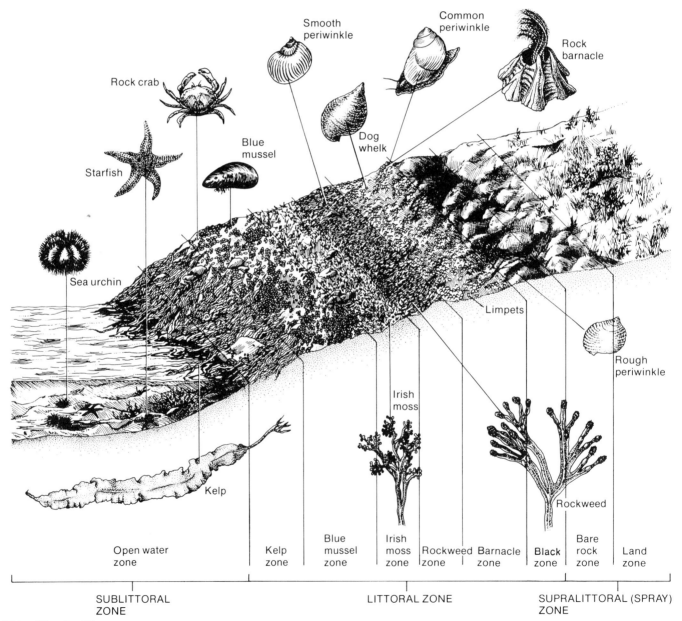

Smooth periwinkle

Common periwinkle

Rock barnacle

Rock crab

Blue mussel

Dog whelk

Starfish

Sea urchin

Limpets

Rough periwinkle

Irish moss

Kelp

Rockweed

| Open water zone | Kelp zone | Blue mussel zone | Irish moss zone | Rockweed zone | Barnacle zone | Black zone | Bare rock zone | Land zone |

| SUBLITTORAL ZONE | LITTORAL ZONE | SUPRALITTORAL (SPRAY) ZONE |

The Land Zone

The land zone is the further of the two from the water. It receives spray from the ocean only during periods of intense wave action. It is dominated by a variety of common terrestrial plants, mainly grasses and herbs. Near the bottom of the land zone, a zone of rock tripe occurs. Rock tripe is a lichen in the genus *Umbilicaria*. When this lichen is dried out, it is black and brittle. But when it is dampened by spray, rain or fog, it absorbs water and becomes green and leathery. Still closer to the water black patches of another lichen, *Verrucaria*, occur.

Lichens consist of a fungus and an alga growing together in a symbiotic relationship called mutualism (see Section 2.4, page 24). The fungal part of supralittoral lichens has a thick cell wall. This helps prevent drying out. Also, the fungal part can soak up many times its own weight in water. As a result, these lichens can live in the dry supralittoral zone. The algal part of the lichen produces food by photosynthesis. Some of this food is stored in the fungus for use when photosynthesis cannot take place. The fungal part sends hyphae ("roots") deep into the rock. These secure the lichens to the rock. The lichens show up clearly as a lichen zone at the bottom edge of the land zone.

The Bare Rock Zone

Below the lichen zone is a bare rock zone. It stretches down to the top of the littoral zone, the highest level reached by the spring tides. In this zone the rocks are normally bare. They are smooth, offering little habitat for organisms. Further, the rocks are wetted only occasionally by spray. Birds and terrestrial arthropods may rest here. The only marine visitor is the rough periwinkle. It may move from the littoral zone through this zone to graze on lichens in the land zone.

Section Review

1. Why is the supralittoral zone also called the spray zone?
2. How have supralittoral lichens adapted to their habitat?
3. Describe two common organisms of the lichen zone in the land zone.
4. Describe the bare rock zone.

17.3   Life in the Littoral Zone

As you walk from the supralittoral zone toward the ocean, you will have little trouble telling when you have reached the littoral zone. The first zone of the many within the littoral zone is the black zone. It stands out, as the name suggests, as a black strip across the shore.

Zonation in the Littoral Zone

Conditions are always changing in the littoral zone. When the tide is out, this zone is a moist, salty, land environment. The rock surface is exposed directly to sunlight, rain, wind, and temperature changes. When the tide is in, this zone is basically a sea water environment. Waves pound and erode the rock. The surging waves supply oxygen and nutrients to organisms. As well, they remove excess carbon dioxide and other waste products.

The tides and waves bring abrupt changes in salinity, temperature, and light intensity to the littoral zone. The organisms that live here must be adapted to the harsh conditions that accompany changing water levels. The organisms in the upper region of the littoral zone experience the greatest changes. They are out of the water, exposed to the sun, drying winds, and land predators, for the longest time each day. Those in the lower region are out of the water for only a short time each day.

Dessication, or loss of moisture, is the most serious problem faced by organisms in this zone. Some organisms cope with this problem by following the ebbing tide seaward. Others have devised methods for trapping enough water to sustain them until the tide returns.

The littoral zone is divided into six subzones. Beginning with the uppermost zone they are, in order:
- black zone
- barnacle zone
- rockweed zone
- Irish moss zone
- blue mussel zone
- kelp zone

These zones are usually separated by sharply defined boundaries. This is the result of intense competition for living space. Let us begin at the uppermost of these zones and move toward the ocean. In each zone we will see how the dominant organisms have adapted to their habitat.

Black Zone

The uppermost of the six zones in the littoral zone is the black zone. Every two weeks the spring tides cover this zone. Also, it is frequently wetted by wave action and spray. Much of the time, however, this zone is dry. It does stay wet enough to support the growth of certain blue-green algae and lichens. These organisms cling to the rock and give it a characteristic black colour. This strip of black looks more like a stain than a community of organisms.

Figure 17-3 shows *Calothrix*, one of the most common blue-green algae in the black zone. It consists of filaments of microscopic cells. Each filament is surrounded by a sticky gelatinous sheath. This sheath sticks *Calothrix* to the rocky surface. It also protects the cells against drying out. Further, it protects the cells against changing salt levels. These vary from 3.5% salt when the tide

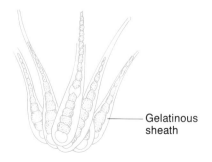

Gelatinous sheath

Fig. 17-3 The blue-green alga, *Calothrix*, magnified 300X.

Smooth periwinkle
Littorina obtusata

Rough periwinkle
Littorina saxatilis

Common periwinkle
Littorina littorea

Fig. 17-4 The three common periwinkles found on a rocky shore.

covers the *Calothrix* to 0% when rain falls on the exposed *Calothrix*.

Calothrix is a nitrogen fixer. That is, unlike most organisms, it is able to use atmospheric nitrogen to make its proteins (see Section 7.2, page 116). As a result, *Calothrix* thrives in the nutrient-poor environment of the black zone.

The rough periwinkle, *Littorina saxatilis*, is the main herbivore of the black zone. It grazes mainly on *Calothrix* and other blue-green algae because of their high nitrogen content. The rough periwinkle has adapted well to the dry environment of the black zone. Its shell is thick to lessen water loss. Further, the opening in the shell is small which also decreases water loss (Fig. 17-4). It is so well adapted that it can stand exposure to the air for over a week. In extremely dry conditions, it seals itself to the rock surface with a mucus.

The green alga, *Enteromorpha*, often grows in tufts in the black zone (Fig. 17-5). Oxygen produced by photosynthesis often collects in bubbles in the tubelike stalks of *Enteromorpha*. When the tide is in, the bubbles buoy up the stalks. They wave back and forth like tiny green fingers above the mat of *Calothrix*.

Barnacle Zone

As we walk further into the littoral zone, we enter the barnacle zone. This zone is covered and uncovered daily by the tides. As the name suggests, the dominant organisms of this zone are barnacles (Fig. 17-6). Barnacles are crustaceans. They live stuck to the rocks and depend on the tides to bring them food. At high tide, the barnacles open up. Appendages emerge and sweep dinoflagellates, diatoms and other protists into the barnacles' interiors (see Fig. 17-2). At low tide the barnacles close up to prevent water loss. Barnacles have lived for as long as six weeks out of water. They let air in through an opening that is small enough to prevent serious water loss.

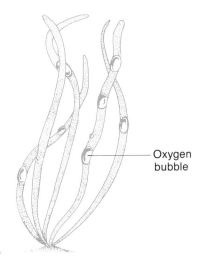

Oxygen
bubble

Fig. 17-5 The green alga, *Enteromorpha*, magnified 3X. (A)

Fig. 17-6 This barnacle, *Balanus balanoides*, lives on the North Atlantic coast. (B)

A

B

Fig. 17-7 When the tide is out, rockweeds droop over the rocky surface to which they are attached.

Also found in the barnacle zone are limpets, dog whelks, common periwinkles and, in some cases, blue mussels. Limpets move about, scraping algae from the rocks for food. Dog whelks are predators. They feed on barnacles, mussels, and periwinkles. The blue mussels in the barnacle zone are usually quite small. Apparently the tides do not bring these filter feeders enough food for maximum growth when they live this far up in the littoral zone.

Rockweed Zone

Just below the barnacle zone is the rockweed zone. This zone is dominated by brown algae called rockweeds. These plants may grow to a length of 2 m in sheltered regions. However, they are usually about 30-40 cm long (Fig. 17-7). The most common rockweeds on North American shores belong to the genera *Fucus* and *Ascophyllum*.

Bladder rockweed, *Fucus vesiculosus*, is probably the most common rockweed on the east coast. Its thick cell walls help it resist water loss when the tide is out. The air bladders on the plant body help buoy the plant up when the tide is in. A disc-shaped holdfast firmly attaches this rockweed to the rocky surface. The bladders are a disadvantage in areas of heavy wave action. (Why is this so?) As a result, bladderless forms of this rockweed often grow in such areas. Species of *Fucus*, both with and without bladders, grow on both coasts of North America.

Knotted rockweed, *Ascophyllum nodosum*, is another common rockweed of the east coast. Note, in Figure 17-8, the locations of the bladders. You can see that these might easily get ripped off in water with intense wave action. As a result, *Ascophyllum* normally grows only in sheltered areas where the water is calm. No species of *Ascophyllum* grow on the west coast.

The smooth periwinkle, *Littorina obtusata*, is the characteristic animal of this zone. It and its close relative, the common periwinkle, *Littorina littorea*, graze on the rockweeds. When the tide is out, the periwinkles often move under the drooping rockweeds where it is moist and cool. Limpets are another common herbivore of this zone.

Irish Moss Zone

Still closer to the water is the Irish moss zone. Irish moss, *Chondrus crispus*, is a red alga. It and another red alga, *Gigartina stellata*, often form a spongy carpet several centimetres thick. This zone varies in colour from purple to green and yellow. It is out of the water for only a few hours each day. As a result, the red alga in this zone are not very tolerant of temperature extremes or periods of dryness.

At low tide, the algae retain water. This forms a good environment for a wide range of invertebrates—isopods, amphipods and decapods. The rock crab, a decapod, is a characteristic carnivore of this zone.

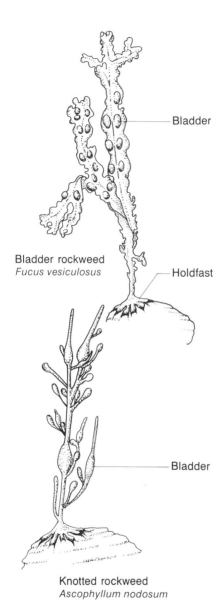

Bladder

Bladder rockweed
Fucus vesiculosus

Holdfast

Bladder

Knotted rockweed
Ascophyllum nodosum

Fig. 17-8 Two common rockweeds, magnified 0.5X. Note how these brown algae use holdfasts to cling to rocky surfaces.

Irish moss contains carrageenin, a substance which has gelling and stabilizing properties. Because of these properties, carrageenin is used in ice cream, toothpaste, chocolate milk, evaporated milk, and body lotions.

Blue Mussel Zone

The blue mussel zone often overlaps into the Irish moss zone. In fact, this zone sometimes extends up through the rockweed zone to the bottom of the barnacle zone. The mussels are often so tightly packed together that no rock surface can be seen (Fig. 17-9). They attach themselves firmly to the rocks with threads made of protein (Fig. 17-10). They do not move about like many other bivalves. The species *Mytilus edulis* occurs on both coasts.

The blue mussel zone is under water most of the time. Even at low tides, wave action may keep it covered. Mussels have adapted well to this watery environment—they are filter feeders. Their respiratory movements pass water over the gills. Mucus on the gills filters out food particles such as phytoplankton, bacteria and detritus.

The main predators of mussels are whelks, starfish and, of course, humans. A whelk bores through the shell and siphons out the mussel's interior tissues. A starfish uses its tube-feet to pry open the mussel's shell. Then the starfish sends its stomach out through its mouth and into the mussel. It digests the interior tissues of the mussel. Then it pulls its stomach back inside again.

Fig. 17-9 The mussels in this area leave little rock exposed. How do you suppose the mussels get enough to eat when they are so densely packed?

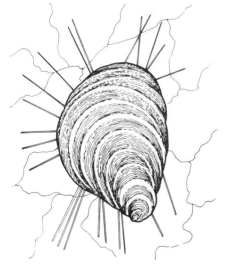

Fig. 17-10 The blue mussel, *Mytilus edulis*. Note the strong protein threads that hold this animal to the rock.

Kelp Zone

The lowest zone of the littoral zone is the kelp zone. This zone is dominated by a forest of the large brown alga, *Laminaria*, one of the kelps (Fig. 17-11). The kelp zone may be uncovered once every two weeks during spring tides. However, even at that time, wave action often keeps it covered. The dense growth of kelp provides food and habitat for a wide range of animals. Limpets, mussels, isopods, amphipods, crabs, and starfish are just a few of the inhabitants. At high tide the starfish leave the kelp beds and move up into the blue mussel zone to prey on the mussels.

Kelp and other brown algae are often harvested for food. Iodine, potash, and other valuable nutrients are obtained from *Laminaria*, *Fucus*, and *Ascophyllum*. Because of their high protein and vitamin content, these plants are also used to feed domestic animals. In addition, they are often ground up to make fertilizer for gardens and fields. A chemical called alginic acid is obtained from brown algae. Alginic acid is used as a stabilizer in ice cream and some types of paint. It is also used as the carrying medium for some antibiotic drugs.

Fig. 17-11 This kelp was recovered from the cold waters of northern Canada. Kelp over 10 m long often wash ashore in the warmer waters off the California coast.

Section Review

1. Describe the variations in abiotic conditions which occur in the littoral zone.
2. Name, in order from driest to wettest, the six zones in the littoral zone.
3. **a)** How often does the black zone receive moisture?
   b) What two main groups of organisms inhabit the black zone?
   c) How has *Calothrix* adapted to black zone conditions?
   d) How has the rough periwinkle adapted to black zone conditions?
4. How have barnacles adapted to conditions in the barnacle zone?
5. **a)** How has the rockweed *Fucus* adapted to conditions in the rockweed zone?
   b) Why are bladderless rockweeds often found in areas with heavy wave action?
   c) Why does *Ascophyllum* normally grow only in sheltered areas?
   d) In what two ways are rockweeds important to survival of the common periwinkle?
6. **a)** Name two red algae that grow in the Irish moss zone.
   b) How is Irish moss used by humans?
7. **a)** Why is it an advantage for mussels to be filter feeders?
   b) Describe how two predators feed on mussels.
8. **a)** Describe how you would recognize the kelp zone.
   b) What uses do humans make of kelp and other brown algae?

17.4 Life in the Sublittoral Zone

Beyond the littoral zone is the sublittoral zone, or open water zone. This zone is seldom exposed, even at low tide. Therefore its temperature and salinity stay fairly constant. Kelps are common in this zone. Their branching hold-fasts attach firmly to the rocky bottom. The bottom is often covered with a variety of smaller algae. Among these algae one can spot starfish, brittlestars, sea urchins, and a host of other fascinating animals. Because of the wide diversity of animals, this zone is a favourite of scuba divers. In fact, it is popularly called the scuba zone.

The exact nature of the animal community in this zone depends on the nature of the bottom, the oxygen concentration, the light intensity, the temperature, and other biotic factors.

If you have not already done so, you can read about the ecology of many of these animals in Section 16.7 of Chapter 16.

Section Review

1. Why is the sublittoral zone also called the open water zone?
2. What plants dominate this zone?
3. Why is there a greater diversity of animal life in this zone than in any zone of the intertidal zone?

17.5 Life in Tide Pools

Tide pools are a common feature of rocky shores. As the tide moves out, water often remains trapped in depressions in the rocky surface. The resulting pools vary in size from that of a dishpan to a room (Fig. 17-12). Tide pools are distinct habitats. They differ from the rocky surface around them and they differ from the ocean. They even differ from one another.

Fig. 17-12 A wide variety of shapes and sizes of tide pools form when the tide recedes from this rocky shore in the Gaspé Peninsula of Québec.

Classification of Tide Pools

Tide pools are classified according to their locations on the rocky shore (Fig. 17-13). A low littoral pool is covered with sea water much of the time. (In an area with a tidal range of 4 m, such a pool would normally be less than 1 m above average sea level.) Therefore its abiotic environment (temperature and salinity) remains fairly constant. Such pools are usually dominated by brown and red algae. Living among the algae is a wide diversity of animals—sea anemones, limpets, periwinkles, whelks, barnacles, isopods, amphipods, starfish, brittlestars, and sea urchins.

Fig. 17-13 Tide pools are named by their locations on the rocky shore.

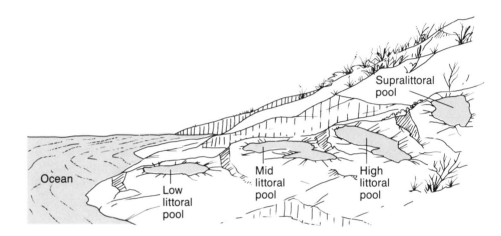

A mid littoral pool is usually 2-3 m above average sea level in an area with a tidal range of 4 m. As a result such pools are flushed regularly with sea water. When the tide is out, however, a mid littoral pool can be a harsh environment. If a heavy rain falls, the sea water becomes diluted. On hot days, evaporation of water increases the salt concentration of the sea water. Further, the water becomes too warm for many organisms. As a result, mid littoral pools have a lower diversity of life than low littoral pools. Mid littoral pools are commonly dominated by large green algae such as sea lettuce (*Ulva*), *Enteromorpha* and *Cladophora*. The brown alga, *Fucus*, is often present. Periwinkles, isopods, and barnacles are common animals in these pools. Those mid littoral pools that are closest to the water may contain starfish and mussels. Figure 17-14 shows one such pool. Many marine animals—sea urchins, sea anemones, and whelks—cannot tolerate the changing conditions of these pools.

A high littoral pool may go many days without having its water exchanged with the sea. In other words, it is near the high tide mark. Freshwater runoff and precipitation can make such pools almost a freshwater environment. The evaporation of water over several days can make the water very salty. Such pools normally contain few large marine organisms. How-

Fig. 17-14 The water in this mid littoral pool was about 0.6 m deep.

ever, they do contain animals such as periwinkles, barnacles, amphipods, and fly larvas that can tolerate the extremes in this environment.

A supralittoral pool is in the spray zone above the high spring tide level. Such a pool is essentially a freshwater environment. It receives only spray from the ocean. Most of its water comes from freshwater runoff and precipitation. Such pools get very hot in the summer and very cold in the winter (in northern latitudes).

Section Review

1. Make a copy of Table 17-1 in your notebook. Complete it to make a summary of life in tide pools.

Table 17-1   Life in Tide Pools

Type of pool	Abiotic Conditions	Main organisms
low littoral		
mid littoral		
high littoral		
supralittoral		

17.6

Adaptations of Marine Algae

All organisms show adaptations to their habitats. Marine algae are no exception. For example, those algae in the upper parts of the tidal range have adapted to long periods of dryness. As well, those in areas of heavy wave action have adapted to that environment. In this activity you will examine some marine algae to see how they have adapted.

Problem

How have marine algae adapted to their habitats?

Materials

fresh or preserved specimens of a few marine algae, for example, rockweed (*Fucus* and / or *Ascophyllum*), *Enteromorpha*, Irish moss (*Chondrus*), sea lettuce (*Ulva*)
dissecting knife
hand lens
probe
tray

Procedure

a. Copy Table 17-2 into your notebook.

Table 17-2 Adaptations of Marine Algae

Name of alga	Habitat	Adaptations	Advantages to alga

b. Get a sample of an alga from your teacher and place it in the tray.
c. Record the habitat of this alga in your table. You can find this information in the earlier sections of this chapter.
d. Study the alga closely. Note its texture (feel), thickness, shape, rigidity, colour, means of attachment to the substrate (its "roots"), and other structural features. You may find it helpful to cut through the alga and examine the cut with the hand lens. Record these features in your table.
e. Repeat steps (b) to (d) with the other algae provided.
f. Complete the "Advantages to alga" column of your table.

A completed table is your write-up for this activity.

17.7 ACTIVITY Adaptations of Rocky Shore Invertebrates

Like the algae you examined in Activity 17.6, marine invertebrates show adaptations to their habitats. In addition to structural adaptations, animals also show behavioural adaptations. This activity uses preserved specimens. Therefore you will be looking at structural adaptations in the laboratory. You can find out about the behavioural adaptations by watching the animals in a marine aquarium or on a field trip. You can read about them in other sections of this book.

Problem

How have marine invertebrates adapted to their habitats?

Materials

preserved specimens of a few marine invertebrates, for example, rough periwinkle (*Littorina saxatilis*), smooth periwinkle (*Littorina obtusata*), common periwinkle (*Littorina littorea*), limpet, dog whelk, blue mussel, barnacle, rock crab, starfish, sea urchin, sea anemone
hand lens
probe
tray

Procedure

a. Copy Table 17-3 into your notebook.

Table 17-3 Adaptations of Marine Invertebrates

Name of animal	Habitat	Adaptations		Advantages to animal
		Structural	Behavioural	

Fig. 17-15 What adaptations does a starfish have that make it possible for it to open up a blue mussel?

b. Get an invertebrate from your teacher and put it in the tray.

c. Record the habitat of this animal in your table. You can find this information in earlier sections of this book. (Use the index.)

d. Study the animal closely. (Do not damage it. Then it can be used by other students in the future.) Note its body covering, colour, adaptations for feeding, adaptations for holding on, adaptations for moving and other structural features (Fig. 17-15). Record these features in your table.

e. Complete the "behavioural" column of your table by observing living animals in an aquarium or on a field trip. (If this is not possible, get the information from earlier sections of this text.)

f. Repeat steps (b) to (e) for the other animals provided.

g. Complete the "Advantages to animal" column of your table.

Discussion

A completed table is your write-up for this activity.

17.8 *FIELD TRIP* Investigating Zonation in the Littoral Zone

You learned in Section 17.3 that the littoral zone has six zones: black, barnacle, rockweed, Irish moss, blue mussel, and kelp zones. In some areas one or more of these zones may be missing. Usually, though, you can see at least four very distinct zones. On this field trip you will work in a group with 3 or 4 other students to investigate the ecology of these zones.

Problem

What ecological relationships exist between littoral organisms and their environments?

Materials

white tray	identification book(s)
hand lens	ball of coarse string (2)
probe	metre stick

Procedure

Note: Remember that you are working among living organisms. Try not to harm them. Watch where you are walking. If you remove organisms for close study, do so carefully. Then return them promptly to their habitats.

a. Prepare a full-page copy of Table 17-4. Your group will need 3 or 4 such copies. (Do not copy the example.)

Table 17-4   Littoral Zone Survey

| Name of organism | Zone | Relative abundance (a,f,o,r) | Habitat description | Adaptations | | Advantages to organism |
				Structural	Behavioural	
rough periwinkle	black zone	f	very dry; receives spray occasionally; covered only by spring tides; smooth rocky surface	thick shell; small opening; colour similar to rocks; looks like a pebble; has a file-like "foot"	seals itself to rock with mucus; moves to suitable environment	lessens water loss; protection against predators; scrapes algae off rocks for food

b. Visit the selected site when the tide is out. Prepare a transect strip as follows. Lay out two strings parallel to one another and 1 m apart. Begin at the water's edge and continue up to the supralittoral zone. Place the strings perpendicular to the water's edge. All your studies are to be done within this transect strip (Fig. 17-16).

Fig. 17-16   The transect strip for a study of zonation in the littoral zone.

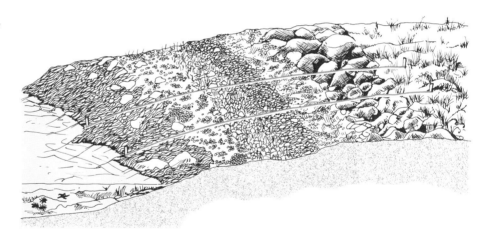

c. Study the kelp zone first. Enter the names of each organism (algae and animals) in your table. Note their relative abundance (a = abundant, f = frequent, o = occasional, r = rare). Then do the studies necessary to complete the rest of the table as outlined in Sections 17.6 and 17.7.

d. Study the remaining zones, in order, as you did the kelp zone.

Discussion

1. a) What abiotic factors show a gradient (gradual change) as you move from the kelp zone to the black zone?
   b) Explain how these gradients cause a zonation of organisms in the littoral zone.

2. Write a paper of about 500 words that describes the ecological relationships that exist on the shore that you studied. Begin by summarizing how the organisms of each zone have adapted in structure and behaviour to abiotic conditions in their zone. Write as many food chains as you can for the shore. Try to draw one food web for the shore. What is the importance of the open ocean and the land zone in the ecology of the littoral zone?

17.9 *FIELD TRIP* Comparing Two Tide Pools

You learned in Section 17.5 that striking differences exist between tide pools at low, mid or high littoral levels. On this field trip you will investigate these differences from an ecological perspective.

Problem

How do low and mid or high littoral pools differ ecologically?

Materials

white tray	metre stick
kitchen sieve	Hach water testing kits for salinity,
hand lens	oxygen, carbon dioxide, pH
probe	Hach water testing kits for all the other
identification book(s)	chemical factors discussed in Section
thermometer	5.7, page 95 (optional)

Procedure

a. Prepare a full-page copy of Table 17-5. Make extra rows for "Other geophysical factors" and "Other chemical factors" as directed by your teacher.
b. Prepare two full-page copies of Table 17-6.
c. Visit the selected site when the tide is out. Select a low and a mid or high pool for comparison.
d. Complete your copy of Table 17-5. That is, do the indicated geophysical and chemical tests for each pool. Each chemical test should normally be done three times. If one value differs greatly from the other two, ignore it. Otherwise average the three trials.
e. Complete your copy of Table 17-6 for each pool. Look back to Sections 17.6 and 17.7 to see how you should conduct your investigations. You may wish to use the kitchen sieve to catch the smaller invertebrates. See Section 12.7, page 187, for techniques. Don't forget to return all organisms to the water!

f. Rinse all metallic equipment with fresh water as soon as possible to lessen rusting.

Table 17-5 Tide Pool Comparison (Abiotic Factors)

Description of area (wave action, freshwater runoff, pollution, type of rock, etc.)

Date_____

Time_____

Weather: Wind speed_____

Wind dir._____

Sky_____

_____

_____

Factor		Low pool	Mid or high pool
Air temperature (°C)			
Water temperature (°C)	Surface		
	Mid-depth		
	Bottom		
Size of pool	Area (m²)		
	Average depth (m)		
Appearance of water (colour, clarity)			
Other geophysical factors			
Salinity (%)			
Oxygen (μg/g)			
Carbon dioxide (μg/g)			
pH			
Other chemical factors			

Table 17-6 Tide Pool Comparison (Biotic Factors)

Location of pool _____ (low, mid or high)

Name of organism	Relative abundance (a,f,o,r)	Adaptations		Advantages to organism
		Structural	Behavioural	

Discussion

1. Account for the differences in abiotic factors between the two pools.
2. Write a paper of about 500 words that explains the differences in the communities of organisms in the two pools.

17.10   *CASE STUDY*   **Comparing Two Tide Pools**

A class of students compared a low and a mid littoral pool as described in Section 17.9. Some of the data from that field trip are recorded in Table 17-7. Study those data closely. Then answer the questions that follow. The day was sunny and the field trip was done between noon and 16:00.

Questions

1. Why are the water temperatures lower in the low pool?
2. Why is the salinity higher in the mid pool?
3. **a)** Account for the unusually high oxygen concentration in the mid pool.
   b) What would you expect the oxygen concentration to be in this pool when the pool is exposed during the night? Why?
4. **a)** Why is the ammonia concentration higher in the mid pool than the low pool?
   b) Why is the nitrate concentration $0 \ \mu g/g$ in the mid pool?
5. Compare the environmental conditions preferred by brown and green algae.
6. Which pool has the greater diversity of life? Why is this so?

17.11   **Human Impact on Rocky Shores**

Rocky shores seem to attract people (Fig. 17-17). Some people are attracted by the rugged beauty of the wet rocks. Others are attracted by the fascinating array of life on the rocks and in the tidal pools. Still others come to collect food such as mussels and clams. Whatever the reason for the visit, the shore ecosystem suffers. Animals and algae get crushed under careless feet. Rare organisms get collected. Many organisms also are eaten.

The rocky shore is a source of food for humans. With careful management it can continue to provide us with food. We should remember, however, that it is also a source of food for both marine and land animals. For example, predators such as starfish move in with the tides to prey on mussels and other intertidal animals. Terrestrial animals such as racoons prey on intertidal animals when the tide is out. Shorebirds also prey on isopods, amphipods, and other small animals. Scavengers eat the dead plants and animals left by the receding tides.

Fig. 17-17 Rocky shores are always interesting to explore.

Table 17-7   Comparing Two Tide Pools

Factor		Low littoral pool (0.3 m above average low tide)	Mid littoral pool
Air temperature (°C)		26	26
Water temperature (°C)	Surface	23	28
	Mid depth	20	24
	Bottom	18	23
Size of pool	area (m²)	9	4
	average depth (m)	0.8	0.4
Appearance of water		clear, colourless	clear, colourless
Salinity (%)		3.5	3.9
Oxygen (μg/g)		7.0	20.1
Carbon dioxide (μg/g)		5.0	1.0
pH		9.2	8.6
Ammonia		0.1	0.3
Nitrate		0.1	0.0
Brown algae		*Fucus* (a); *Alaria* (a); *Laminaria* (r)	*Fucus* (o)
Red algae		*Chondrus* (f); *Rhodymenia* (f); *Ceramium* (f)	*Hildenbrandia* (o)
Green algae		none	*Ulva* (f); *Cladophora* (a); *Enteromorpha* (a)
Molluscs		limpet (f); dog whelk (o); mussel (f); common periwinkle (a); smooth periwinkle (f)	rough periwinkle (a)
Arthropods		amphipod (a) isopod (f); barnacle (a)	amphipod (a); barnacle (f)
Echinoderms		starfish (f); brittlestar (o); sea urchin (r)	none
Cnidarians		sea anemone (f)	none

Pollution by sewage, oil spills, and industries can devastate the rocky shore ecosystem (Fig. 17-18). We often dump wastes into the ocean assuming that, because of the large size of the ocean, the pollutants will do no harm. Yet onshore currents often build up lethal concentrations of pollutants along the shore.

Section Review

1. In what three ways do visitors to rocky shores affect life there?
2. Describe how rocky shore organisms are important to organisms from other ecosystems.
3. Why are rocky shore ecosystems often damaged unintentionally by pollution?

Fig. 17-18 Intertidal animals and many algae can be killed by pollutants such as sewage. Raw sewage runs from homes onto this shore. Also, a large city nearby pollutes this shore with its effluents. Little life except brown algae was found here.

Main Ideas

1. A zonation of organisms exists within the littoral zone.
2. A rocky shore has three main zones: littoral, supralittoral and sublittoral.
3. The supralittoral zone has two main zones: land and bare rock.
4. The littoral zone usually has six main zones: black, barnacle, rockweed, Irish moss, blue mussel and kelp.
5. The organisms in each zone have adapted to the unique abiotic factors in that zone.
6. Tide pools are classified according to their locations on the rocky shore as low littoral, mid littoral, high littoral or supralittoral.

Key Terms

intertidal zone

littoral zone

sublittoral zone

supralittoral zone

tide pool

zonation

Chapter Review

A. True or False

Decide whether each of the following statements is true or false. If the sentence is false, rewrite it to make it true. (Do not write in this book.)
1. The intertidal zone is always under water.
2. The sublittoral zone is also called the spray zone.

3. Organisms in the upper part of the littoral zone must be well adapted for moisture retention.
4. The black zone consists mainly of blue-green algae and lichens.
5. Starfish prey on mussels, oysters and other bivalves.
6. A low littoral pool usually has a greater diversity of life than a mid or high littoral pool in the same location.

B. Completion

Complete each of the following sentences with a word or phrase that will make the sentence correct. (Do not write in this book.)
1. The intertidal zone is also called the ▨▨▨▨ zone.
2. Of all the periwinkles, the ▨▨▨▨ periwinkle is best adapted for water retention.
3. When the tide is out, barnacles decrease water loss by ▨▨▨▨ .
4. Brown algae are not easily washed away by wave action because they have ▨▨▨▨ .
5. Irish moss is an important source of a gelling agent called ▨▨▨▨ .
6. A ▨▨▨▨ pool is essentially a freshwater environment.

C. Multiple Choice

Each of the following statements or questions is followed by four responses. Choose the correct response in each case. (Do not write in this book.)
1. The lower part of the land zone within the supralittoral zone is dominated by
   a) lichens   c) herbs and grasses
   b) blue-green algae   d) brown algae
2. The most serious problem faced by organisms in the littoral zone is
   a) predation   c) abrupt changes in salinity
   b) dessication   d) extremes of temperature
3. The rough periwinkle is well adapted to life in the
   a) kelp zone   c) rockweed zone
   b) Irish moss zone   d) black zone
4. Which of the following are quite commonly used for food by humans?
   a) kelp, mussels and starfish
   b) kelp, mussels and Irish moss
   c) sea urchins, mussels and sea anemones
   d) sea lettuce, kelp and sea urchins
5. If pollution killed the rockweeds in the rockweed zone, which organisms would likely disappear from that zone?
   a) barnacles   c) common periwinkles
   b) Irish moss   d) blue mussels

Using Your Knowledge

1. **a)** Why is the littoral zone also called the intertidal zone?
    b) Explain why a zonation of organisms exists in the littoral zone.
2. **a)** Explain why rock tripe is able to live in the supralittoral zone.
    b) Why does this lichen not occur in the littoral zone?
3. Suppose you visited a rocky shore and saw every rough periwinkle "glued" to a spot in the black zone. What would you conclude about past environmental conditions? Why?
4. The stalks of *Enteromorpha* usually extend up into the water during the day. Late at night, however, these stalks are often lying on the rocky bottom. Why?
5. A place on the north-east coast of North America has bladderless *Fucus* and no *Ascophyllum* in the rockweed zone. What is a likely characteristic of this place?
6. **a)** In what two ways are rockweeds important to periwinkles?
    b) State three ways that blue mussels have adapted to their environment.
7. **a)** Draw two food chains which likely exist in the blue mussel zone.
    b) How might these food chains be affected if pollution killed the starfish?
8. Explain why a low littoral pool usually has a greater diversity of organisms than a high littoral pool.

Investigations

1. Research the life cycle of a rocky shore invertebrate. Write a paper of about 150 words on your findings.
2. Mark several rough periwinkles with a small spot of nail polish. Note their positions on the shore. Return in a week and see if the periwinkles have remained in the same zone and location.
3. You may have seen barnacles or mussels on sea walls or pier supports. Investigate the relationship between their position and the tidal range.
4. Look for empty mussel shells that have a hole bored in them by a dog whelk. It will be a small neat hole. Where are the holes located? Is the shell thick or thin in this location?
5. Visit a rocky shore on a sunny hot day. Count the number of common periwinkles living on 1 m² of rockweed. Mark the study area. Return on an overcast cool day and repeat the count. Explain the difference.
6. Prepare a demonstration of the gelling properties of Irish moss by making blancmange as follows. Obtain a handful of fresh Irish moss. Wash it well then add it to one litre of milk. Cook the resulting mixture for 30 min in a double boiler. Then remove the Irish moss by pouring the mixture through a collander. Add enough sugar and vanilla to obtain the desired flavour. When the blancmange is cooled, it will become a firm jelly. Happy eating!

18 Sandy Shores

The sandy shore, in contrast to the rocky shore, appears barren of life (Fig. 18-1). But life does exist here. Most of the organisms, however, live beneath the surface. Like other coastal life, these organisms have adapted to the harsh conditions that accompany the changing water levels. This chapter describes some of these organisms and their adaptations. It also looks at the human activities which are affecting sandy beaches.

Fig. 18-1 The sandy shore may appear barren of life. But many organisms are adapted to living deep in the shifting sand.

18.1

Abiotic Factors and Zonation

Zonation

Figure 18-2 shows a beach profile. The sandy beach has three main zones—offshore, foreshore, and backshore.

The offshore zone, (also called the subtidal or sublittoral zone) is that area below the level of low tide. It extends out to the edge of the continental shelf. This zone may range from a metre to a kilometre in width. Sand bars and troughs occur here.

Fig. 18-2 Profile of a sandy beach and the adjacent dune area. ▶

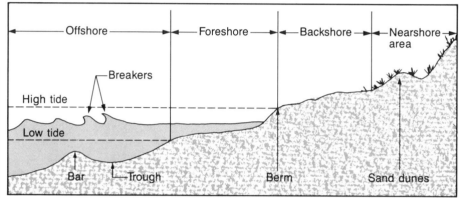

Fig. 18-3 Swash marks on the foreshore of a beach.

The next zone inland is the foreshore zone, (also called the intertidal or littoral zone). In general, it is a flat sloping surface. It is alternately covered by tidal water and exposed to air. A berm marks the upper limit of high tides. A berm is a nearly horizontal portion of the beach. It is formed from materials such as driftwood deposited by wave activity. The foreshore is also the zone of swash and backwash. Here waves rush back and forth over the beach. When the wave reaches its highest point on the beach, water percolates into the permeable sand. Thin wavy lines of fine sand and other debris are left behind. These are called swash marks (Fig. 18-3).

The third major zone is the backshore or supralittoral zone. It extends from the berm to the coastline. Beach shores are commonly bordered by a zone of perennial vegetation, dunes, cliffs or other coastal features. Except in storms, waves seldom reach this area.

The Sandy Shore

Sandy shores are in a constant state of change and motion. Every wave on a sandy beach lifts and moves quantities of sand. During the stormy winter months, high-energy waves erode the beach. Much of the sand is carried away and deposited offshore as sand bars. This action lowers the level of the beach. Sometimes it even exposes the underlying rocks. However, during the

Fig. 18-4 Coastal sand dunes are deposits of wind blown sand.

308 Chapter 18

calmer summer months, the smaller waves tend to wash the sand back on the beach. The beach usually returns to its former level.

Sand may also be transported to beaches from adjacent areas by longshore currents. Mass transport of sediment by longshore currents is commonly called the "river of sand". These currents run parallel to the shore. They are produced by waves being deflected at an angle by the shore.

The dry sands on the highest parts of the beach may be carried by winds. Strong onshore winds blow beach sands inland, often forming coastal sand dunes. A sand dune is a ridge of sand deposited by the wind (Fig. 18-4). This area of the shore, beyond the beach, is often called the nearshore zone.

If you have ever walked along the beach after a violent storm or high tide, you would have noticed much debris. Floating objects, masses of seaweed, small shells, and subtidal animals are cast ashore by waves and tides (Fig. 18-5). This is the ideal time to search for sea shells, but violent storms make life difficult for organisms. Only specialized animals can live in this turbulent world. The rest of this chapter looks at how life is adapted to living in the three zones of a sandy beach.

Fig. 18-5 Wave action, like this, often casts debris onto the shore.

Section Review

1. Where is life generally found on a sandy shore?
2. **a)** Name the three major zones of a beach.
    b) Write a brief note describing each of these zones.
3. **a)** What is a berm?
    b) What are swash marks?

18.2   Life in the Supralittoral Zone

We will study the three main zones of a sandy shore by taking an imaginary walk from the supralittoral zone on the right of Figure 18-6 to the water's edge. Let us begin by taking a close look at the supralittoral zone.

Plants

Shifting sands make life almost impossible for plants in the supralittoral zone. Sometimes small tufts of grass take root along the upper tide or drift line. An occasional plant from the adjacent sand dune community may also live here.

Animals

Very few species of animals live in this arid region of the beach. Those species that do live here are mostly arthropods. They seek protection from the intense heat and light by burrowing. Many insects and amphipods find food and shelter in the plant and animal debris deposited along the upper tide line.

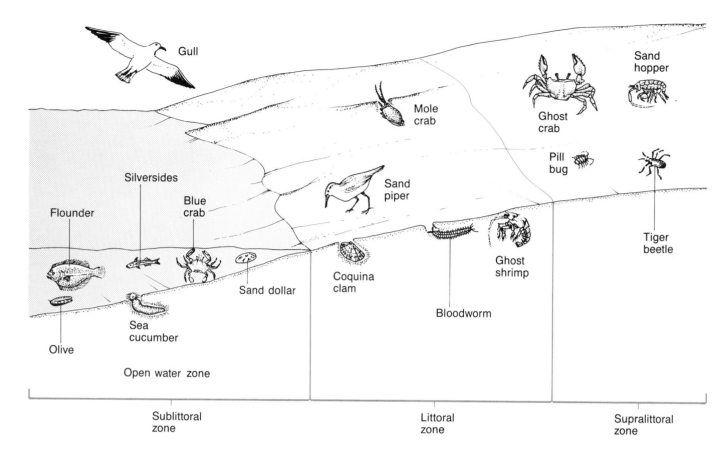

Fig. 18-6 Zonation on a sandy shore along the North Atlantic coast.

Let us look briefly at some of the animals which inhabit the supralittoral zone.

Ghost Crab Ghost crabs (*Ocypode*) are most common in warm and tropical regions. Their light colouration lessens absorption of heat. As well, it helps to camouflage them against the sand. The ghost crab can run faster than any other crustacean (Fig. 18-7).

To avoid the daytime heat, this crab burrows deeply into the sand. At night it scavenges on dead and decaying matter washed onto shore. Because it feeds at night, the ghost crab is called a nocturnal scavenger.

The adult ghost crab may live and act like a terrestrial animal. However, it is still a marine organism. It depends on the ocean for respiration. Each day it must wet its gills with the ocean water. It also depends on the ocean for reproduction. The female ghost crab returns to the ocean to spawn.

Sand Hopper The sand hopper, or beach flea (*Talorchestria*), is an amphipod. It can grow up to 6 cm long. The sand hopper survives the heat of the day and high tides by digging a small burrow. Sometimes it seeks shelter under seaweed debris. If disturbed, the sand hopper leaps from its hiding place. This is how it got its name. As the tide falls during the hours of

Fig. 18-7 A ghost crab.

darkness, thousands of sand hoppers emerge from their burrows. They scavenge on dead plants and animal matter in the littoral zone.

Pill Bugs   The supralittoral zone is also inhabited by pill bugs, also called sow bugs. Pill bugs are small isopods. They burrow just beneath the sand surface. They are active scavengers. Small isopods, less than 1 mm long, also live in the pore spaces between the sand grains.

Insects   Fast-running tiger beetles are common on the sandy beach. Kelp flies and other insects on the sandy beach provide a food source for various birds.

Section Review

1. **a)** What plants are found in the supralittoral zone of the sandy shore?
    b) Where is most life found in this zone? Why?
2. **a)** Name three organisms that live in the supralittoral zone of the sandy shore.
    b) For each organism, describe adaptations for food-gathering and adaptations for protection.

18.3　Life in the Littoral Zone

Phytoplankton and Plants

There are no permanent plants in the littoral zone. The shifting sands offer them no foothold. Instead, the chief producers are phytoplankton. Great numbers are washed ashore with the advancing tides. They serve as the base of food chains for intertidal animals.

Animals

Unlike the rocky shore, the surface of the sandy shore appears barren of life at low tide. But beneath the surface, life exists, waiting for the next high tide. By burrowing into the sand, organisms are protected from many environmental stresses. These include exposure to sun, heat, cold, wind, and rain. They are also safe from the pounding waves and ever-shifting sands.

Few animals are adapted to living in such harsh conditions. Those that have succeeded occur in large numbers. They are either proficient burrowers or fast crawlers that scurry back and forth with each wave. They are also rather small in size.

Because food is abundant, there is no serious competition for food sources. The microscopic life found on and among the sand grains is an important food source. As well, plant and other debris are continuously thrown up on the beach. Let us look briefly at some of the common animals associated with the littoral zone of the sandy shore.

Fig. 18-8 Mole crab scraping food particles off its antennas.

Mole Crab   The mole or sand crab, *Emerita*, is a fascinating little creature. This crustacean is 3-5 cm long. Great numbers live buried in the top layer of sand. They are carried in unison up and down the beach with the tide.

Unlike other crabs, the mole crab moves only backwards. Each time a wave advances, it burrows backward into the shifting sands. It always faces the surf. As the wave recedes, it extends its antennas, filtering the water for suspended plankton. Food particles are scraped off as the antennas are drawn through the mouth parts (Fig. 18-8).

Coquina Clam   The coquina clam, *Donax*, is a small triangular-shaped clam. Its smooth thick shell can withstand the pounding of the surf. Each clam has a slightly different colour pattern.

Coquinas live in clusters just below the surface of the sand. There are often several hundred per square metre. As the waves wash them out of the sand, they burrow back beneath the surface. They extend their siphon tubes above the surface of the sand to filter small organisms out of the water. Some species move up and down the beach with the tides. The small hydroid, *Clytia*, often grows on the clam's shell. It extends above the sand surface. This gives away the hiding place of the clam.

Other clams which burrow more deeply into the sand are also found on many sandy shores. Among these are the razor clam, *Siliqua*. These are sought after by gourmets. On the California coast, the razor clam is replaced by the pismo clam, *Tivela*.

Bloodworm   The bloodworm, *Glycera*, is a bright red worm about 4-6 cm long. These worms live in colonies just below the surface of the sand. Often there are as many as 30 000 worms per square metre.

The bloodworm is nick-named the "breakthrower". When searching for food, it extends and contracts a tubelike organ from its head. This is called a proboscis. It is used to capture small worms and small invertebrates.

Predatory Visitors   Shorebirds are often abundant along the sandy shore. Gulls and terns fly along the shore in search of food. Sandpipers and plovers race up and down the beach with the waves. They probe and snatch tiny crustaceans from the sand when the waves recede (Fig. 18-9). Cliff swallows sweep over the shore, capturing flies and other insects over the sands. Many migratory birds also stop by to feed and rest. At night many mammals visit the beach in search of food. Among them are skunks, racoons, and rodents. Various coastal fish move in at high tide to feed.

Beach Mating   Several marine species move on the beach to mate or lay eggs. Large sea turtles come on shore to lay their eggs in the sand (Fig. 18-10). When the eggs hatch, the young head towards the ocean. Many are eaten by predators before they reach the ocean.

Fig. 18-9 Gulls scavenge for food on the sandy shore.

Thousands of grunion, a silver smelt-like fish, spawn on the southern California beaches. This spawning occurs just after the highest spring tides, from the end of March to about August. The female burrows into the wet sand and deposits her eggs. The male then fertilizes them. Then both return to the ocean. During the next spring tide, the eggs hatch. The young fish are carried to the ocean with the receding waters.

Section Review

1. What are the main producers of the littoral zone? Why?
2. Where is most life found in this zone? Why?
3. **a)** Name three organisms that live in the littoral zone of the sandy shore.
   b) For each organism, describe adaptations for food-gathering and adaptations for protection.
4. What mammals commonly visit the sandy shore to feed?
5. Name two animals that come on shore to mate or lay eggs.

Fig. 18-10 These sea turtles come ashore to lay their eggs.

18.4 Life in the Sublittoral Zone

Phytoplankton and Plants

Phytoplankton are the main producers of the sublittoral zone. In fact, they are the most important producers of the sandy shore ecosystem. They are usually very abundant and provide food for the many filter feeding animals.

Large plants and attached seaweeds generally do not grow here. The sand does not provide a solid base for anchorage. Powerful ocean waves would easily upset them.

Zooplankton and Animals

Numerous zooplankton are carried in with the currents and waves. Among these are copepods, isopods, and amphipods. Larval forms of crabs, worms, starfishes, and sea cucumbers are also common. As well, swarms of jellyfish drift inland during certain seasons.

Many animals burrow into the sand. Here they are safe from the pounding surf. Among these animals are blue crabs, clams, sea cucumbers, and sand dollars. Some swimmers burrow temporarily into the bottom. However, few animals that build permanent tubes or burrows live here. The ever-shifting sand quickly clogs and covers their burrows.

Other animals are more tolerant of turbulent waters. For example, the tube feet of starfish help the starfish to maintain secure suction against the substrate. Some animals are efficient swimmers. Flounders, killifish, and silversides are common predatory fishes. They feed on small fishes and invertebrates.

The rushing waves prevent detritus from settling on the sandy bottom. Therefore, very few deposit or detritus feeders live on this bottom. Instead, many sublittoral animals are filter feeders.

Section Review

1. What are the main producers of the sublittoral zone? Why?
2. What animals are commonly found in the sublittoral zone?
3. How have these animals adapted to the pounding surf?

18.5 ACTIVITY Adaptations of Sandy Shore Invertebrates

Marine invertebrates show both structural and behavioural adaptations to their habitats. This activity uses preserved specimens. Therefore you will be looking just at structural adaptations in the laboratory. You can find out about the behavioural adaptations of some of the animals by watching them in a marine aquarium or on a field trip. You can read about them in other sections of this book.

Problem

How have marine invertebrates adapted to their habitats?

Materials

preserved specimens of a few marine invertebrates, for example, mole crab, ghost shrimp, clam, sea cucumber, sand dollar, pill bug, sand hopper, bloodworm, lugworm
hand lens   probe   tray

Procedure

a. Copy Table 18-1 into your notebook.

Table 18-1   Adaptations of Marine Invertebrates

| Name of animal | Habitat | Adaptations | | Advantages to animal |
		Structural	Behavioural	

b. Get an invertebrate from your teacher and put it in the tray.

c. Record the habitat of this animal in your table. You can find this information in earlier sections of this book. (Use the index.)

d. Study the animal closely. (Do not damage it. Then it can be used by other students in the future.) Note its body covering, colour, and its adaptations for feeding, holding on in the shifting sands, burrowing, and moving. Note any other interesting structural features (Fig. 18-11). Record these features in your table.

e. Complete the "behavioural" column of your table by observing living animals in an aquarium or on a field trip. (If this is not possible, get the information from earlier sections of this text.)

f. Repeat steps (b) to (e) for the other animals provided.

g. Complete the "Advantages to animal" column of your table.

Fig. 18-11 What adaptations does a clam have that make it possible for it to obtain food when burrowed in the sand?

Discussion

A completed table is your write-up for this activity.

Investigating Zonation in the Littoral Zone

18.6   *FIELD TRIP*

You learned in Section 18.3 that most of the animals which live in the littoral zone are efficient burrowers or fast crawlers. Others visit the beach in search of food or a mate. As a result, the animals are often difficult to find. On this field trip you will work in a group with 3 or 4 other students to investigate the ecology of the littoral zone of a sandy beach. Be patient and look closely.

Problem

What ecological relationships exist between littoral organisms and their environments?

Materials

white tray	identification book(s)
hand lens	ball of coarse string (2)
probe	metre stick

Procedure

Note: Remember that you are working among living organisms. Try not to harm them. Watch where you are walking. If you remove organisms for close study, do so carefully. Then return them promptly to their habitats.

a. Prepare a full-page copy of Table 18-2. Your group will need 3 or 4 such copies. (Do not copy the example.)

Table 18-2 Zonation in the Littoral Zone

Name of organism	Relative abundance (a,f,o,r)	Habitat description	Adaptations		Advantages to organism
			Structural	Behavioural	
mole crab	o	dry, hot sand at times; covered daily by tides; sands shift	antennas trap food	burrows into sand; faces surf; extends antennas above sand	lessens water loss; protection from tides and predators

b. Visit the selected site when the tide is out. Prepare a transect strip as follows. Lay out two strings parallel to one another and 2 m apart. Begin at the water's edge and continue up to the supralittoral zone. Place the strings perpendicular to the water's edge. All your studies are to be done within this transect strip. You will have to dig carefully into the sand to locate burrowers.

c. Work from the water's edge inland. Enter the names of each organism in your table. Note their relative abundance (a = abundant, f = frequent, o = occasional, r = rare). Then do the studies necessary to complete the rest of the table as outlined in Section 18.5.

Discussion

1. Is there a zonation of organisms, either on or below the surface, as you proceed landward? Explain.

2. Write a paper of about 500 words that describes the ecological relationships that exist on the shore that you studied. Begin by summarizing how the organisms have adapted in structure and behaviour to the abiotic conditions in this zone. Write as many food chains as you can for the shore. Try to draw one food web from the chains. What is the importance of the open ocean and the land zone in the ecology of the littoral zone?

Human Impact on Sandy Shores

The sandy shore is most famous as a recreational area. It is also home for many organisms. As well, it plays an important part in biochemical cycles. The products of decomposition are washed back to the ocean by waves and tides. Thus the sandy shore supplies offshore waters with phosphates, nitrogen, and other nutrients. However, life in the sandy shore is threatened by pollution, industrial development, and overharvesting. Toxic chemicals, pesticides, and heavy metals can kill or damage marine life. When some chemicals become concentrated, marine life can be unfit to eat. Large oil spills can leave kilometres of beaches blackened. Oil adheres to bird feathers, thereby preventing the bird from flying, makes them sink in the water and sometimes poisons them. It kills fish and numerous other coastal organisms. As a result, recreational facilities along the coast are often ruined.

Many organisms are forced to move to another area when a beach becomes a popular holiday resort. Offroad vehicles can crush life both on and below the surface. Sometimes "breakwaters" are built offshore to prevent waves from damaging swimming areas. These barriers can prevent fishes and turtles from coming onshore to lay their eggs.

Various crabs, clams, shrimp, turtles, and fish are collected for food and as souvenirs. However, in many instances overharvesting endangers certain species. How do you think we should cope with overharvesting?

Section Review

1. State three reasons why the sandy shore is important.
2. Briefly summarize how humans are threatening the existence of life on the sandy shore.

Main Ideas

1. A sandy shore has three main zones: littoral (foreshore), supralittoral (backshore), and sublittoral (offshore).
2. Shifting sands and waves prevent large plants from taking root along the sandy shore.
3. Most animals burrow into the sand for protection against the environmental stresses.
4. The organisms of each zone have adapted to the abiotic conditions of that zone.
5. Life on the sandy shore is threatened by pollution, industrial development, and overharvesting.

Key Terms

backshore

foreshore

littoral zone

longshore currents

nocturnal scavenger

offshore

sand bar

sand dune

sublittoral zone

supralittoral zone

Chapter Review

A. True or False

Decide whether each of the following statements is true or false. If the sentence is false, rewrite it to make it true. (Do not write in this book.)

1. No plants grow on the sandy shore.
2. The sand hopper is a filter feeder.
3. Phytoplankton are an important food source for intertidal animals.
4. Many animals burrow into the sand for protection.

B. Completion

Complete each of the following sentences with a word or phrase that will make the sentence correct. (Do not write in this book.)

1. The main producers of the sandy shore are ░░░░░░░ .
2. Organisms that feed at night are called ░░░░░░ .
3. Two organisms that occupy the supralittoral zone are ░░░░░░ and ░░░░░░ .
4. The small ░░░░░░ often grows on the shell of the coquina clam.

C. Multiple Choice

Each of the following statements or questions is followed by four responses. Choose the correct response in each case. (Do not write in this book.)

1. Two common inhabitants of the littoral zone are
    a) starfishes and periwinkles
    b) mole crabs and bloodworms
    c) ghost crabs and pill bugs
    d) gulls and sand dollars
2. The mole crab is different from other crabs in that it
    a) only moves backward
    b) burrows upside down in the sand
    c) visits the supralittoral zone to feed and mate
    d) has one oversized claw
3. The function of the proboscis of a bloodworm is to
    a) dig a burrow
    b) assist movement
    c) assist breathing
    d) capture food

Using Your Knowledge

1. Why are the inhabitants of the sandy shore generally small in size?
2. The number of species found on the sandy shore is few. However the number of individuals is many. Why is this so?
3. List the organisms found on a sandy shore according to their feeding types: filter feeders, detritus feeders, scavengers, predators. Which type dominates in each zone of the beach?
4. Many beaches annually lose vast quantities of sand. Discuss three ways by which this problem can be controlled.

Investigations

1. Research the life cycle of a sandy shore invertebrate. Write a paper of about 150 words on your findings.
2. Find out which organisms of the sandy shore are favourite foods of seafood gourmets.
3. Fill a bucket or large jar two-thirds full of sand. Top it up with sea water. Compare the burrowing techniques of two hard body and two soft body marine invertebrates by placing *one* organism at a time into the bucket or jar. Which method is most efficient? Which organism burrows the quickest? How do they free themselves if they become covered with too much sand by wave action? How do burrowing animals know when to retreat into the sand before the approach of the next incoming tide? Write a report on your findings. Don't forget to return the organisms to the water!
4. The marine flatworm, *Convoluta roscoffensis*, moves up on to the beach surface at low tide allowing its symbiotic algae to photosynthesize. Find another example of a symbiotic relationship on a sandy shore.
5. Make a collection of empty shells found on the shore. Label each shell with the locality, habitat, and date of collection. Using a shell identification guide book, identify each shell.
6. Walk along the sea shore. List all debris washed up on the shore or lying in the water. Divide your list into things that are there as a result of human activity and things that are there naturally. Which list is longer? Account for your data.
7. Find out the effects of major oil spills on marine and coastal life. How are oil slicks and beaches cleaned up? Who is in charge of cleanup in your area? Have any fines ever been issued? Write a 300 word report on your findings.

19 Salt Marshes, Mud Flats, and Estuaries

The salt marsh, mud flat, and estuary together make up one of the most productive of all ecosystems. They contain an abundant and diverse community of organisms. They also provide a nursery for many other marine and freshwater organisms. Unfortunately, pollution and industrial development are quickly reducing this productivity.

In this chapter you will study the characteristic abiotic and biotic properties of salt marshes, mud flats, and estuaries. As well, you will learn how human activities are affecting these areas.

19.1 Abiotic Factors and Zonation

Zonation

As in the rocky and sandy shores, a zonation of life is found in the salt marsh. This zonation is determined by tides and salinity. It varies from place to place. Within each zone, organisms are adapted to the specific environmental conditions of that zone.

The salt marsh has three main zones: sublittoral, littoral, and supralittoral. The sublittoral and littoral zones are often referred to as the low marsh. The supralittoral zone is known as the high marsh

The low marshes are younger. They are developed on mud and silt. They are flooded at least once each day (Fig. 19-1).

Fig. 19-1 View of a low salt marsh at high tide.

The high marshes are older. They have a drier sandy substrate. They are submerged only during high spring tides and storms. Thus they are more terrestrial in character.

Below the marsh vegetation and extending out to low tide level, there is generally an area of mud or sand flats. These tidal flats are intertidal habitats. Mud flats also occur along the upper portions of estuaries.

Salt Marshes

Cutting through the tidal flats are many channels or creeks. It is through these channels and creeks that seawater enters and drains from the marsh with the tides. Pond holes called **pannes** also occur. Tidal currents usually leave the marsh water turbid and full of silt.

The salt marsh is continuously changing. During high tide, dense vegetation slows down water movement. This causes deposition of mud and silt contained in overlying water. With time, decaying plant material and sediment accumulate. These in turn elevate the marsh, making it no longer intertidal. Other plants then invade the habitat, and a new type of community eventually develops.

The oxygen supply in the water is generally sufficient. However, it is absent in the mud. Bacterial decomposition in the mud quickly depletes the oxygen. Then hydrogen sulfide accumulates in the mud. This gives marshes a characteristic rotten-egg odour.

Fresh water flooding and tidal cycles can cause wide changes in salinity. Evaporation increases the salinity of the water. It can also leave heavy salt deposits in the mud. Fresh water runoff during the spring helps to reduce salinity. The tidal cycles also cause wide ranges in temperatures in the marsh. The marsh becomes very hot when the tide is out and cools when the tide returns. Thus salt marsh organisms must be able to withstand wide ranging temperatures, variations in salinity, limited oxygen, and tidal cycles (Fig. 19-2).

Fig. 19-2 How do you suppose the blue crab withstands the changing conditions of the salt marsh?

Mud Flats

Tidal waters prevent mud flats from completely drying out. However, water temperature fluctuates considerably during the tidal cycle. In the summer, the sun heats the mud flats during low tides. Cooler water is brought in with the incoming tides. In the winter the reverse occurs.

Like the salt marsh, the range of salinity is wide. Evaporation causes high salinity in small tide pools. During heavy rains, salinity may decrease.

Estuaries

Continuous Change   Estuaries are continuously being reshaped. River-carried sediments help to form deltas. Due to the Coriolis Effect (see Section 15.3 page 237), silt and mud tend to be deposited on the left shore. With time, mud flats develop. As well, ocean currents, tides, and winds erode the coastline. If more material is deposited than is carried away, barrier islands, sand bars, and lagoons result.

Salinity   Salinity varies horizontally and vertically. It can also vary with the season and the amount of rainfall. Thus organisms living in the estuary must be adapted to such changes.

Horizontally, the least saline waters are at the river entrance, and the most saline waters are at the mouth of the estuary (Fig. 19-3). Vertically, salinity may be stratified, with a layer of fresh water on top and a layer of dense salt water on the bottom. The salinity may be homogenous, since strong winds and currents can mix the water from top to bottom.

The salinity also varies throughout the year. The salinity is highest during the summer and during periods of drought when less fresh water flows into the estuary. It is lowest during the winter and spring when runoff is high. Any sudden changes in salinity can have a profound effect on life of the estuary.

Fig. 19-3 Estuarine salinity increases from river entrance to open ocean.

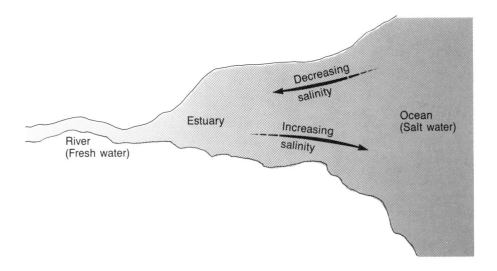

1. What factors determine the zonation of life in the salt marsh?
2. Distinguish between low marsh and high marsh.
3. Describe the network of tidal flats and channels in the salt marsh.
4. Does succession occur in a salt marsh? Explain.
5. Explain why the mud flat is considered a harsh environment.
6. Describe how salinity varies horizontally, vertically, and seasonally within an estuary.

19.2   Life in the Supralittoral Zone of the Salt Marsh

Salt marshes have a wide variety of plant and animal species which occupy a large number of niches. The abundance and type of life is influenced by both water depth and salinity. Many ocean organisms also begin their lives in salt marshes. For this reason, the marshes are often called "the cradles of the ocean". This wide diversity helps to make the salt marsh one of nature's most self-sustaining ecological systems. Let us begin our study of life in the salt marsh with the supralittoral zone.

Plants

Figure 19-4 shows the zonation of plants in the supralittoral zone of an Atlantic coast salt marsh. This vegetation is basically terrestrial. However, its growth is not as vigorous as growth in the low marsh. The reason is that nutrients are not as plentiful here.

The uppermost zone is the shrub zone. It is dominated by marsh elder (*Iva*) and groundsel (*Baccharis*). In the autumn, groundsel is covered with flowers which look like small cotton balls. Thus it is often called "cotton bush".

Several other plants grow here. These include bayberry (*Myrica heterophylla*) and wax myrtle (*Myrica cerifera*). Also common are goldenrod (*Solidago*) and pink flowered sea hollyhock (*Hibiscus*).

Grasses and rushes grow in the uppermost part of the marsh. Common grasses include reed grass (*Phragmites*), panic grass (*Panicum*) and red top grass (*Agrostis*). Where there is fresh water, the spikerush (*Eleocharis*) and narrowleaf cattail (*Typha*) are usually found.

Just below the shrub zone is the black grass zone. It is so-called because the dark green grass (*Juncus*) turns almost black in the fall.

Still closer to the water is the *Spartina patens* zone. *Spartina patens* is also called salt meadow hay. It is a small, fine-leaved grass. It usually grows to a

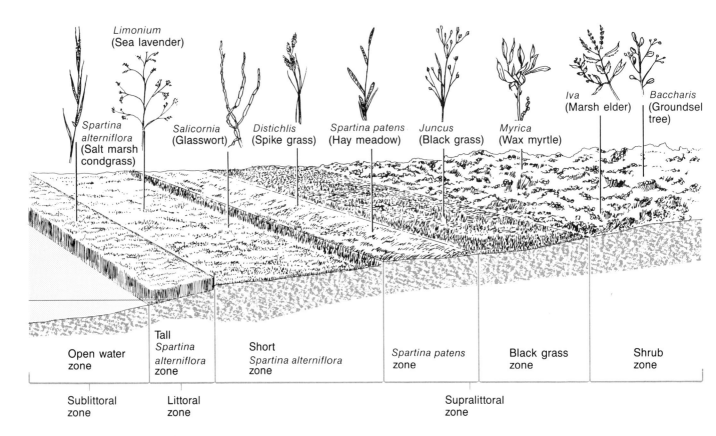

Fig. 19-4 **Zonation of plants in a New England salt marsh.**

height of up to 1 m. Because it grows very densely, few other plants grow with it. *Spartina patens* is commonly grazed or harvested as a forage crop for cattle. When *Spartina patens* ages, it usually falls over. This forms a mat through which the next year's growth emerges. Blue-green and green algal mats may form on the fallen leaves. Together, these mats help to keep the soil moist.

The spike grass, *Distichlis spicata*, also dominates the high marsh. It often grows with the short form of *Spartina alterniflora* and with *Spartina patens*. Spike grass is usually found in the wetter, more saline parts of the high marsh. It can withstand higher concentrations of salt than *Spartina patens*.

The lowest zone of the supralittoral zone is the short *Spartina alterniflora* zone. This plant is a yellow grass. The decrease in nutrients at this location may account for its reduced growth.

Growing among the short *Spartina* are sea lavender (*Limonium*), sea blite (*Suaeda*) and spearscale (*Atriplex*). Seaside plantain (*Plantago*) and glasswort (*Salicornia*) also occur here. The thick, fleshy stems of the glasswort can be pickled and preserved. They are considered a delicacy.

Animals

The animal life of the supralittoral zone changes almost as quickly as the vegetation. The marsh snail *Melampus* is a common scavenger of this zone.

Fig. 19-5 The marsh snail *Melampus*.

This tiny coffee bean coloured snail generally lives at and above the tide line. At low tide, *Melampus* occurs in high numbers at the base of *Spartina patens* (Fig. 19-5). Here it feeds on small algae and detritus. Just before high tide, *Melampus* moves back up the stem.

The marsh crab replaces the fiddler crab of the littoral zone. It resembles the fiddler crab, but the male has two tiny claws instead of one large and one small claw. It burrows in the upper region of the marsh. It feeds on the outer leaves of cordgrass. It also eats dead and small living animals.

The meadow mouse often nests among *Spartina patens*. It feeds heavily on the grasses. The grasses and shrubs provide food and shelter for many birds. The redwing blackbird, for example, nests in the dense growths of marsh elder and groundsel. In the remote stands of these shrubs, nests of smaller herons and egrets are often found. The willet and the seaside sharp-tailed sparrow replace the intertidal clapper rail and seaside sparrow.

Section Review

1. **a)** Name in order the four zones of plants found in the supralittoral zone of an Atlantic salt marsh.
    b) For each plant zone, list the dominant and commonly occurring plants.
2. Briefly describe the animal life of the supralittoral zone.

19.3 Life in the Littoral Zone of the Salt Marsh

The organisms that live here must be adapted to the harsh conditions that accompany the changing water levels. They must tolerate sudden changes in salinity, temperature, and oxygen.

Plants

The littoral zone is dominated by the tall smooth cordgrass *Spartina alterniflora* (Fig. 19-6). This is the most abundant large plant of the marsh. Plant growth is generally more vigorous in the lower marsh. It is here that the most nutrients are received from tidal waters.

Spartina alterniflora is a very coarse, green-leaved grass. It can grow to a height of 3 m. It is tallest along the edge of tidal creeks and channels. It becomes progressively shorter toward the high marsh.

Adaptations *Spartina alterniflora* has a wide range of salt tolerance. It is semisubmerged in salt water at high tide. At low tide it is exposed to the sun. It has adapted to these conditions by selectively absorbing sodium chloride from the water. The salt is concentrated in its cells. Then it is excreted

Fig. 19-6 Salt marsh cordgrass is the most abundant and important grass of the salt marsh.

Fig. 19-7 A marsh periwinkle on the stem of cordgrass at high tide.

through special salt-secreting cells in the leaves. When the surface water evaporates, sparkling salt crystals remain behind. These are later washed away during high tide.

Oxygen is absent in the mud, but is abundant in the surface waters. *Spartina alterniflora* has adapted to these conditions with a series of hollow tubes running throughout the plant. These carry oxygen from the leaves to the roots.

Because of the lack of oxygen, marsh sediments are high in sulfides. Sulfides are toxic to most plants. However, *Spartina alterniflora* has the ability to take up sulfides. Then they are converted within the plant to useable sulfates.

Importance *Spartina alterniflora* is the most ecologically important large plant of the marsh. It is the major source of detritus for the community. About half of this detritus is carried away by tides. It then becomes a significant part of the estuarine food web. This plant also provides food and cover for both marine and terrestrial animals. Because it grows in thick stands, it helps to reduce erosion. Waterfront property owners often plant *Spartina alterniflora* within the littoral zone of their shoreline to reduce the eroding effects of wave action.

Algae Algae cover the entire littoral zone substrate. The upper region supports blue-green algae. The middle region has mainly brown algae. At the low tide mark, red algae dominate. Tiny algae also live on blades of marsh grass.

Animals

Some of the inhabitants are permanent residents. Others are seasonal visitors. Still others come to feed at low or high tide.

The marsh periwinkle, ribbed mussel, and marsh fiddler crab are permanent residents amongst the tall *Spartina alterniflora*. Let us take a brief look at them.

Marsh Periwinkle At high tide, the marsh periwinkle moves up the stem of *Spartina* (Fig. 19-7). It does so to avoid drowning and to escape from predators. At low tide it moves back down and onto the mud. Here it feeds on algae and detritus.

Ribbed Mussel The ribbed mussel partly buries itself in the mud. At high tide it opens its shell to feed. It filters plankton, bacteria, and organic detritus from the water. When the tide recedes, the shell closes.

Marsh Fiddler Crab If you have ever visited the salt marsh at low tide, you would have seen an army of fiddler crabs running across the mud. The male is identified by its one oversized claw (Fig. 19-8). It is thought that the male uses its large claw to beckon a female mate. Marsh fiddler crabs live in burrows. They have both gills and lungs. Thus they can endure periods of high tide. They are omnivores and, as a result, fare well in the diverse habitat of the salt marsh.

Visitors   When the tide is in, many fish, crabs, and turtles spread over the marsh to feed. When the tide is out, many predaceous animals invade the marsh from the landward edge. The sharp claws of the racoon allow it to dig for mussels and crabs. Herons, egrets, and gulls feed on small fishes, crustaceans, insects, and frogs. The willet, tern, and ibis also fly in to feed.

Some birds nest among *Spartina*. Two of the most common are clapper rails and seaside sparrows. Their diets include sandhoppers, aquatic insects, and fiddler crabs. The diamond-backed terrapin is another common resident. It hibernates in the marsh mud.

Insects   Numerous insects also occupy the marsh. Two of the best known inhabitants of this zone are the salt marsh mosquito and the greenhead fly. The mosquito breeds in the still marsh pools. The greenhead fly lays its eggs on the stems of *Spartina*. Any person who has visited a salt marsh can tell you what these two insects like to eat. You never forget the bite of a greenhead fly!

Fig. 19-8 The male marsh fiddler crab is easily recognized by its one oversized claw.

Section Review

1. What is the dominant plant of the littoral zone of the salt marsh?
2. Describe three adaptations of *Spartina alterniflora* to the harsh conditions of the littoral zone.
3. State three reasons why *Spartina alterniflora* is important.
4. **a)** Name three animals that live amongst the *Spartina alterniflora*.
   b) How have they adapted to the rise and fall of the tide?
5. What animals commonly visit the littoral zone in search of food during low and high tides?

19.4   Life in the Sublittoral Zone of the Salt Marsh

Plants and Phytoplankton

Phytoplankton are plentiful in the sublittoral zone. This is due to the abundance of nutrients. These are made available from decomposing marsh grass and other debris. Waves and currents prevent large algae and grasses from establishing here. Occasionally kelp is washed in from nearby communities.

Animals

Zooplankton are also abundant in this zone. Estuarine waters flowing through the marshes are nursery grounds for larval and juvenile stages of many marine mammals. Included are such animals as the flounder, squid, and sand shrimp.

Several subtidal dwellers move onto the marsh at high tide to feed. The killifish, for example, feeds on a variety of small invertebrates and plant vegetation. The sand shrimp and blue crab also come in to feed.

Section Review

1. Distinguish between the low marsh and high marsh.
2. What phytogenic organisms live in the sublittoral zone of the salt marsh? Why do they live there?
3. What animals live in the sublittoral zone of the salt marsh?

19.5   *ACTIVITY* Adaptations of Marsh Plants

All organisms show adaptations to their habitats and salt marsh plants are no exception. They have adapted to the wide ranging temperatures, salinity, limited oxygen, and tidal cycles. Many have also adapted to the strong sunlight and the exposure to winds and strong wave action. In this activity you will examine some marsh plants to see how they have adapted.

Problem

How have marsh plants adapted to their habitat?

Materials

fresh or preserved specimens of a few marsh plants, for example, *Spartina alterniflora, Spartina patens*, seaside plantain (*Plantago*), glasswort (*Salicornia*)

dissecting knife   hand lens   probe   tray

Procedure

a. Copy Table 19-1 into your notebook.

Table 19-1   Adaptations of Marsh Plants

Name of plant	Habitat	Adaptations	Advantages to plant

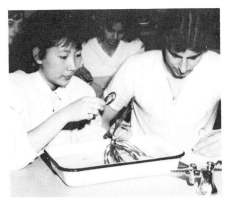

Fig. 19-9 Carefully observe how each plant's stems, leaves and roots are adapted to living in the salt marsh.

b. Get a sample of a marsh plant from your teacher and place it in the tray.

c. Record the habitat of this plant in your table. You can find this information in the earlier sections of this chapter.

d. Study the plant's leaves, stems, and roots closely. Note their texture (feel), thickness, shape, height, rigidity, colour, and other structural features (Fig. 19-9). You may find it helpful to cut through the plant stem and examine the cut with a hand lens. Record these features in your table.

e. Repeat steps (b) to (d) with the other plants provided.

f. Complete the "Advantages to plant" column of your table.

Discussion

A completed table is your write-up for this activity.

19.6   Life in the Mud Flat

Plants and Phytoplankton

Wave action keeps the tidal flats relatively free of plants. Instead, mats of blue-green and green algae typically cover the mud flats. However, on the sandier portions of the flats, green, brown, and red seaweeds often grow. These are most abundant in the sublittoral zone. Some species extend into the littoral zone. Several species remain covered by water in the tidal pools. Occasionally, the sublittoral eel grass (*Zostera*) extends into the lower littoral zone. Marine seaweeds and grasses provide protective cover and a home for many small animals. They also trap silt and prevent it from washing out to the ocean.

The main producers of the tidal flats are phytoplankton. Large numbers are continuously brought in with the tides and currents.

Mud flats act as sinks for energy and nutrients. Tides and currents carry inorganic nutrients and detrital organic matter, often from nearby marshes, to the mud flats. Inorganic nutrients provide sufficient minerals for the plants of the mud flats. The organic detritus provides an important source of energy for the animals of the mud flat.

Animals

The tidal flats are home for a wide variety of animals. The species present vary with the substrate and geographical location.

In general, the young stages of many marine animals develop among the sublittoral grasses and seaweeds. There they find protective cover. The adult stages of annelids (segmented worms), molluscs, and crustaceans are often abundant on the flats (Fig. 19-10). They live in close association with the bottom. Like all life within the littoral zone, they have adapted to the harsh conditions that accompany the changing water levels.

Fig. 19-10 Clumps of mussel on a mud flat at low tide.

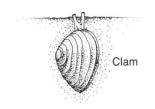

Clam

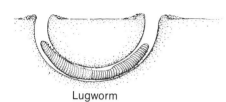

Lugworm

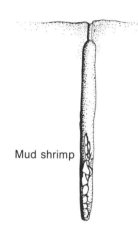

Mud shrimp

Fig. 19-11 Mud flat organisms burrow in a variety of ways.

Fig. 19-12 Some fish that visit the mud flats at high tide to feed.

Burrowers Few organisms remain on the exposed surface at low tide. Some move with the tides to the sublittoral zone. However, most burrow into the substrate. Among these are worms, clams, shrimps, and snails. Burrowing provides protection from predation and desiccation (drying out).

Depending on the type of substrate, some burrowers retreat into permanent or temporary burrows or tubes. The tube openings look like "chimney tops" and often dot the tidal flat surface by the hundreds. The tops of some worm tubes are camouflaged with seaweed and small shells. Other organisms like the mud snail burrow only slightly into the mud. Still others move freely through the substrate (Fig. 19-11).

Lugworms (*Arenicola*) live in permanent U-shaped burrows. They tunnel their way through the mud-sand substrate. Often their burrows are 30 cm or more in depth. Their burrows are identified by the coiled sediment castings deposited near the entrance.

Most tube builders and burrowers have some means of obtaining oxygen and food. Clams extend their siphons into the water above the substrate. Oxygen and food are then drawn in. The plumed worm extends its head and much of its body out its tube opening. It catches tiny invertebrates by moving its proboscis in and out. The mud shrimp gets its food and oxygen by creating a current of water with its swimmerettes. Tiny hairs covering the first two pairs of legs help filter the water for plankton and detritus.

Feeding Types Four different types of feeding mechanisms are found on the tidal flats. Filter feeders feed on suspended plankton. Among the filter feeders are some worms, clams, shrimps, mussels, and oysters. Deposit feeders extract algae, fungi, and bacteria from the bottom sediments. These include certain species of worms, crabs, shrimps, sea urchins, and sand dollars. Predators on the flats include crabs, shrimps, and whelks. The major scavengers are snails.

Fish When the tide is in, numerous fish invade the flats (Fig. 19-12). Some are seasonal visitors. Others are common year round. The silversides and killifish, for example, are generally abundant year round. Menhaden, flounder, and rays are a few of the many other common tidal visitors. They feed on plankton, vegetation, and tidal flat animals.

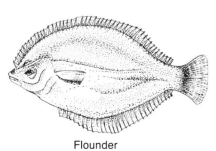

Flounder

Killifish

Silversides

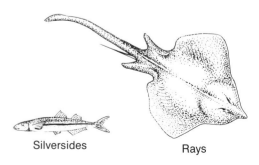

Rays

Birds Many birds also visit the tidal flats. Wading birds, such as the heron and egret, hunt for fish in shallow waters. Deep-probing shorebirds use their beaks to search for worms and clams in the mud. Diving and floating birds swim underwater to gather plants and animals along the bottom. Large birds of prey, such as osprey and bald eagle, dive for fish and other prey. They usually reign over the tidal flats as top carnivores.

Section Review

1. **a)** What types of producer cover the exposed mud flats? Explain.
   b) What type of vegetation is commonly found growing in the sandier sublittoral zone of the flats?
2. Where does most life exist on the tidal flats? Why?
3. **a)** Name four organisms that burrow into the substrate.
   b) Describe how two of these burrowers obtain their oxygen and food.
4. **a)** Name the four types of feeding mechanisms found on the tidal flats.
   b) Give one example of each feeding type.
5. Briefly describe the variety of fishes and birds that commonly visit the flats to feed.

19.7   Life in the Estuary

Estuaries provide habitats for a wide variety of plants and animals. The abundance and diversity of organisms is partly a result of the large quantity of nutrients available. Fresh water carries nutrients from the land. Sea water carries nutrients from the ocean.

Several factors control the distribution of life in the estuary (Fig. 19-13). These include salinity, temperature, and oxygen. Light, nutrients, and substrate are also important factors. Of all these factors, salinity is the most critical. Because of tidal movements, the salinity constantly changes. Salinity tolerances restrict many freshwater organisms to the upper parts of the estuary. In contrast, many marine organisms are restricted to the lower parts, next to the ocean. Some organisms, however, occur only in areas where conditions change daily. Let us look briefly at some of the characteristic life found in temperate region estuaries.

Fig. 19-13 Six important factors that affect the distribution of life in the estuary.

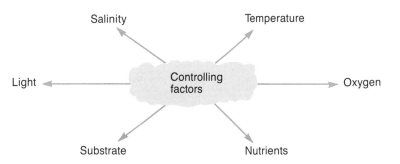

Plants and Phytoplankton

Phytoplankton occur throughout the estuary. Their numbers change with the tides and seasons. In summer they are most numerous near the surface and in low-salinity areas. In winter they are more uniformly distributed. When nutrients are present in sufficient amounts, phytoplankton (algal) blooms may result. Diatoms, along with other producers, serve as a food source for many invertebrates and fish.

Mats of blue-green and green algae often cover the surface of estuarine mud flats. The brown alga, rockweed, may attach itself to rocks or other solid objects.

A plant zonation can be seen in many estuaries. In the shallow waters, eelgrass (*Zostera*) and wigeongrass (*Ruppia*) commonly occur. Cordgrass (*Spartina alterniflora*) and glasswort (*Salicornia*) usually grow in the littoral zone (Fig. 19-14). Where salinity is reduced by seepage of fresh water, reed grass (*Phragmites*) and salt marsh bulrush (*Scripus*) often occur. In the upper regions of the estuary, various rooted freshwater plants penetrate into the brackish water.

Animals

Adaptations   Estuarine animals are faced with two problems. They must be able to maintain their position during tidal movement. They must also make adjustments to changing salinity and temperature. Only animals that can adapt to these variable conditions survive.

Animals have adapted in many ways. Clams and some worms and shrimp bury themselves in the mud. Barnacles, oysters, and mussels hide inside their tightly-closing shells. They also securely attach themselves to hard surfaces. Other organisms occupy crevices around sessile organisms. Many small invertebrates and fish migrate to areas where conditions are more suitable.

Distribution   Most marine species are adapted to living in high salinity waters. But in many coastal and estuarine areas, salinity gradients exist. In general, as the salinity decreases, the number of marine species declines. Thus fewer species penetrate upstream. In areas where fresh water enters, freshwater species are most abundant. A few freshwater species can tolerate brackish conditions.

Most species have an optimum salinity range within which they grow best. Outside this range, populations decline. Often one subspecies replaces another subspecies.

Types   The majority of estuarine organisms are marine and benthic. Many organisms common to mud flats and salt marshes occur here too.

The oyster is the most prominent member of the estuarine community. Oysters attach themselves to solid surfaces in the littoral zone. At low tide, the oyster beds are exposed (Fig. 19-15). Oysters may also form reefs. They cluster together, usually on top of shells of past generations.

Fig. 19-14   As in the salt marsh, cordgrass is a dominant plant in the estuary. This cordgrass is called big cordgrass and can grow 4 m tall in low salinity waters.

Over three hundred species are associated with oysters. Barnacles, sponges, and bryozoans attach themselves to the oyster shells. The oyster crab strains food from the oyster's gills. One species of snail feeds on body fluids and tissue debris from the oyster's mouth. As well, a wide variety of life lives between and beneath the oysters.

Many fish enter the estuaries to breed and lay their eggs. Atlantic salmon, sturgeon, and shad spawn in freshwater streams. The striped bass spawns where fresh and salt water mix. As the larvas and young fish mature, they move downstream to more saline waters. Other species, like the croaker, spawn at the mouth of the estuary. The larvas then travel upstream to feed in the plankton-rich low salinity areas.

Some fish, like the killifish, spend most of their time in the estuary. They spend the winter months in deeper waters, or they bury themselves in the mud. Sticklebacks can live in both fresh and salt water. Other fish including the bluefish and mackerel enter the estuary only to feed.

Fig. 19-15   An oyster bed.

Section Review

1. What factor is responsible for the great abundance and diversity of estuarine organisms?
2. **a)** List six factors that control the distribution of estuarine organisms.
   b) Which abiotic factor is the most critical in an estuary?
3. **a)** Describe the plants and phytoplankton commonly found in an estuary.
   b) Which plant species are also found in salt marshes and mud flats?
4. **a)** What two problems are estuarine organisms continuously confronted with?
   b) Choose three estuarine organisms. Describe how each has adapted to living with these problems.
5. How does salinity affect the distribution and abundance of marine and freshwater species in the estuary?
6. **a)** The oyster is the dominant organism about which life revolves in an estuary. Explain.
   b) Briefly describe the variety of fish that spawn in, live in, and visit an estuary to feed.

19.8   Human Impact on Salt Marshes, Mud Flats and Estuaries

Destruction

The future of many salt marshes and estuaries is seriously threatened. Industrial development and pollution upset the ecological balance. This often results in great losses of productivity and fertility along the shore. In some cases, it even leads to the extinction of species. Let us look at a few ways by which we are destroying these wetlands (Fig. 19-16).

Fig. 19-16 How humans are destroying salt marshes and estuaries.

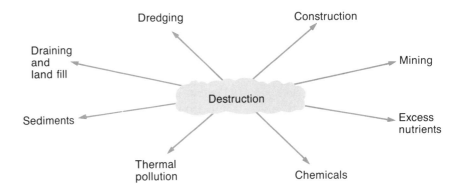

Land Fill Many marshes are lost because they are drained and filled in. This creates land on which we can build houses, industries, and airports. But it also destroys the habitat of many marsh and estuarine organisms.

Mining Other marshes are destroyed by mining. They are mined for minerals, oil, sand, and gravel.

Construction Dams and irrigation projects interfere with spawning migrations. Channel dredging and construction activities often change the pattern of water circulation. As well, changing the shape of the estuary to make a harbour can cause changes in local salinity. All these changes affect local ecology.

Sediments Large quantities of sediments are introduced daily to coastal waters. They come from construction, dredging, tidal currents, and erosion. Suspended sediment causes turbidity. This can inhibit photosynthesis. It also smothers gill-breathing animals and burrowers. As well, it chokes nonselective sediment feeders.

Chemicals In many places coastal life is being poisoned by pesticides and industrial wastes. Concentrations of pollutants increase at each step in the food chain. Even the dumping of sewage is taking its toll. Pollution leads to a decreased diversity of species. Only those species that can tolerate the pollutants are present in large numbers.

River pollution has greatly reduced the annual yield of oysters. Oysters tend to collect and concentrate the pollutants, making them unfit to eat. Many fish which live in polluted waters also contain high concentrations of dangerous chemicals. Also, they often contain pathogenic (disease-causing) bacteria.

Since DDT began to be used as an insecticide, blue crabs and fiddler crabs have become rare in some marshes. Populations of shrimps, amphipods, and birds of prey have also declined.

Excess Nutrients Coastal waters tend to have higher nutrient concentrations than open ocean waters. Thus coastal waters are more productive. For example, salt marshes are among the most productive ecosystems on earth. There are several reasons for this high productivity. Tides continually carry out waste and bring in nutrients. The meeting of fresh and salt water traps and concentrates nutrients. Few nutrients are tied up in biomass for very long. As a result, the salt marsh is able to supply most of its needs and still have matter and energy to spare. Some of this extra productivity is fed into tidal flats and estuaries and, eventually into the open ocean.

Problems may arise if the rate of nutrient supply suddenly begins to increase rapidly. Algal blooms can result. Then uneaten algae sink to the bottom. These and other organic materials accumulate. Their decomposition by bacteria requires oxygen. But often bacterial decomposition depletes the oxygen supply faster than it can be replaced. Then animals die. Only anaerobic bacteria can survive. These produce hydrogen sulfide gas which has a characteristic rotten-egg odour.

Overharvesting Clams, oysters, mussels, and scallops are common inhabitants of mud flats. They are sometimes overharvested for food and for their shells (to be used for decorations). Many estuaries provide rich fisheries. However, any mismanagement may result in a decline of fish populations.

Thermal Pollution Many industries use water as a coolant or for steam power. The heated water is commonly returned to the aquatic environment. This is known as thermal pollution. The increased water temperature lowers the oxygen content. This change can eliminate some local species. Even nonlethal temperatures may disrupt biological systems. For example, they may affect the timing of gamete production. Also warmer waters often attract new species of fish to the area.

Solutions

As you have seen, salt marshes, mud flats, and estuaries are important marine ecosystems. Yet they are disappearing rapidly. Preservation, wise management, and pollution control can help prevent further unnecessary destruction. Some state, provincial, and federal governments have already passed laws regarding their management. Others have not. Governments exist to serve the people. Therefore if you care about these wetlands, voice your concerns to the government.

Section Review

1. **a)** List seven ways in which humans are destroying salt marshes, mud flats, and estuaries.
   b) Discuss the effects of each of the seven ways on the marsh-mud flat-estuarine ecosystem.
2. What action can be taken to help prevent unnecessary destruction of these marine habitats?

Main Ideas

1. Coastal life has adapted to the harsh conditions that accompany the changing water levels.
2. Salt marshes are called "the cradles of the ocean". They are among the most productive ecosystems on earth.
3. Distinct zones of plants cover the salt marsh and estuary. Plant life is generally absent on mud flats.
4. Of the many factors controlling the distribution of life in an estuary, salinity is the most critical.
5. A high nutrient supply helps to maintain an abundant and diverse estuarine community.
6. Industrial development and pollution threaten the future of many salt marshes and estuaries.

Key Terms

black grass zone

high marsh

low marsh

salt meadow hay

shrub zone

Spartina alterniflora zone

Spartina patens zone

Chapter Review

A. True or False

Decide whether each of the following statements is true or false. If the sentence is false, rewrite it to make it true. (Do not write in this book.)
1. High marshes are flooded twice each day.
2. Large algae and grasses grow in the sublittoral zone of salt marshes.
3. The common name of *Spartina alterniflora* is salt meadow hay.
4. Mud flats are generally overgrown by salt-tolerant vegetation.
5. The killifish is a common inhabitant of salt marshes and estuaries.
6. Salinity greatly influences the distribution of life in the estuary.

B. Completion

Complete each of the following sentences with a word or phrase that will make the sentence correct. (Do not write in this book.)

1. The producers which cover mud flats are ▨▨▨ .
2. The male marsh fiddler crab is recognized by its oversized ▨▨▨ .
3. In general, the number of marine species ▨▨▨ from the mouth of the estuary to upstream regions.
4. To avoid desiccation, many worms and shrimp retreat into ▨▨▨ .
5. The Atlantic salmon and shad visit the estuary to ▨▨▨ in freshwater streams.
6. Mud flats act as sinks for ▨▨▨ and ▨▨▨ .

C. Multiple Choice

Each of the following statements or questions is followed by four responses. Choose the correct response in each case. (Do not write in this book.)

1. The dominant plant of the low marsh is
   a) short *Spartina alterniflora* c) *Distichlis spicota*
   b) tall *Spartina alterniflora* d) seaweed
2. The dominant organism in the estuary about which life revolves is the
   a) mussel b) clam c) oyster d) mud snail
3. Two animals that live amongst the tall *Spartina alterniflora* are
   a) marsh snail and marsh crab
   b) marsh periwinkle and seaside sparrow
   c) killifish and meadow mouse
   d) ribbed mussel and marsh fiddler crab
4. The abundance and type of life in the salt marsh is primarily influenced by
   a) salinity and tidal cycles
   b) tidal cycles and oxygen
   c) temperature and salinity
   d) turbidity and temperature

Using Your Knowledge

1. a) Make a table that lists the plants and animals found in salt marshes, mud flats, and estuaries.
   b) What organisms are common to all three habitats?
2. Are freshwater organisms able to live in an estuary? Explain.
3. Why are salt marshes one of the most productive ecosystems on earth?
4. a) Draw two food chains which likely exist in the littoral zone of the salt marsh.
   b) How might these food chains be affected if pollution killed the algae in the area?

5. Discuss the effects of industrial development and pollution on salt marsh and estuarine ecosystems.
6. If you were in charge of management of salt marshes and estuaries, what regulations would you enforce? Why?

Investigations

1. Select one salt marsh or estuarine invertebrate not discussed in this chapter. Research its life cycle, feeding habits, and adaptations to its environment. Write a report of 300-500 words on your findings.
2. Collect mud from surfaces exposed by tides. Examine small portions in wet mounts under a microscope. What kinds of organisms do you see? What are their roles in the marine ecosystem?
3. Design an experiment to test the effect of different concentrations of salt solutions on meadow and salt marsh plants. Perform the experiment. Be sure to include a control. Submit a formal lab report.
4. Obtain a stem (with leaves) of both a freshwater and a salt water plant that have wilted as a result of sitting in a saturated salt solution. Place the stems in a container of fresh water for one day. Can the wilting process be reversed in both plant types? Write a short report explaining your observations.
5. Measure the salinity and temperature at half-kilometre stations along an estuary. Begin about two kilometres upriver (or further, depending on the estuary) and move towards the ocean. Record your results in a table and construct a graph of the results. Write a short report discussing the significance of your data.
6. Find out what branch of your government is responsible for the management of salt marshes and estuaries. What are the government's policies? What changes would you recommend?
7. Find out what measures are being taken to help reduce the quantity of nitrogen and phosphorus compounds being released into coastal waters in your area.
8. Visit one zone of the supralittoral zone of the salt marsh. Record the name and relative abundance of each organism (plant and animal) you observe. Describe their habitats. Collect comparable data from another zone in the supralittoral zone. Which organism(s) are common to both zones? Which organisms are found in only one zone?

Index